FIRESIDE

Successful Investing A COMPLETE GUIDE TO YOUR FINANCIAL FUTURE

By the staff of **United Business Service**

With Introductory Chapters on The Art of Prudent Investing by **David R. Sargent**, President

Editor **Ronald K. Mills**
Associate Editor **Carolyn McIntyre Finnegan**

A Fireside Book
Published by Simon and Schuster
New York

Copyright © 1979, 1981 by United Business Service Company
All rights reserved
including the right of reproduction
in whole or in part in any form
First Fireside Edition 1980
Published by Simon and Schuster
A Division of Gulf & Western Corporation
Simon & Schuster Building
Rockefeller Center
1230 Avenue of the Americas
New York, New York 10020
FIRESIDE and colophon are trademarks of Simon & Schuster

Designed by Irving Perkins
Manufactured in the United States of America

10 9 8 7 6 5 4 3 2 1

Library of Congress Cataloging in Publication Data

ISBN 0-671-42775-X

Contents

8 / Contents

10 / Contents

Editor's Note

Successful investing is as much an art as a science. Indeed, it probably is more art than science. As with any art, consistent success usually rests on a foundation of basic knowledge. It requires mastery of certain fundamentals.

This volume is designed to provide that foundation for those who are just embarking on a serious program of investing. But it is more. It is designed also to serve as a basic reference tool for seasoned investors, a source to which they can turn for answers to specific investment questions and reviews of subjects on which they may have become hazy.

Compilation of such a body of information and knowledge, as you might well imagine, is no small task. We have approached it here on a team basis. The members of the professional staff of United Business Service who have contributed to this work bring to it a widely diversified expertise.

They bring impressive credentials to the task, as well. A doctorate in economics. Several masters' degrees in business administration. Chartered Financial Analysts. A Certified Financial Planner. They also bring experience. Collectively, their years in the business, investment, financial, and academic fields approach 250.

We have attempted to give as sprightly a style as possible to the writing, a task that frequently tried our talents. We hope you will find it readable and readily comprehensible.

Insofar as possible, we have tried to steer clear of material that is likely to become dated. We want this to remain a valid reference work for many years. For instance, in our discussion of tax shelters, we tell you what a tax shelter is, how it works, and when one is likely to be of service to you. But we do not get into the specifics of oil and gas participations or cattle feeding programs, because the vagaries of Congress might well render them obsolete before the ink is dry. We do not venture opinions on the investment potential of any specific company, and any references to the past performance of the securities of any company are made for illustrative purposes only. Despite our care, it is inevitable that events and the passage of time will take their toll.

Special acknowledgment must go to Stanley M. Rice, Sales Vice-President for United Business Service, who conceived the idea of this book, then left us free to do it in our own way. Sam Meyerson and the other editors and designers at Simon and Schuster deserve credit for transforming our manuscript into a creditable volume.

I owe a personal debt of gratitude to Carolyn Finnegan, who served as associate editor on this project. Her careful attention to detail ferreted out countless errors and inconsistencies. Her editorial suggestions proved invaluable and have greatly enhanced the quality of this book.

Likewise I am indebted to Elizabeth Breed for transforming our sometimes impossible scratchings into an intelligible manuscript, maintaining in the process not only her sanity but her sense of humor. Her devotion to the task made my job immeasurably easier and more pleasant.

As a reader, you will be grateful for the excellent work of Patricia A. Ganley and Jacqueline Caliri, who compiled the index. Their careful and painstaking effort makes this a much more valuable resource than it otherwise would be. For that, and for their always cooperative spirit in tackling such tasks, I am most appreciative.

My thanks would not be complete without mentioning my colleague Clarence R. Smith, who performed many of my regular duties while my efforts were directed toward completion of this book.

And a special, tender word of appreciation is due the most important "unofficial" member of the team, my wife, Lenore, whose patience and loving support were indispensable.

Happy reading . . . and successful investing.

Ronald K. Mills
Editor

Boston

Unless otherwise credited, all charts appearing in this book are from Securities Research Company, a division of United Business Service.

How to Use This Book

A REFERENCE tool is only as good as its ability to yield the desired information quickly and efficiently. So, the first thing we provide in this volume is a detailed table of contents. This will give you a quick scan of the topics covered in each chapter.

In addition, we have taken special pains to compile a thorough and extensive index. It is designed to steer you quickly to the various subjects covered in the book.

Likewise, we have taken special pains with the organization of the book. Familiarity with its layout will help you zero in more quickly on the information you desire. This will be the case particularly if you are intending to use it primarily as a reference work. Novice investors will do well to start at the front and work quickly through, then go back and spend more time on the areas that cover their gaps in knowledge.

The book has been written so that each chapter and section follow logically after the ones preceding. It is designed to guide the novice in an orderly progression through primer material and on to increasingly more advanced and sophisticated information.

Here is a synopsis of each of the book's seven sections.

Part I—The Art of Prudent Investing—can best be described as an expression of investment philosophy. In these four introductory chapters, David R. Sargent, President of United Business Service, sums up the tenets that have guided the company's investment advisories over more than half a century. Buy for the long term. Buy common stocks for capital growth. Buy them for a rising pattern of dividend growth. Choose your investments carefully and stick with them. Avoid fads. Be content to grow wealthy slowly—but surely.

Part II—Your Investment Alternatives—provides a detailed description of the various investment media. Equities. Bonds. Convertibles. "Governments." Tax-exempts. Mutual funds. Options. Commodities. Gold. Tax shelters. Real estate. In these chapters you will find complete information on the mechanics of these various investment areas. How they work. When they work best. Their potential benefits—and pitfalls.

Part III—How to Make Your Choices—describes the various tools used by investment analysts and how you, too, can use them. It tells you how to read and use charts. It explains the various market averages, how they're compiled, what they show—and don't show. It tells you how to read an annual report. It gives you an industry-by-industry survey of what to look for as you evaluate investments in each. Finally, it tells you where to get good investment advice.

Part IV—Mastering the Strategies and Tactics—shows you how to use the tools described in the preceding section. It gives you a set of rules for sound investing. It explains how the stock markets work. How to use options. How to invest profitably in commodity futures, and how to avoid big losses in them. How to spot tomorrow's investment winners today.

Part V—Taking Care of the Housekeeping—gets into the day-to-day "care and feeding" of your investment program. It explains how to choose a broker. It tells how commissions are calculated and how you can save on them. It lists the various ways you can hold your securities certificates, when it's best to leave them with your broker and when it's best to take possession yourself. It gives you a list of ways to make periodic additions to your investment program—dividend reinvestment plans, payroll savings, mutual fund programs, stock dividends and rights, annuities. Finally, it gives you some pointers to help you steer clear of Uncle Sam's tax shoals.

Part VI—Investments and Your Financial Plan—weaves your investments into your total financial program. It helps you get the plan in order. It provides a guide for building a college education fund. It shows you how to create a retirement nest egg. It relates your investments to your estate plan. Finally, if you are single or a woman, it addresses some of the special problems your financial plan involves.

Part VII—Speaking the Language of the Bulls and Bears—is an extensive and exhaustive glossary of investment, economic, business, legal, and financial terms. You'll find it a valuable reference as you encounter the arcane and esoteric terminology of these worlds.

Part I THE ART OF PRUDENT INVESTING

Chapter 1 Overview

MOST PEOPLE want to remain poor, and do. They deliberately avoid financial prosperity. Think of the number who rent apartments instead of buying houses, for example, when everyone alive today should know that home prices have risen every year since memory begins, except for a brief period during the Depression of the 1930s.

The mortgage householder can deduct his interest payments and real estate taxes from his income before taxes, so Uncle Sam is really helping him pay his "rent." The real rent payer pays his share of his landlord's interest and taxes but gets no deduction; the landlord gets it. The landlord gets the profit on the apartment or house as it rises in value. So does the homeowner. What does the rent payer get from a boom in property values? An increase in rent.

Yet millions of people pay rent, by preference. Other millions borrow but once. They take out a mortgage to finance their first home, because there's no other way to get a home, then bear down to pay off that mortgage. "Neither a borrower nor a lender be," quoth their mothers, so they push to retire the mortgage early. Think of all the World War II GI's who sacrificed to get rid of their GI mortgages and the 4 percent rate they carried. What do mortgage lenders now demand? Three times that amount. Few of us today are likely ever to see 4 percent mortgage money again.

Lessons Not Learned

Even those who have profited from the post–World War II plunge into real estate have not learned much of a lesson. How many people do you know with two houses, one for living and one for investment? The writer has a friend with a paid-off mortgage and a swollen passbook account. When the house next door came on the market we urged the friend to borrow and buy it for investment. The advantages were easy to see—deductible tax and interest costs, plus depreciation and a steady flow of rental income. Long term there was the virtual assurance of profit through capital gain.

What was the response? A sardonic smile and the cynical remark, "No thanks, and I suppose the next urging from you will be to buy stocks instead." True, that's what we did urge, the point being to buy something, for the road to wealth must in great part be traversed via the ownership of things—real estate, businesses, equities, and the like. The more you buy with bank money the more leverage you have, and the faster the progress can be. But buying things with borrowed money does involve risk, and we'll talk more on that later in this book.

Why don't people buy things? Why do they tend to squirrel money away into "safe" places like the local savings and loan association? Why do they determinedly turn their backs on the chance to make money? Because they are pessimists. They fear the future. They don't believe things will work out. They give everything a negative interpretation. They lack faith. "I would never open a store on that corner." "Convertibles are too dangerous. What if you rolled over?" (How many convertibles have you seen roll over? How many sedans, for that matter?) "Flying scares me." "The weather has been so bad this winter that corporate earnings are sure to suffer—and if this cold weather does break, the floods could be disastrous."

Worry, worry, worry. NATO can't hold. Britain is collapsing. The Arabs have us by the throat. Inflation is heating up again. Interest rates are sure to rise. Consumer debt is too high. Who can afford to buy a house or car at these prices?

There is always something to worry about, and concentration on such uncertainties or unfavorable possibilities prevents action. People don't make decisions, investments, or money. A pity.

The Power of Positive Thinking

The optimist, statistically a rare bird, has a leg up. He assumes from the start that America was here when he was born and probably will be when he dies. If he's wrong in this main assumption, he will lose more important things than his money. He looks around for opportunities. When the pound sterling falls to an "all-time low," he takes a trip to London—a bargain. He doesn't simply mutter darkly, "Britain's had it," and keep his cash in the bank.

When inflation threatens, he buys something like stocks or real estate to try to offset the impending decline in the dollar's buying power. Consumers generally do exactly the opposite, which is the very worst thing for them to do. When inflation threatens, they cram their extra money into bank accounts. If the stock market falls, optimists look for bargains while the pessimists are predicting even lower prices. Most people never seem to learn from the turtle that you cannot make any progress unless you stick your neck out.

The optimist can, and often does, go too far. He might expect to get rich quick. He often thinks he can pick stock market winners, and has been known to get so far out on a borrowed-money limb as to be cut off by a falling stock market or interrupted cash flow. Despite experience that tells him there are no wizards on Main Street, he frequently believes there are some on Wall Street.

For you, the key is to think positively. But temper your optimism with prudence. Weigh the possible gains and risks, then go ahead, making haste slowly. That's the road to riches.

People tend to think alike. When times are prosperous, everyone feels good, usually too good, and lots is done to excess. Too much borrowing, spending, and speculating often bring on a corrective recession of some sort in business, and folks turn to living sensibly. But they feel worse. They don't feel as if they are living sensibly, but more as if they are being forced to live at penurious levels.

This happened to investors in the 1970s after the stock market had stumbled along for several years between 800 and 1000 on the Dow Jones Industrial Average. Despite the steady rise in corporate earnings and dividends, the feeling grew that something serious was the matter. A longtime subscriber wrote us, "I have been with United Business Service for more than twenty years and never before have written to ask a question. Over the years, you at UBS have generally taken the position that in the longer range investments in sound American companies will provide the best hedge against inflation and the route to happiness and prosperity. Looking backward, you have always cited ample proof in support of your positions, but my question is, looking forward, are we seeing the end of an era, a whole new ball game to which old rules and precedents no longer apply?"

He continued: "Should we all be in gold, or other things that the political sector can't take away from us by destroying their value? Or should we be short in the market, or just hiding in our cellars, waiting for the holocaust? We have to remember that the mighty Roman Empire was not destroyed by the barbarians as some would have us think; it was destroyed by the politicians and the citizens who no longer fought to preserve their rights."

Beware the Ideologues

As we wrote to him then, "Such fears are fanned by magazine articles which claim among other things that corporate profits are illusory, that if the replacement costs of plant and equipment currently being depreciated were considered in setting up depreciation charges, there would be no corporate profits. This widely discussed canard always appears in inflationary and worrisome times, when the market is low. No one worries about accounting procedures in roaring bull markets."

The last time this fear of replacement costs of plant and equipment surfaced was in the late 1940s as a result of war-induced inflationary surges in price. What actually followed, of course, was one of the biggest jumps in corporate profits ever and an all-time great bull market which swept the Dow from under 200 in 1949 to more than 500 in 1956.

Or, take the article by two professors who write convincingly of the end of the private corporation, the victim of too much government. The SEC, FTC, FDA, EPA, and Justice Department, not to mention a horde of lesser controllers at state and local levels, are regulating business into oblivion, they argue. The authors simply ignore the more than doubling in corporate profits and the same jump in dividends over this last decade of increasing federal, state, and local concern for what business does to and for the nation.

It is amusing, as an aside, to note how often those who deplore any restrictions of the marketplace are those who never themselves took a chance therein. They write off the sad demise of the free enterprise system as they peer out safely from within the tenured walls of academia and nonprofit organizations.

In the same league are, of course, the gold and silver bugs. These are essentially ideological in their approach to economics: "Gold has intrinsic value. Silver almost does, too. So switch from depreciating dollars and pounds and hie to the precious metals." The stark fact that such metals are simply commodities and are worth only what the marketplace says they are worth is beyond belief to such ideologues.

Gold was a great hedge against inflation when it was turned loose on the market and soared from $35 to $195 per ounce. It was not when it fell back to $110 or less in the next two and a half years. The yellow metal also did well for holders when it bounced back up again from there to the dizzying height of $875 per ounce in early 1980. Lots of gold buyers were bruised, however, when the metal fell to $500 later that spring.

The truth is, the future is always impossible to foresee. Who predicted Watergate, Vietnam, double-digit inflation, OPEC's oil prices, a 20 percent prime, or the corn-killing heat wave of '80?

During these unsettled years, our big corporations and their shareholders have prospered. So they should again in the next decade. Meantime, as the chart below shows, it has been a generation since stocks on average sold so cheap. Maybe this is the last chance for another generation to get the best for the least!

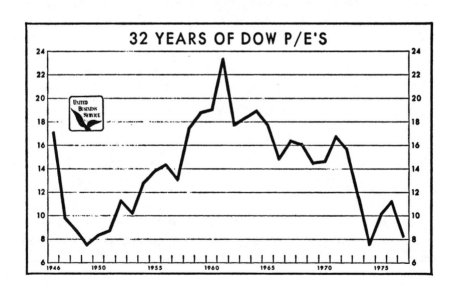

32 YEARS OF DOW P/E'S

Be Positive, Be Patient

The moral is, of course, to think positively (with prudence), and when everyone else is waiting for the future to become obvious, buy the good stocks you see on the bargain counter. But you must be patient, too. Sometimes the stocks you buy will move up rapidly, but more than likely they won't. The time factor is always unknown. Just buy the shares of a company that has a good record and seems to have as good a prospect, and sit with it.

One Wall Street sage once admitted that he'd made more money with the seat of his pants than with his security analysis. In short, buying and holding beat trading over the long term. Below are a couple of true-life examples of what one sensible lady did with her patience and positive thinking.

She bought 100 shares of Dresser Industries in March 1954 for $2,339. This was split two for one twice, giving her a total of 400 shares. She bought another 300 shares in September 1966 for $7,590, and another 200 in March of 1974 for $9,950. The total holding was then 900 shares. After she had given away 200 of her lowest-cost shares, her remaining 700 were split two for one, giving her 1,400 shares with a total value of $56,000 as of the end of 1977. Her net cost was $18,710.

Her experience with Emerson Electric was even more impressive. She bought 100 shares in December 1949 for $1,200 and another 100 through rights in April 1953, for $1,810. After several stock splits, she had 2,432 shares at the end of 1977 worth $79,000. Her total cost, $3,010, was barely more than the annualized dividend of $2,918.

She always told us she was too busy running the farm to trade. "I just buy and hold," she said. Too bad more people don't do likewise.

What's in This Book for Me?

The purpose of this book is to acquaint the unacquainted with the path to financial prosperity and to encourage the timid to take a chance. We'll look at all sorts of investment vehicles, as the Wall Street sophisticates call them—stocks, bonds, convertibles, Governments, municipals, mutual funds, etc., with an eye to showing you what's available, what they're good for, and how to tell which ones are for you.

Chapter 2 On Planning Your Investments

MOST PEOPLE are, and sadly will forever be, planless. Or if they have a plan, it will be a one-track route to a passbook account or to the local broker. Few are the savers who sit down and consider first what their dollars should do for them and, second, given those needs, what their options are. All too often the savings habit perpetrated on the hapless individual in his prepuberal elementary school years by the local savings institution is simply carried over into adulthood. The Lord's Prayer, the Pledge of Allegiance, and a passbook account are all part of the good clean life.

Life insurance is introduced later to the adult who in money matters really doesn't know much more than he did in the third grade. He succumbs to "You do care for your wife and kids, don't you?" Or, "This policy will get you to a happy retirement in Florida when both you and it mature and are ready for endless summer."

No one usually comes around to explain the leverage in real estate, or the growth potential in common stocks. The nearest the average person gets to the vast, complex, and at times lucrative bond market is a recommendation from the Personnel Department that he consider a payroll deduction for Series E Savings Bonds. The exhortation to buy E Bonds offering a modest 6 percent return is made even when long-term Treasury bonds could be bought at the local bank around the corner to yield 9 percent or more.

The truth is, most of those giving such advice don't know much about money or savings and rarely have financial plans of their own. They, too, stumble from one financial misconception to the next. So have a plan. Figure out what you need and what's available, then set up a program that approaches both. This should be a loose, easily adjustable program for the removal from the spending stream of a few dollars, more or less regularly, and the storage of these dollars in places where they should do the most good for all concerned.

Where Should You Save?

Let's look at some of the options casually referred to above. First, the passbook account. Great for the beginning. The interest rate is fair. You can have the money any time (with the passbook and proper identification, of course). The savings bank is perfect for the dollar you may need tomorrow or next fall. But for the long pull, forget it.

Inflation takes the joy out of saving. When this writer joined the working world three decades ago, the clerical starting wage in Boston was around $22 per week. Today it is over $150 and one could suspect that today's beginner is not much wealthier than yesterday's. Thus, the poor soul who squeezed a dollar out of a meager pay envelope thirty years ago for a savings account would be withdrawing a dollar worth less than a seventh as much today. So the savings account, whatever its other blessings are, is no long-term investment.

Neither is insurance, and for the same reason—inflation. Insurance is for protection, whether from the premature demise of the principal breadwinner in the family or the flaming destruction of the family home. So buy it that way, for protection against financial loss and not as an investment, and you'll be OK.

Real estate can be a good investment. Rarely have real estate prices *on average* fallen; but there are lots of exceptions to the "rule" in real estate, as a good many pretty stuffy bankers found out with the ill-managed real estate investment trusts (REIT's) in the 1970s. In real estate you have to know the territory, and for the average person that generally is limited to his own back yard.

Thus, for practical purposes, most of us buy the house we live in, and maybe one in the country, but that's about it, and properly so. We have more about real estate later on in this book, but for now we can probably agree simply that it is not a major investment preoccupation for most of us.

There are other choices for those with miserly inclinations. French peasants buy gold napoleons and bury them in the back yard, a relatively tiresome practice for the average American family that moves every few years. Furthermore, there is no interest income here and an obvious risk of theft in this break-and-enter society of ours. Certainly you have read of the man who kept his packages of tens and twenties in an old stove until a kindly neighbor came in and used the stove to burn the trash.

The small investor can have difficulty with bonds, if only because they tend to come in relatively large dollar amounts. Bond dealers prefer to work with $25,000 units and really jack up the price when you talk about anything under $10,000. But the larger investor should review the opportunities in the bond market, particularly where income is of paramount concern.

We'll deal in depth with all sorts of bonds—corporate, government, municipal, convertible, deep discount—later in this book, but for now we'll treat them generally as one savings option. Bonds are a loan by you to the issuer. That issuer agrees to pay you a fixed rate of interest and to give you your money back on a certain future date.

This means that a bond has much the same weakness as a savings bank account. It leaves you vulnerable to the ravages of inflation. The dollar you get back is nowhere near as good as the one you originally lent or deposited. It won't buy as much. A good bond will usually give you a better return than the savings account, but the bond will move up and down as interest rates fluctuate. So the savings account and a quality bond are at about a stand-off with one another and, because of their vulnerability to inflation, not particularly attractive for very much of your long-term savings dollars.

Why You Can't Ignore Stocks

Short of diamonds, art, or some other esoteric storehouse of value, there's not much left in the way of choices for the saver but common stocks. Lots of people stay away from common stocks because they always go up and down in value, sometimes with alarming speed. Stocks can also at times fall to zero and disappear, a most disheartening experience for the holder.

All of us have heard of people who "lost everything" in the great stock market crash of 1929. Few of us hear of the good solid investment gains enjoyed by thousands upon thousands of sensible buyers of good common stocks. As with a happy family life, a good investment experience does not make TV prime time.

So we tend to hear the horror stories of stock ownership, and, unless educated to the contrary, we stay away from common stocks. It is a shame, for the investment in common stocks is about the only way most savers can hope to offset inflation. Sometimes stocks do not rise enough to match the loss in purchasing power of the dollar, and sometimes in a roaring bull market stock values soar far ahead of the inflation rate.

Stocks were a marvelous inflation hedge during much of the 1950s and 1960s, when the market rose impressively and inflation ran at a modest 2 to 3 percent annual rate. Any long-term chart of the Dow Jones will show that. Any chart will also show that the market did not do so well versus inflation in the 1970s. For a number of years the Dow Jones Industrial Average ranged along between 800 and 1000, taking stockholders nowhere, while the rate of inflation ran at 6 percent or better. (In 1974, the inflation rate soared to 11 percent and in early 1980 nearly doubled that pace as it hit 18 percent.)

But what most stock-fearing savers fail to realize is that there is more to owning stock than profits or losses. There is dividend income, which tends to rise yearly. Back in 1977 our *United Business and Investment Report* carried the following editorial to illustrate that point, and it bears repeating here.

According to the 1976 economic figures, all we lost last year [to the ravages of inflation] out of our dollar saved was about a nickel. The consumer price index rose but 4.8%.

This compares well with the more than 9% experience in 1975 and seems but a trifling amount when compared to the whopping "double-digit" rate of 1974. But even 4.8% goes a long way toward obliterating the savings

| | Dividends | |
	Then	Now
American Electric Power	$2.00	$2.10
American Tel. & Tel.	3.40	4.20
Exxon Corp.	2.65	3.00
Middle South Utilities	1.26	1.38
Mountain States Telephone	1.52	1.88
Tenneco Inc.	1.76	1.88
U.S. Fidelity & Guaranty	2.48	2.64
Washington Water Power	1.56	1.76

bank return on a dollar saved, and it also puts a big hole in the 8.5% return available on an A-rated bond.

Inflation doesn't do any particular favors for common stock dividends either, but it can be offset by dividend increases. Just by way of illustration, consider the experience of the portfolio recommended [in 1975, as shown in table, preceding page].

Each company increased the dividend—some by just a little, but the overall rise was 13.3%, nearly three times the rate of inflation. And these increases are not the last to expect, for these companies characteristically boost dividend rates frequently.

Exxon and American Telephone have increased their rates seven times in the past decade while American Electric Power and Middle South can claim ten. Washington Water Power is the champ in this group with twelve boosts in ten years.

The moral is clear. Even if the Dow has trouble clearing 1000, rising dividend payments will take much of the sting out of inflation.*

Stock Values Go Up and Up

Another thing folks tend to overlook is that the intrinsic values behind good stocks go up along with dividends. As the economy of this country grows, so do the sales and earnings of our leading corporations. Gross national product, for instance, amounted to $233 billion in 1947. Thirty years later, the GNP figure was $1,900 billion. Part of this impressive change was inflation, of course, but part also represented incredible industrial growth and a huge surge in the standard of living.

Naturally, business participated in this growth. Some would even claim that business created this materialist surge. In any event, stockholders participated in it, while savings bank depositors did not. General Motors, for example, reported revenues of $3.8 billion and earnings of $288 million in 1947, versus $47.2 billion and $2.9 billion three decades later. Small wonder that the stock which sold at 10 at the midpoint of 1947 sold at 78 at mid-1976.

Other leading companies fared as well or better. Consider this random sample of some well-known blue chip issues in the 1970s. Note how values rose even though the market for the shares moved largely sideways:

* *United Business and Investment Report,* February 22, 1977.

	Revenues*		Earnings*		Stock Price	
	1970	1979	1970	1979	1970	1979
American Tel. & Tel.	$16,955	$45,400	$3.99	$8.04	50	53
Caterpillar Tractor	2,128	7,163	1.69	5.69	32	55
Int'l Business Machines	7,504	22,863	1.79	5.16	65	65
Sears Roebuck	9,262	17,514	1.50	2.54	32	18
Weyerhaeuser	1,233	4,423	.93	4.02	22	37

* Millions of dollars.

Of course, having determined that common stocks represent your best long-term investment savings option, you shouldn't just trot down to your corner broker and start investing in stocks. You can, to be sure, but you shouldn't. You need a plan which accommodates such variables as your income, your family responsibilities, your housing needs, reasonable insurance protection, short-term spending protection (savings accounts), and long-term investment objectives (college, retirement, etc.).

Rough these figures out and you'll have an idea of what part of your spending stream is savable, and how much of that you will likely have available for the purchase of common stocks over the years ahead.

Chapter 3 Investment Risks—Defined and Contained

"I ABHOR risk," wrote the senior legal type for a large life insurance company. "I want to know that a dollar saved today will be around tomorrow and the day after that." So his savings plan was strict and sober—straight life, paid-up annuities, and, of course, plenty in the local savings bank. "No use putting all your eggs in one basket." That is the picture of the supercautious saver.

His pattern and program of saving might be OK if his circumstances are acutely straitened. Let's suppose a man has a limited amount saved and limited life expectancy, plus a large and young family. Under such circumstances, there is little hope of recouping any dollars lost. His needs will be large and long term, while his source of income is likely to be near term. Obviously, such a fellow would have to play his investment-savings cards close to his chest.

But if he is not in such dire straits, he would be foolish to stay so close to the ground. A small flight, so to speak, into common stocks would give him some hope of protection from inflation. Put another way, where savings are concerned, there's always an element of risk. Money in common stocks can swell or shrink as the market rises and falls. Money in bonds can do much the same as interest rates wax and wane. Money in the local savings and loan association can shrink in value as inflation pushes up the cost of living.

If risk is inevitable, it is worth studying. What sorts of risks are there, how should they be offset, how much can you take in the way of chance, what is tolerable and intolerable as far as a risk is concerned, is one man's risk another man's opportunity? In this chapter we will run through some of the typical risks all of us face today. Then we will show you some ways to balance them. We'll also try to show you how to recognize your risks and opportunities and, more important, how to determine just how much risk you can and should assume.

33

The Inflation Risk

First, what sorts of risks are there? The biggest risk to anyone, of course, is his own mortality. This the intelligent soul tries to keep under reasonable control with moderate living habits, good medical care, and, if he's inclined, prayer. But financial risks are more complicated. Savers are perpetually on the horns of this dilemma. If they buy securities, the market for them may go down and their savings will shrink. If they don't buy securities, if they just hold on to their dollars, they'll stand a good chance of seeing those dollars shrink in purchasing power, if not in numbers. Outside of your own perishability, inflation is likely to be the major threat to your security and to that of every other denizen of the Western world.

Inflation is *the* enemy. It is the biggest and surest risk most of us ever face, for no currency in the financial history of mankind has failed to lose purchasing power over the years, sometimes at a fast furious rate as in Germany right after World War I and at other times quite sedately as in the early 1950s in this country, when the dollar only lost about 2 percent of its value annually to higher prices. In fact, during that period the late Professor Sumner Schlicter of Harvard Business School argued for more inflation as an economic stimulant and a producer of a faster rise in the standard of living.

It is doubtful if even Dr. Schlicter would like the raging inflation-

	Start*	After 45 Years
Bread	$ 0.25	$ 2.25
Round Steak	1.49	13.39
Potatoes (1 lb.)	0.13	1.17
Butter	1.25	11.23
Toilet paper (4 rolls)	0.79	7.10
Man's suit	85.00	763.73
Woman's dress	30.00	269.55
New house	34,980.00	314,296.00
Malibu coupe	4,588.00	41,223.00
Regular gas (1 gal.)	0.599	5.38

* St. Louis prices in early 1977.

ary pace of the post–Vietnam war era when the nation struggled with price inflation rates of 6 to 12 percent. It is equally doubtful that we'll ever again get back to the Eisenhower era's 2 percent that became so dull to some. Even if we get partway back, say to an annual 5 to 6 percent rate, we'll have some real problems.

The table on the preceding page shows what a 5 percent rate will do over 45 years, the working lifetime of the average man or woman.

To keep pace with this, a $3 hourly wage would become $26.96 after 45 years. Clearly, investments which did not have a chance to move along too would be disastrous.

The Interest Rate Risk

Though inflation is the major risk, there are other, usually smaller, risks in setting out to defeat or even partially offset that prime threat. Prices of stocks and bonds fluctuate, for example, and when they fall below your purchase price, the loss seems real even though it is only on paper. Some people can't take such losses, even temporary ones, on paper. Our "I abhor risk" friend is one. Others can, and thus they are able to use stocks and bonds to beat inflation.

Let's take a look at the risk in bonds. First, a bond is simply a certificate which represents a loan you have made to a company, say General Motors, or to the United States government, a state, or a city. One obvious risk is that the borrower might not pay you back. This is unlikely, given the nature of the borrowing organizations suggested above, and has happened rarely in modern times. Furthermore, bonds are rated. So you have a good idea before you buy one how much chance there is of anything occurring like default—failure to repay principal or interest.

The real risk in a bond is a rise in interest rates. Bonds are issued initially at a fixed rate of interest. But from there on they trade at a price where the current yield is equal to that of the bond market generally. The General Motors Acceptance Corporation 8⅝s of 1985 will sell at 100 if interest rates generally are running close to the 8⅝ percent coupon, or the $86.25 annual interest payment on the $1,000 face value bonds. But if rates rise to 10 percent generally, the bond price will fall to 86¼ ($862.50) so the $86.25 payment will represent a 10 percent yield to a new investor adding such a bond to his portfolio. Conversely, if interest rates should fall to 7 percent, the GMAC 8⅝s would rise to 124 or thereabouts, the increase needed to make the $86.25 interest payment produce a yield of 7 percent.

Since the prospect of profit is not a very scary one, we'll concentrate on the risk of loss of principal due to rising interest rates. This risk can be greatly reduced by keeping the maturity of the bond you buy short. For example, the GMAC bond discussed above matures in 1985, and was a ten-year bond at issue. This means you get the bond's face value back in a few short years, regardless of where interest rates are then. Thus, if interest rates are up between the time you buy and the time the bond matures you can simply ignore the paper loss, knowing that when the maturity date comes you will get your money back.

The other risk in bonds is that inflation protection is small. You "lend" 100-cent dollars and get back maybe 80-cent or 90-cent dollars when the bond matures, depending on the degree to which inflation has eaten away at the dollar's purchasing power during the years you held the bond. A portion of this loss, to be sure, is offset by the coupon, because the interest rate offered on a bond reflects in part the general level of inflation. We'll have much more on bonds later in this book, so we can end here by simply stating that the risks in bonds—default, rising interest rates, and inflation—are by no means intolerable.

The Market Risk

Everyone knows that the risk in common stocks can be enormous. We have already noted how the stock market crash of 1929 beggared many investors overnight. In fact, most people think the risk in stocks is so great that buying stocks is just like betting on horses. They believe that savers go to the bank and gamblers to the stock market. While nearly everyone is familiar with the 1929 experience, how many of them know that thousands of investors who held common stocks in 1929 still held them in 1939 and were doing very well indeed?

That is because good stocks—the shares of our leading corporations, like General Motors, General Electric, Eastman Kodak, etc.— go down in a bad market, but not out. When investment sentiment, the business cycle, or whatever, improves, good stocks come back. So the little old lady in Boston's Back Bay who held American Telephone, United Fruit, United Shoe, General Electric, and the like in 1929 was doing all right in 1939. Her shares had come back in price, and in most cases her dividends were better.

If the big risk in stocks is in a rising and falling market, it can largely be offset by long-term holding. Don't worry when the market goes down; it will eventually come back, and your good stocks will come with it. A second risk in stocks reflects the soundness of the companies they represent.

A national figure once made the unfortunate comment "If you've seen one slum you've seen them all." You will be no more correct if you consider one stock to be just like another. Stocks vary widely in appeal, popularity, price stability, and dividend characteristics, as well as in risk and reward. Before entering the stock market with your dollar saved, you should review these differences carefully, for on Wall Street what's good for the goose isn't necessarily good for the gander.

How Much Risk for You?

Which brings us to you and your risk-taking ability. We touched on this earlier in this chapter. If the money you save is small in amount and your needs pressing and near term, you have to be a lot more careful than if you are in the opposite and more enviable position. If you barely have your son's tuition in hand and the bill is due in six months, you don't put the money in any common stock, not even in Ma Bell. Who knows what surprise could come around the corner to upset the stock market, albeit temporarily, and leave your tuition fund badly dented?

On the other hand, if you have your son's tuition in hand and he's only seven years old, you would be foolish not to buy some Exxon or GE with it. By the time he gets to college, it could be two or three times as big (so also the tuition bill). Better yet, you may have saved even more, so you can let your GE or Exxon stock ride to even higher long-term levels.

In the final analysis, the amount of risk you take depends on you and your circumstances. The richer, younger, and least depended upon by others can take bigger chances than the poorer, older, and most leaned on, obviously. The commission salesman should save more carefully than the tenured academician. The fellow with six kids has to play it safer than the man with none and a working wife.

Put another way, invest in stocks only that money you do not expect to need in the foreseeable future. Start with the shares of the best companies, picking those that represent the fastest-growing areas of the economy, rather than the clearly more mature industries—health care rather than autos, for instance.

Spreading Your Risks

By all means, diversify. This means spreading your money over a number of different companies and industries. You never get rich quickly this way, for one stock will sag when another soars. Neither will you go broke, for the same obvious reason. A Wall Street tycoon once said the way to make money was to put all of your eggs in one basket and then "to watch the basket like hell." Well, maybe it worked for him, but for the rest of us diversification is a must.

It makes saving more fun, too. To hold the shares of a number of companies is entertaining. It makes you feel like part of the big world. You can stick out your chest when "your" company comes up with a new miracle drug for the common ulcer, and can shrink in shame when your company is caught bribing the Japanese Diet. Owning stocks puts you right out there in big business with the millionaires, tycoons, and corporate brass who make things happen.

There are other risks within the stock market beyond that of price or rising and falling markets. There is the risk of obsolescence—of corporate managements or products. Things go out of style. Double knits did that in the 1970s. Or conditions change to make a product less attractive to the buying public. This happened to motor homes when the Arabs quadrupled the price of oil. The private auto put street railways and many railroads out of business. There are things we consider commonplace today which will be uncommonly unnecessary tomorrow.

There is risk in too much of a good thing. The first discount stores were highly successful. Soon they became chains, then more chains. After a while there were too many of them and lots went under. If an industry appears to be "the rage," stay away. Political shifts can add risk, too. Think twice before investing in a company doing business abroad. It's one thing to make pharmaceuticals in England, France, or Germany. It's quite another to mine copper in Peru, drill oil in Libya, or to refine chrome in Rhodesia.

Politicians are important at home, too. Electric utilities know this all too well. All of them have to appeal to various governmental agencies for rate increases. The company with a friendly regulatory climate is usually a much better investment than one in the opposite situation. Similarly, think twice before investing in an industry whose product runs counter to national policy. Producers of gas-guzzling cars, dirty coal, and strip mining equipment have suffered this way in recent years. Lastly, politicians have an unnerving way of reversing themselves, to the endless discomfort of some companies and their shareholders.

No discussion of risk is complete without an avuncular admonition to common stock buyers that life itself is risky, as well as is the stock market. Just as you adjust to the adverse mortal possibilities as you live out your three score and ten, you have to adjust to the risks inherent in stock ownership. Don't worry about a sharp drop in the Dow. Don't be rattled by the television anchorman's sonorous announcement on the evening news that "stocks fell sharply today on Wall Street."

Just remember that if you buy the "best," stay reasonably diversified, and hold for the long pull, you are bound to win. The country is growing, the economy is expanding, and our leading companies are going right along, too. So also will their shareholders, with ever rising dividend income and stock prices.

Chapter 4 **Building Your Portfolio**

THERE ARE two ways to build your portfolio—all at once, or gradually. Most of us have to use the latter method as we painfully extract a few dollars at irregular intervals from our family's spending stream. Those who get to do it all at once are usually widows who are the beneficiaries of their husbands' insurance policies.

Investing Defensively

We'll show you how to do it both ways in this chapter. We'll also show how people with different circumstances can meet those varied circumstances with differing investment portfolios. Let's start with a "for instance." A woman came to us in 1948 as a middle-aged widow whose children were grown and gone. She was housemother at a local college (no co-ed dorms in those days) and had, therefore, "free" board and room and little need for her modest salary. Neither did she have much in the way of assets. So she had to be careful with her savings and yet could buy stocks because she appeared likely to have no immediate need for the dollars she could save. We told her to buy a stock each time she had saved $500 or $1,000, and gave her suggestions of very good companies in relatively "defensive" industries. Until she retired in 1958, she followed our plan.

By "defensive" we mean rather steady businesses which are relatively unaffected by the ups and downs of the business cycle. A good example of this is a telephone company. People seem to use the telephone in good times and bad. Revenues for the industry never go down, and when their costs go up and threaten earnings, the companies simply seek—and almost always get—rate relief. So their earnings records are excellent and their dividends secure.

Ma Bell, for example, was famous during the depressed 1930s for paying her $9 dividend each year while many companies were falling by the wayside. In recent years she has done even better by shareholders, with eight increases in twelve years. Rochester Telephone has boosted its rate almost yearly over the same period. Another good record is that of Central Telephone & Utilities, whose dividend rate in 1977 was 108 percent above the 1967 level. Such increases take care of a lot of inflation.

Other defensive industries include the big retail chains (Federated Department Stores), small loan companies (Beneficial), food suppliers (CPC International), household products (Colgate, Procter & Gamble), banks, and, believe it or not, tobacco companies. These are industries whose products are in relatively steady demand. You rarely cut toothpaste purchases because times are tough, and, as the record shows, smokers smoke no matter what. This group is further favored by the steady rise in population and average hourly income. This means there is a yearly gain in the number of dollars flowing their way.

Then there is always the neighborhood power company. These are in much the same position as the telephone people. Revenues rise regularly along with rates, and enough faster than costs to permit almost annual dividend increases. So we urged our widow to buy some of the more interesting electric utility issues, those of companies serving the more rapidly growing sections of the country.

After a decade her portfolio, into which she had put about $13,000, contained these companies:

Company	1948 Value	1958 Value	1978 Value	30-Year Gain (%)
American Cyanamid	$ 1,560	$ 8,259	$ 8,080	+ 417.9
American Telephone	1,650	2,475	3,877	+ 134.9
Beneficial Industrial Loan	1,817	6,081	8,646	+ 375.8
Federated Dept. Stores	700	3,330	8,640	+1,134.3
General Motors	1,180	5,940	7,050	+ 497.5
Lowenstein & Sons	440	791	586	+ 33.2
National Lead	1,020	10,281	2,990	+ 193.1
Northern States Power	1,044	2,552	3,016	+ 188.9
Phillips Petroleum	580	1,930	4,620	+ 696.6
Tennessee Gas Trans.	1,584	7,078	8,597	+ 442.7
Texas Utilities	1,040	5,219	6,400	+ 515.4
Yale & Towne	550	2,023	8,625	+1,468.2
TOTALS	$12,585	$55,959	$71,127	+ 465.2

She already had a decent capital gain on these securities in 1958, an even more impressive one in 1978—and that after some sharply down markets. Her portfolio is now much larger because of stock dividends and splits. In fact, only one of her holdings failed to split its shares in those thirty years. Over the years, too, her dividend income kept pace, increasing 443 percent from $907 in 1948 to $4,921 in 1978. Interestingly enough, the yield on the total portfolio backed off slightly to 6.97 percent from 7.2 percent in 1948. Only when bond yields got up to 9 percent and 10 percent and her eightieth birthday passed did she capitulate to anything of a fixed-income nature, and over the long haul did very well. Incidentally, Beneficial Industrial Loan is now Beneficial Corporation, Tennessee Gas is Tenneco, National Lead is NL Industries, and Yale & Towne is Eaton Corporation.

Investing Bit by Bit

Here's another "for instance," from a California woman who really had it made, financially anyway. She wrote us:

I do not know much about the stock market but it has always fascinated me and I want to get into it. This is my situation.

I am female, 52 years of age (but I look 45), working for the State of California at $1,000 a month. I hope to retire in ten years if not before.

I have no properties and rent for $200 per month. My expenses are nil. I can live on $400 per month because I am single and have men friends who pay for all entertainment and most of my meals. My auto is paid for. I can live on the balance of my paycheck after all deductions are made plus income from a note.

I am deferring $700 a month on the State deferred income plan which is deposited with the Great Western Savings & Loan. The state also offers the T. Rowe Price Growth Stock, Inc., and Price New Income Fund, Inc. According to your reports these are excellent mutual funds. Would you advise me to diversify and take some of that $700 and invest it in Rowe?

I also have a $10,000 note out which pays 10% annually and can be recovered at any time. I would like to invest this money also.

I have $3,000 in savings for emergencies. I have good medical coverage through the State.

I am sure there are a lot of other gals like me who need guidance on how to invest their incomes so they will be able to be independent in their later years. Any advice you can give me would be appreciated.

Obviously, here is someone who should buy stocks. Her savings program is impressive, yet it offers no protection against inflation. The $700 per month deferred income could shrink substantially in purchasing power by her sixty-second birthday. So would the note she had out. So we told her first to switch her monthly savings to T. Rowe Price Growth Stock Fund, a no-load mutual fund with a broadly diversified list of leading common stocks in the underlying portfolio.

Because the fund was huge, $1.44 billion under management at the time, we told her it would probably continue to bump along about with the market, no great shakes maybe, but lots better than Great Western Savings & Loan could offer. Then we suggested that as additional cash became available for investment, she should buy a few stocks of her own. She would, in effect, be building her own mutual fund.

We further pointed out that she didn't have to be too conservative in her stock selections, because her current money needs were slight. After all, think of all the free meals she could boast of. So the list we sent along to this woman was not quite as somber as it was to our housemother friend. Here it is:

Abbott Laboratories	Burroughs
American Express	Minnesota Mining
Anheuser Busch	Schlumberger Ltd.

"Start with the A's and buy them alphabetically, or in any other order that pleases," said we, "for they are all good long-term growth stocks. Abbott Labs is big in health care, an industry that prospers in good times and bad. American Express and Anheuser must be familiar to you. Burroughs is computers, 3M is tapes, adhesives, graphic systems, abrasives and the like. Schlumberger is huge in oil field services—an energy crisis beneficiary—and is a growing factor in electronics as well."

We never learned whether our "youthful" correspondent did what we suggested, but we certainly hope so. That is one of the drawbacks to life as an investment adviser. Folks generally never tell you whether they have followed your advice or not, unless of course it didn't work out very well. As elsewhere in the human condition, nothing flies as fast as word to the adviser that his advice has caused losses. (John Milton put it better: "For evil news rides post, while good news baits.")

Investing to Preserve Capital

In another instance, a widow came to us with a $50,000 insurance check, a $10,000 passbook account, and about $7,500 in common stocks, one of which was Scudder Duo-Vest, the no-income highly leveraged fund managed by Scudder. She was in her fifties, which meant a life expectancy of 25 years or so, had her own mortgage-free home and no job. Her situation was a great deal different from the California woman's discussed above.

For one thing, she had no men friends to buy her meals. With no job, neither did she have the many attendant fringes that employment usually involves. She needed eating money now and could take few chances. So we told her to split her investment funds in two, putting half in bonds and half in stocks. This program would offer more income now, of course, for the average high-grade bond yield in these inflationary times runs nearly twice that of common stocks. The trade-off, quite obviously, is that the portfolio half in bonds offers the holder only half the protection against inflation as the all-stock program.

We will not go into the bond solutions required, except to say we kept the maturities fairly short, ten to twelve years. As for stocks, we split again about evenly between growth and income issues. Our widow's current income needs were just too pressing to allow as much emphasis on long-term growth as we would have liked.

Of the stocks she received from her husband's estate—Tenneco, Burroughs, Georgia-Pacific, American Telephone, and Scudder Duo-Vest—we sold only the fund, because it was oriented toward capital gains and offered no income. Clearly it was not for her. Tenneco and Telephone would give her good income, and the other two good long-term growth possibilities. To these we added other issues to the tune of $27,000, with about the same amount in bonds. The excess over the $50,000 insurance check came out of the savings account. We thought $4,000–$5,000 in savings ample for an emergency fund. When all was said and done our widow's portfolio looked like this:

No. Shares	Cost	Value	Dividend	Yield
100 American Natural Resources	41	$ 4,100	$ 264	6.4%
40 American Telephone	60	2,400	152	6.3
200 Bank of America	24	4,800	160	3.3
20 Burroughs	90	1,800	14	0.8
100 Georgia-Pacific	33	3,300	80	2.4
200 Koppers	23	4,600	180	3.9
200 Louisiana Land & Exploration	28	5,600	240	4.3
100 Tenneco	34	3,400	188	5.5
200 Texaco	27	5,400	400	7.4
		$35,400	$1,678	4.7
5 high-grade bonds		$27,000	$2,295	8.5
savings account		$ 4,500	$ 225	5.0
Totals		$66,900	$4,198	6.3%

You can see here how the bonds "sweetened" the income. You can see also how we stuck to big-name issues and balanced between income and growth potential. It's obvious why we sold the Scudder and why we did not buy more of Burroughs. It is probably also easy to justify our reduction in the savings account in the light of the large investment in high-grade bonds which are almost as easily available if a financial pinch develops.

There Are Men, Too

Men invest too, of course, and some of them have the same opportunities and restrictions as the women we have used as examples. Others are in a different environment and can take real chances in the hopes of big gains. Income they have in surplus, dividends they do not need. A high-income small-town family attorney came to us over a period of years, and after a while he had this list of stocks:

American Home Products	Louisiana-Pacific
Caterpillar Tractor	MAPCO
Eastman Kodak	Mesa Petroleum
First Pennsylvania Corp.	Mountain Fuel Supply
General Signal	Peabody International
Georgia-Pacific	St. Louis–San Francisco
Houston Natural Gas	Westinghouse Electric
K mart	

A review of these names will show some to be solid blue chips (American Home, Kodak), some to be chancy (Westinghouse, Mesa Petroleum, Louisiana-Pacific), and some to be in the middle (Caterpillar, Frisco, Georgia-Pacific). Although the dividends on these shares went up over the years, the average yearly percentage return never ran much over 3 percent, and the high-yielding stocks in the list were usually the companies in trouble, as was First Pennsylvania, along with a lot of other banks in the 1970s.

Some of the blue chips gave our man grief, too, at times. Probably his biggest heartbreaker was Eastman Kodak, which he bought at 75, saw it soar to double his cost and then plunge to less than 60. But on the average his well-diversified portfolio did what he wanted it to do—produce capital gains and minimum income.

Don't Marry Your Stocks

The last pearls of wisdom we have to offer on building your portfolio are on how to watch it after it is built. Even though you subscribe to the "buy good stocks and hold them long term" philosophy of investment, there are times when stocks should be sold. You do not do so when you think the market in general will go down, but you do when there is evidence that a company's position is deteriorating, its market is shrinking, its products are becoming obsolete, or some other demonstrably unfavorable situation is developing.

Let's try an example. Suppose you had owned Skyline or any one of the other leisuretime motor-home makers when the Arab oil boycott hit in 1973. The sharp jump in the price of fuel that autumn was clearly a permanent development and just as clearly reduced the market for heavy fuel-consuming pleasure vehicles. Times had changed, and to the disadvantage of Skyline, so you should have sold the shares.

That same revolution in the energy world made coal mining companies such as Pittston or Westmoreland Coal much more attractive. Again, it doesn't take genius to see such shifts. Often the changes are much subtler and harder to see, but when you see them it is wise to move.

Adjust for Your Changing Needs

Another cause for switching is when a stock no longer fills your financial bill. While our lawyer friend is a big earner, it is fine for him to hold low-yield stocks. But what about the same fellow in retirement? Taking chances on stocks when you are young is one thing, and quite another in those golden years. As your need for safety and income increases, you gradually switch from the Louisiana-Pacifics to the Tennecos. It is only good sense to do so.

Keep Good Records

Last, it is imperative to keep records. There are all sorts of record-keeping books available, and it is easy to log the number of shares you have and what you paid for them. There is a place to put down the dividend payment dates, amount paid, etc. The tough thing is to make yourself do it. But without such records you are at the mercy of the company's computer as far as your dividends are concerned and the Internal Revenue Service when you sell.

To sum up, building your own portfolio is easy, it can be fun, and it certainly will be rewarding. First, figure out who you are, financially speaking, then put together a list of securities that brew up into your cup of tea. After that, ride with your portfolio long term, making changes only as they appear necessary. It is a great way to financial independence.

Part II YOUR INVESTMENT ALTERNATIVES

Chapter 5 Equity Investments: "A Piece of the Action"

IF EVER there was an affordable and convenient way for most of us to participate directly in the free enterprise system, it is through the acquisition and holding of common stocks. Your single share of General Motors represents an actual ownership stake in that industrial behemoth. As even a most fractional owner, you enjoy certain rights —and you assume certain risks. We'll get into those rights and risks in this chapter as we explore the pros and cons of investment in common stocks. We'll also introduce you to ways other than common stock ownership that allow you to establish equity positions in a company: preferred stock, warrants, rights, and put and call options.

The Concept of Ownership

Let's expand a bit on the ownership concept, zeroing in first on common stocks. Your share of common stock represents something of intrinsic value, a piece of equity in the company. As that intrinsic value rises and falls, so does the worth of your investment. You have committed a portion of your wealth to the fortunes of the company. If you have chosen the company wisely—or fortuitously—each dollar invested has the potential of rising exponentially in value as the company prospers. You are not merely being paid for the privilege of letting the company borrow your dollars.

Because your investment is in something of intrinsic value, you have in effect untied it from monetary value. When you convert it back to monetary value by selling it, you will get what it is intrinsically worth in current dollars—or at least what a buyer perceives as its worth. This is completely without regard to what it was worth in dollars when you acquired it. If the company has been growing as fast as the economy in general, or faster, the intrinsic value likewise will have grown. The dollars you receive when you sell will have equal or greater buying power than those you used to purchase the investment.

Contrast that with the situation when you merely lend your dollars to the company via purchase of a corporate bond. In effect, when you redeem your "loan," you get the same number of dollars back. In the meantime the buying power of those dollars may have shrunk, leaving you with less valuable dollars.

It is important that you have a firm grasp of the equity concept and comprehend the difference between being an owner and being a lender in order to understand the value of common stocks as a hedge against inflation. By being an owner, you tie your investment more closely to ongoing economic conditions, whereas by being a lender you keep your dollar tied to a post sunk into the ground on the day you made the loan. The latter can go only as far as its short leash allows.

It is also important that you understand the risk-reward differences between ownership and lending. As an owner, just as you stand to gain when the business prospers, you stand to lose your stake if it should collapse. You are also at the mercy of the market when you sell your equity, for, in the final analysis, it is worth what the market says it is worth, regardless of its intrinsic value.

As a lender, your assets are protected against such loss (unless, of course, the business fails completely and defaults on the loan), but you replace that risk with the risk that the worth of your dollar and what it earns will not keep pace with rising prices.

Common Stocks: Rights and Risks

A corporation offers shares of its common stock to the public as a means of raising capital. If it is a company's initial offering, or if it is an offering of previously unissued shares, it is called a primary issue. Shares which are outstanding and offered in a block by one or more holders are referred to as secondary offerings; proceeds of these do not accrue to the company. In return for your investment, you receive a stock certificate that along with providing evidence of ownership has other legal characteristics. The certificate contains a serial number, the name of the registrar or transfer agent, and the par or stated value of the stock. It should be noted here that in the case of common stocks, par value has little, if any, relationship to the market value of the stock. The certificate also informs you that as a shareholder you have no financial obligation to the corporation. This means that should some corporate liability arise, that liability would not extend to you.

Along with certain legal protection, you enjoy various rights as a shareholder. First, unless you hold stock that is specifically designated as nonvoting, you have voting rights, meaning you are entitled to vote on such things as the selection of an accounting firm and merger proposals. Most of these matters are dealt with at a company's annual meeting. Since you could own shares in dozens of corporations, you could spend a good part of your time attending such meetings. As this is usually neither possible nor desirable, when an important matter is to be voted, a corporation distributes a proxy statement to its shareholders. This is a legal document which permits you to choose someone (a proxy) to vote for you. It is usually mailed to the stockholder, along with information pertaining to the particular matters to be voted on. A card is included where you can indicate your preference in the matter at hand.

As a shareholder you are also entitled to receive dividends on a pro rata basis. A corporation is not legally obligated to pay a dividend on its common stock, but when the directors declare a dividend, every shareholder receives an equal amount per share of stock.

Also, as a stockholder you retain the right to protect your proportionate interest in the corporation. For instance, if you own 100 shares of a company which at some point, say, decides to increase the amount of its outstanding stock by 15 percent, you have a preemptive right to purchase 15 additional shares. If you decide to exercise this right, your initial proportionate share of ownership in the corporation has not been reduced despite the increase in the number of the shares outstanding. Those rights, by the way, have a value of their own; should you choose not to exercise them, you can sell them to someone else. This usually must be done within a certain time or the rights expire. More on rights and their cousins, warrants, later.

Finally, although you have no legal financial obligation to the corporation, in cases of bankruptcy or liquidation the corporation has an obligation to its common stockholders. In such cases, the corporation's first responsibility is to its creditors—to those who have lent it money. After they have been paid, the holders of preferred stock are entitled to the par or stated value of their shares; that's one reason it is called "preferred" stock. If anything remains, it is then divided among the common stockholders on a pro rata basis.

Picking the Right Stock

OK, you ask, now that I know what a common stock is, how do I go about choosing from among the thousands of stocks available? How do I determine in which corporation I want to own shares?

The answer is the key to successful investing—choosing stocks that meet your individual investment needs. It is not an altogether simple task, as any professional analyst, portfolio manager, or investment adviser will tell you. However, in the case of common stocks, understanding a few basic characteristics can be beneficial in helping you make your investment decisions.

First, you should know that the two most important aspects of a common stock's value are quality and earnings. Determining the quality of a common stock is more difficult than determining the quality of, say, a bond. But a common stock is usually graded on the basis of the corporation's historic earnings performance as well as its future earnings outlook. Has it shown healthy growth in the past? Have earnings been stable? What are its prospects in the years ahead? The stock's performance in the market is an important criterion, too. Does its price tend to remain relatively stable or does it tend to be volatile?

Watch Dividend Performance

Of more than passing interest to the common stockholder, naturally, is the company's performance on dividends. As we said earlier, a corporation is not legally required to pay dividends on its common stock. However, since the regular payment of a dividend increases the attractiveness of its stock, a corporation tries to provide them whenever possible. The most common form is a cash payment. Such payments are usually made quarterly, but they can also be made more or less frequently. The corporation's directors decide how much will be paid.

At this point it might be helpful to define some of the terms that are used in conjunction with dividend payments. First, the directors *declare* a dividend of a specific amount. The dividend is said to be payable to *holders of record* (in other words, owners of the stock) as of a certain date. The *payment date* is the actual date that you, as a shareholder, will receive the dividend. The *ex-dividend date* determines whether the buyer or the seller receives the dividend.

As a shareholder, you should also be aware of two other types of dividends: the *stock dividend* and the *stock split*. Neither of these actually changes your proportionate ownership in the corporation. A stock dividend is stated as a percent dividend. For example, a corporation declares a 2 percent stock dividend. If your initial holding amounted to 100 shares, you would own 102 shares after the dividend was paid.

How Stock Splits Work

Now take the case of a stock split. Say a corporation declares a 2-for-1 split. This means that if you were originally holding 100 shares you would have 200 shares after the split. But since all other shareholders would likewise have twice as many shares, your relative ownership position remains the same. The value of your investment would not change, either, for the new shares would trade at half the cost of the old ones. Reducing this trading price, in fact, is the main reason for stock splits; a corporation generally uses a split to trim the stock's price to what it considers to be a more marketable trading range. It is important to keep in mind that when you receive a stock dividend or when your stock is split, your interest in the corporation has been neither increased nor decreased. Also, the total value of the stock has not been affected, nor has the earning power of the corporation been diluted.

How to "Value" a Stock

Speaking of value, how can you place a specific "value" on a common stock? How do you determine at what price the stock should be bought? When can it be considered overvalued and best sold? Let's talk more about a point we mentioned earlier—the discrepancy that sometimes exists between a stock's "intrinsic" value and the value that the stock market places on it. In determining a stock's intrinsic value, you look at such things as the corporation's balance sheet (assets, liabilities), its debt, capital requirements, earnings, dividends, future prospects, and management. In choosing a stock, you try to pick one whose intrinsic value appears greater than the value the market has currently placed on it. Other factors sometimes used to evaluate a stock are book value (net worth), liquidating value, and price-earnings ratios. We give you a much more detailed description of these tools and how to use them in Chapter 23.

Be Aware of the Risks

Let's now talk more about some of the risks involved in investing in common stocks. One of the largest is also the most difficult to combat, for it frequently is fickle, unpredictable, and illogical. That factor is market psychology. Generally speaking, a rising trend in prices will occur when there is an attitude of optimism (economic, political, social) on the part of investors (the market). On the other hand, declines occur when investors take a pessimistic stance. Changes in basic market psychology can be seen in the fluctuations that occur from day to day in the stock market.

On a more individual level, as mentioned previously, a particular stock's price will be affected by such things as earnings, dividends, and future prospects. The risk lies in the fact that these elements change and that unforeseeable events occur. Take, as an extreme example, the case of Marine Midland Banks. Due to some unforeseen real estate investment trust (REIT) losses, Marine Midland earnings in 1975 plunged to $1.19 a share vs. 1974's $3.20. During the same year, its stock plummeted from a high of 20 to a low of 10. These REIT losses continued into 1976, and earnings fell again, to $1.04 a share, and the stock sank to a low of 8¾. Also at this time Marine Midland cut its quarterly dividend from 45¢ to 20¢. So you can see how abruptly the tide may turn for certain corporations. Of course, the higher the quality of the stock, the less inherent is the risk involved. The high-quality stocks tend to be much less volatile, and while "quick" profits will probably not be forthcoming, what is saved on the nerves might be worth it to some investors.

Preferred Stocks

The more conservative investor might be better able to sleep at night with preferred stocks instead of common. Preferred stocks reside in a sort of no man's land between bonds and common stocks. Some would say these hybrids embrace the least favorable characteristics of both, for they have neither the enforceable claim of a bond nor the share in profits of a common stock. Although preferred stock is an equity security representing ownership in a corporation, holders do not have a vote (except under certain conditions) nor do they have pre-emptive rights.

"Preferreds" must have some redeeming features, or they long ago would have passed into oblivion. For individual investors, that appeal is seated in the generous returns usually available in preferreds. Though the dividend may not enjoy the same guarantee that bond interest does, it takes preference over common stock payments. This is a right that usually is stated in the issuing company's charter, as is the right of the preferred holder to corporate assets in liquidation ahead of the common stockholder. But for the corporate investor, new-money preferreds (those issued since 1942) offer a tax break. In order to avoid double taxation, a taxable corporation may deduct 85 percent of dividend income derived from investments in other taxable corporations.

The market behavior of straight preferreds is much the same as that of bonds; both are fixed-income investments and therefore interest rate sensitive. This is not the case with convertible preferreds or participating preferreds. Their market price patterns more closely follow those of the common stock—convertibles because they may be exchanged for shares of common, and participating because under certain conditions they participate in dividend growth with the common. We mentioned above that preferred shareholders in certain cases may be allowed a vote. That generally happens when the preferred dividend has been omitted for a stated number of quarters. Still other types of preferred stock may accumulate unpaid dividends which have to be cleared before common dividends are paid.

More recently, utilities—the principal issuers of this genre—have offered preferred stocks with sinking funds, giving holders the illusion of eventually getting their money back. Under the terms of the sinking fund, the issuing corporation will retire a stated percentage or dollar amount of the total issue each year until the entire issue is retired. This fund may be satisfied by open market purchases made when the issue was trading well below par value and held in the company treasury to satisfy sinking fund requirements several years hence. Thus, a shareholder could hold the preferred to the bitter end without a single share being called early. Of course, he would be free at any time to sell the shares on the open market.

Rights and Warrants

In counterpoint to the staid preferreds is an array of more speculative equity-related investments—rights, warrants, and options. Let's look first at rights and warrants. As is true of common stocks, a corporation issues rights and warrants to obtain additional capital. To obtain it quickly, a rights offering is usually made. Under the terms of a rights offering, a shareholder is entitled to purchase a limited amount of additional stock, usually at a preferential subscription price during a fixed period of time (usually within a month of issuance). During this period the stockholder can either exercise his rights and buy the stock, or he can sell his rights to others, who, in turn, may exercise them or sell them. Or, if he is careless, he can merely allow the rights to expire unexercised or unsold. Money down the drain. It is in the buying and selling of rights and warrants that the speculation occurs.

Warrants, like rights, give the shareholder the privilege of purchasing additional shares of stock at a fixed price during a specific period of time (usually several years in the future). As mentioned previously, common stock prices tend to fluctuate widely over a period of time. There is considerable risk involved in trading either rights or warrants, but because rights involve a shorter period of time, they are of a less speculative nature.

Here is an example to help you understand how warrants work and how they are evaluated by the market. XYZ Corporation's common stock has a current market price of $40 a share. XYZ issues warrants that will permit owners to purchase one share of common at $35. At these prices the warrant has a theoretical value of $5 (current market price of common minus subscription price). If the common should double in price to $80 a share, the warrant should be worth $45 ($80 less $35). As you can see, a far greater percentage gain would have been made if you had owned the warrant (800 percent) than if you had held the common (100 percent).

Warrants generally sell at premiums over their theoretical value in rising markets, reflecting their greater leverage. By the same token, if the common begins to fall, the warrant generally falls at a more rapid clip.

As a buyer of rights or warrants, you assume all the risks without the benefits of the common stock ownership. You are entitled to no dividends, you have no voting rights or any of the other rights of the common stockholder. In other words, you do not participate in the ownership of a corporation. Any return you receive on this type of investment is based solely on price appreciation.

Puts and Calls

Now let's look at another method of investing also linked to the price action of common stocks: put and call options. A put is an option to *sell* a specified number of common stock shares at a specified price (the striking price) during a specified period. A call is an option to *buy* a specified number of shares at a specified price within a specified period of time. Put and call options may be both sold (written) and bought, and we discuss them in greater detail in Chapter 14.

The major attraction of option trading is the great leverage it provides. An option can be bought or sold at a fraction of the cost of its underlying stock (usually 3 to 8 percent), and small swings in the price of that stock can generate larger gains or losses for the option trader. The field, therefore, has been a magnet for speculators.

But conservative investors, if they know what they are doing, can make use of options, too: in guaranteeing market position and obtaining stock at what may amount to a discount price, in hedging against unpredictable turns in an uncertain market, and in generating greater income. We'll tell you more about how to do it in Chapter 32.

Meanwhile, as a general rule, we think your best bet in staking out a position in the equity markets is through common stocks. In the next two chapters we give you more specific information about how to find the stocks you need to fulfill your investment aims.

Chapter 6 How to Find Growth Stocks

LET'S ASSUME that at this point in your life you do not need any extra income, you are beginning to think about funds for the kids' college education and your own retirement. With the evils of inflation hacking away at your hard-earned savings, you want today's invested dollars to grow sufficiently to meet your future needs. What you are looking for is a good growth stock.

"Fine," you say. "How do I tell a good growth stock from any other stock? Where do I look for them? How do I evaluate them?"

What Makes a Growth Stock

Let's take a look at some of the characteristics that distinguish a growth stock from the other general categories of stocks, those that emphasize dividend payments (income stocks) and those whose prices tend to rise and fall in line with the economic cycle (cyclicals). For a start, we can tell you that growth stocks are generally found in companies that offer products and services with particularly favorable long-term growth potential. Managements tend to be aggressive and are constantly searching for new products and eying growing markets. As such, they place a good deal of emphasis on research and new-product development. Also, they generally exhibit an ability to achieve consistent and above-average sales and earnings growth.

On the other hand, dividend growth might be less dramatic because a good portion of earnings is plowed back into the company rather than paid out to investors. Thus, a growth stock more often than not will have a below-average yield. It should be pointed out, however, that a low yield today could mean a higher return tomorrow. By reinvesting its earnings, the company hopes to increase its profits over the years, which in turn means higher dividends for investors. For instance, between 1967 and 1976 Coca-Cola increased its dividend payment by almost 200 percent, yet the stock's current yield remained below 4 percent.

Growth Stocks and Economic Trends

One of the most difficult tasks in choosing a growth stock is knowing what areas of the economy do in fact possess unusual growth potential. It's difficult, but by no means impossible. In the absence of a crystal ball, you have in your daily newspaper one of your best information sources. What phases of life does it discuss the most? What are people talking about? What trends are developing in our society? What deep-rooted changes are emerging?

In the late 1950s and early 1960s, for example, it was becoming increasingly evident that computers were going to play a big part in our future. At that time, Burroughs was still grinding out its adding machines. But it was also moving toward other electrically operated equipment and on to electronic machines for the accounting trade. It then began getting into computers for banks and other financial institutions. Far-sighted individuals who bought this stock in 1965 would have seen their investment grow by 1,500 percent in ten years.

This illustration brings up another important point about growth stocks: "Patience is a virtue." Again using Burroughs, let's assume you purchased the stock in the early 1960s, when the shares sold in the teens. In 1964, five years after the company began its transformation into a high-technology concern, the stock was down to 11. No one could have faulted you for selling out that year. Although the promise of computer excitement was still there, the company had as yet failed to make much money on it, and without earnings—the sine qua non of stock prices—there was no market performance. Then, in late 1964, earnings turned up, and in January 1965 the stock moved from 12½ to 16. A year later it had nearly doubled, and in five years the stock had gained tenfold.

So, through just this one example, and there are countless others, you see the rewards that can be reaped from finding an area with future promise and being patient enough to stay with it.

Timing Your Buys

With growth stocks, as with any other investment, timing is an important key to success. You have to determine the best time to buy—and to sell. While there is no sure formula, a few considerations should prove helpful. The ideal time to buy is when a company is still in its early stages of development. There is, of course, more than average risk involved, since emerging companies are smaller and lesser known, and their success has not been firmly established. But their stocks do tend to be more reasonably priced than those of companies that have carved a niche.

On the other hand, a company's chronological age is not necessarily significant. Some well-established corporations fit the criteria for a growth stock because of their proven ability to introduce new product lines and find new markets. A good example is Philip Morris. For years growth had been based on cigarette sales. Then in 1969 it acquired Miller Brewing. Philip Morris applied its skills as a marketer of consumer products to this new line, boosting Miller's position in the industry from eighth to third and its market share from 4.5 to 15 percent. In the process, the company's growth rate jumped from 15 percent to more than 20 percent annually within a decade. This example vividly demonstrates that a company's age has less to do with its growth than its ability to recognize growing product areas and then to capitalize on them.

Of course, an investor must be willing to pay a premium for a well-established growth company, such as American Home Products, Burroughs, Coca-Cola, or Eastman Kodak, which sold at 37 to 42 times earnings in 1973. But these same companies are also sensitive to market declines—as amply demonstrated by their price-earnings ratios, which fell to around 10 by the close of the decade. The key is to choose a stock with an above-average growth record which is selling at a reasonable multiple of earnings. While this takes a bit of watching, it can be done.

Finding the answers to a few simple questions should make the selection easier. Does the company have a product or service with exceptional long-term potential? Does management reinvest earnings? Is a reasonable return on capital realized? Is capitalization of a size that will allow for future expansion? Does management have a piece of the action via stock ownership? What portion of net goes to research and development? Is the price-earnings multiple reasonable vis-à-vis the company's record and potential? If most of these questions rate a positive answer, you may well have uncovered a worthwhile growth situation.

Timing Your Sells

Even long term growth stocks should be sold at certain times and in some situations. Performance of the market as a whole is not generally one of the criteria. Major market turns are difficult to spot and they seldom coincide with the tops and bottoms in an individual issue. The 1973 bear market was a year old before the blue chips gave ground. What you should be on the watch for are changes in the prospects for a firm—new competition, new laws, new products. If something in the fundamental outlook for a corporation develops, a switch may be indicated.

There are many examples of this principle at work, but one of the best was Scott Paper back in the 1960s. Scott was the foremost maker of premium tissue and toweling. The company's record was one of dynamic growth. The stock was a blue chip growth favorite and sold at lofty price-earnings ratios. The company had **a** huge and growing market pretty much to itself. Then Procter & Gamble moved in. It bought a Midwestern outfit named Charmin and took off after Scott's tissue and toweling customers. This shook the Scott management at the time. To have the expert marketers at P&G after your customers would scare anyone.

Here, then, was a perfect example of fundamental change. Scott went from being virtually alone in a rich market to being eyeball to eyeball with one of the world's toughest competitors. The market saw this and the Scott price-earnings multiple tumbled. Investors who sold then were doing the right thing for logical reasons. The fundamentals of Scott had changed.

In conclusion, if your investment objective is to beat inflation, then growth stocks could be the route for you. But remember, patience may be required. The table opposite illustrates comparative short- and long-term performances of cyclical and growth stocks over a ten-year period. As you see, the rewards for perseverance can be great.

	Price Dec. 1974	Price May 1976	% Change Dec. '74– May '76	Price May 1966	Price May 1976	% Change May '66– May '76
Growth Stocks						
Am. Home Products	33	32	− 3	13	32	+ 146
Am. Hospital Sup.	26	35	+ 35	14	35	+ 150
Coca-Cola	53	80	+ 51	40	80	+ 100
Disney (Walt)	21	54	+157	4	54	+1,250
Eastman Kodak	63	100	+ 59	65	100	+ 54
Int'l Bus. Mach.	168	254	+ 51	143	254	+ 78
Average			+ 52			+ 99
Cyclical Stocks						
Aluminum Co., Am.	30	53	+ 77	56	53	− 6
General Motors	31	69	+123	83	69	− 17
Int'l Paper	36	72	+100	27	72	+ 167
Norfolk & Western	61	78	+ 28	112	78	− 30
Union Carbide	41	68	+ 66	64	68	+ 6
U.S. Steel	38	78	+105	43	78	+ 81
Average			+ 76			+ 9

Chapter 7 Common Stocks for Income

IN THE previous chapter you learned the benefits of investing in growth stocks. But what if your prime objective is income—you're looking for a little extra "bread money"? Many retired people with fixed incomes find themselves in this category. While bonds and preferred stocks are popular investment vehicles for those seeking income and safety, you should not make the mistake of ignoring common stocks as a valuable means of obtaining extra income. Many of these issues provide high current yields and have the potential for future dividend increases as opposed to the fixed rate of return on bonds and preferreds. They offer the possibility of some capital growth as well.

Although the need for additional income might be of the utmost importance, with the cost of living constantly edging upward, you should not pick a stock solely on the basis of current dividends. You won't gain any ground by purchasing one of today's high yielders if there is little potential for future dividend increases.

Look Beyond Current Yield

There is, of course, more risk involved with a common stock than, say, a bond, but the risk can be reduced by choosing stocks that have exhibited steady and dependable earnings and dividend growth over the years. The key, again, is not just to look at current yield. You must look to the past record, too. Is there a long history of consistent dividend payments? What has the dividend growth record been like? What are the prospects for dividend growth in the future? Again, careful attention must be given to price. What is the stock's price-earnings ratio? Is it high or low in terms of current earnings and future prospects and in terms of other stocks in its industry? As with any other common stock investment, an income stock should

be chosen on the basis of quality and growth, and not just because
it is enjoying a high level of current income.

Actually, choosing income stocks is a relatively easy matter compared to selecting growth stocks. First you look for a business that
is steady, something that by nature tends to do well despite the
prevailing economic climate.

Get a Line on Telephone Stocks

The telephone business is a fair representative of this type of industry. We pointed out in an earlier chapter how people tend to use
the telephone as much in bad times as good. With the number of
people and the level of popular affluence rising year after year, so
are telephone revenues.

The only major problems the telephone business encounters ema-
nate from inflation and politics. The former pushes up costs of both
labor (through increases in wage levels) and capital (through higher
interest rates). Politics enters when the company seeks rate relief
from the squeeze of rising costs. In the wake of the consumer movement, regulatory authorities frequently think first of the consumer's
reluctance to pay more for telephone service and second, if at all,
of the stockholder's right to a fair return on his investment. After
all, in the popular lexicon the user is poor, the stockholder rich. But
these problems have been surmounted time and again, so the
earnings-dividend experience of telephone companies' shareholders
has been passing fair.

When most of us think of "telephone" stocks, nine times out of
ten the name that leaps to mind is American Telephone & Telegraph. No doubt about it, good, solid, dependable old "Ma Bell" has
performed admirably and faithfully over the years, and should continue to do so well into the future. In the decade between the mid-
1960s and the mid-1970s, she boosted her dividend five times. But
some of the smaller so-called independent companies did even better. Rochester Telephone, for example, increased dividends 14 times
in a dozen years in that era. These smaller companies should not be
overlooked as possible income stocks. So when you're putting together an income portfolio, take a look at the current yields of and
prospects for these "telephones":

> Central Telephone & Utilities   Mid-Continent Telephone
> Continental Telephone   Rochester Telephone
> United Telecommunications

Plug into Electric Utilities

Like the telephones, electric utilities are worth consideration as income investments. We say this even though they have trouble these days getting environmentalists to let them expand generating facilities, because of too much air pollution by fossil fuel plants and too much thermal pollution by nuclear ones. In spite of these problems, the industry's leading companies have enviable dividend records.

The table below lists dividend payments of Florida Power & Light over a twenty-year period. It shows why utility stocks have appeal for income year in and year out, even when the stock market fails to behave.

In short, the 1961 buyer of Florida Power & Light common enjoyed dividend increases every year. By 1980, the dividend had increased by more than 400 percent. When this increase is compared with that of the consumer price index, the most widely used measure of inflation, it shows that this utility's dividends handily outpaced

Year	Dividend	Year	Dividend
1961	$0.53	1971	$1.06
1962	0.59	1972	1.10
1963	0.63	1973	1.16
1964	0.69	1974	1.33
1965	0.72	1975	1.44
1966	0.78	1976	1.56
1967	0.84	1977	1.66
1968	0.90	1978	2.00
1969	0.96	1979	2.32
1970	1.02	1980	2.72

the rise of prices in general. During the two decades, the dividend compounded at an 8.5 percent annual rate while the consumer price index moved ahead at a 5.2 percent annual compound rate.

This type of inflation-beating dividend growth has been exhibited by several other of the companies listed below. If electric utility stocks appeal to you as income possibilities, any of these perennial favorites would bear investigation.

Florida Power & Light	Public Service of New Mexico
Houston Industries	Southern California Edison
New England Electric System	Tampa Electric
Northern States Power	Texas Utilities
Public Service of Indiana	Wisconsin Electric Power

Tap a Water Company

One little-known and often overlooked group that offers steady income plus some hope of profit over the long pull is the water utilities. Just as certain as death and taxes is our steady uptrend in water consumption. This has been regularly reflected in a similar annual increase in water utility revenues and, in most cases, earnings. Of course, water company profits per share are never likely to explode, but no matter how bad the times, neither are they likely to dry up. Water is just about the last commodity we would forgo. Thus, water company shares have an appeal for safety and, generally speaking, high yield.

Other industry groups come and go as candidates for an income list. When in disfavor, stocks in some industrial groups can sell to yield nearly twice what they do when they have caught the public favor. Gulf Oil, for example, sold above 40 for much of 1968 and 1969, when the dividend was $1.50. This made for a yield of 3.75 percent. By 1973 the oils were out of favor, partly because earnings fell and partly because it looked as though the Arabs would take over everything, and the same dividend, still amply covered by earnings, provided a yield of 6.5 percent. General Motors yielded about 5 percent on a $5.25 dividend in 1965. Eight years later, the yield was 8 percent on a dividend of the same size.

It's perfectly logical to buy temporarily unpopular stocks for income as long as you can be reasonably certain that the dividend is safe and that the company has a good earnings-dividend record. Do not, however, buy a stock for high yield when the earnings-dividend performance is erratic, for that very irregularity may account for the temporarily generous return. The market will be telling you in those instances that it "ain't safe."

Inflation and Income Stocks

A word is warranted at this point on inflation and income stocks. One of the reasons income stocks return a high yield in times of rising prices is the very inflation itself. When inflation intensifies, stock prices fall at first, particularly those of income-type stocks. They fall with the bond markets as lenders say, in effect, "If you want my money now you will have to pay me a decent return, plus what those dollars will likely depreciate per year."

A 12 percent prime rate reflects just this equation—so much for a "real" return and so much to offset inflation. The income group generally comes to terms with current inflationary reality. For instance, many of the other growing electric utilities yielded less than 5 percent for years. But in 1974, when the inflation rate reached the two-digit level, these issues on the whole yielded 10 percent or more.

As the foregoing demonstrates, choosing stocks for income can be a relatively simple process. Just be sure that you pick companies in stable businesses with histories of consistent and rising dividend payments, and an apparent capability of raising dividends in the years to come.

Chapter 8 Corporate Bonds

A GOOD many conservative investors have long believed that the only really "safe" security is a stolid corporate bond, and would never think of putting their money into anything else. Indeed, the 1974 surge in interest rates and concomitant decline in stock prices won a lot of theretofore more venturesome investors into that camp.

Nevertheless, most common stock investors still blanch at the thought of investing in bonds, and one reason is because fixed-income securities represent unfamiliar territory. We shall seek to span that knowledge gap in this chapter. There is no real mysticism to bonds. Neither are bonds always as "safe" as they seem, and we'll get into that a bit here, too.

Simply Stated, They're Loans

Stripped of their esoterica, bonds are no more than credit instruments and merely represent a loan by the investor to the issuing company. When a corporation wishes to build a plant or finance equipment purchases, it may do so by floating a bond issue, which is no more than taking out a loan composed of tradable evidences of debt.

There are several reasons why a corporation will choose to sell bonds rather than offer the public more shares of common stock. For one thing, the registration procedures and expenses of issuing bonds generally are less burdensome than those involved in issuing stock. For another, the company might not wish to dilute any further the equity of outstanding common shares. Or, the company's assessment of the existing investment and economic climate tells it that bonds would be easier to sell than stock, or less costly in the long run.

Corporate bonds come in several styles. They can be mortgage bonds backed by liens on specific assets. They can be issued for specific purposes, as when railroads or airlines float equipment trust certificates. Most frequently, however, they are in the form of debentures, which means they are backed by a pledge of the earning power of the corporation rather than by a lien on specific corporate property.

However, these mortgage bonds, trust certificates, and debentures share many common characteristics. They all are, as we said above, tradable evidences of debt; they usually come in denominations of $1,000, and so can be readily bought and sold by investors. They all carry a fixed interest rate (coupon) on their face. They all have a predetermined expiration date when the loan must be repaid (maturity).

The precise nature of the bond and the specific terms of the "loan" agreement are contained in the bond indenture. Besides noting the type of bond being issued and fixing the coupon and maturity date, the indenture might also reserve the issuing company's right to retire, or "call," the bond at a specified date and price in advance of maturity. It might also note whether all bonds of the particular series will be issued at once or serially. It would give specifics on how the bonds would be called. Sometimes if an entire issue is not called, those bonds chosen for retirement are picked on the basis of serial number; often they are chosen by lot. The indenture also will identify the name and address of the trustee, usually a bank, that administers and oversees the bond issue, making sure all terms and conditions are met, that interest payments are made on time, and the like.

The "Mechanics" of Bonds

Bonds may be issued in "registered" form, which means the name and address of the current owner are kept on file by the corporation. It sends periodic interest payments directly to the owner, and no one else may offer the bond for sale or redemption. The registered owner of a called bond is notified directly. This is the safest and most convenient way for you as an investor to hold bonds. Bonds can also be issued in "bearer" form, which means in effect they are owned by whoever has them in his possession. Thus, they are virtually the same as cash. No proof of ownership need be demonstrated to redeem them or to collect interest. Interest is indeed collected by snipping little coupons from the bond certificate at stated intervals in that stereotyped procedure that conjures up images of wealthy little old ladies and gents stooping over a table in a vault doing just that. After they're clipped, the coupons can be presented to a bank for payment.

Bonds are issued and traded in $1,000 denominations and quoted in terms of "par" (100). Thus, a bond quoted at 98 sells at $980, one quoted at 101½ sells at $1,015, etc. Because bond interest is fixed, prices must adjust up or down to reflect prevailing interest rates. Sometimes such an adjustment is made even as the bond is being issued. Suppose an issuing company wants the bond to pay only 6 percent interest, while the prevailing interest rate is 6.25. As an inducement, instead of selling the bond for $1,000 and being committed to paying $62.50 a year in interest for the life of the bond, the company will sell it initially for $960 and pay $60 a year in interest. This will give the buyer an effective rate of 6.25 percent as long as he holds the bond. That is called an "original issue discount." Though the buyer paid only $960 for the bond, he will collect $1,000 when it matures. The difference is reported as income ratably over the life of the issue, with the holder's cost basis rising each year by the amount of reported income.

Marketplace Determines Yield

Once the bond has been issued, whether it sold initially at par or at a discount, the marketplace takes charge of its price fluctuations. Suppose you buy a bond at par that pays 7.5 percent interest. Each year as long as you hold the bond you will receive a $75 interest payment. If bond yields in general rise to 8 percent, your 7.5 percent bond would drop in current value to $940, because that's all a potential buyer would be willing to pay in order to reap the 8 percent he could get elsewhere. On the other hand, if bond yields generally dropped to 7 percent, you could get $1,070 if you sold your bond. A bond that sells below par is said to be selling at a "discount." One that sells above par is said to be selling at a "premium."

Yields Trending Upward

Over the past four decades, the overall trend in bond yields definitely has been upward. Back in 1950, Moody's AAA Corporate Bond Composite Index returned less than 3 percent. In the mid-1970s, that yield had jumped to nearly 8 percent in the wake of a serious credit crunch. There are times when interest rates go down sharply, usually when the economy enters a recession. Bond prices then move up quickly. When interest rates stop falling, though, the advance in bond prices slows markedly, then stops, too.

International economics will play an indirect role in bond prices and interest rates in the years ahead. Arab claims on the dollar stemming from their oil exports to us, currency fluctuations caused by floating exchange rates, and our inevitable entanglement in the web of worldwide inflation will pose ongoing uncertainties. However, with continued expansion of the U.S. economy and gradual growth in economic activity, interest rates can be expected to move unevenly higher in the years to come.

How do you as a bond buyer protect yourself in such an investment and economic climate? One way is to buy shorter-term bonds, sticking pretty much to those with maturities of ten years or less. Such bonds tend to hold price fluctuations to more moderate proportions. Another way is to manage your bond portfolio in such a way that you are not left holding outdated bonds at deep discounts. Try to keep your portfolio heavily represented in bonds with coupon rates closely approximating prevailing interest rates.

How do you judge a bond's quality? If you're up to it, you can examine the corporation's debt structure, its financial statements, its credit rating, and other complex factors and make an assessment on your own. More likely you'll do what most of the rest of us do—you'll look to the rating services and bow to their judgment. There are two that are widely quoted: Moody's Investors Service and Standard & Poor's.

Both use similar criteria in determining the relative quality of bonds available for public sale, those representing the least risk to the investor being rated highest. Consequently, U.S. Treasury issues backed by the federal government's awesome taxing power are at the top of the pile. Close behind are those of the various federal agencies which, though they are not specifically backed by the government, carry the weight of moral obligation of the government not to allow them to go into default.

Some top utility and industrial corporate bonds carry highest ratings, too; Exxon and American Telephone are examples. As bonds go down the rating scale, risk rises. In compensation for that added risk, investors demand a higher yield. The higher the bond's rating, the more closely its yield will tend to reflect changes in interest rates in general. On the other hand, yields on bonds carrying lower ratings will be much more heavily influenced by changes in the credit rating or profitability of the issuer.

This table shows you the rating scales used by Standard & Poor's and Moody's:

Standard & Poor's		Moody's Investors Service
AAA	Highest quality	Aaa
AA	High quality	Aa
A	Good quality	A
BBB	Medium grade, some speculative aspects	Baa
BB ⎱ B ⎰	Speculative, but with some defensive qualities	Ba
CCC ⎱ CC ⎰	Highly speculative	B
C	Bonds on which no interest is being paid or which already may be in default	Caa
D	Lowest rating	C

Both rating services are highly regarded in the financial community, and either one can be relied upon as you make your bond-buying decisions. However, for the purposes of uniformity, we shall use the Standard & Poor's ratings throughout this book.

Generally speaking, most investors buying for income should go no lower than BBB-rated bonds. If you go much lower than that, you put your capital in jeopardy; and, after all, the primary reason you're interested in investing in bonds is to protect that capital. Any additional yield provided by more speculative issues would be more than offset by the additional risk undertaken.

Different Kinds of Yields

As we noted earlier, bonds are issued with a specific interest rate printed on the face of the certificate. This is called the "stated," or "nominal," income. However, as we also noted, the price you actually pay for the bond, whether at its issue or in the aftermarket, determines the true yield the bond is earning for you. This yield, the amount of annual interest payment in relation to the price you paid, is called the "yield on cost." Another important figure is "current yield"—the coupon rate divided by the current trading price for the bond. If a bond stands a chance of being called before maturity, there is a "yield to call date" to consider. Finally, there is a "yield to maturity."

If you buy a bond at par when it is issued and hold it until it matures or is called and you get your principal back, all four yields will be the same. However, that is not a likely sequence, so you have to apply one or another of the available yields to your investment to determine its standing in your portfolio.

Generally speaking, the current yield will give you the truest reading, for it tells you how much income that holding is generating in comparison with other income investments.

If you hold the bond until it is called or until it matures, the yield to call date or yield to maturity will be of some consequence to you. That's because these figures take into account the premium or discount at which a bond is trading and the realization that this premium or discount must be amortized from purchase date to maturity.

For instance, if a bond trades at 107, you pay a $70 premium. When the bond is called or matures, you will sustain a $70 loss, for you will receive only the $1,000 face value of the bond for which you paid $1,070. That $70 loss must be offset against the income you will receive over the remaining life of the bond. On the other hand, if you bought the bond at 93, you will receive a $70 profit when the bond is retired.

These yield-to-call or yield-to-maturity figures allow you to make a quick comparison of the bond's possible return with the potential return of all other bonds carrying an endless variety of interest rates, maturity and call dates, and prices. The computation is more involved than most of us want to bother with, so we consult tables that have been especially constructed to provide this information. Your broker should be willing to look it up if you ask. These yields, as well as current yields, are frequently included in bond quotations.

Bonds—Why and When?

Bonds have appeal, despite their tendency to fluctuate in price as interest rates change, because they do offer better defensive qualities than common stocks; hence, they really can represent an anchor to windward in your investment program. Because their return is fixed, they can provide a firm dollar foundation on which to build an income portfolio. That fixed return is useful, too, if you should wish to use securities as collateral for a loan. Often bankers will lend you a greater percentage of the face value of a bond than they will on the common stock of the same corporation.

But the fixed return of bonds also represents their greatest drawback. This is particularly so in an inflationary environment such as we have seen in recent years and which we can expect to continue into the foreseeable future. The continual erosion in the dollar's purchasing power has raised havoc with fixed-income investments, and today's investor cannot begin to keep pace with rising prices if he stakes his entire claim on fixed-income securities. That's why it is our judgment that bonds should compose no more than a modest portion—perhaps 30 percent at most—of your portfolio.

Because conditions change, no bond, not even those of the very highest quality, can be put away and forgotten. Contrary to many investors' impressions, bond holdings should be watched closely, less for changes in quality deterioration or interest payment reliability than for shifts in the overall level of interest rates. Federal Reserve policy, the availability of credit, the volume of bank loans, corporate liquidity, and a host of other outside factors all have an important bearing on the prevailing level of interest rates, and these have a far greater and more frequent impact on high-grade bond prices than changes in the interest-paying ability and credit rating of the issuer.

Consequently, if you choose to include bonds in your investment program, you have to remain alert and ready to shift positions according to your perception of overall interest rate and bond market trends.

Chapter 9 Convertible Securities

SOME STOCKS, as we have seen, offer the double attraction of good yield plus moderate capital gains potential. So does another form of investment security—the convertible.

Logically enough, the convertible derives its name from the fact that it can be converted into, or exchanged for, another investment security—common stock in all but the rarest of cases. Also, it can come in the form of a bond or preferred stock. In either event, the convertible can be swapped for a specified number of common shares—often within a specified time period, after which the conversion privilege is "no longer" and the bond or preferred sells on its merits as a fixed-income investment.

To some degree at least the convertible enables the investor to have his cake and eat it, too. If the common stock goes up, the convertible will go up—though probably at a slightly slower gait, and provided that the common is not selling many points above the conversion price. (More on that below.) Of course, stocks also go down, but the convertible almost always provides a better yield than the stock it can be swapped for, and this higher return limits its downside risk. If it is high enough, it can even provide a "floor," beneath which the convertible will not fall, no matter what the stock does.

This is a rather esoteric area of investment, abounding with terms such as "conversion basis," "conversion value," "premium," "parity," etc. It's really not very complicated, but much of it seems to be a mystery to the average investor—the person who just might find the convertible much to his liking if he understood what it was all about.

How They Work

So, let's try to unravel the mystery. Below we have tabulated four convertibles, two bonds, and two preferred stocks, using prices and yields that were prevailing in mid-1980. The table is of the type you can expect to find whenever convertibles are touted by investment advisers, brokers, and the like.

	Price	Yield	Common Stock Price	Conversion Basis (Shares)*	Conversion Value†	Common Stock Yield
Bonds						
Caterpillar Tractor 5½s, 2000	113	4.9%	56	19.80	111	4.3%
K mart Corp. 6s, 1999	86	7.0	26	28.17	73	3.5
Preferred Stocks						
Bristol-Myers $2.00 Pfd.	47	4.3	43	1.06	46	3.7
Weyerhaeuser $2.80 Pfd.	49	5.7	37	1.21	45	3.5

* Number of common shares which would be acquired if conversion privilege were exercised.

† Market price of common stock multiplied by number of shares to be obtained in conversion.

First of all, remember that the Caterpillar and K mart bonds, like all bonds, are quoted on the basis of 100, though they bear face values of $1,000; hence, one Caterpillar convertible would actually cost $1,130 rather than $113. Now, let's get to the individual columns in the table.

Price and yield, of course, require no explanation. Under "conversion basis," we have the number of common shares you will receive for each bond, or each preferred share, if you convert. In the case of the Cat bonds, each can be swapped for 19.80 shares. The holder of the Bristol-Myers $2.00 preferred can exchange each share for 1.06 common shares.

The "conversion value" is simply the number of common shares you can acquire through conversion (or the conversion basis) times the price of the common. In other words, it's the value of what you will get if you convert. Again in the case of Cat, the conversion value is 19.80 shares times 56, the market price of the common—or 111. With Bristol-Myers common selling at 43, the conversion value of the $2.00 preferred is 46—or 1.06 times 43.

Common stock yield, obviously self-explanatory, is lower in all four cases than that of the convertible. If it weren't, in all likelihood it would pay you to convert.

The Conversion Premium

Before we get into the techniques of how to convert, it would behoove us to discuss the all-important conversion premium. The premium is simply the percentage by which the price of the bond or preferred exceeds its conversion value. If the price is equal to conversion value, then the convertible is selling at conversion parity. If by some quirk the bond or preferred is trading below its conversion value, it is at a discount.

Therefore, the premium is just that. It's simply what you pay for the conversion privilege, over and above the value of the common stock into which you can convert. In the case of the Cat bonds, you pay 113 for the right to swap for stock worth 111. Thus, the premium is 1.8 percent or 113 divided by 111. And, of course, you are also paying the premium for the "right" to receive higher income. The 4.9 percent yield on the Cat bonds is modestly above the 4.3 percent being offered by the common.

In buying convertibles, the size of the premium is always an important consideration. Generally it isn't a good idea to pay a premium of more than 20 percent, but there are no hard and fast rules. For example the K mart 6s of 1999, in the table, sell at a fairly high premium of 18 percent ($86 \div 73$) but are certainly not without appeal. Their yield of 7.0 percent is double the 3.5 percent of the common. Thus they provide a means of participating in a good quality fast-growth situation, and at the same time reaping an attractive return. Such an opportunity is not often available.

Weyerhaeuser is a similar case. Here the premium over conversion value is 9 percent ($49 \div 45$), a bit more than that of Bristol-Myers or Caterpillar. But this is another quality growth investment, and there is a clear-cut (though smaller) income advantage in buying the preferred—5.7 percent vs. 3.5 percent from the common.

The other two convertibles in the table are also attractive from a statistical standpoint, since their premiums are quite small (only 2 percent in each case). However, the yield differentials are also smaller. But there is, of course, more to picking a good convertible than figuring out its premium and yield. Caterpillar, though a fine company and an industry leader, is subject to cyclical influences. Its long-term earnings trend has been a highly favorable one, but there have been a few ups and downs along the way. Thus, the future price action of the Cat bonds and stock *may* (one never knows!) be more volatile than that of, say, Bristol-Myers.

Generally speaking, a convertible is not much better or worse than the stock it can be swapped for. While such factors as premiums, yields, expiration of conversion privilege, etc., must be carefully weighed, it is the investment appeal of the company and its common stock that overshadows everything in importance.

How and When to Convert

Some mention should perhaps be made of how convertibles can be converted, and when it is especially advisable to do so. Most convertible certificates, be they bonds or preferreds, carry on their reverse sides a small section which the owner must fill in and sign (everything is well explained) and then send along to the company's transfer agent—the address of which is given. If there is no such section on the back of the certificate, the holder can either contact the company directly or turn it all over to his broker.

As to *when* it's best to convert, it pretty well boils down to this: So long as the convertible provides better income, stay with it. But when dividends on the common stock are raised to the point that you can improve your income by converting, then do so. Of course, there is no guarantee that dividends will continue to be paid at the new higher rate. That's up to the company directors from quarter to quarter. But if prospects are good, as they should be if dividends have just been increased, it's most likely that payments will be maintained at the new rate.

A good example of a time-to-convert situation is provided by American Telephone, the time early 1977. AT&T has a $4.00 convertible preferred, each share of which can be swapped for 1.05 common shares. As long as AT&T was paying common dividends at a $3.80 annual rate, it was slightly advantageous to stick with the preferred, since the common you could obtain through conversion would bring you only $3.99 annually ($3.80 × 1.05) vs. the $4.00 you were getting on the preferred.

However, in February 1977, Telephone hiked its common dividend to a $4.20 annual rate. This meant that the 1.05 common shares obtainable through conversion would now be paying $4.41 a year. Moreover, there was no price advantage in holding on to the preferred, since it was selling at conversion parity—or, in this case, at 1.05 times the price of the common. Conversion was in order.

There is, of course, another time when conversion is called for, and that's when the conversion privilege is about to expire. This may happen when an issue is called for redemption, but in some cases the convertible "lives on" as a straight bond or preferred after the exchange period has run its course.

Again an example might clarify matters. In June 1977, Mesa Petroleum called for redemption its $1.60 convertible preferred, at a price of $26.75 a share, on July 11. Through July 8, each preferred share could be converted into 0.985 share of common, which was then selling around 34. Obviously, it was more to the holder's advantage to convert the preferred (then around 33) than to wait for it to be called.

In this case, however, conversion meant a sizable reduction in current income, since Mesa's indicated common dividend was only 40¢ annually. Thus, the holder had another option. He could sell the preferred and buy something else. But whatever his preference, he had to act by July 8, when the conversion privilege expired. Otherwise he was out roughly $7 a share.

Their Uses—and Limits

Convertibles, like stocks, come in all sizes and colors. Some are issued by strong, growing companies and carry high-quality ratings. Some are highly speculative. Clearly, a bond or preferred selling closely in line with its conversion value is much more appealing than one selling well above. In the latter case, the conversion privilege may never be of any real value. The attraction of convertibles—which are, after all, fixed-income securities—may also be influenced by the level of interest rates.

Well-chosen convertibles can provide inflation protection, long-term growth, relatively better price protection on the downside, and, in almost all cases, greater income than the underlying common stocks. A successful investor once described them as "like spinning a coin and saying heads I might lose a little, tails I could win a fortune." Maybe that's an overly rosy assessment, but convertibles do deserve consideration by the patient investor.

Chapter 10 Investing in Uncle Sam

You would be hard put to find anyone but an unreconstructed pessimist to argue with the statement that obligations of the United States government are just about the safest investments in the world as far as preservation of your dollar is concerned. As long as Uncle Sam retains control of the presses that print the money, there is virtually no doubt that interest and principal on these obligations will be paid when due.

The safety of "Governments" in terms of preserving the buying power of that invested capital is quite another thing. With inflation running at annual rates of 7 percent and upward, and yields on these government securities remaining moderate by comparison, the purchasing power of the assets committed to them will continue to shrink. In other words, you pay for one kind of "safety" with another. It's that trade-off of risks we talked about in earlier chapters.

An understanding of these risks and trade-offs is necessary if you consider U.S. government obligations as candidates for your investment program. Sometimes they do indeed have a valid place—because you want some safety of capital, or you want an assured rate of return for a specified period, or you have a tax problem they can help solve.

When the New York Stock Exchange was founded in 1792, its main business was dealing in U.S. government issues. Ever since then, they have been actively traded and enjoy the best market of any security in this country and probably in the world. Millions of dollars' worth can be bought and sold in a few minutes. Most of the trading is now done in the over-the-counter market, though these issues are listed on the New York Stock Exchange.

How "Governments" Work

"Governments" come in a wide variety of sizes, shapes, and styles. Before we get into their specifics, let's take a short detour and explore the structure through which they are issued and administered. All securities that are issued directly by the federal government come from the Department of the Treasury. Hence, they are also frequently called "Treasuries." The Treasury sells these securities to raise money to pay its bills, either in anticipation of tax revenues or because such revenues are insufficient to cover the bills.

The government also buys as well as sells these securities to help control the supply of money floating around in the economy. But that job is done by the Federal Reserve Board, a fiefdom unto itself, charged with the well-nigh impossible task of keeping the country's monetary and credit machinery chugging smoothly across the balance beam between too much growth and too much inflation. When the Fed wants to shrink the size of the money supply, it sells securities, thus taking out of circulation the money investors use to buy those securities. Conversely, if it wants to expand the money supply, it buys up these obligations, releasing dollars into the nation's spending stream.

The Fed also acts as the nation's central banker. It does this through the twelve Federal Reserve banks spread out around the country. These banks administer the Federal Reserve Board's monetary, credit, and banking policies. They also serve as the "bank" for the Treasury Department by handling the details of selling and purchasing its various marketable securities. You can deal directly with your nearest Federal Reserve Bank if you wish to buy or redeem U.S. government obligations. (More on the specifics of buying and selling them is included in Chapter 36.)

Bills, Notes, and Bonds

Back to those securities. Although they provide an almost endless variety of yields, maturities, and denominations, Treasury obligations are divided basically into three categories: bills, notes, and bonds.

Each week the Treasury auctions off 13- and 26-week bills and every four weeks, 52-week bills. The bills are sold at a discount from par, the difference representing the interest to the buyer. Until 1970, these bills came in denominations as low as $1,000. But when a surge in short-term interest rates lured millions of dollars from savings accounts into Treasury bills that year, the minimum denomination was jacked up to $10,000 to keep small investors from draining thrift institutions dry. Because of their relatively short maturity, they present practically no market risk.

If you can't come up with the $10,000 entry fee for bills and you find Treasuries attractive for short-term investments, take a look at Treasury notes. They range in maturities from one year to ten years, and some come in denominations as low as $1,000, though the more common minimum is $5,000. Their yields, too, are generally comparable with those provided by bills.

For longer-term investment, Treasury bonds are available. They may be issued for any length of time, with maturities generally ranging from 5½ to 25 years, though they are usually issued for at least ten years. They come in registered or bearer form and in denominations ranging from $1,000 to $1 million.

Some U.S. obligations are callable at par before maturity, on four months' notice. This fact is indicated in their description—for example, the 4¼s of 1987–92.

Besides these marketable issues, the government offers a variety of other special-interest securities. The most common are U.S. Savings Bonds. If you're old enough, you'll remember them as the "war bonds" of World War II. For many years, these have been available only in the E and H series (and after 1979 only in the EE and HH series). A full discussion of their special features appears in Chapter 36.

Other nonmarketable issues are available for persons building tax-sheltered retirement funds under the Keogh and Individual Retirement Account programs. These United States Retirement Plan bonds are available in denominations as low as $50. Interest is compounded semiannually and payable when the bonds are redeemed. In accordance with Keogh and IRA rules, redemption may not take place before age 59½ without tax penalties to the owner, unless he can demonstrate complete disability. Federal income tax is deferred on these issues until they are redeemed. They are exempt from state and local income taxes.

Federal Agency Bonds

In addition to these direct obligations of the United States, there is a wide variety of securities called "instrumentalities of the United States government." These are securities issued by official or quasi-official offshoots of the government called federal "agencies." These agencies were first used in the 1920s to provide capital for federally sponsored activities or federally guaranteed programs outside the regular budgetary structure. Their growth has mushroomed in late years. As recently as 1965, interest-bearing obligations of agencies amounted to about $17 billion. Only eight years later, in 1973, the total had soared to more than $70 billion. By mid-1980, it was well on the way to $200 billion and still climbing.

Many obligations of these agencies do not carry a direct federal guarantee. But a strong moral obligation is attached to honoring them, and it is inconceivable that the government would ever allow a default on any of them. Therefore, from the standpoint of safety of principal, they are virtually as solid as obligations specifically guaranteed by the government.

The best known of the government-sponsored enterprises and agencies are the Federal Home Loan banks, the Federal Land banks, the Federal Intermediate Credit banks, the Federal National Mortgage Association, the Government National Mortgage Association, and the Tennessee Valley Authority. In 1973, Congress created the Federal Financing Bank in an attempt to bring a measure of order to the chaotic structure of federal agency financing. Its aim was to provide a single vehicle through which a score of smaller and lesser-known agencies could raise capital. In 1974, its first year of operation, its outstanding debt was $4.5 billion. By 1977, that debt had climbed to $30 billion and by mid-1980 was near $80 billion.

At times federal agency securities have provided noticeably higher yields than direct United States obligations, and when this occurs, they do indeed bear serious consideration. Generally, though, the spread is rather small. These issues do not have quite as good a market as Treasury issues, but this should not pose any particular problem unless you are an investor dealing in millions of dollars. However, unless the spread is half a percentage point or better, you're probably just as well off to stick with Treasuries.

A Word on Taxability

Before leaving Governments, we should take note of the tax implications attached to them. Income earned on them is fully taxable at the federal level. Treasuries and most agency obligations, however, are exempt from state and local income and property taxation, though those of the Federal National Mortgage Association, Government National Mortgage Association, and the Export-Import Bank are not. The state and local tax situation is a point to consider when comparing Governments with corporate bonds and other taxable securities, particularly if you live in a high-tax state.

Although their income may escape state and local taxes, U.S. government and agency securities are subject to excise, gift, estate, and inheritance taxes levied by the states. They are also subject to federal gift and estate taxes.

We should not neglect to mention here a class of Treasury bonds which bear a special privilege with regard to federal estate taxes. This feature, which allows them to be applied at par against the estate tax obligation even if they were bought at a discount, has earned them the nickname of "flower bonds." Although law prohibits issue of any new bonds carrying this special feature and none have been issued since 1971, there are still several outstanding, should you wish to acquire some in the course of your estate planning. Here is a list of flower bonds still available.

3¼s of June 1978–83	4s of February 1988–93
3¼s of May 1985	4⅛s of May 1989–94
4¼s of May 1975–85	3s of February 1995
3½s of February 1990	3½s of November 1998
4¼s of August 1987–92	

Since government obligations are at the top of the quality list, their market action depends wholly upon fluctuations prevailing in interest rates. The swing of that price action depends in large part upon the amount of time to maturity; the shorter the maturity the less will be the price swing. As a bond approaches maturity, its price will begin to stabilize right around par. Prices of obligations subject to call will be influenced by that factor. For example, in times of falling interest rates, high-grade bonds will tend to rise in price but their call price will limit the extent of such advances; noncallable issues, on the other hand, will not be so constrained.

To preserve investment flexibility, we recommend that if you include Governments in your portfolio you choose those with maturities of ten years or less. This will help minimize the market risk should you find it desirable or necessary to sell them before they mature.

But keep in mind that despite the ultimate safety of U.S. government and agency obligations in terms of marketability and preservation of capital, they possess the same serious drawbacks in protecting against inflation as do other bonds, because both income and principal are fixed.

Chapter 11 Investing in Tax-Exempts

It's bad enough that inflation chews away a sizable chunk from any increases you might enjoy in your income. But then comes the tax man and applies a bite of his own. Your rising income pattern catapults you rather swiftly into the loftier tax brackets. In many cases the resulting tax boost, along with inflation's nibble, sets you further behind than you were before your "raise."

With this "double-indexing," so to speak, is it any wonder that more investors are turning with attentive eyes to state and local bonds? If they can't do anything about inflation's incisor, at least by holding the bonds they can avoid some of the tax man's molar, since interest earned by state and local bonds is exempt from federal income taxation.

Indeed, one of the reasons "municipals," as they have come collectively to be known, are free of federal income tax is so they can offer lower interest than taxable securities and still attract capital. In the lower tax brackets, an investor would be better off to buy taxable securities, because even after the taxes were paid their higher yield gives a better return.

When Are They Profitable?

At what point do the tables turn? When does it become more profitable for you as an investor to buy tax-exempts than to hold taxables? The answer depends on three things: your tax bracket, the prevailing yield on taxable securities, and the prevailing yield on tax-exempts. We'll give you a table and a simple mathematical formula in a bit that will help you determine when you have reached that point.

When we say tax bracket, we do not mean the percentage of your income you actually pay to Uncle Sam, but the amount you would pay on every dollar earned above your present taxable income, based on the Internal Revenue Service tax tables. Thus, if you're in the 34 percent bracket, 34 cents of your next dollar of income would go for federal taxes.

Besides your own tax bracket, the relationship between yields on taxable and nontaxable securities in the marketplace will determine the relative merits of either alternative. As an average, tax-exempts yield somewhere around 65 percent of what taxable bonds yield. Thus, if bond yields in general are running 8 percent, yields on tax-exempts will be running around 5 percent. In such a relationship, you can expect the tables to turn in your favor when you reach the 36 percent tax bracket.

In the aftermath of New York City's flirtation with default in 1975, investor confidence in all tax-exempts took a severe beating. If the Big Apple could go to the brink of fiscal collapse, what about Orange City, Iowa, or Lemon Grove, California? Suddenly, all municipals were suspect. The only way to assuage investors' doubts was to crank up yields. At the height of the scare, tax-exempt securities were providing yields within 85 percent of those provided by taxables. Hosts of hitherto diffident investors were leaping into line to buy tax-exempts. To accommodate those lacking the wherewithal to buy bonds outright, or who wished to diversify their limited assets, tax-exempt unit trusts sprang to the forefront of investor interest. Later, after a propitious change in the tax laws, municipal bond funds seized the hearts and minds of rapacious investors. (For more on the "muni-funds" and unit trusts, see Chapter 13.)

Meanwhile, New York City refused to die. Slowly, with the help of time, the gods, Uncle Sam, and high-coupon bonds, it edged away from the brink. As it did, confidence began to creep back into the municipal bond market, and the yield relationship to taxables resumed a more traditional stance.

However, the experience opened the eyes of many more investors to the possibilities offered by tax-exempts. Ironically, this newborn interest was developing at a time when the federal government was stepping up efforts to wean state and local entities away from tax-exempts. Since any transition to fully taxable municipal bonds will be many years in the coming, tax-exempts will be around for a while for investors who might find them attractive and useful.

So we get back to the broad question of deciding when they are of value to you and then to the more specific question of how to pick and choose them if you want to include them in your portfolio. The table below shows how the advantages of tax-exempt securities increase as the tax bracket escalates.

Tax Bracket	Tax-Exempt Yield of:				
	4.5%	5.0%	5.5%	6.0%	6.5%
	is equivalent to taxable yield of:				
28%	6.25%	6.94%	7.64%	8.33%	9.03%
29	6.34	7.04	7.75	8.45	9.15
31	6.52	7.25	7.97	8.70	9.42
32	6.62	7.35	8.09	8.82	9.56
34	6.82	7.58	8.33	9.09	9.85
36	7.03	7.81	8.59	9.38	10.16
40	7.50	8.33	9.17	10.00	10.83
42	7.76	8.62	9.48	10.34	11.21
50	9.00	10.00	11.00	12.00	13.00
60	11.25	12.50	13.75	15.00	16.25

If you want to work the figures out for yourself, here's the formula. To determine the equivalent taxable yield on a tax-exempt, divide the stated interest by 1.00 minus your tax bracket. Thus, a 5 percent tax-exempt bond for some one in the 40 percent bracket would be equivalent to an 8.33 percent taxable bond:

$$\frac{0.05}{1.00 - 0.40} = 0.0833$$

What Kinds of Bonds Are There?

The safest of all tax-exempt securities are those offered by municipalities under the Department of Housing and Urban Development (HUD) and guaranteed by federal subsidies. Don't confuse these with bonds issued by the various state housing authorities, which have neither federal nor state backing.

General obligation bonds, also called "full faith and credit bonds," are next safest because they have the full taxing power of the state or municipality behind them. However, they run the gamut from safe to speculative, depending on the solvency of the issuing body.

Revenue bonds, which depend on such things as tolls and user fees for their income, are more risky because they do not have taxing power behind them. If their fees do not generate the necessary income to service the obligations, they can go into default.

Industrial development bonds are first cousins to revenue bonds. They are issued by a state, community, or authority to build a facility for a company whose lease payments cover interest and principal. The corporation puts its credit on the line and gets financing at tax-exempt rates. They were created to provide incentives for investment in local economic development projects and particularly for providing capital to install pollution control equipment in existing plants. Because corporations are easier to analyze than municipalities, these issues generally are snapped up rather quickly. As a result of their popularity, Congress has limited individual issues to $5 million.

Assessment bonds are issued for specific projects and paid for by assessments levied on property owners in the benefited area. The quality and value of the property on which the assessments are levied determine the safety of the bonds.

Tax revenue or bond anticipation notes are offered by communities in expectation of incoming revenues. They are usually short term and offer low yields. Their short maturities and high quality make them attractive to commercial banks, and, generally speaking, they trade at roughly half the return available on taxable commercial paper.

Marketability Can Be a Problem

There is no central marketplace for the quarter of a trillion dollars' worth of outstanding municipal debt. Bonds are traded by telephone among countless brokerage dealers. There are no commissions, but neither are the prices of most bonds listed anywhere. You are at the complete mercy of the dealers, who inventory bonds for their own account and have a major stake in profiting from markups and discounts.

Moreover, there is no strict definition of a round lot in the municipal market. It is any amount that is large enough to get the dealer to narrow his spread between bid and asked price. Generally $25,000 is considered a round lot, but sometimes it can be $50,000 or $100,000.

With many thousands of entities issuing and continually floating and retiring bonds of varying maturities and interest rates, the factors affecting these securities reach infinite proportions. Because institutional and individual investors frequently purchase and hold these securities for long periods, the market is not nearly as liquid as that for common stocks or corporate bonds.

Marketability thus becomes a concern of the potential municipal investor. Generally speaking, it is best to avoid small-town securities that might be difficult to sell without a price concession should you need to dispose of them prior to maturity.

Issues floated by larger governmental subdivisions are rated by Moody's and Standard & Poor's and appear regularly in the Blue List, an inventory of bond offerings published each trading day by Standard & Poor's and circulated among municipal bond dealers. The obligations of many smaller towns, school and utility districts, and authorities, on the other hand, will appear in the listings only infrequently. Generally speaking, any bearing an A rating or better may be considered safe.

How Do You Judge Them?

But you must remember there is a great deal more to picking municipal bonds than selecting the largest yield and collecting income. Auditing standards are inferior when compared with those of the corporate world. Though financial statements are improving, issuers frequently publish inadequate reports. Ratings are sometimes unreliable measures of credit risks, as the New York City episode so clearly demonstrated.

Therefore, you are much more on your own as you evaluate tax-exempts than you are with corporates. Good information is hard to find, so the rating services are a helpful starting point. But you should get a prospectus on any bond you might consider purchasing, and you should watch the financial statements for news of litigation or legislation that might influence the quality of the bond.

Beyond that, what should you look for in a municipal bond? With general obligation debt, the object is to discover how heavily indebted the issuing municipality already is relative to its real assets and its economic power. Important considerations must include an assessment of the largest employers and taxpayers, population growth, personal income levels, and operating revenues.

If you look at revenue bonds, pinpoint the sources of income. As a rule of thumb, be sure there is at least $1.20 in income for every $1.00 in debt service (interest costs). If revenues tend to be highly cyclical, you might want to add a greater cushion. Then try to determine the order of liens; see what is pledged to whom.

Revenue bonds include water and power issues backed by receipts from users (industrial, commercial, and residential utility customers). Besides the companies' financial track records, you also must assess the rate-relief history of the state's regulatory agencies.

Bridge, turnpike, and tunnel bonds are secured by tolls. Revenues from such tolls might be adversely affected in the future if the country should experience skyrocketing prices or shortages of gasoline.

Hospital bonds are popular with some investors because they usually derive about 90 percent of their revenues from federal Medicare and Medicaid programs. There is growing evidence that Congress might put a damper on some of these payments in the future. Malpractice suits are another cloud on the horizon. Also, they have limited marketability and might be difficult to sell if you should wish to do so.

Housing and finance authority bonds are issued by local agencies principally to build middle-income housing. Sometimes they include college dormitories, mental health facilities, and nursing homes. Rental payments usually provide the security, but individual arrangements can vary considerably. As noted above, these are not to be confused with federally guaranteed Department of Housing and Urban Development securities.

Airport bonds are covered by leases to airlines. As with toll-oriented issues, sharp increases in energy prices and a slowdown in the overall economy could affect the airlines' ability to cover the lease payments.

Many sports complexes have been financed by municipal bond sales, and these are generally covered by ticket sales. Proliferation of major-league sports franchises and difficulties experienced by some of these franchises should constitute a warning flag to wary investors. Legislation that stripped most of the tax-shelter allure from investment in sports franchises should also be weighed when looking at such bonds.

We should not proceed without mentioning specifically the bonds of Puerto Rico. They may have to be chosen with greater attention to potential risk than those of other governmental bodies, but they do possess an attractive feature that should not be overlooked: Income from them not only is exempt from federal taxes but also from taxes in all states and municipalities.

Which Ones to Buy?

Once you've decided that tax-exempts belong in your investment program, you're faced with the decision of how to stake your claim. Do you want to hold the bonds themselves? Or leave the selection to the professionals? If you choose to go with the pros, do you want an unmanaged unit trust? Or a managed municipal bond fund?

If you don't feel confident of your expertise and you have no adviser to consult, or if you have less than $25,000 to invest, you might do best to stick with the funds. Many offer minimum investments as small as $1,000, and for that you get a broadly diversified portfolio, which minimizes your risk.

Bond fund or unit trust, what's the difference? A bond fund has no set expiration date; maturing bonds are sold or replaced and the fund continues in existence long after its original portfolio has matured or changed. Not so with a unit trust, which consists of a set portfolio split into $1,000 units. As the components of its portfolio mature, unit holders receive their prorated share of the principal.

If you're going to invest in tax-exempts, you should try to reap fullest measure from the exemption. This means you must explore your own state's and municipality's tax treatment of them. Most states, if they levy taxes on income from securities, will exempt that income generated by obligations issued within the state. The same is true of local taxes. So if this is a factor, you should try to find "home grown" tax-exempts—ones issued in the state in which you live.

You have to watch this angle when investing in the unit trusts or bond funds. While these funds are allowed by federal law to pass the tax exemption on to you, some state and local governments have not been going along. This means they will tax all of the income generated by the fund—including that from bonds issued within your state. If local or state law penalizes you on that score, think about going with bonds themselves instead of a bond fund. Or look for a unit trust wholly invested in bonds from your own state; there will be no tax problem with these.

When Shouldn't You Use Them?

Here's another important point to consider as you ponder the possibility of investment in tax-exempts. If you have loans outstanding, the interest deduction on these might be in jeopardy to the extent that it matches income from municipals. The Internal Revenue Service takes a hard line on this point, disallowing such deductions where it can show even the slightest connection between the loan and the holding of tax-exempts. Loss of such deductions might negate most, if not all, of the benefits of owning municipals.

There are other times, too, when tax-exempts might not fit into your investment picture, even if you are in a high tax bracket. They are subject to gift, estate, and inheritance taxes and thus have some drawbacks in estate planning. A forced sale in an estate settlement could result in loss of principal, particularly in the case of a municipal for which no ready market exists. Younger beneficiaries in lower tax brackets might rather have assets showing more promising returns.

If your income fluctuates a great deal, tax-exempt bonds might help you one year but hurt the next. However, if you anticipate substantial growth in your income over the next several years, you might want to acquire municipals during times of high interest rates when their yields are attractive.

In the final analysis, though, tax-exempts are vulnerable to the same criticisms we have voiced earlier about other fixed-income investments. If they possess any protection against inflation, it is strictly limited. In a highly inflationary environment, they can, in fact, lose ground. The prospect so alluring to many taxpayers of depriving Uncle Sam of some tax revenue must be weighed against the possibility of obtaining greater gains elsewhere. Giving Caesar his due can frequently be more profitable in the long run.

Chapter 12 Mutual Funds

THE CONCEPT of forming a company to execute in collective investment the pooled assets of like-minded investors is a relatively recent development. As early as 1823 a New England life insurance company possessed features that resembled those of an investment company. The first recorded precursor to what we know today as mutual funds was organized a few years later by King William I of the Netherlands.

But it wasn't until 1868 that the first bona fide "mutual fund" came upon the scene. In that year the Foreign and Colonial Government Trust was formed in London to provide "the investor of moderate means the same advantages as the large capitalists, in diminishing the risk of investing in Foreign and Colonial Government stocks, by spreading the investment over a number of different stocks."

If the mutual fund idea was rooted in Europe, it blossomed into full flower across the Atlantic. The first bud appeared in the United States in 1893 with the appearance of the Boston Personal Property Trust. It was followed in 1904 by the Railway and Light Securities Company. Both were organized as closed-end investment companies. In 1954, the latter converted to an open-end investment company and changed its name to Colonial Fund, under which it still operates. We shall distinguish between closed-end and open-end funds and define other terms in a moment. First let's complete our historical perspective.

The early 1920s witnessed the appearance of the mutual fund as we know it today, offering a self-liquidating feature, prudent investment policies and restrictions, diversification, a published portfolio, and an uncomplicated capital structure. Massachusetts Investors Trust, the first of the modern genre, was introduced in March 1924. Then came State Street Investment Corporation, also in 1924. These were followed in 1925 by Incorporated Investors, now Putnam Investors Fund. From modest beginnings, these three funds have become giants with assets in the hundreds of millions of dollars.

By 1929, there were 19 open-end funds with assets totaling only about $140 million. Growth was slow through the Depression-ridden 1930s, so that by 1940 combined assets of mutual funds were less than $500 million. The next three decades witnessed phenomenal growth, and by the end of 1972 net assets of the industry had mushroomed to $60 billion, representing more than ten million shareholder accounts. Falling markets and net redemptions served to lower the total to only $34 million in 1974. However, by mid-1980 the industry was well along the recovery path with $53 billion of net assets, excluding $76 billion worth of money market funds.

Even so, it should be noted that while the mutual funds have been credited from time to time as having a significant influence on the direction of the stock market, their assets generally have accounted for less than 7 percent of the market value of all stocks listed on the New York Stock Exchange.

What Is a Mutual Fund?

Now let's get a handle on what a mutual fund is—and what it isn't. Legally speaking, there is no such thing as a "mutual fund." That's merely a name coined to embrace a variety of investment companies and investment trusts created for the mutual investment under professional management of assets contributed by several individuals. A mutual fund—or, more technically, an investment company—is a corporation; and, as with other corporations, the individual investor's interest in it is represented by shares of stock. If the assets under management increase in value, the investor's capital will increase accordingly. Should the assets' value decline, the prorated net value of each share will likewise decline.

A mutual fund thus is basically different from, say, a savings account, where a depositor is guaranteed a fixed rate of return and will be able to withdraw all of his principal when he desires. A mutual fund investor is an owner, not a lender; he shares in the profits and losses and in the income and expenses.

However, there are some differences in the way they are taxed that distinguish investment companies from other corporations. Where all of the income from a conventional corporation is subject to federal income taxation, most of it is passed on to shareholders in an investment company. In order to qualify for investment company status, a fund must comply with the provisions of the Investment Company Act of 1940. That comprehensive piece of legislation provides the foundation for regulation of the mutual fund industry and establishes standards of income distribution and diversification of assets.

Briefly, to operate as a regulated investment company and enjoy the tax benefits attached thereto, a fund must distribute at least 90 percent of its income each year to its shareholders. The remaining 10 percent or less is used to cover operating expenses and other overhead and is subject to corporation taxes. Shareholders pay income taxes at their own individual rates on the income passed along to them.

To assure diversification and to prevent the possibility that an investment company would acquire a controlling interest in a corporation, the law prohibits it from investing more than 5 percent of the value of its total assets in the securities of any single company or from holding more than 10 percent of the voting securities of any one company.

Closed-Ends and Open-Ends

The first mutual funds were closed-end funds. Closed-end funds still exist but are now known as publicly traded investment funds. They differ in a number of respects from open-end funds. The primary difference, though, is in the way the shares of the fund are created.

In a closed-end fund, the number of shares to be offered for sale is fixed at the outset; the fund operators may not create new shares on demand. An open-end fund, on the other hand, may create and sell its shares on a continuous basis; if an investor wishes to purchase fund shares, the new shares are created as needed.

Another important difference is that open-end funds stand ready to buy back, or redeem, outstanding shares at a price based on the market value of the portfolio at the time of redemption. Closed-end funds do not buy back their shares from investors. Investors, in fact, have no direct buying or selling contact with the closed-end fund except when reinvesting distributions in additional shares. Instead, they buy and sell fund shares on a securities exchange or in the over-the-counter market, just as they would do with any common stock. The broker who handles the transaction charges the same commission as he does for any similar transaction involving common stock.

Load Versus No-Load Funds

Open-end funds fall into two major categories: load funds and no-loads. They resemble each other in every way but one. Load funds are sold with a sales commission (the "load"), typically about 8.5 percent. This figure is expressed as a percentage of the total purchase price; that is to say, net asset value plus the sales charge. Thus, as compared with stock commissions, which are based on the sums actually invested, the sales charge for mutual funds is understated. For example, if you purchased shares in a load fund for $1,000, only $915 would actually be invested in securities. The remaining $85 would go to the sales organization. If you divide that $85 by $915, the amount invested, you get 9.3 percent. Looking at it another way, if you want a full $1,000 in securities earning money for you, you must pay the fund a total of $1,093.

In respect to performance, there is no appreciable difference between that of the load funds and of the no-loads. Why, then, should you as an investor pay the load? Mutual fund salespersons will proffer any number of arguments to justify the load. Probably the most common is that over the long run the growth of the fund will reduce the effective cost of the sales charge to a minimum.

In rebuttal, you can't always count on such growth, even over a relatively long period. Even if you amortize the load over a nine-year period, it amounts to about 1 percent a year. If load and no-load funds are performing in lock step, it's pretty hard to justify even a 1 percent "penalty." Performance of mutual funds in recent years has not been so spectacular as to justify ignoring the effect of the load on your nest egg.

Another argument put forth in defense of the load is that it carries an element of service for the investor. The salesperson or broker to whom the load is paid stands ready to answer questions, give advice, and help iron out any kinks that might develop with regard to your fund account. You have to ask yourself whether the cost of such an implied service is justified. In the final analysis, the price of a fund, whether you pay a sales commission or not, is secondary to choosing a fund with a good long-term performance record and investment aims in accord with your own.

Advantages of Mutual Funds

There are a number of sound reasons why small investors and large investors lacking access to investment counsel should explore the advantages of buying and holding mutual funds. Among them:

Professional management. When you buy a fund you benefit from the expertise of full-time money managers who watch over the fund's portfolio and make all the necessary decisions as to what to buy, sell, or hold. Of course, the experts can make mistakes—some of them are beauties—and as among doctors and lawyers, some mutual fund managers are bright, others are not. In general, however, the leading funds are run by high-caliber people with substantial experience in investments.

Division of risk. A typical fund spreads your investment dollar over many different industry and company stocks and securities. Thus a disaster in any one or a few of them does not mean a calamity for the fund as a whole. For example, a $1 billion fund such as T. Rowe Price Growth Stock is invested in more than 50 different stocks, none of which accounts for more than 5 percent of the fund's total market value at the time of purchase.

Information. How a mutual fund has performed is a matter of record. Mutual funds are unique in the fact that they publish information as to their performance and it is readily available. Thus the layman, by reading the prospectus and shareholder reports, can compare one fund with another and make a decision as to which to buy. This is not the situation, say, with bank trust departments and stockbrokers.

Freedom from emotional involvement. All too often the individual investor is swayed by the influence of one or a few well-motivated but poorly informed friends who are only too free with their stock market advice. Also, lacking expert knowledge, the individual may make investment decisions at times on the basis of headlines, rumors, and the fears and emotions of the moment. Investing in the stock market is for cool heads only, and it is one place where a little of the wrong knowledge can lead to big losses. When you buy good mutual funds, you can sit back and relax and, to paraphrase the Greyhound ad, leave the driving to them. The time and effort needed to choose and follow a good fund and keep on top of its fortunes, compared with the time and effort required for keeping track of individual stocks, is as minutes are to hours.

Freedom from housekeeping. Aside from the emotional aspect of investing, there's the problem of mechanics. If you own stocks, you have to protect the certificates unless the account is in a street name. There may be proxies to sign, rights to exercise, decisions to exercise or sell warrants, and on and on. Then there's the headache at income tax time. At the end of each year, mutual funds provide shareholders with information as to the total of dividends and other distributions made during the year and certain pertinent tax information. On a day-to-day basis, the status and value of your mutual fund account can be determined at a glance from the mutual fund quotations in your newspaper.

Automatic reinvestment of income dividends and capital gains distributions. One of the principal advantages of mutual fund investment is that dividends can be automatically converted to additional shares, thus compounding your investment. Contrast this with the situation when you own a few thousand dollars worth of each of several stocks. The dividend checks might be so modest that it would be difficult or expensive to reinvest them in additional shares. All too often dividend checks are frittered away, and the investment loses the benefit of compounding. The reinvestment feature of mutual funds is a form of forced saving and can make a big difference over the long run.

Instant diversification. It takes as little as $250 to start a typical mutual fund account. Additional investments can likewise be made in small amounts and at any time. When you buy shares in a mutual fund you buy a pro rata share of many different corporations in a number of different industries. To achieve similar diversification as an individual investor even in a small way would entail considerable time, to say nothing of commission expenses. Furthermore, funds purchase stocks in such large quantities that they almost always qualify for minimum sales commissions.

Exchange privileges. Most of the larger investment companies sponsor a variety of funds which offer a broad range of investment objectives, services, and programs. Thus a shareholder whose investment goals have changed may be able to switch part or all of his principal from one fund to another within the same "family." In addition, this exchange may be done by mail, telegram, or even telephone. The exchange privilege is only one of a number of shareholder services that make mutual funds an increasingly useful adjunct to financial planning. Tax-sheltered retirement plans and systematic investing and withdrawal plans are other features of the modern mutual fund, making it a comprehensive and convenient investment for the individual of moderate means.

Cost of Ownership

Every form of investment has its negative side, mutual funds included. Fund ownership is no free ride; there are costs and fees. We've already discussed the sales charge in the case of load funds. Not so obvious are management fees which average about 0.5 percent per year of assets for load funds and no-loads alike. In some instances the management fee is reduced as the fund's net asset value increases. Besides the management fee, there are a number of smaller charges for administrative services, directors' compensation, shareholder servicing, custodian fees, legal fees, reports to stockholders, and the like.

The total of the management fee and the housekeeping costs expressed as a percentage of net assets constitutes the fund's expense ratio. These ratios vary considerably depending on the size of the fund and other factors. For example, at T. Rowe Price Growth Stock they have averaged less than 0.55 percent annually in recent years. Aside from efficient management, the low expense ratio reflects the benefits of size, for this is a fund with assets numbering in the hundreds of millions of dollars. Contrast that with the 1.5 percent and more per year for Pennsylvania Mutual in recent years. But that fund is a midget compared to Price Growth. Since many expenses are fixed, they understandably represent a larger portion of the cost of running a small fund than a large fund. What you look for is a declining trend in the expense ratio as assets grow over the years. Otherwise the fund is not managed efficiently, and expenses may become a heavy drain on performance.

Reading the Prospectus

The Securities Act of 1933 requires delivery of a prospectus (essentially an abbreviated form of registration statement) prior to or with any solicitation of an order for mutual fund shares. The prospectus "tells it all"—something about management and its background, such unfavorable facts as there may be, including litigation and problems with the Securities and Exchange Commission, as well as a host of figures relating to income and expenses, dividends and gains (or losses), portfolio turnover, assets and liabilities, and the portfolio of investments.

In most cases, the funds have taken great pains to word their prospectuses in such a way that the average investor, with careful reading, can find out more about a fund's potential than he can glean from a similar reading of the annual report of an industrial corporation. Only when you buy a new issue, with its accompanying prospectus, are you in a position to learn as much about a corporate common stock.

The prospectus opens with a statement about the fund's primary objective. Thus the prospectus of Financial Industrial Income Fund states: "The basic investment goal of the Fund is to obtain the best possible current income while following sound investment practices."

The prospectus then elaborates on the fund's investment aims and gives information as to the minimum starting investment ($500 in the case of Financial Industrial Income) and the minimum subsequent investment, which is generally under $50. Early in the prospectus is a statement of per-share income and capital changes for each of the past ten years. That will give you an idea of the fund's investment income and expenses, its dividends, and its net realized and unrealized gains (or losses) on securities. The statistical tables that accompany this information show changes in net asset value and various financial ratios, such as the ratio of expenses to average net assets, and the ratio of net investment income to average net assets. It may also show portfolio turnover.

The prospectus goes on to outline the fund's investment limitations. For example, among other restrictions Financial Industrial Income may not: "Sell short or buy on margin. Borrow money in excess of 5% of the value of its total net assets, and when borrowing it is a temporary measure for emergency purposes. Buy or sell commodities, commodity contracts, or real estate (however, securities of companies investing in real estate may be purchased) ... Invest in any company for the purpose of control or management. Buy other than readily marketable securities. Purchase securities if the purchase would cause the fund to have more than 5% of the value of its total assets invested in the securities of any one company, or to own more than 10% of the voting securities of any one company (except obligations issued or guaranteed by the U.S. Government)."

Next comes information about the fund's investment adviser, plus the names and backgrounds of officers and directors. Information on the "how-to's" follows: How to purchase shares, how to redeem shares, how to exchange shares, and how to transfer shares. Then come statements about the fund's dividend policies, dates dividends are paid from investment income if and when earned, and perhaps a few remarks on the tax status of dividends and capital gains distributions.

The prospectus winds up with a statement about its investments, including a breakdown as to the proportion of the portfolio in common stocks and bonds as well as the number of shares and the market value of each holding as of the statement date. The prospectus may also provide the cost of each investment, thus enabling the reader to see at a glance the major trouble spots. Other statements about assets and liabilities, along with notes to the financial statements, bring up the rear.

The Pulse of Portfolio Turnover

The frequency with which securities are bought and sold is a vital measure of a fund's health. By itself, however, it does not tell all you need to know to evaluate a fund's prospects. You might call it a financial heartbeat. Thus, a rapid heartbeat may be shown by a vigorous individual enjoying healthful exercise, or in someone else it may be symptomatic of a morbid condition. A performance fund may show a substantial portfolio turnover rate and good performance all at the same time; a similar turnover rate for a fund that never goes anywhere suggests both poor portfolio management and a heavy drain on net assets from brokerage commissions and related expenses.

Many funds do include statements as to turnover rates in their prospectuses. Unfortunately, you sometimes have to do a good deal of hunting to find them. If the turnover rate is nowhere to be found, there is a comparatively simple way of determining it: Divide the lesser of purchases or sales of investment securities by the average of net assets for the period in question. The numerator of this common fraction may be found in notes to the financial statements under the heading "Purchases and Sales of Securities." Under that heading in a semiannual report of T. Rowe Price Growth Stock Fund was the following: "Purchases and Sales aggregated $70,970,090 and $67,-369,885, respectively, for common stock. Sales of Federal agencies and certificates of deposit aggregated $2,000,000 and $17,024,813, respectively." The numerator in this instance is $67,369,885.

For the denominator, refer to the "Statement of Changes in Net Assets" under which in the example are net assets at the beginning of the period of $1,112,897,758 and net assets at the end of the period of $1,209,754,151. The average of these two amounts is $1,161,325,955. The resulting fraction—and all of this is made infinitely easier with a pocket calculator—reduces to 5.8 percent as compared with a stated turnover of 5.9 percent. That's not bad for an approximation.

One added complication. It is important that you exclude transactions in government securities and short-term notes from the computation. That was no problem in the example above, because the amounts for purchases and sales were stated for common stock. Funds provide the necessary information in a number of ways. For example, in a report for Financial Industrial Income, the notes to financial statements put it this way: "During the year, purchases of investment securities aggregated $63,059,813 and sales aggregated $66,822,877 (excluding corporate discount notes)."

An Important "Don't"

There is nothing to be gained by acquiring mutual fund shares immediately prior to dividends or capital gains distributions. To the contrary, to do so can hurt you.

Here's how. Apart from the ups and downs of the stock market, asset value gradually increases to the extent that portfolio securities are a source of interest and dividend income to the fund. If portfolio holdings appreciate, so much the better, for this also builds up asset value. To the extent such appreciation is realized, it becomes a source of capital gains distributions. Dividends from investment income and capital gains distributions are paid to the shareholder who buys the shares before the ex-dividend date. In other words, the ex-dividend date is the day on and after which the buyer of a share is not entitled to a previously declared dividend.

An investor who purchases fund shares shortly before an ex-dividend date will receive the dividend, to be sure, but it will be a hollow benefit. The pitfalls are spelled out in the prospectus, but while some funds take pains to explain the matter in some detail, others slough it off as a minor detail. This is unfortunate, because in a strong market the payments can be big and the tax consequences important.

The prospectus of the Johnston Capital Appreciation Fund has one of the best discussions on this point we have ever read. Here's how they put it:

Prior to purchasing shares of a fund, the impact of dividends or capital gains distributions which are expected to be announced or have been announced but not paid should be carefully considered. Any such dividends or capital gains distributions paid shortly after a purchase of shares by an investor prior to the record date will have the effect of reducing the per share net asset value of his shares by the amount of the dividends or distributions. All or a portion of such dividends or distributions, although in effect a return of capital, are subject to taxes, which may be at ordinary income tax rates. The individual should consult his own tax adviser for any special advice.

No one wants to pay taxes on someone else's gains, yet that is the situation if shares are purchased just prior to a capital gains distribution. Moreover, in the case of a load fund, the total sales charges would be needlessly high

Funds in Your Future?

There you have some of the basics about mutual funds—where they came from, how they work, what to look for in evaluating one, how to read a prospectus. As you must have concluded from the foregoing, it's not exactly a matter of running your finger down a list of funds, finding one whose name intrigues you, and buying it to hold for keeps.

As with any investment decision, you have to know first what your own objectives are. Then you must find the proper vehicle—or, more frequently, vehicles—for meeting those objectives. Mutual funds can and do play an important part in achieving the investment goals of millions of Americans. How well funds do for you as an individual investor depends in large measure on how skillfully you have chosen the funds in your portfolio.

Just as you must evaluate other investments as to quality and the type and extent of risk each embodies, you must do the same with mutual funds. Some funds are better managed than others. Some place more emphasis on safety of principal than others. Some trade off quality of their holdings for higher yields or the chance of greater growth.

What Kind of Fund?

If you are a risk taker at heart and like a fast ride for your buck, look at the performance funds. If you buy for the long haul and have in mind a nest egg for retirement many years hence, you should stick with the sound quality growth funds. If you want some current income while waiting for the day you cash in your shares, you should try to find funds that combine good current income with a potential for growth. Finally, if income is all-important to you and you will settle for little or no growth in the process, bond funds may be for you.

A list of good quality growth funds would include these:

David L. Babson Investment Fund	Pioneer Fund
Johnston Capital Appreciation Fund	Putnam Investors Fund
National Investors Corp.	T. Rowe Price Growth Stock Fund

Here's a sampling of funds that stress high current income:

David L. Babson Income Trust	American General Bond Fund*
Northeast Investors Trust	Fort Dearborn Income Securities*
Rowe Price New Income Fund	Montgomery Street Income Securities*

Here are some that emphasize both growth and income:

Affiliated Fund	Financial Industrial Income Fund
American Mutual Fund	Guardian Mutual Fund
Decatur Income Fund	Windsor Fund

Here's a potpourri of funds that tend to invest in speculative stocks. These funds are not for the faint at heart:

Acorn Fund	Pioneer II
Mathers Fund	Putnam Voyager Fund
Over-the-Counter Securities	Scudder Special
Value Line Special Situations	

Again . . . Diversify

For the same reason you choose a mutual fund to diversify your portfolio and thereby spread your risks, you should not put all of your investment eggs in the same mutual fund basket, either. By avoiding that trap, you will cut your losses should a fund you are holding undergo a management crisis, lose its "magic touch," or just plain hit a patch of poor luck.

* Publicly traded investment fund

Chapter 13 Specialized Investment Funds

COLLECTIVELY, MUTUAL funds compose a dynamic, ever-evolving industry. Sponsors have been resourceful in bringing out new products to fit changing market conditions. In recent years, new types of funds have been devised, particularly in the income area, which may be of greater interest to some readers than the conventional equity types which are the backbone of the industry.

This section is devoted to a rundown of funds for specialized objectives. Few of these funds can stand alone in an investment program, but they can be used with other funds or securities to "fine tune" your portfolio to your particular financial needs.

Money Market Funds

A soft stock market and hefty returns of 10 percent and higher combined to give the money market funds a lot of appeal when they were introduced in 1974. Two dozen or so were started that year, and investors salted away more than $3 billion in them by the end of 1975. Some observers reasoned at the time that when short-term interest rates declined, investors would rush to redeem their money fund shares and pour their assets into the stock and bond markets. But when rates did come down, withdrawals did not reach the calamitous stage that had been feared.

Increasingly, small businesses, corporations, and others who would be unlikely to shift to stocks or savings banks found these funds to be convenient repositories for their cash reserves. Also, brokers began putting their own money and that of their customers into the funds as a temporary parking lot for subsequent reinvestment in stocks. Extensive use was made of these funds as a temporary haven for the tuition receipts of schools and colleges. Thanks to infusions of money from a growing body of institutional investors, the money market funds passed the acid test of reduced interest rates in pretty good shape.

Money fund assets swelled to more than $70 billion in 1980, reflecting the appeal of their inflation-paced yields to some four million investors. Among the larger of these funds are Dreyfus Liquid Assets, Fidelity Daily Income Trust, Merrill Lynch Ready Assets Trust, The Reserve Fund, and Scudder Managed Reserves.

Index Funds

The Vanguard Group introduced the First Index Investment Trust—the first index fund to be offered to the public—in August 1976. This fund, in common with a number of other index funds that are not available to the general public, seeks to provide investment results that correspond to the price and yield performance of the Standard & Poor's 500 Composite Stock Price Index. The trust holds more than 400 of the issues in the S&P.

Although the investing public has not warmed up to the notion of indexing, a number of major institutional investors have. The main target of the index fund marketers is the giant pension fund market. With tens of billions of dollars of assets, over half of which are invested in equities and with yearly contributions tending to run to more billions, the money flowing into private pension funds each year is roughly equivalent to a third or more of the total assets of the mutual fund industry.

A growing number of corporations, such as American Telephone, Exxon, and Ford, have already put hundreds of millions of pension fund dollars into indexed portfolios. Some say that as much as 30 percent of pension fund assets will ultimately end up under similar "passive" management. The rationale for index funds is rooted in the foolishness of the late 1960s, when supposedly prudent and experienced institutions started to chase after high-risk situations to provide quick profits. The bear market of 1969–70 ripped off the veneer and revealed the speculative nature of this search for instant stock gains and led some to question the judgment of many portfolio managers. Along came 1973–74 and the severe drubbing of quality growth stocks, the so-called nifty fifty which had been bid to unsustainable heights on the basis of unrealistic earnings estimates. Again the judgment of money managers was questioned. Just as the bear market of 1973–74 plowed under the wisdom of buy-growth-at-any-price policies, so did the deep furrows in portfolio values prove fertile for the popularization of the index fund concept. Then came the Employee Retirement Income Security Act (ERISA), which provided the final blow to the imprudent management of pension monies.

Although a fund may mimic a popular market average in a low-cost manner—index funds are "managed" by computer programs—there are many mutual funds that have outperformed any and all market averages over the long term. If you are content to ride the coattails of the Standard & Poor's 500 and have no hopes of ever doing better than average in your investments, then index funds are for you. Otherwise, stick to managed mutual funds, where good judgment pays off in good performance.

Managed Municipal Bond Funds

Until the Tax Reform Act of 1976, there was no way a conventional mutual fund could invest in tax-free municipal bonds and pass the tax-exempt status of the interest earned on those bonds through to its shareholders. Unit trusts, reviewed below, were able to pass through this tax exemption, but it was necessary to change the tax laws to cover conventional mutuals.

With the change in the law, mutual fund sponsors lost little time in introducing managed municipal bond funds. Within two years, more than thirty funds were offering shares to the public. Incoming cash was piling up at the rate of a million or more dollars a day at a number of the funds and soon sales on an industry-wide basis were up to an annual rate of $2 billion.

As was the case with money market funds when they were new, the tax-exempt bond mutuals have drawn their share of critics. Some say that they are potentially unstable investments because any rush to redeem would reveal the poor marketability of portfolio holdings. However, partly because of their concern over marketability, the leading funds have tended to build their portfolios around readily marketable, generally high-rated securities.

Management fees for municipal bond mutuals are in the same ball park as conventional stock funds, about 0.5 percent of assets. There are sundry other expenses, just as there are in all funds, but these operating expenses, though small, are still greater than the very low expenses associated with tax-exempt unit trusts. Moreover, the latter are unmanaged, hence have no management fees. The difference in charges between tax-exempt bond mutuals is a yearly cost and gives the unit trust an advantage in respect to yield to investors.

Muni fund managers say that any difference in yields over the long run will be more than offset by the benefit of skillful management. On the other hand, critics of the new funds cite a lack of experience in the management of large municipal bond portfolios. Better to have no management, they say, than bad management. Fund managers retort that such views are nonsensical; they already have knowledgeable people on the payroll and if any additional strength is needed they know where to get it.

Most of the larger municipal bond mutual funds are no-loads and feature monthly or quarterly dividends paid in cash or automatically reinvested in shares as elected, redemption (without charge) at net asset value, exchange privileges, and periodic reports including state-by-state breakdowns of income.

A representative list of muni funds would include Dreyfus Tax Exempt Bond Fund, Federated Tax-Free Income Fund, Fidelity Municipal Bond Fund, IDS Tax-Exempt Bond Fund, Kemper Municipal Bond Fund, Merrill Lynch Municipal Bond Fund, Oppenheimer Tax-Free Bond Fund, Rowe Price Tax-Free Income Fund, Scudder Managed Municipal Bonds, and Vanguard Municipal Bond Fund.

Unit Trusts

Unit trusts, taxable or nontaxable, are similar to conventional funds in the sense that they are means by which investors can obtain a pro rata share of a widely diversified portfolio, thereby benefiting from lower risk through diversification. However, there are important differences. The portfolios of unit trusts are fixed; no new bonds are added after the initial offering. Shares in the trusts are called units, each unit representing $100 to $1,000 principal amount of underlying bonds. Large securities dealers such as Merrill Lynch, Pierce, Fenner & Smith and John Nuveen & Company sponsor unit trusts. After assembling the portfolios, they offer them to the public with a sales charge ranging from 2 to 4½ percent. The bonds are deposited with a trustee, a major bank, shortly before the offering.

Although they are under no obligation to do so, sponsors maintain a secondary market in their units. Prices will fluctuate according to the market value of the underlying bonds, which in turn depends on the general level of long-term interest rates and the market's response to rating changes by Moody's and Standard & Poor's. No trading of the portfolio bonds is allowed, the funds existing as self-liquidating trusts until all or most of the bonds reach maturity or are otherwise retired. The proceeds from securities that mature or are called are distributed rather than reinvested. Typically, checks representing interest income minus necessary expenses of the trust are mailed to investors monthly.

Dozens of corporate bond and municipal unit trusts have been launched by brokerage houses over the past several years, with assets totaling more than $15 billion. The portfolios come in all sizes, generally falling in the $15 million to $65 million range. Two to four dozen different issues may be included, with fixed maturity dates in the 1980s for intermediate-term trusts, to the early years of the next century for the typical long-term portfolio.

They feature, as noted above, low operating expenses (generally under 0.2 percent of assets) and no management fees. This does not mean that unit holders get economy class treatment. As their conventionally managed counterparts do, the unit trusts furnish their holders with detailed reports such as annual statements summarizing unit value and specifying the amounts distributed from both the interest and principal accounts, plus such other information as may be needed for payment of taxes and other matters.

If you do hold unit trusts, you should be sure to pay attention to these statements, particularly when you prepare your tax returns. Many investors do not realize, or else they forget, that the checks they receive from a unit trust can represent a return of principal as well as interest income. As a result, they inadvertently pay an income tax on the returned principal or spend it instead of holding it out for reinvestment.

Gold Funds

Investor demand for funds that invest in gold stocks is a reflection of the instability in world political, monetary, and social conditions. During 1973–74, when inflationary expectations were strong and foreign exchange fluctuations uncertain, gold-bullion and gold-mining shares were purchased in large amounts by speculators as well as by investors attempting to protect the purchasing power of their savings. Thus ASA Ltd., one of the major funds that invest in the shares of gold-mining companies, was up 208 percent in 1973–74, whereas both the average fund as well as the popular market averages were deep in the minus column.

ASA and other gold funds have substantial investments in South African gold-mining shares. Thus economic and political conditions in that nation bear importantly on the outlook for gold funds. In recent years this has been a factor of instability, South Africa having been dealt severe blows by soaring oil prices, inflation, riots, and racial unrest.

Other risks of investing in gold funds are tied to the hazards of gold mining as such. Supposedly rich lodes can give out. Mine shafts can become flooded. Periods of reduced inflation or downward pressure on gold prices stemming from large-scale sales by nations with major gold reserves also pose financial risks. Thus in 1975–76 the performance of gold funds was poor, to say the least. However, they did very well in 1977–79, outperforming all other categories of funds during that inflationary period.

Among the more widely known gold funds are ASA Ltd., International Investors Incorporated, Precious Metals Holdings, Research Capital Fund, and United Services Fund. ASA and Precious Metals Holdings are publicly traded investment funds.

We talk more about gold in Chapter 16.

Foreign Funds

Apart from the highly specialized gold funds, there are other investment companies that invest in the shares of foreign corporations. They are less interested in the outlook for a particular commodity than they are in prospects for growth in the economy of an entire nation. Such funds are diversified as to industries and companies, just as are conventional funds that limit their investment opportunities to stateside securities.

Japan has proved to be a particularly fruitful source of above-average performance for foreign funds. That country's spectacular economic growth since the end of World War II has enabled Japan

Fund, whose shares are traded on the New York Stock Exchange, to show above-average growth since its inception in 1962. That fund, which invests exclusively in Japanese companies, rose 137 percent for the ten years, 1970–79. Not many other funds did as well in that period of essentially sideways movement in the domestic stock market.

Templeton Growth Fund was in second place with 441 percent growth, topped only by International Investors. An open-end fund with a load charge, Templeton invests on a global scale, with United States, Japan, and Canada taking top billing. Geographic diversification at Scudder International Fund, a no-load fund, has tended to favor Japan, various European nations, and Australia. On the other hand, Canadian Fund, a load fund, depends, as does Japan Fund, on the economic well-being of one nation. Not surprisingly, the fund's chief emphasis is on natural resources, particularly petroleum and metals and mining.

Specialty Funds

These tend to limit their investments to the stocks of certain related industries or other areas of special interest. Century Shares Trust, a load fund, was the first specialty fund, organized in 1928 to invest in insurance company and bank stocks. Since then funds have been introduced that specialize in such areas as chemicals, electronics, and aerospace.

The risk here is that most industries have or eventually develop cyclical patterns; if you get in early, you may very well show above-average gains. But the history of the stock market is rife with examples of industries that flower for a few years only to wither, if not die. Sometimes there's a rebirth leading to a more mature phase where sustained growth can be achieved. Sometimes an industry will show growth over several decades, then level off or become so diffused with other industries that its original unity is all but lost in a maze of regulations, new products, and services.

For example, National Aviation Corporation was founded about a half century ago as a means by which investors could participate in the anticipated growth of commercial aviation. The idea was to pick the winners among the many companies competing for capital in a young field. Now, as a maturing industry, commercial aviation has seen its growth settle back to about the same pace as the economy as a whole. Moreover, aviation securities have become increasingly volatile, and the aviation investor, unless he is extraordinarily nimble, is finding it difficult to show consistent capital gains performance from year to year.

Rather than subject its performance to the deeper air pockets of the modern aviation industry, the fund in 1976 changed its investment policy so that over a period of time it would be able to invest up to 75 percent of its assets in companies which utilize technology extensively in their operations or product development. Along with the change in policy came a change in name to National Aviation & Technology Corporation.

Other specialty funds have avoided being caught within the narrow confines of particular fields by broadening their definitions. An example is Chemical Fund. To quote from its prospectus, the fund is "designed for investors who seek long-term growth of capital and of income, rather than high current income, through investing in companies that are engaged in the chemical, chemical process and related scientific fields." At Chemical Fund, this does not mean exclusively companies such as DuPont, Allied Chemical, and the like. Under the portfolio heading Physical Chemistry are found Burroughs, Hewlett-Packard, IBM, and Texas Instruments.

Dual Funds

Sponsors of mutual funds never lack imagination when it comes to forming funds with a new twist. For example, in the mid-1960s a spate of dual funds issued forth. These funds, less than a dozen of which are publicly traded, were launched with a good deal of promise and fanfare. The stock market was giving a good account of itself at the time and the new funds, resplendent with speculative features, were expected to provide the best of two worlds—big gains for the capital shares and big income for the income shares. Here's how the idea works. Basically, dual funds are publicly traded investment companies with a differernce. They have two classes of stock, capital shares and income shares, with equal amounts of each. The capital shareholders are entitled to all of the capital appreciation (if any) but no income. In contrast, the income shareholders receive all of the income from the portfolio holdings. Thus each class of stock ends up utilizing double the money it has invested. The income shares, though not entirely free from risk, have generally given a good account of themselves over the years, but the capital shares have given investors a fast run for their money—both ways. Examples of the genre include Scudder Duo-Vest, Leverage Fund of Boston, and Gemini Fund.

Funds That Invest in Funds

As we said, fund sponsors have not lacked for ideas. The natural extension of their excursions into the imagination are funds that invest in—are you ready?—mutual funds.

One fund we know of that tried this approach invested in performance-oriented funds in fair as well as foul weather. That fund and a companion money market fund were "switch funds," so named because shareholders were able to telephone in their orders to shift capital without commissions between a venturesome fund and a parking lot for cash.

The concept lacked staying power; the Securities and Exchange Commission didn't see eye to eye with the sponsors, and sent the funds to the grave.

Hedge Funds

Most funds do not sell securities short, but hedge funds are a conspicuous exception. These funds as a matter of policy always keep a portion of their portfolios in a "short" position, so that if the stock market plunges, at least they will show a profit on their "shorts." On the other hand, if the market advances, their "longs" should move up. It sounds great in theory but in practice the results have been less than spectacular.

Funds for Special-Interest Groups

A number of funds are known not by what they invest in but rather by whom they sell shares to. These investment companies for special-interest groups include such funds as Elfun Trusts, a no-load for past or present employees of the General Electric Company; PRO Fund, organized, as the prospectus puts it, "to offer shares of a professionally managed mutual fund to participants in retirement programs for self-employed persons, generally professional men and women"; and the Lutheran Brotherhood Fund, a growth-income fund sold to Lutherans.

Chapter 14 **Options**

To UNDERSTAND options is to be privy to some of the deepest and most arcane secrets of the gods of finance. To employ this knowledge for profit is to be the object of awe among the great unwashed who mill and churn in the courtyards of the temples of investment. To presume to employ it without proper initiation is to invite almost certain financial disaster.

Fewer still are those who possess the capacity to convey this esoteric and mysterious wisdom by means of spoken or written word. It is thus with due humility that we embark on this chapter.

The first step in your rite of passage is an introduction to the exotic and suggestive language of options. Puts. Calls. Strips. Straps. Straddles. Spreads. Naked options. Naked short puts. Trapezoidal hedges. The list goes on.

The basic concept of options is simple enough. They are used in many businesses as a matter of course. Option contracts are nothing more than obligations to buy or sell a given piece of property at a stated price within a specified time period. A real estate purchase and sale agreement is an option contract and if you've ever bought or sold a house, chances are you used one.

CBOE: Order from Chaos

Until the Chicago Board Options Exchange (CBOE) opened its doors in April 1973, trading in puts and calls was a haphazard venture. Each contract was individually negotiated by brokers for the buyer and seller. Once an investor was into a contract there was little opportunity for his transferring it to a third party. This process still goes on, of course, and many sophisticated investors still do their options trading that way. But the average investor can probably operate most profitably and most conveniently by confining his options activities to the CBOE and other exchanges that handle such trading.

Initially, the CBOE traded only call options, and those on only 16 stocks. By mid-1977, it was listing options for stocks of more than 100 companies, each offering three expiration dates and at least as many different striking prices. We'll define these terms as the explanation proceeds.

Investors, always eager for new ways to make a killing, latched on to options with such enthusiasm and with such obvious profit to the CBOE that other exchanges soon were clamoring for a piece of the action. By 1980, the American, Pacific, and Philadelphia stock exchanges were sitting comfortably on the options bandwagon. It seems only a matter of time before options appear on the Big Board. In all, calls were listed on about 300 stocks, and puts on about half that number, in 1980. Eventually, puts should be available on all stocks with call options.

The establishment of a central marketplace for trading options eliminated some of the less desirable aspects of the previously existing unorganized options arena. The CBOE introduced a systematized method of setting striking prices and expiration dates for contracts. In addition it provided liquidity and visibility for these transactions. The same system is followed by the other exchanges on which options are traded.

Purchases and sales are handled in much the same way as they are for common stocks. An order is placed with your broker and is executed on the floor of the exchange. Once an order between a buyer and seller is matched, their connection is severed and the Options Clearing Corporation steps in to become buyer to the seller and seller to the buyer. In this way both parties to the contract are free to take whatever subsequent action they choose, independent of one another. Thus, contracts may be closed out at any time prior to expiration by making an offsetting trade. Furthermore, the Options Clearing Corporation, which serves all the option exchanges, guarantees that stock will be delivered if the option is exercised *and* that the seller will be paid.

While the various option exchanges are auction markets, not all of them use the CBOE system of competitive market makers. This was a major innovation of the new exchange. The two functions normally handled by the specialist were separated. A board broker took over the brokerage function of executing limit orders placed by floor brokers. Competing market makers were assigned to take over the specialist function of trading for their own accounts to stabilize the market. This tends to make the CBOE a more efficient market, with premiums heaving closely to supply and demand balances.

Now, into the mechanics.

Call Options

A call is an option to buy 100 shares of the underlying stock at a specified price, known as the "exercise price" or "striking price," within a specified time period. Unless the Clearing Corporation makes a change to reflect a stock split, one option contract is for 100 shares of the underlying security. Striking prices are set at five-point intervals on or around the trading price for stocks selling below 50 and usually at ten-point intervals for those above 50. A new option series is initiated nine months prior to its expiration date, so that at any given time three contracts with the same exercise price are available on one underlying stock, with maturities three months apart. Options with the same expiration date may be offered with several different striking prices.

When the striking price is above the current trading price, the call is said to be trading "out of the money." A strike below market price would mean the call was "in the money." When market and striking prices jibe, the option is "at the money." Although premiums—the price you actually pay for the option—generally run from 5 to 12 percent of the price of the underlying stock at the time of the option's introduction, this figure then varies with supply and demand and with time. Options are wasting assets in that they have a limited life span beyond which they have no value.

If the premium, which is paid to the seller (also called the "writer") of the option, and the option striking price are equal to the current price of the stock, that option is said to be trading "at parity." The premium will tend to move point for point with the share price only when the option is at parity. Prior to that the premium will rise less than point for point, since the leverage value is reduced at parity and thus the demand for that call dries up.

In a rising market, the demand for options increases as the number of sellers decreases. This increase in demand under normal circumstances tends to enlarge the premium. In a declining market, the reverse is true, causing the premium to narrow.

The relationship between the striking price and the stock price has an important influence on the size of the premium. A call with a striking price of 40 on a stock trading at 50 is understandably worth more than a call with a strike of 60. A call approaching its expiration date which stands little chance of being exercised at a profit will move down in value and expire worthless.

Another factor which influences the price is an approaching ex-dividend date. It is just prior to this date that options are most frequently exercised by option buyers eager to collect the dividend. In order to prevent the stock from being called away, the writer may buy an offsetting call to close out his contract. This tends to enlarge the premium prior to the ex-dividend date as demand exceeds supply.

These various influences can be clearly seen in the accompanying chart of Citicorp common stock and three of its call options. The shaded bands represent the amount by which the call is trading above parity, or its tangible value. The effect of time is obvious; the "fat" in the premium is trimmed away as the calls approach expiration. In fact, the April call traded below its tangible value (parity) about a month prior to expiration, a clear warning to option writers that exercise was a strong probability. The July call, trading well above its parity value in January and again in March, shows very succinctly the vital influence of time in the level of a premium. Since this option was then trading "at the money," it had no tangible value; its only asset was time.

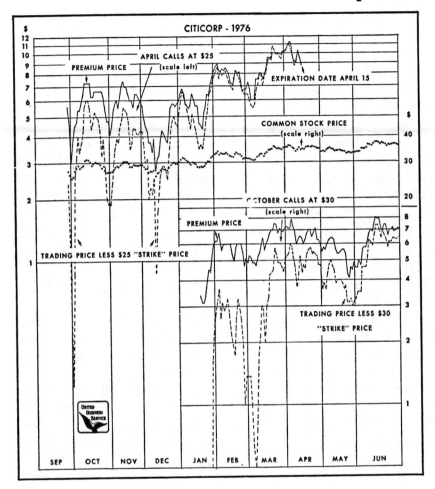

When to Buy and When to Sell Calls

The call option *buyer* is looking for a rise in the price of the underlying security. If the stock does indeed rise, he may choose to exercise the call and buy the stock at its strike price, which is lower than the current market price. Or he could liquidate the call by selling one bearing the same date and striking price. It is the latter transaction that is most commonly used, since this does not entail the expenditure of additional capital.

In such an event, he will have realized a short-term capital gain. However, if he chooses instead to exercise the option and actually acquire the shares, no taxable event will have occurred as long as he keeps the shares. But his cost basis for these shares will be increased by the premium paid for the option. Thus, if the call was bought at a premium of 5 and exercised at 30, the cost basis will be 35 and the exercise date becomes the purchase date for tax purposes.

When the underlying security moves contrary to expectations and it becomes clear that a loss is inevitable, the trader is usually best off to take some action rather than allowing the call to expire worthless. He should make a closing sale transaction in order to reduce the extent of the loss. However, he should be sure to make his move before the proceeds from the sale sink below what he would have to pay the broker in commissions. Either an expiration or a closing sale is a short-term capital loss. A covering transaction that would reduce the loss may or may not be possible, depending on whether a buyer exists for that particular series.

A *writer* (seller) of covered options is generally interested in generating a greater return from his long-term holdings than would be possible from dividends alone. When a call is written against securities already owned, it is referred to as "covered."

Writing "naked" options, where the underlying stock is not owned by the seller, is quite another matter. This highly speculative technique will produce a profit if the stock declines or remains constant, but the profit is limited to the amount of the premium received. On the other hand, if the stock rises, the potential for loss is unlimited, as it is on a short sale. Then the writer must either make a closing purchase transaction to liquidate his contract or buy shares at market to cover when the call is exercised.

Options and Margin Requirements

Option writing programs, covered or otherwise, are executed in margin accounts. Margin agreements give the broker a lien on the assets in the account and assure the proper delivery of shares or cash as required. Options currently have no loan value in a margin account. Writers of naked options must maintain sufficient cash or loan value in their accounts to fulfill their obligation in the event of a call.

In a sideways or declining market when profits are difficult to come by, an option writing program can generate additional cash flow from a portfolio. However, the market does not always perform as expected, and the call writer may be faced with delivering securities he would prefer to hold. Rather than incurring a large capital gains tax liability, he could purchase new shares to satisfy the call obligation.

Avoiding Unwanted Exercise Notices

A call can be exercised at any time up to expiration; the writer has *no* choice in the matter but to give up the shares he promised to sell. If he really doesn't want to sell, he can watch for and heed certain early warning signals. The chance of exercise is higher prior to an ex-dividend date, since the buyer will want to own the stock and collect the dividend. Also, as a call reaches parity, the instance of exercise increases; and, of course, a profitable call would never be allowed to expire unexercised.

To avoid having to deliver shares, an investor must make a closing purchase transaction in the same call series before an exercise notice is received. Exercise notices are delivered to member firms by the Options Clearing Corporation and are assigned on a random basis to members. Brokerage firms may use either a random selection method or may assign exercise notices on a first in, first out basis. You should check to find out which method your broker uses, since it could have a strong bearing on when to close out a questionable option. Once an exercise notice is received, the writer's choices are narrowed—the underlying stock must be delivered, be it shares already owned or new shares purchased to cover. At that point, the offsetting option transaction is no longer possible as a means of liquidating the call.

It is usually more profitable to write call options in a declining or trendless market than in a rising market. An up market favors the call buyer. While an "in-the-money" call may earn the writer a larger immediate cash advance, this type of contract stands a greater chance of being exercised. Similarly, for a call buyer an "out-of-the-money" option is the least costly but also the most likely to expire worthless.

Balancing these risk-reward factors when there may be a dozen or more choices for one stock is not easy. One good rule of thumb is not to reach too far, settle for the middle of the road, particularly in writing calls.

Put Options

Having completed a strikingly successful four-year trial of trading call options, the exchanges won permission from the Securities and Exchange Commission in June 1977 to begin a pilot program of offering put options. Initially, trading was limited to 24 issues distributed among the five exchanges.

Contrary to what you might surmise at first thought, puts are not simply the reverse side of calls. They are totally separate and distinct transactions. Where a call option gives the buyer the right to purchase shares of the underlying stock from the writer, a put option gives him the right to sell (or "put to") the writer those shares.

Let's take a closer look at how puts work. A trader who expects the stock market to decline might buy a put option on some stock he is holding to lock in a lower limit on the decline of that stock. Remember, the put he bought gave him the right to sell those shares at a specified price. Generally this is done by buying the put with a striking price at or above the current market price. If the market price declines below that level, he can exercise the put to cut his losses. Of course, in his expectation of a market decline he could have written a call option on the stocks he was holding, as we explained in the preceding section. Conversely, should the trader expect a rise in the stock market, he could write a put or buy a call.

Buying Puts—When and Why

Buying a "covered" put—one purchased against stock actually owned—allows the trader to put a floor on his losses should the market decline, a point we made a moment ago. However, he might also buy a put without actually owning the underlying shares and make money in a falling market. In this case, as the market declined according to his expectations, before the put expired he would sell a put of the same series and expiration date. At that point, the put he sold would be commanding a higher premium than the premium he paid at purchase. The difference in these premium prices would represent his profit.

In exercising a covered put, a buyer need not necessarily deliver the shares he actually holds, though, of course, he has the right to do so. If he expects the market to recover and wishes to retain his position in that stock, he might do as the buyer of the uncovered put did and write a put with a higher premium to close out his contract.

If the market goes up contrary to the put buyer's expectations, the loss is limited to the cost of the put—the premium. Just as the buyer of a call option need not let it expire worthless, a put buyer may limit his loss if the stock rises by selling the put at a lower premium than he originally paid. In general, this is a prudent policy. In this case the loss is limited to the difference between the premium paid and the premium received on the covering trade.

There are tax implications in put trading that you should understand before embarking on such a program.

Writing Puts

The writer of a put is taking a greater risk if the market moves against him. In this event he will be required to take delivery and come up with the cash for shares at a price well above market. This disconcerting situation could occur at any time up to the expiration date of the option contract. The cost basis on these shares will be the exercise price minus the premium received.

The put seller may be motivated by a desire to generate cash in a trendless market. The put expires worthless and the writer pockets his premium. He may also wish to acquire stock at a price below the current market. In this case he writes a put with a striking price at market and pockets the premium. When the stock drops, the put buyer exercises and the writer acquires stock with his cost being strike minus premium. Puts should only be written against sufficient cash to purchase the shares when exercise occurs.

Unlike call premiums, which rise as the share price rises, put premiums rise when the share price drops. Premiums tend to be higher for the more volatile stocks, which also holds true for call premiums. Time has the same value with puts as with calls.

A Growing Market

In 1974, the first full year of an organized options market, more than 300,000 contracts were written and only one in six was exercised. Two years later, eight times as many contracts were written, 2.6 million. Whether it was because conditions were more favorable or traders more discriminating, one contract in three was exercised that year.

Although increasing institutional participation is a factor in the growth of the options market, this sector is thought to account for only 10 percent of the total trading. Aside from the strictures that have been placed on money managers and pension fund administrators by the prudent man provisions of the Employee Retirement Income Security Act of 1974 (ERISA), institutions heretofore had been held back by tax considerations. Mutual funds must derive at least 90 percent of income from investments to qualify for pass-through tax exemptions. Under previous IRS rulings, option premiums were ordinary business income, not investment income. But this tax treatment was revised in the Tax Reform Act of 1976, when such premiums were specifically classified as short-term capital gains. This development cleared the way not only for institutional option writing programs but also for an influx of new mutual funds called "option income funds."

Summing Up

Broadly speaking, options may be used to guarantee market position, to obtain stock at prices below those on the shares currently, to limit losses, to hedge against unpredictable turns in an uncertain market, and to generate income or cash flow.

To help you get a handle on these somewhat confusing trading techniques and to help clarify for you the risk-reward parameters of options trading, the accompanying table places these concepts in perspective.

Utilizing options as a part of your investment program can be conservative investment strategy. Conversely, it can be equally as speculative as short selling, with an unlimited loss potential. It is not a technique which should be attempted without full understanding of its uses, values, and risks. For a more detailed discussion of the myriad strategies possible with options see Chapter 32.

Market action necessary for profitable option trades:

Call Options	Put Options
Buyer: Rising market	Buyer: Declining market
Seller: Declining or sideways market	Seller: Rising or sideways market

Market action that will result in losses on option trades:

Call Options	Put Options
Buyer: Sideways or declining market	Buyer: Sideways or rising market
Seller: Rising market	Seller: Declining market

The amount of risk or reward in a given option position:

Option Contract Position	Possible Loss	Possible Gain
Call buyer	Cost of premium	Unlimited
Call seller, covered	Cost of buy-back*	Premium received
Call seller, naked	Unlimited	Premium received
Put buyer	Cost of premium	Unlimited
Put seller	Cost to buy in*	Premium received
Spreads, straddles, or combinations	Unlimited†	Unlimited†

* For the writer of a covered call or a put, the extent of the loss may be limited by making an offsetting sale. If no covering option is purchased, the loss is more a matter of lost opportunity than of cash loss; he cannot participate in a rise on the call side and must take delivery of shares at a price above market on a put.

† Depending on type of spread, straddle, or combination transacted.

Chapter 15 Commodities

MENTION THE word "commodities" to the average investor, and if there isn't a totally blank look on his face, chances are his reaction to the topic will be strongly negative. Either he will know someone who has lost heavily, or he will regale you with a horror story or two about a hapless investor who awoke one morning to find a truckload of eggs or a few thousand bushels of grain on his doorstep. He may even have read about the great salad oil swindle, the losses in cocoa and silver trading that destroyed an American-owned Swiss bank, or more recently, the shellacking a large U.S. grain exporter took in the soybean market. He may even have lost money himself on a flyer.

To our Mr. Average Investor, the commodity market is a hot ticket and not for him—and quite possibly he is correct. After all, many of these stories are rooted in fact. Tino DeAngelis did bankrupt one of the leading brokerage houses of the day (Ira Haupt) with his watered-down salad-oil tanks back in 1963. In the process, he gave the American Express Company a major fright as well. Paul Erdman became a successful author after his Swiss subsidiary of the United California Bank of Los Angeles lost 200 million Swiss francs—$80 million at the exchange rates of the day—trading in cocoa and silver in 1969–70. An American grain company, Cook Industries, dropped $60 million in the soybean pits in 1976–77. Moreover, many an untimely delivery, although not on anyone's front doorstep, has bloodied a speculator or two caught napping. So if our average investor gets just a little nervous thinking about commodities, it is understandable. There are few quicker ways to part an investor from his money than the futures market.

Man's urge to speculate, however, is well documented throughout history. Thus, while the average investor is quite right to stand at arm's length, those among us with the willingness to apply common sense, a good deal of discipline, a little scholarship, and some spare cash will find the futures game not beyond their ability to understand or trade. They will also find it highly exciting, potentially very profitable, and in some cases not much more dangerous than the stock market. Now let us look more closely at this wild horse called the commodity or futures market and see what it is all about.

Historical Evolution

The futures market that is so widely traded today in reality is an offshoot of the cash or "on-the-spot" market that traces its roots back to the early Greek and Roman trading empires or perhaps further, since there is evidence that Sumerians had a rudimentary system of credit backed by grains or metals 3,000 years before Christ.

Many of the basic rules of futures trading are clearly traceable to the law merchants' code that evolved out of the well-organized European medieval fairs. Highly complex futures trading systems also existed in Japan in the 1600s. But the rapidly expanding commerce of the city of Chicago in the 1850s was the primary catalyst that led to the development of the modern commodity exchange and to the popularity of trading in "time" or "forward" contracts.

The Civil War was a particularly important formative period. Rising grain demand and price fluctuation stimulated use of forward contracting on the Chicago Board of Trade, a cash grain trading exchange formed in 1848 to handle and promote Chicago's booming commerce.

Time or forward contracting was not an idea born in the United States, however. It evolved from "to arrive" contracts which, in turn, were refinements of *lettre de faire* documents used in the twelfth century and earlier. Forward contracting was not quite futures trading, although the distinction is slight. The earlier types of contracting, including forward contracting, were entered into for the express purpose of receiving title at some specified date to the actual goods. The parties to these documents were connected to the business, and nearly all such financial agreements ended in transfer of titles and delivery of the base commodity.

When war conditions, harvest glut, and winter shortages of grains began to create large price fluctuations as well as highly attractive profit situations, it was only natural that the more adventurous investors outside of the commodity business would be attracted. They were. But then the game changed. The new players were not interested in making or taking delivery, but rather in assuming a risk to reap a profit. As a result, each contract passed through many hands. Thus the concept of trading for purposes other than taking title became firmly, though unofficially, established in Chicago during the Civil War years. With speculators now involved, and deliveries the exception rather than the rule, forward trading became the futures trading of today.

In late 1865, shortly after the end of the war, the Chicago Board of Trade passed its first rules on the subject of time trading, providing, among other things, standardization of delivery, margin deposits, and prescribed terms of payments. In practice, if not in name, forward or time contracting merged into futures trading and the era of the modern commodity exchange had begun.

The Commodity Exchange

The modern day commodity exchange and futures trading have evolved over a long period to fit the developing commercial needs of the country. Each exchange, however, evolved on a separate, if somewhat parallel, track, and each is highly individualistic. Generally, the older exchanges are state chartered. The Chicago Board of Trade was chartered by the Illinois State Legislature in 1848 and is the oldest and largest of the U.S. exchanges. The newer exchanges are organized under membership corporation laws.

Despite the variety in size and individualistic nature of the two dozen or more active domestic exchanges, they are all fundamentally similar. The primary objective of the modern commodity futures exchange is to provide and to regulate a marketplace for members to trade in futures contracts. Basically, this entails providing the physical trading space, establishing the rules and regulations to conduct trading, setting the operating hours, providing the information for the standardized contract, seeing that prices and market information are recorded and disseminated to guarantee the financial obligations of exchange members in connection with futures commitments, and settling disputes between members. In addition to their futures trading activities, some exchanges also provide extensive cash market services such as sampling, grading, weighing, and inspection.

Organization of the Exchanges

U.S. commodity exchanges are voluntary associations of persons interested in buying and selling commodities. Whether they are state chartered or corporately organized, only individuals are eligible to become members of a U.S. commodity exchange. There are no company memberships. In practice, however, companies often do control a membership. Many members are employees of large companies whose businesses are closely linked to exchange commodities—large brokerage houses, grain processors, meat packers, and exporters. The company furnishes the money to purchase the membership provided the individual agrees to give it up if he leaves their employ.

Only members can trade on a commodity exchange, and therein lies one of the two principal reasons for buying a seat on an exchange—access to the trading floor. The floor trader pays only clearing costs (which will be explained later) and receives a commission from nonmembers to fill orders. The other reason to purchase a seat is economic, provided one is a large enough trader to justify the costs involved. Membership for trader-members unable or unwilling to become floor traders entitles them to a reduced commission rate, usually about half the nonmember rate.

To provide the facilities and services required, commodity exchanges need some source of revenue. U.S. exchanges are nonprofit organizations that exist only to facilitate futures trading of members, not to make money. But they do have expenses to meet, and must remain as solvent as possible. This is generally accomplished through a combination of investments, dues, fees for services, and, if necessary, member assessments.

The Clearing House

Guaranteeing the financial commitment that each member makes when buying or selling a commodity futures contract is an important but difficult task. To do this, exchanges have developed corporations called clearing houses to take the opposite side of all trades and to guarantee all contracts. The clearing house, in effect, becomes the buyer to all sellers, and the seller to all buyers. By so doing, it is able to insure that each contract will be honored. The section on margins later in this chapter explains how the clearing house maintains financial integrity for each contract.

The clearing procedure begins at the end of each trading day. All exchange members send their trading cards to their respective clearing member. There is a card for each side of a transaction containing the details of the trade. The clearing member posts this information from the cards on trade confirmation cards and forwards them to the clearing house. The clearing house takes the confirmation cards from all the clearing members and matches up each purchase and sale for names, prices, delivery months, and quantities. The match-up must be exact. If there are any discrepancies, the clearing house makes up a duplicate unmatched notice, called an out-trade, and sends a copy back to the two parties to resolve. Most out-trades are resolved. If they cannot be resolved by the start of the next day's trading, the clearing house rejects the unmatched trade. Rejected out-trades then go into the exchange's arbitration process for final settlement.

Not all members of an exchange belong to the clearing house, but all clearing house members must be members of the exchange. The clearing house is a stock company, and clearing house members buy stock in relationship to the amount of clearing business they do. All trades must be cleared through a clearing house member. In addition to purchases of stock, a substantial cash deposit must be made to the guarantee fund of the clearing house corporation. Like the exchange itself, the clearing house is a nonprofit organization and generates its operating capital through fees and from interest on invested capital.

The Standard Commodity Contract

Another equally important creation of the exchange is the standard commodity contract. "To arrive" trading, the forerunner of forward and then futures trading, was replete with pitfalls for everyone. Shipments came in all sizes and grades, depending on what the seller happened to have on hand, and settlement was a nightmare. Each transaction needed to be individually negotiated as to the specific terms of payment, delivery point, and so on.

To put everyone on an equal footing and to simplify trading, the standardized contract was developed. Traders now only need to be concerned with the price and number of contracts during trading hours.

In brief, each commodity contract represents a firm legal agreement between the buyer or seller and the exchange's clearing house. The buyer agrees to accept delivery on a specified amount of a commodity when the contract is tendered (delivered). Conversely, the seller agrees to deliver the commodity detailed in the contract sometime during the delivery month. Only a small percentage of contracts are actually delivered, since the bulk of traders in a futures contract are either speculators who have no need for cash commodities or hedgers (producers or consumers of the commodity) who are using the market to shift risk temporarily to the speculator. Indeed, the risk-shifting function of the futures market is one of its main economic justifications.

With few contracts being settled by delivery, a method is needed to dissolve the contractual obligation. A simple one is used. The buyer or seller takes an equal, but opposite, position in the same delivery month. This is called offsetting, and negates the original purchase or sale. It can be done at any time before the contract goes off the board (terminates). During its lifetime, a commodity contract, despite its deliverability, is merely a bookkeeping entry. A commodity contract, therefore, is not a tangible item like a stock certificate; and when you first buy and then sell or sell and then buy the same contract, the net result is zero.

There are many commodities traded, and each has specific requirements to maximize its usefulness to the people who are in the cash business—the farmers, packers, manufacturers, and others, collectively known as the "trade." This is an important consideration even though most contracts are offset before delivery. No one is 100 percent sure of what makes one cash commodity a successful futures market while another fails. There are guidelines: a large supply and demand that is uncertain, adaptability to standardization and grade, relatively free flow of supply to terminals, and a low degree of perishability, to mention a few. But there are exceptions to these guidelines, especially with regard to perishability. One thing is clear, however; trade acceptability is a significant factor for success. If the trade cannot economically use the contract to hedge, it is less likely to survive.

The details vary for each commodity but in general a contract will cover the following items: (1) The quantity (trading unit) being traded. (2) The grade. (3) Termination of trading and delivery date. (4) Daily minimum and maximum price fluctuations allowed. (5) Description of par delivery grade, the grade of commodity specified for delivery. (6) Premiums and discounts for nonpar delivery. (7) Trading limits—number of contracts that can be bought and sold in one day. (8) Position limits—the number of contracts a trader can hold in one single delivery month, and in all months together. (9) Delivery points. Essentially, every facet of entering into, making, and taking delivery of or exiting from the commodity futures market is covered in a standard contract.

Margins

In the earlier description of exchange operations, the subsidiary clearing house emerged as the party to all commodity transactions, that is, it became the buyer to all sellers and the seller to all buyers. From this vantage point, the clearing house can and does control the financial integrity of its members and their contract commitments. We have already mentioned that each clearing house member buys stock and deposits a large amount of cash into the corporation's guarantee fund. Each member is also required to post a performance bond to the clearing house for each net open position. This payment is called margin and affects not only clearing house members but nonmembers as well.

There are four basic classifications of margin. The first is called "standing margin" and is the amount of money a clearing house member keeps on deposit (to assure settlement of the contract) with the clearing house for each net open position (long or short) at the end of the trading day. If the member firm, for example, has 500 long May copper and 500 short May copper, its net position is zero and, theoretically, no standing margin is required. (In practice, a clearing house member would always keep a sizable deposit in his account whether it is needed or not.) On the other hand, if there were only 400 long May copper, the firm would be net short 100 contracts, and would be required to post standing margin to cover this net open position. Standing margins are fixed by the governing board of the clearing house and must be current before each day's trading begins.

The second type also affects the clearing house member and is called "variation margin." If a market is particularly active and moves against the member's position, his standing margin would need to be supplemented to keep it at full value. The clearing house can call for variation margin money at any time to cover price changes, and the member must provide the money by certified check within one hour.

Like most cost-of-business items, margins are passed through the system to the nonmembers of the clearing house and on to the nonmembers of the exchange. Although the clearing house sets the rate that member firms pay, what they in turn request from individual traders is left to their discretion. This, incidentally, accounts for the differences you will encounter when asking different brokers about margins on the same commodity.

Use of the word "margin" to describe up-front money in commodities differs significantly, by the way, from its use in the stock market for speculator-investor accounts. Stock margins are the minimum amounts of money an investor can put down to buy shares. He then must borrow the balance of the cost of the stock from the broker to complete the transaction. As a result, the stock investor pays the broker interest on the borrowed funds until the position is terminated or the "loan" is paid off.

In contrast, commodity margins at the brokerage level are similar to those at the clearing house level—they are primarily a performance bond to assure proper settlement of the contract. The commodity broker does not put up the difference between margin and the value of the commodity contract as does the stockbroker, so no interest is required of the commodity investor.

The first level of margin at the customer end is called "original margin." Unlike a stockbroker, a commodity broker will not buy or sell a commodity before he has your money in hand; there is no

-day settlement period. Typically, margins will run between 5 and 10 percent of the face value of a commodity. But they can be much higher, depending on the volatility of the commodity and how close the specific contract is to expiration. For example, most margins are increased when the contract reaches its delivery month.

Since it would be inconvenient for brokers to demand hourly variations in margin from their clients, but since it could be dangerous for them not to adjust for adverse price changes, brokers usually take a range approach. At the upper end is the original margin, and at the lower end is "maintenance margin." You need original margin to initiate the trade, but the broker will not ask for additional money until your account falls to the maintenance level. At that point, the broker will send a written notice, or margin call, to you requesting enough money to bring the entire position back up to the original margin level. If you are unable or unwilling to meet the margin call, the broker can close out the position.

Leverage

The commodity margin system is a particularly important aspect of futures trading, for it provides the main attraction for speculators—leverage. With a margin rate of 10 percent, it takes only a 10 percent change in the commodity's price to give the speculator a 100 percent gain or loss in his trading equity. The speculator is also permitted to use equity gains in open trades to purchase additional positions at no cost. For example, assume the margin on one hog contract (30,000 pounds) is $1,200, and the current commodity price is 40¢ a pound. If the price of hogs should advance to 44¢ a pound, the equity gain would be $1,200. Until the trade is offset, the $1,200 would be only a paper profit. However, if he wishes, the trader can buy a second hog contract at 44¢ without adding any extra money. The paper profit would cover the second margin requirement. With two positions working for him, the hog market need only advance to 46¢ a pound to give the speculator enough for a third position. Leverage, of course, is a two-edged sword. A decline of 3¢ a pound would leave the trader with virtually no gain; a decline of 4¢ would leave him with a loss.

Open Interest

When a trader buys or sells a contract, until he offsets the trade or settles it through delivery, he is said to have an "open position." In each market there will be a number of these open positions, and collectively they are referred to as the commodity's "open interest." Open interest is reported along with the volume of sales and the prices each day. Since there are always two sides to each contract— a long interest (representing contracts that have been bought) and a short interest (those that have been sold)—a figure of 100 for open interest would mean there are 100 longs and 100 shorts currently holding positions in that commodity. The significance of open interest will be discussed in Chapter 33.

Hedging

We have talked mostly about the speculator up to this point. But futures markets are real, not just artificially created arenas for gambling. They are backed by cash commodities, and grew out of the need of the producers and manufacturers engaged in processing the commodity to protect themselves from adverse price changes. The use of the commodity market by the people in the business or trade is called hedging, and is the backbone of the futures industry. A hedger, then, is an individual or company that either has the commodity to deliver or who wishes to receive delivery of the commodity. Whether they actually make or receive delivery is immaterial. A hedge, or hedging, is taking a position in the futures market that is equal to but opposite from an existing or soon to exist position in the cash market. To facilitate hedging activity, a must for a successful futures market, exchanges usually set margins for bona fide hedgers below those for speculative accounts, give them lower commission rates, and eliminate position limits.

Because hedging involves the cash market, the hedger is not concerned with changes in the futures price per se. His interest is with the relationship between the cash price and the futures price. This mathematical difference between the two prices is called the "basis."

Usually, the basis is given as an amount above or below the futures prices. If a farmer can get $2.50 per bushel for corn at his local elevator, and corn for December delivery is selling for $2.75 on the Chicago Board of Trade, the farmer's basis that day would be "25 under."

Hedging is an extremely complicated topic—and beyond the survey nature of this chapter. However, generally, a hedger is interested in eliminating as much of the risk associated with price fluctuation as he can, and he does this by putting on long or short hedges in various combinations. So that you will have some idea of what a hedging operation is about, we have conjured up two highly simplified hypothetical examples to illustrate a short and long hedge.

The Short Hedge

It is July, and farmer Jones has planted 1,000 acres of corn that he expects will be ready for harvest in September. The weather has been good, and his yield history suggests that he will get 100 bushels per acre, or 100,000 bushels by harvest. His production costs are running about $2.00 per bushel. Unfortunately for our farmer, the crop looks good all over the state, and it appears that prices will fall by harvest time. Currently, the local elevator is buying corn for $2.35 per bushel. Farmer Jones looks at the futures market and sees that corn deliverable in December is selling for $2.55 per bushel. That makes his basis 20 under.

If the forecasters are correct and corn does fall, Mr. Jones could end up not only with less profit, but possibly no profit at all if the market dipped below $2.00 per bushel. To protect his current margin of profit of 35¢ a bushel (production cost of $2.00 subtracted from elevator price of $2.35), farmer Jones decides to put on a short (selling) hedge. He sells 20 contracts (grain contracts are in units of 5,000 bushels each) of March corn at $2.55 per bushel. Now, no matter what happens to the actual price of corn, if the basis holds up, farmer Jones will have his 35¢ a bushel. If the cash market falls, what he loses at the elevator or terminal when he sells his corn will be offset by an equal gain in his short futures position. If the price of corn should go up, the loss in the futures position would be offset by the gain in the cash price. The table illustrates the principle.

PROFIT-LOSS EFFECT ON A SHORT HEDGE UNDER VARYING MARKET CONDITIONS

(This illustration assumes that corn costs farmer $2.00 per bushel to produce.)

Unhedged	Profit (Loss)	Hedged — Effects of a hedged position in a changing market if basis* remains stable	Profit (Loss)	Effects of a hedged position in a changing market if basis* changes	Profit (Loss)
Sale now at market price of $2.35	35¢		35¢		35¢
Sale in December at market price of $2.10	10¢	Cash price $2.35 Futures price $2.55 Net	35¢ 0¢ 35¢	Cash price $2.35 Futures price $2.60 (basis: 25 under) Net	35¢ (5¢) — 30¢
Sale in December at market price of $2.60	60¢	Cash price $2.10 Futures price $2.30 Net	10¢ 25¢ 35¢	Cash price $2.10 Futures price $2.25 (basis: 15 under) Net	10¢ 30¢ — 40¢
Sale in December at market price of $1.95	(5¢)	Cash price $2.60 Futures price $2.80 Net	60¢ (25¢) 35¢		

* Basis is difference between market price and futures price.

The Long Hedge

Assume once again that it is July. ABC Milling has just landed a large contract with a local bakery to supply it with flour. A price has been agreed upon for the flour, but the baker wants half of it delivered next January. ABC Milling based production costs and the flour sales price on the current cash wheat price of $2.75 per bushel. January delivery, however, means ABC will need to buy additional wheat in December. To protect itself against adverse price changes over the five-month period, the milling company turns to the futures market. The price for a December contract is $3.00 per bushel, which gives ABC a basis of 25 under. By purchasing (long hedging) enough December wheat contracts to fulfill its raw material needs, the milling company, like farmer Jones, can eliminate much of the risk of changing prices.

The two examples assume that the basis is flat and that the hedges performed perfectly, although in practice they seldom do. As the price goes up and down, the basis also changes, sometimes narrowing, sometimes expanding. These contractions in the basis can be quite costly if they move against the hedger's position. Furthermore, the above examples assume the hedger is seeking only protection from price changes. Recent studies indicate hedgers expect to profit from a hedge in the same manner that a speculator expects to profit from an outright futures position. Thomas A. Hieronymus makes a convincing argument that hedging is, in fact, another form of speculation.*

The Trading Floor

Naturally, the trading area for each commodity will differ from exchange to exchange. Nonetheless, they all have common elements. There will be a specific area designated on the floor where each commodity trades. These individual trading areas within the larger complex are called "pits" (or sometimes "rings"), and there is only one to a commodity. Some are elaborate octagonal platforms with

* *Economics of Futures Trading—For Commercial and Personal Profit*, Commodity Research Bureau, New York, 1971.

ascending steps on the outside, and descending steps on the inside. Others are simply handrails formed into a circle. There is a telephone area near the pits for floor brokers (or their telephone people) to receive orders from the firms they represent. There is, in close proximity, a table or platform containing one or more market reporters. Their job is to monitor the changing price picture, then to transmit it to the exchange's quote board system and to the ticker services which send prices all around the country and abroad. There is a quote board system—easily viewed panels or blackboards containing the size and price of the last trade for each contract.

Now that you are familiar with the structure of a modern commodity exchange, let us look at what happens when the bell rings and commodity trading's special brand of pandemonium takes over. For the sake of simplicity, the following description of a commodity trade is a compendium of several markets. Procedures differ from exchange to exchange, but the path an order takes is basically similar in all markets.

It all begins when trader Joe decides to enter the futures market. We will assume he is not a member of the exchange and that he wants to buy ten contracts of May XYZ commodity at 45. His first step is to call his account executive and give him the buy order. The AE writes out the buy slip for 10 May XYZ at 45 and then sends the order ticket to the brokerage firm's order room. The order room time-stamps the slip and then calls or wires the information to the exchange that handles XYZ commodity. At the exchange, the order is received, time-stamped, and passed on to the floor broker's telephone person stationed at one of the many phones on the trading floor. The phone attendant writes up the order and sends it by messenger or hand signal to the floor traders. All commodity trading is done by public outcry. Needless to say, with several hundred brokers on the bigger exchanges aggressively shouting at one another, it is sometimes difficult to execute orders. To augment the yelling, therefore, hand signals are also used. There is a hand signal for both prices and quantity. The combination of shouting and hand waving often gives a commodity pit a frantic look, but it is remarkably orderly and efficient.

The floor broker with order in hand then goes to the necessary pit and via voice and hand signal makes trader Joe's bid. Fortunately for trader Joe (or possibly not), another floor broker has a matching sale order and shouts or signals, "Sold." Meanwhile the market reporter notes the transaction and sends it off to the quote board and to the ticker system if it is different from the last trade. The two brokers get together and fill out their trading cards before moving back into the pit to fill another order. Trader Joe's floor broker also sends the completed order ticket to the floor phone person, who sends it back through the system to trader Joe. The time between the receipt of the order and its execution is only a few minutes.

Government Regulation

Where large sums of money are at stake, man can be very creative and devious in his pursuit of it. Thus, along with the advantages of having a futures market for agricultural products, Americans also have suffered through an assortment of abuses, most notably those involving the cornering of markets and manipulation of prices by wealthy traders.

The first federal foray into regulating the commodity futures market came in 1884. Since then, there has been a steady stream of legislation passed largely on a "crisis" basis; when the horse has bolted, Congress has locked the door. The Grain Futures Act came in 1922. This act was amended and strengthened somewhat in 1936 and renamed the Commodity Exchange Act; it also extended federal regulations to nongrain commodities. The act created the Commodity Exchange Authority (CEA), which applied its rather limited powers to futures trading until 1974. That year, Congress created a stronger watchdog, one tailored after the Securities and Exchange Commission that regulates the stock market. The Commodity Futures Trading Commission (CFTC), armed with a much broader mandate than its predecessors, is still flexing its new muscles as it explores every facet of the commodity business. Its presence is certain to bring some deep-seated and far-reaching changes in the years ahead.

Chapter 16 Gold, Inflation, and Your Dollars

GOLD HAS been popular with humankind almost as long as the species has existed. It has been used to beautify, buoy, and bribe for centuries. It has been on center stage of the human drama since time immemorial. "Saint-seducing gold," Shakespeare called it in *Romeo and Juliet*. "Though wisdom cannot be gotten for gold, still less can it be gotten without it," said Samuel Butler a couple of centuries later.

The chance of finding gold opened up the American West, and the subsequent preoccupation of this nation with the yellow metal gave William Jennings Bryan the opportunity to declaim, "You shall not press down upon the brow of labor this crown of thorns. You shall not crucify mankind upon a cross of gold," at the National Democratic Convention in Chicago in July 1896.

There's No Fence or Fortress...

Just why the love of gold ran so commonly through the breast of Egyptian and Etruscan, Aztec and Andalusian, Butler and Bryan, is hard to say. Perhaps because it was easy to find, often simply rolling along in streams. Or easy to work, for gold is very soft and malleable. Or maybe it was the color which first bewitched humankind.

Whatever the reason, gold was long popular and, being much desired, had real value and, having real value, conferred real power to its possessor, as Mr. Butler observed. Enhancing the elevated status of gold has been the low status of official money, particularly paper money. Thanks to the widespread inability of governments to live within their incomes, currencies have always depreciated.

... Against an Ass Laden with Gold*

Who can count, for example, how many times currencies have retreated to near zero values and disappeared in modern times? The German mark did so twice within one human lifetime. How many banks have failed in the Western world since 1900, taking depositors' money into oblivion? The runaway inflation in Germany after World War I simply eliminated the hard-working, rigorously saving middle class and paved the way for social and political disasters of even worse proportions.

Anyone who has had the foresight or ability to convert bank deposits or currency to gold during such periods of financial holocaust has survived. Those who "trusted" the system and its money perished. Small wonder, then, that the financial vicissitudes of the twentieth century further elevated gold in the minds and hearts of men. Here was something that you could count on. It was tangible, had "intrinsic value," and was a permanent haven for wealth.

The Gold Standard

So strong was the faith in gold and so weak the trust in paper money that the latter had to be tied to the former to have any credibility. Europe and the United States went on a so-called gold standard, meaning that a dollar, pound, or franc was worth a specific amount of the metal. As long as this was the case, the paper money became as good, or almost as good, as gold. The trouble with the gold standard was the cost it exacted in terms of economic, social, and political upheaval.

Here's the way the gold standard works, in theory. As a nation prospers on the upside of a business cycle, domestic wages and prices tend to rise to a point where some other nation has a competitive advantage in the domestic market. Domestic consumers then begin to buy imported products. The exporting nation exchanges

* *Familiar Letters,* James Howell.

the currency received from the sale of its goods for gold, which it takes home.

As the domestic market loses gold—the base of the domestic money supply—that money supply shrinks. A smaller money supply turns the business cycle down, a depression ensues, wages and prices fall as unemployment and the number of idle plants rise. Domestic prices then become competitive in foreign markets and domestic companies begin to prosper by selling in those foreign markets.

Foreign currencies are swapped for foreign gold, which is brought home and monetized. Paper money is printed to match it, and the money supply is increased, which leads to boom conditions again. Wages and prices move up as prosperity returns, only to make domestic products vulnerable to foreign competition once again and the boom ends in another bust.

Obviously, no social or political fabric could stand one wrenching depression and soaring boom after another. Thus, the gold standard was really honored more in the breach than in the observance early in this century. The Great Depression really did it in, and the United States under President Franklin D. Roosevelt finally abandoned it in 1933.

Gold and the Dollar

The United States led the Western world out of the Depression, whether thanks to FDR or to the consequences of Hitler's imperialistic designs for Germany. Thus, for most of our lives, we in the United States have automatically assumed a patronizing attitude toward the rest of the world. We drove big cars on 25¢-a-gallon gasoline while most Europeans were still on bicycles. We had indoor plumbing, central heating, and a radio in nearly every room, while our closest competitor in terms of living standards offered its hardworking citizenry chamber pots, coal stoves, and a wireless in the local pub.

The dollar was the world currency, having replaced the British pound during World War II. It was pegged to other currencies and to gold at $35 per ounce by an agreement struck at Bretton Woods,

New Hampshire, in 1944. Any foreign nation that did not want the dollars earned from sales of goods to us could turn them into gold. Few did. It was American products they wanted, first to rebuild their war-shattered countries, then to give them the consumer prosperity we had long taken for granted.

During that period we could, generally speaking, go wherever we wished, using the English language and the American dollar almost as handily in Manila or Madrid as in Muncie or Mamaroneck. In addition, we sold our excess steel and radios to the world's "natives" and bought what we wished of their coffee, copra, and copper. Much of the world was dependent on us. If we failed to buy enough from them, their prices fell and near starvation followed. Even Europe was sufficiently dependent on the U.S. economy to give credence to the statement that "when the United States gets the sniffles, Europe gets pneumonia."

U.S. trade dominance produced a flow of gold to this country. The yellow metal was a luxury Europe could scarcely afford when their citizens were clamoring for food, clothing, and shelter first, and then later, autos, dishwashers, and color TVs. Today's big gold hoarders, the Arabs, were in worse shape with their oil selling for next to nothing and producing barely enough revenue to keep them in tents and camels. In the years following World War II, we had most of the world's gold in expensive quarters underground at Fort Knox, Kentucky. Even big gold-producing countries such as South Africa and the Soviet Union turned their gold into dollars so they could buy U.S. products and technology. So in those years, when a few foreign countries sidled up to our gold window with some excess dollars to swap, hardly anyone paid any attention.

But things began to change in these early postwar years, too. First came the Marshall Plan, which funneled U.S. dollars into the rebuilding of European facilities.

Second was the "trade, not aid" philosophy developed by the Eisenhower administration which encouraged our purchase of European and "third world" products as a way of stimulating their economic growth enough to diminish their need for our aid. All of this worked, helped in no small way by the unswervingly hard work of the ordinary men and women of Germany and Japan. Thanks to their "grit" and our enlightened economic policy, Europe and Japan rose from the rubble of war to economic heights in a far shorter time than anyone predicted. It wasn't long, in national terms, before Germany and Japan became real competitors with the United States in world markets.

During the decade or two immediately following World War II, we sold, or exported, much more than we bought, or imported, in the world marketplace. This excess of exports over imports was used to finance all the U.S. troops we had stationed in Europe to keep the peace. We also used the excess to finance the building of Caterpillar Tractor plants in Scotland and Burroughs facilities in France. But as the prosperity we had encouraged, and in part financed, waxed, the need for our dollars to buy goods from us waned.

Our so-called trade surplus—the excess of exports over imports—narrowed and financed less and less. By the time the Vietnam war had escalated, we were spending more for foreign military actions than the U.S. economy earned in the world market. Our balance-of-payments surplus became a deficit. This meant a growing number of dollars were being held abroad, dollars that foreigners increasingly had no need to spend here for the things we made.

Thus, the move to exchange dollars for gold steadily gained momentum. Our gold reserves sank drastically, causing great alarm. The first to panic were those with no trust in "paper money." These are people who believe that gold, unlike all other commodities, has an "intrinsic" value. As far as they were concerned, erosion of the U.S. store of gold was fast reducing the value of dollars to mere paper.

Then came the smart money men. These were the financial experts in the big multinational companies who dealt daily in large amounts of pounds, yen, lira, and marks, as well as dollars. If the dollar was losing its international appeal, they reasoned, why shouldn't we keep as much of our working capital in other more popular and stronger currencies? So they swapped dollars. Then came all sorts of speculators, big and little, all trying to "make a buck" (if you will!) selling dollars.

The Dollar Is Cut Free

By the summer of 1971, the dollar was in real trouble. The Nixon administration realized this and did three things. First, it closed the gold window. No longer would our dwindling gold supply be used to repatriate dollars. Second, it unpegged the dollar. From now on, said the White House, in effect, gold buyers can pay what they wish for the yellow metal; the price of gold will have no bearing on the dollar. As part of this, Washington let the dollar float in a free market. The dollar was no longer in a fixed relationship with foreign currencies. The price of both gold and dollars in foreign currencies fluctuated according to the dictates of supply and demand. Third, it slapped controls on domestic wages and prices in a frontal assault on the raging inflation that was plaguing the U.S. economy. This was in part to help consumers at home, but also to show Europeans and others skeptical of the dollar that we were facing squarely our inflation and balance-of-payments problems.

Because of this inflation at home and the adverse balance of payments, the dollar had really become overvalued. In part, too, the dollar had started out overvalued after World War II to help our "trade, not aid" policy. An overvalued currency is one that buys more in a foreign country than it does at home. That's why traveling in Europe was such a bargain in those days. It's also why Volkswagens were so inexpensive and popular for U.S. drivers. By 1971 this overvaluation of the dollar had become so obvious that everyone had to recognize it, and did.

Gold rose immediately from $35 an ounce, the price for nearly four decades, to $42 or so, a gain of 20 percent. Also escalating were the West German mark, the yen, and most other Free World currencies. The dollar sank closer to a realistic value. It was allowed to fluctuate, to seek its own level, free to move with supply and demand rather than to be artificially adjusted by the high priests of the international monetary world, the central bankers.

Our problems, however, did not dissipate as rapidly as we had hoped. Gold continued to strengthen, albeit erratically, as did the prices of most other Western currencies, along with the Japanese yen. The dollar, in short, continued to melt. This did not help the stock market. No one likes to think that his currency is falling. Probably much of the concern is because most investors do not really understand why dollars go up and down in value.

Recurring "panics" occurred, including a substantial one in early 1973. Treasury Secretary George Shultz announced a major easing of wage and price controls, following a big jump in farm and food prices for two months in a row. This immediately rekindled fears in the hearts of European central bankers of more inflation here, and the dollar fell apart. Gold leaped to around $126 an ounce or more, nearly four times the old official $35 price. Wall Street got the jitters, too, but the fears were misplaced. As we wrote then:

Of course, as Treasury Secretary George Shultz said as recently as December, the problem of too many dollars in Europe and Japan is not ours, but theirs. Just because they have sold us so many Toyotas and VWs that they are loaded with dollars is not our concern. They can always use these dollars to buy Chevrolets, General Motors common, or anything else of the like that is available for purchase or investment in this country. Trouble is, they want to have their cake and eat it too. They want to export heavily to the United States without commensurate imports from us, and they want the dollar to stay firm on foreign exchanges. To keep the dollar up they, the foreign nations, must buy billions in the marketplace. What they ideally ought to do, of course, is let the dollar fall where it will, which would make our products more competitive, theirs less, our exports up, theirs down, and the dollar strong again. But this costs jobs and isn't popular. So there they are—between the devil of too many dollars and the deep blue sea of unemployment. Meantime, the stock market sinks nervously.*

U.S. on the Bargain Counter

Sink the market did, although the declining dollar was far from the only reason. For the next few weeks the dollar became truly undervalued—you could buy more of life's needs in New York with dollars than you could with an equivalent amount of marks in Frankfurt or francs in Paris. This was a good thing for us. Detroit sold more cars, West Germany sold fewer. By early 1975, for example, the VW Beetle had advanced in price on the U.S. market to nearly $3,500 versus $3,300 for a close U.S. competitor. (Compare this with the $1,800 Beetles of 1963.)

Our foodstuffs became so inexpensive for foreigners that our surplus sold out overnight, bringing a prosperity to the farmer that he

* *United Business and Investment Report,* February 12, 1973.

hadn't enjoyed for decades. Our balance of trade soared as exports boomed and our balance-of-payments deficit disappeared. The pleasure was not unalloyed, of course, as the surge in exports was accompanied by a surge in prices.

Everything we had here really ended up on the bargain counter for foreigners, all because the dollar "collapsed." The dollar remained free to float at levels dictated by supply and demand, clearly the healthiest thing for the economy. Finally, the stock market took heart, or at least began to worry about other things as investors saw that a declining dollar did not hurt them. Meantime, gold stocks— the shares of gold-mining companies—had gone through the roof.

Investing in Gold

A glance at the accompanying chart of gold-mining shares shows graphically what happened when Washington unpegged the dollar from gold. The group doubled in price from 1966 to 1969 on a speculative bubble but soared nearly sixfold when supply and demand were allowed to set the price. The big surge in 1973–74 reflected in part the rise to world economic prominence of the members of the Organization of Petroleum Exporting Countries (OPEC). When the OPEC oil price was quadrupled, the flow of money—Western money —into their coffers was quadrupled, too.

GOLD MINING STOCKS

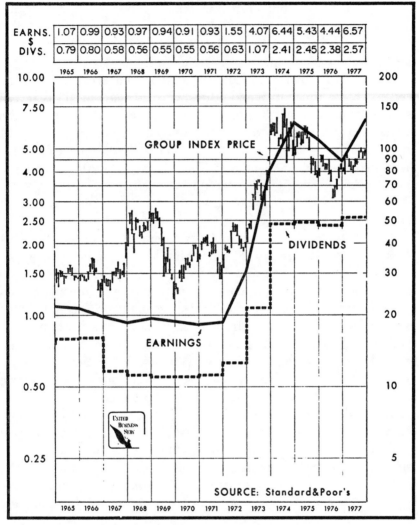

EARNS. $	1.07	0.99	0.93	0.97	0.94	0.91	0.93	1.55	4.07	6.44	5.43	4.44	6.57
DIVS.	0.79	0.80	0.58	0.56	0.55	0.55	0.56	0.63	1.07	2.41	2.45	2.38	2.57

GROUP INDEX PRICE

DIVIDENDS

EARNINGS

UNITED BUSINESS SERV

SOURCE: Standard&Poor's

When, in 1974, the U.S. Congress made it legal once again for Americans to own gold, the Arabs saw this as a chance to increase their wealth even more. They—and other currency speculators—rushed out and bought a lot of yellow metal. All this attention pushed the price of gold almost to $195 an ounce by the end of 1974, giving the mining companies a nice surge in earnings. It was not surprising to see Campbell Red Lake, for instance, go from 10 to 50 in the early 1970s as earnings per share went from 25¢ to roughly $1.75. Then the gold bullion bubble burst, as bubbles always do, and prices plummeted to a low of $103 in August 1976. Obviously, gold wasn't much of an inflation hedge in that twenty-month period. As the chart shows, gold-mining shares fell, too.

Although the love for gold dies hard in the breasts of central bankers, French peasants, and others who have a cynical distrust of the ability of political institutions to balance budgets, gold is no longer of monetary importance. Gold-mining countries such as the Soviet Union, South Africa, and Canada will continue to sell the metal in order to finance imports. The International Monetary Fund and the U.S. Treasury will remain on the sell side of gold markets. The yellow metal is a commodity now, just as copper, corn, and soybeans are.

Admittedly, gold differs from other commodities in the way people are willing to squirrel it away. Most aboveground gold is just that, hidden away for a rainy day. Who among us would be willing to store tons of soybeans or copper ingots forever? If people should ever lose this mystic love for the yellow metal, the price could plunge over the long term, for industry use represents only a fraction of the available supply. Nevertheless, gold will tend to move up when inflation fears are rampant and down when world finances appear to be under control. All the hoarders are not yet gone. The long-term balance of market forces favors higher gold prices.

Industrial demand for gold is destined to keep rising along with the economic growth of the West, for gold is an excellent electrical conductor and a well-nigh-indispensable ingredient of the supersensitive electronic technology of our times. Gold-mining shares, therefore, are likely to continue in a volatile long-term uptrend, reflecting higher metal prices translated into better mining company profits.

The market performance of the shares will be enhanced by inflation jitters and depressed by labor and political turmoil in gold-producing nations. They will reflect generally the things that help or hinder all freely traded common stocks. One might guess that earnings progress for this industry, given the problems of dirty and dangerous working conditions, might be substantially slower than that for companies in computers, health care, banking, and brewing.

Investment Outlook: So-So

Generally speaking, therefore, gold-mining company shares have no more than average appeal. However, if you wish to speculate in gold, if you prefer the yellow metal to greenbacks, do so in mining company shares rather than gold bullion itself. There is a ready market for gold stocks, easy storage of the certificates, and, usually, dividend income.

Owning gold bullion, on the other hand, is expensive. You must pay to store and insure it. It represents negative income, if you will. It offers no dividends, and is much more difficult to market when you want to sell. Following is a brief description of what we regard as the four best gold-mining company issues, all traded on the New York Stock Exchange.

ASA Ltd., unlike the mining companies discussed below, is a closed-end investment company, based in Johannesburg, South Africa. The portfolio is made up of investments in some two dozen South African mines. Given the race problems and politics of the Union of South Africa, the shares of ASA Ltd. carry considerable risk. The stock is extremely volatile and in recent years has lagged behind the three discussed below.

Campbell Red Lake Mines Ltd., controlled by Dome Mines, is a leading low-cost Canadian gold producer. Output has grown impressively over the past several years, yet ore reserves as of the end of 1976 totaled 1,734,400 tons, an increase of 97,300 tons from a year earlier. (Ore reserves are important for any extractive company.) Earnings reflect output, costs, and price. Because of the volatility of bullion prices, profits per share have bounced about in recent years, dividends have been erratic, and the shares themselves have swung over a wide price range.

Dome Mines Ltd. is a large and relatively high cost Canadian gold-mining company but does have a substantial investment in two low-cost producers, Campbell Red Lake and Sigma Mines. Reserves of ore totaled 1,890,000 tons as of December 1976 for the Dome properties, to which must be added those of Campbell Red Lake, see above, and 1,231,740 tons for Sigma. Market performance of the shares in recent years has been almost identical with that of Campbell Red Lake common and should continue so over the foreseeable future.

Homestake Mining Company is the largest U.S. producer. Operating results for the company are affected in a major way by lead and zinc prices, since these metals account for nearly 70 percent of operating profits. Silver and uranium mining also are part of the Homestake picture. Nevertheless, Homestake common tends to move with other gold issues and should continue to. Reserves of all metals mined are ample.

The Glitter of the Kaffirs

Not satisfied with risking all on the gold-mining shares listed on the NYSE, which represent mostly Western Hemisphere mines, some brokers, traders, and eternally gullible investors went off after the shares of South African gold producers in 1974.

These are companies working within the Union of South Africa's apartheid social structure. Tense race relations mean even tenser labor-management problems. Black miners working in 100-degree temperatures deep underground for white managements in the clean air above ground can become understandably restive. When they do, white government police move in. Eleven protesting miners were shot and killed in 1973. In February 1974, three mines—Free State Geduld, Welkin, and Western Holdings—had 61, 47, and 34 percent, respectively, of their miners walk off the job.

In short, these stocks, called "kaffirs" (for the native tribes in the area), offer all of the risks of Dome and Campbell Red Lake, plus a tinderbox racial situation. In addition, good reliable information on reserves, taxes, and routine operating statistics is very hard to come by. For this reason, they are much cheaper in relation to earnings. But cheap or no, our advice is, if you must gamble on gold, use NYSE-listed issues.

Enter the Krugerrand

Proving that where there is a market enterprising promoters will find a product, savers are now offered a means of buying gold coin-shaped ingots minted by the Republic of South Africa weighing one troy ounce, the basic weight on which gold prices are quoted. Krugerrands can be bought at the world gold-ounce price plus a modest charge for "coinage and distribution," one at a time if you are a small investor or by the dozen if you are a financial "biggie."

Krugerrand holders can always find what their hoard is worth simply by multiplying the number of pieces they own by the world price, quoted daily in the financial press. A further encouragement offered investors by the thoughtful vendors is their availability. They can be purchased in many banks, brokerage offices, and coin dealerships.

Krugerrands are not the only such gold pieces minted primarily for hoarders, though they are probably the most widely known now, thanks to the massive advertising campaign to which we have been subjected. Others include the Mexican 50 peso, Austrian 100 corona, and Hungarian korona, each of which weighs in at about an ounce, and the Austrian four-ducat, weighing about half an ounce. Incidentally, you can frequently buy these for less of a premium than you'd pay for the Krugerrand, though you might have to look harder to find someone who deals in them.

But again, where's the appeal? These coins can get lost or stray or be stolen. They offer no income and could go down in price as well as up. Our feeling on Krugerrands, pesos, coronas, koronas, ducats, kaffirs, and gold stocks is that you should let someone else have them. The game, as has been said in other contexts, just isn't worth the candle.

Chapter 17 Tax Shelters

THERE IS nothing illegal or immoral about using tax shelters to keep Uncle Sam's hands off as much of your wealth as possible. After all, he's the one who makes the breaks possible, and, in general, there is some good reason for them. Tax shelters were born when the federal government decided to use the power of taxation as a tool of economic policy as well as a means of generating revenue.

Hence, when Washington wanted to promote home ownership, it allowed individuals to deduct from their taxable income the cost of borrowing the price of a house. To encourage people to invest in the equity markets to provide capital to fuel the country's growing economic machine, it gave them a break on their long-term capital gains. More recently, to make it easier for them to put something aside for their later years, it provided tax incentives for retirement savings. Even U.S. Series EE Savings Bonds can be regarded as tax shelters, for the taxes on the interest they earn may be deferred until a future time when a taxpayer's tax rate might be lower than during his peak earning years.

On a more sophisticated level, the government provides tax incentives to induce investment in such risky ventures as oil-well drilling and exploration. It provides other tax-saving devices to lure money into capital-intensive industries to help promote their development.

Inevitably, these mechanisms tickle the imaginations of those who would stretch, bend, and squeeze them into forms of dubious merit to provide advantages where none were specifically intended. The result has been a string of tax shelters in such diverse areas as motion picture production, vineyards, pecan groves, and professional sports team franchises.

So, we have two kinds of tax shelters. Those that bear the express blessing of the federal government and those that have been created on the thready fringes of the legislative cloth of which the tax code is sewn. If you explore tax shelters with serious intent, you can feel relatively secure in sticking to those areas of specific endorsement. But if you venture into the territory of the benders and stretchers, caution lights and warning bells should go off in your head to alert you to your vulnerability.

"Shelters" Versus "Loopholes"

Thus, in their purest form, tax shelters are not tax "loopholes." Loopholes are unintentional gaps in the tax structure through which clever taxpayers and special-interest groups can wiggle to unfair advantage. However, shelters can outlive their usefulness or provide more tax breaks than justified to achieve the desired results. Sometimes, too, they can give more advantages to certain taxpayers, particularly high-income ones, than the public at large or "reform"-minded groups deem fair. Congress then puts its shoulder to the legislative wheel and changes the rules.

A good example of that has occurred in recent years as Washington, riding the crest of a reform wave, has conducted major surgery on the tax-shelter laws in the name of righting such inequities. "Hobby farming" was one target. Persons with high incomes subject to stiff federal income taxes would purchase farms and then not work them, having no intention of showing profit. Their ownership of the farms entitled them to the tax breaks available to legitimate farmers. The farms they did not work or worked only enough to create losses produced large tax deductions, which they then applied to their regular income, thus sheltering that other income from taxation.

Another maneuver used by tax-shelter investors has been to deliberately pile up huge deductions in the early years of an investment, applying them against regular income, then in the later years of the investment, when the large deductions no longer are available, selling out. Or, they would take accelerated depreciation allowances available in the early years, then sell to other investors, who would be able to start depreciating the asset all over again. Uncle Sam was the loser, of course, but so were all the "little" guys and gals who had no legitimate way of reducing their taxes.

What tax reformers have been attempting to do is take the unfair advantages out of the tax-shelter laws while leaving in the bona fide incentives. Special-interest groups have their own ideas of which investments are bona fide, and they subject lawmakers to massive lobbying barrages which cannot help but color the final outcome of such legislative efforts. The thrust of Congress in its "reform" phase of recent years has been to place ceilings on deductions, in general limiting them to the amount of capital actually at risk. Congress also has tightened up on preferences, those things which are given favored tax treatment. It has instituted minimum taxes, to assure that everyone pays at least something. It has written "recapture" provisions into the law to require tax-shelter investors to pay back any "accelerated" depreciation deductions if they sell out too soon.

Tax "reforms," it seems, are a never-ending preoccupation of Congress, at least of late years, and tax "shelters" a perennial target of the "reformers." So it is quite likely that tax-shelter rules will be in a rather constant state of flux at least in the years immediately ahead. This does not mean that shelters will be unavailable, or that legitimate ones will not be encouraged. But it does mean that investors will have to exercise more care in participating in them and will have to depend more heavily on professional help.

The uncertain state of tax-shelter rules also makes it impossible in a discussion such as this to get into the specifics of any tax-shelter program or, indeed, to go much deeper than a general explanation of what tax shelters are, how they can (and cannot) be used, who can use them most profitably—and who should stay away from them.

"Savings" Versus Risks

Perhaps the biggest danger is that in the process of "saving" taxes, a shelter will yield losses far in excess of the savings. Tax shelters—and when we talk of them here we refer to more sophisticated vehicles than the simple ones mentioned at the outset—should be reserved for the experts and those willing to seek expert counsel in the desired area. They also should be entered into only with a full understanding of the risks involved. For the most part, they should be employed only by persons in high enough tax brackets to make the risks worthwhile, those with sufficient wealth to be able to add capital if needed to avert failure of the investment and to assume those losses if they become inevitable. In other words, tax shelters are not the place to gamble your first savings dollars.

Even if an investor could easily stand a loss, there should be reasonable expectation of gain. Therefore, when searching out a tax shelter, the most important consideration should be the basic validity of the investment itself, not the tax breaks it might generate. Unfortunately, this seemingly obvious point is too frequently overlooked. In the long run, the careless investor—crapshooter, really— would have been better off to have given his money to charity, where at least his deduction would have been guaranteed and the size of his gift determined at the outset.

How Shelters Work

Those admonitions aside, let us turn to the mechanics of tax shelters. There are four ways in which they can work for you. First, they can create tax deductions in excess of the income they generate, affording the opportunity to apply them against other income. This is becoming more difficult to accomplish as Congress tightens the rules, but opportunities still exist in some areas. Second, they can defer taxes until some later date when you expect to be in a lower bracket. Third, they can convert ordinary income to long-term capital gains, which are taxed at lower rates. Fourth, they can provide leverage, which by using borrowed money will multiply both the yield on your own capital and the effectiveness of deductions. Virtually all tax shelters make use of one or more of these mechanisms.

Say you want to invest in real estate because you have always heard it is an excellent tax shelter. You cast about for the right piece of property and you light upon an apartment building. You're able to put down 20 percent of the purchase price and you plan to borrow the rest (leverage). Although you would only have 20 percent of the property's value actually at risk, you'd be able to write off all the expenses of maintenance and of operating the property against the income generated by the property, and even against your other income if the deductions were high enough. You'd also be able to depreciate the property, adding to your tax break. Say the property shows only a 3 percent profit after all expenses. Because of the leverage, that return on your 20 percent investment would be a respectable 15 percent.

If conditions are right, you might be able to take accelerated depreciation on the property, which means taking a larger deduction against income today in exchange for an earlier retirement of your depreciation allowance and, hence, larger taxes in the future (tax deferral). At any rate, the appreciating value of the property is not subject to taxation until you sell it, further deferring your tax liability.

Finally, as you have been taking the depreciation allowances on the property, you have been reducing its cost basis. When you sell it, the proceeds in excess of the cost basis are taxed as a capital gain. To the extent your depreciation allowances offset ordinary income you have converted that ordinary income to capital gains.

Beware of Lurking Dangers

What's wrong with that? Your investment scored on all four counts as a tax shelter. Well, suppose a major developer came to town and threw up a hundred new apartment units, offering them at rents far below what you could afford to charge. Demand for your units would decline and you might find yourself with a rash of vacancies. You expect a few from time to time, but too many for too long can place your investment in jeopardy. If you don't have enough rental income, you'll have to dip into your own pocket to come up with the mortgage payments or risk the loss of your investment through foreclosure. Furthermore, the presence of the new units diminishes the marketability of your property. So instead of appreciating in value it might even decline. Finally, if you have taken accelerated depreciation, you might be subject to some tax recapture even if you have to sell the property at a loss or go through a foreclosure.

The point is, there are risks involved, even in the "safest" tax shelters.

The illustration assumes a direct participation in the tax-shelter investment. To secure the loan, you might have had to put up additional collateral beyond the property itself. In the event of failure, your other assets would likewise be at risk, creating the possibility of even further losses.

To confine their liability to the amount of capital invested, most tax-shelter investors use limited partnerships. If a partnership is put together properly, it is not regarded as a separate tax entity, and its partners are taxed individually on the basis of their proportionate share. The limited form is chosen because it puts a cap on the limited partner's potential liability. The limited partners are not actively involved in the management of the investment, leaving that task to a paid manager, the general partner, whose liability, by the way, is unlimited.

Remember, too, that the manager is generally also the promoter. He'll be paid for his efforts whether you lose your shirt or not. You have to ask yourself why he is offering you such a deal. Since you would be placing your assets under his care, you must examine his qualifications and track record. Is he knowledgeable in his field? Has he managed similar projects successfully in the past? Are his performance projections realistic? Is he putting up some equity money, too?

Study Your Exits

Investors seeking tax shelters frequently forget or do not realize that it is as important to consider their means of getting out of the investment as it is to enter. Timing is important, for the reasons we noted above, particularly regarding the effects of deferred taxation and the realization of capital gains. There are other considerations, too. Assuming that increasing amounts of capital are required to "save" the investment, when does it become more prudent to bail out than to pour good money after bad? Obviously it makes more sense to explore these matters before embarking on such a voyage than after you're on the verge of shipwreck. Unless you're an expert in tax law, you should seek qualified counsel. In fact, as we noted at the outset, tax shelters are not for amateurs, and if you think they can help you, among the first steps you should take is to have a professional render an opinion and lay out both the entry and exit choices for you, showing you the possible benefits—and potential liabilities.

A responsible tax-shelter promoter or salesperson will not allow you to invest without first making inquiries as to your tax bracket and income or other resources and mentioning in some detail the risks that are present. But these are sure to be accompanied by the inevitable promises of potential gain that will be conveyed with more persuasiveness.

Test Your Decision

Therefore, before committing any of your resources to such sophisticated tax shelters as real estate, oil- and gas-drilling participations, cattle feeding, master phonograph recordings, or motion pictures, you should make doubly sure that certain tests are met:

Do you have a firm grasp of exactly how the proposed tax shelter works, how it generates its income and tax breaks?

Are you fully aware of the risks involved?

Do you have a sufficient amount of other, more "secure," savings and investments?

Could you afford to lose your entire tax-shelter investment if that should occur?

Do you have sufficient resources to commit more if necessary to "rescue" your original stake?

Does the proposed shelter provide a reasonable expectation of success and profit?

Are you in a high enough tax bracket—and will you be in one long enough—to make the tax breaks worthwhile?

Are the potential rewards high enough to justify the risks, or could you reap as much with less risk elsewhere?

Have you examined the full implications of the shelter, including your exit options?

Does the shelter manager have a successful track record in similar ventures?

Finally, do you possess the psychological makeup to assume the risks involved? Could you sleep at night while your assets were thus committed?

In general, we take an extremely cautionary stance on tax shelters, preferring to steer most investors along safer courses. But we cannot deny the fact that for some individuals, well-considered tax-shelter programs can indeed play a valuable part in their investment port-folios. We can only emphasize the need to examine each proposed shelter with the utmost care and weigh its potential gains against the potential risks, with special attention to the risks.

Chapter 18 **Real Estate**

"Of all millionaires, ninety percent became so through owning real estate," Andrew Carnegie, the steel tycoon, once observed. He went on to advise: "The wise young man or wage earner should invest his money in real estate." This country's history is generously peppered with examples of the fortunes that can be made in pursuit of that investment. John Jacob Astor became the richest man in America in the early 1800s as the "landlord of New York." William J. Levitt foresaw the need for low-cost housing for GI's returning home from World War II, and mass-produced them into the Levittowns that have become a part of our landscape and language, making himself comfortably well off in the process. William Zeckendorf fathered scores of flamboyant real estate projects, wheeling and dealing himself into and out of several fortunes.

Not all of us need aspire to such heights to enjoy the fruits of real estate investment. Even if you confine your involvement to owning your own home, you stand to add substantially to your net worth as you dutifully make mortgage payments over the months and years. Home ownership, in fact, is the most common form of real estate "investment." For most homeowners, their house represents their largest single asset. Furthermore, it is likely to be an appreciating asset in dollar terms, for it represents a tangible entity with intrinsic value. It tends to hold its true worth, regardless of what inflation does to the buying power of the dollar. In many cases, it tends to rise in "real" value, as well, particularly if it is well located and of a type eagerly sought by potential buyers.

Another type of home ownership that is gaining in popularity, particularly with the rise in housing and energy costs, involves taking a stake in multifamily residential property. There are two basic forms: cooperative apartments and condominiums. With a cooperative, you own a share of the entire property. Whatever tax considerations apply to the whole package apply to you as well. With a condominium, you own your apartment outright, just as if it were a single family residence, with your own individual tax considerations. In addition, you are a joint owner of the common parts of the property. In both a cooperative and a condominium, you share in the maintenance costs of the common property through assessments which you have a legal obligation to pay. As with a single-family house, you build equity as you make your monthly payments, and if the property is well maintained and favorably situated your stake will rise in value over the years.

But beyond the appeal of home ownership, one basic reason for the popularity of real estate as an investment vehicle is the federal government's use of its powers to provide incentives for good-quality housing for all. Recent legislative history is dotted with incentive-inducing provisions. The Housing Acts of 1949, 1965, and 1968, for example, provided mortgage insurance programs, rent subsidies, and the massive urban renewal programs. While their effectiveness has been debatable, these acts do indicate an inescapable governmental involvement in the fate and fortune of the housing industry.

Successes—and Failures

There have been astounding successes and resounding failures in real estate investment in recent years. Two of the strongest areas—farmland and the single-family home—have been able to provide excellent protection against a sharply rising cost of living during the late 1960s and early 1970s. On the other hand, the performance of the hapless real estate investment trusts during the same period tells quite another story.

Favorably located real estate has always been a profitable area of investment. It will become even more so in the years to come as the earth's resources continue to shrink in proportion to its population. Various studies by prominent institutions have shown an inherent long-term need for new homes far above the level of the 1965–75 period. Some of the demand will come from replacement of aging or dilapidated homes, urban renewal, and the acquisition of second homes. But perhaps most significant is the projected swelling in the prime home-buying age group—25 to 44—that will likely carry well into the 1980s. This dividend of the baby boom of the 1950s will mean that, despite the rapidly rising cost of a single-family home, demand will continue to keep prices on a rising trend.

Regardless of your investment objective, real estate can be a contender for inclusion in your portfolio. The following paragraphs discuss some of the more important forms and their investment characteristics.

Investing in Raw Land

Land investment can encompass anything from the most arid prairie land to fertile farming acreage. Speculation in land has provided magnificent fortunes—but also sizable losses. A speculator in land is looking ahead to some possible change in the usage of the piece of property. Either it must be seen to have potential for homes or it must promise to provide some form of future income. Potential industrial, commercial, residential, or recreational uses can have a major impact on land values. Farming acreage has appreciated at an explosive rate, benefiting particularly from farm expansion in the corn belt and higher crop prices. These land values could go even higher, but the potential investor must be aware that increases already have far exceeded the rise in the farmer's own income. Thus, one flag of caution has been raised.

Speculating in raw land is extremely difficult, and dreams of quick profits can obscure the all too numerous pitfalls. Raw land not only provides no current income but it entails additional costs while it is being held, for such things as financing and taxes. This means that such an investment must appreciate in value by at least 10 percent a year just to break even. That can be an especially tall order. Furthermore, raw land is an extremely illiquid investment and should never be purchased with funds that might be needed quickly. In addition to these drawbacks, you may find you have to work hard to make your speculation succeed. You might have to exert influence over zoning or even a community's total master plan.

If you are undeterred by these potential obstacles, your best approach is to stay close to home, where you can more easily appraise development and growth prospects. There are land development companies that purport to provide real estate investments for you—usually in parts of Florida or Arizona. These programs have been sprinkled with more than their fair share of development problems. At times promised amenities have been nonexistent or slow in coming. Government regulation has not always fully protected investors. Do not expect that your investment in raw land will be a quick road to riches.

Rental Property

Apartment living offers an appealing lifestyle for a growing number of Americans, discouraged by the ever rising cost of owning a residence or perhaps simply because of the convenience. Investing in rental property thus constitutes a large and expanding market that ranges all the way from leasing a single-family home to participations in large apartment complexes with all the amenities—swimming pools, tennis courts, and sauna baths. Investment in rental property can bring substantial economic benefits, though there are often numerous management headaches as well. As a landlord, you face the problems of keeping up with maintenance, finding tenants, collecting the rent, and handling complaints about the all-night parties in 4B. If you're not up to those tasks, you can hire someone to manage the property for you, but this cuts into your profits.

In seeking a rental property, it is well to keep in mind the rule of thumb that monthly rental income should total about 1 percent of the purchase price—as a bare minimum. This effectively removes most single-family homes and as a practical matter makes it hard to justify anything less than three units.

There are some distinct advantages to this form of investment. Apartments can generally be financed with a relatively small down payment of 20 to 30 percent of the purchase price, affording considerable leverage on the investment. The down payment is generally smaller if you make the building your home, too. Indeed, leverage is one of the major benefits of investing in rental property, for it magnifies your rate of return on the appreciating value of the property. But there are tax advantages that can have an even greater effect on your profits. We'll discuss them later in this chapter.

In purchasing rental property, make your selections carefully. Avoid those that show evidence of structural flaws or other conditions which might cause hefty maintenance expenses later on. Location is another important consideration. The deterioration of a neighborhood could seriously erode your capital and diminish the property's earning power. Don't be afraid to get a professional appraisal of the property's worth, either. Consider a professional property manager to help in the day-to-day affairs. This of course would likely be uneconomical for a two- or three-family home. Thus, it is best, when possible, to invest in a larger building of five or more units, since economies of scale cut your overhead per unit. You are also less vulnerable to losses should one of your units go unrented for a while. Speaking of vacancy rates, you should study the rental market in the area in which you propose to invest to be reasonably sure you won't be stuck for long with empty units. There will be vacancies from time to time, to be sure, but too many will play havoc with your bottom line.

Business Property

Investing in business property takes several forms. Office buildings, shopping centers, and warehouses are among the most familiar alternatives. Business property provides certain advantages over apartment rental. The commercial tenant is generally more stable and is looking for a location around which he can build a profitable business. He takes better care of his property and, barring extreme financial emergency, pays his rent on time. Some of the drawbacks include the more expensive maintenance services you as a landlord must provide. Vacancies are usually harder to fill, and may require such things as the dismantling of a customized office.

One approach to investing in business property is to buy and convert a marginal suburban retail operation into an office building. This has worked successfully for a good many real estate investors. Others have profited from current conditions by buying and converting vacated gasoline service stations into offices or stores. But the outstanding business property investments recently have been in regional shopping centers. The largest of these can encompass one million square feet or more of store area and serve a customer base of about 250,000 people. They usually have a magnet store or two to act as the main drawing card. Smaller community-type shopping centers may cluster around a supermarket and a drugstore. The investors in the properties have taken advantage of the shift of population from the downtown areas of major cities to the suburbs. Reasonably priced land close to rapidly expanding outlying areas can offer the speculator a good opportunity.

The shopping center owner attempts to build a long list of good-quality tenants with long-term leases. His compensation is generally in the form of a minimum rent plus a certain percentage of gross sales above minimum volumes. Because of the specialized nature of this field, shopping centers are best left to professional developers, though smaller investors can frequently invest through participation in joint ventures and limited partnerships (more on them below). A bad experience with a particular key tenant, such as the bankruptcy of W. T. Grant, can affect profits, as happened with Hubbard Real Estate Investments in 1975.

Investment in shopping centers is possible through common stock ownership. A handful of companies specialize in the field; General Growth Properties and Rouse Company are two leaders.

Real Estate Investment Trusts

Real estate investment trusts (REIT's) are one form of indirect participation in real estate that allows investors to escape management headaches. A proliferation of REIT's came in the wake of a 1960 change in the tax laws. That change made it possible for REIT's to pass federal income tax consequences through to investors in the same fashion as mutual funds, providing they distributed at least 90 percent of their income each year.

In the years immediately following that law change, many REIT's did exceedingly well by their investors. Popularity reached faddish proportions during the late 1960s and early 1970s. Promoters, eager to cash in, put together projects of dubious merit that were snapped up by equally eager investors. As long as the economy remained robust, they could survive. But at the slightest sign of slump, they collapsed like so many houses of cards. Indeed, even the strongest of the REIT's took some hard knocks under the barrage of shifting long- and short-term interest rate relationships, rising unemployment, soaring operating costs, and rent control. The rapidly rising short-term interest rates played havoc with financing arrangements in the mid-1970s and spelled doom for many of the highly leveraged REIT's.

As a result of this drubbing, REIT's got a bad name in the investment community. They were slow to recover as investors overlooked the real lessons of that assault and battery, the lessons we're preaching over and over in this book: Look askance at quick-buck schemes and fads, do your homework to be sure the basic investment is founded on rock and not sand, and once the commitment has been made, keep an eye on it. REIT's might still have a place in your investment portfolio, and you should not let the shakeout of the mid-1970s obscure their possible merit now. You should, however, realize that they are more speculative as investments than high-quality common stocks or corporate bonds, and their potential for much higher returns is coupled with a higher potential for loss. You should also remember that some REIT's are better than others, and seek out only those with the more solid reputation if you do decide to invest.

Real estate investment trusts, like mutual funds, sell shares to the public to raise their capital. Instead of investing in a portfolio of stocks and bonds as do mutual funds, they invest in real estate and mortgages. REIT's, like closed-end mutual funds, do not redeem their shares; rather, the shares are bought and sold over the counter or on the stock exchanges.

REIT's come in two basic forms—equity trusts and mortgage investment trusts. Equity trusts own property outright and seek their profits from rental income and capital gains. Mortgage investment trusts make long-term mortgage loans to large real estate buyers and intermediate and short-term construction loans to builders and developers. It was within this latter segment that the excessive proliferation and subsequent shakeout occurred.

The main attraction of REIT's is that they are able to pass on all the tax advantages of real estate ownership to their investors. Since they are not allowed to reinvest their earnings to provide growth, they rely heavily on borrowed funds to make their profits. Typically, a REIT will have 20 percent in equity, 40 percent in long-term debt, and 40 percent in bank loans and commercial paper.

The mortgage trusts were hit hardest by the economic downturn of 1974–75, mostly because of their involvement in shorter-term, risky construction loans. Their long-term low-interest loans were being carried by short-term high-cost money. Meanwhile their risky short-term loans that might have offset this imbalance were defaulting. These loans had given them handsome returns during the credit crunch of 1969–70, when more conventional sources of capital dried up. But as credit loosened and interest rates fell, traditional lenders again became more competitive. Many of these REIT's became overburdened with an excessively high level of nonearning investments and property foreclosures. Bankruptcies befell some, and investors in a good many others were left hanging on the ropes as share prices plummeted and dividends dried up.

Equity trusts fared better during this period, but they are not without their speculative aspects. Since they invest directly in property and depend to a large extent on a continuing flow of rental income, they can be hit hard by excessive or prolonged vacancies. Eagerness to grab a piece of the action can cause overbuilding in a certain area. Untimely institution of rent controls can slap a ceiling on the income potential of a project. A venture can flounder because of a poor location or because of the loss of a principal tenant.

As you can now see, there is more to investing in REIT's than merely picking one off the shelf. You have to evaluate the merits of individual trusts by a careful study of a number of factors, including examination of their past performance, their capital structure, their investment objectives, and their management. Then you have to find those that mesh with your own objectives and be sure they continue to do so.

Real Estate Syndicates

The syndicate or group participation is another popular form of real estate investment. Most of these take the form of partnerships, but some are corporations. They raise capital by selling participations or shares. They use this money to purchase heavily mortgaged rental property, and apply the resulting cash flow to pay off the debt and even to pay tax-free dividends "out of capital." They use accelerated depreciation to reduce or avoid income taxation. When this has been used up, they sell the property at its appreciated value, applying the special capital gains rules to reduce the taxes on their profits. They then start all over with a new project. Real estate syndicates are also used as vehicles for property development and land speculation.

Most of them take the legal form of limited partnerships rather than general partnerships. Under a general partnership, all partners bear equally in the risks and rewards of the venture. This means all partners can be held liable for losses in excess of their actual stake in the project. Under a limited partnership, on the other hand, the limited partners are liable only to the extent that they are invested in the project. A general partner puts the deal together and manages it, for a consideration, which he is paid regardless of how well or how poorly the venture goes. However, a well-conceived and properly managed project can bring highly expert management to bear, with rewarding results for the limited partners.

As we discussed in our chapter on tax shelters, it is sometimes easy to become so caught up in the potential tax advantages that the basic investment aspects are overshadowed. Before committing any of your own capital to such a venture, you should be sure it will stand on its own merits as an investment. Beware of deals that sound too good to be true, and be sure to take a close look at the track record of the management. There have been cases of deception and mismanagement that have cost investors dearly.

Tax Considerations

As we have pointed out before, favorable federal tax rules provide one of the primary advantages of investing in real estate. Mortgage interest payments and outlays for property taxes are deducted from income before computing the tax. If the deductions exceed income generated by the real estate, they can be applied against other income. In the case of rental property, maintenance costs are also deductible, and special rules on depreciation may be applied. Healthy tax deductions are available on construction-period interest costs.

It is not uncommon—or illegal—for investors to show a "tax loss" while actually enjoying a healthy cash flow. Investors might also be writing off depreciation for tax purposes while the property is actually appreciating in value. This appreciated value is taxed at preferential capital gains rates when the property is sold. It is possible to defer the tax on these gains by swapping the property for other, similar property in a tax-free exchange or, in the case of a personal residence, by replacing one with another of equal or greater value. Persons 55 and older may be excused from most or all of the gain on their principal residence when they sell.

If you invest in real estate, you must keep one eye closely glued on Washington. Changes in the tax rules may have a profound effect on your investment, and you will have to adjust your strategy accordingly should they occur. Real estate, whether it is raw land or a shopping center complex, is not an investment that can be acquired and forgotten.

Who Should Invest—and How?

Since this discussion is general in nature and intended only to give you a broad picture of the various areas of potential real estate investment, we have not attempted to provide the mechanics of specific investment packages. However, the question must inevitably come to your mind: "Should I be in 'real estate'?"

To answer that question, you must first answer these:

Are you in a relatively high income tax bracket (say, 40 to 70 percent) so that the tax deductions provided by real estate investments can provide substantial shelter of other income?

Do you expect to be in these high brackets for the next ten to twenty years?

Can you afford to tie up your assets for long periods in order to take full benefit of the shelter (and in order not to sustain possible penalties for early withdrawal)?

Then you must explore the various types of risks and rewards inherent in the various types of real estate investment. Low-income federally assisted housing is riskier than private residential projects. New construction programs are riskier than established shopping centers. And so on.

Finally, as with any other tax shelter, unless you yourself are an expert, you should seek impartial expert advice before committing your assets. You should understand precisely what the investment involves, how much capital you will be expected to commit, how and when you will get it back, what kind of a return you can reasonably expect, and what might go wrong to cause you to lose all or part of your stake.

Part III HOW TO MAKE YOUR CHOICES

Chapter 19 Forecasting with the Cyclical Indicators

FORECASTING IS a complicated process. Even the most expert forecasters are sometimes quite wrong, and ordinarily they are only partially accurate. Yet, like eating, forecasting is something that has to be done. Every action that each of us undertakes implies a forecast. Buying the week's groceries involves forecasting family needs as well as implying certain expectations about price behavior during the week. The actions of buying, selling, or even holding stocks all imply certain forecasts about stock prices.

The decision, then, is not between forecasting and not forecasting. Investors must forecast, and in so doing they must rely heavily on the work of others, at least for the needed data, and ordinarily for interpretations of those data.

Newspapers and business publications frequently carry reports of forecasts, with the fall of the year usually the most popular time for such reports. Investment advisory services, in most cases, carry forecasts, at least in summary form, throughout the year.

A forecast that appears each month is the one implied in the government's *composite index of leading indicators*. This forecast results from the long-range efforts of a few economists to find a group of economic indicators that tend to move up or down in advance of the movements of general business. The reports of the behavior of this index are widely watched, and the individual investor can advantageously pay some attention to these reports. However, the index is far from infallible, and most professional economists consider it to be only one of several forecasting tools available to them.

The index of leading indicators now being used by the U.S. Department of Commerce turned down four months before the 1953–54 recession, twenty-three months before the 1957–58 recession, eleven months before the 1960–61 recession, eleven months before the 1970 recession, and five months before the 1973–75 recession. The index also turned down in 1950–51, 1961, and 1966. None of these downturns was followed by a full-fledged recession, although the 1966 economy is often described as one that experienced a mini-recession. The declines in the leading indicator index mentioned here were all drops lasting several months, and a chart of the index displays innumerable meaningless squiggles, as well.

Actually, the index now in use wasn't even in existence on the dates cited above. The present index, introduced in 1975, is an improved version which, when computed historically, produced the results noted above. The index used earlier failed to foreshadow the 1973 downturn, largely because several of its components were expressed in current dollars and were still pointing upward, reflecting the influence of inflation, when business actually was softening.

Leading Indicators: A Dozen Precursors

The revised index of leading indicators has twelve components, all tested for historical reliability in moving ahead of periods of general business expansion and contraction. The data for the components are gathered monthly and assembled into a combined index. The combined index measures departures from the base year (1967) value of 100. However, when the combined index is first published, data for all twelve components are not available. For example, in any given year the index for May, published in June, is based on only ten components and is subsequently revised in July when the other two components become available. Also, revisions in some of the components are made over a period of several months, leading to revisions of the combined index on those occasions.

The Twelve Leaders _____

> Average workweek of production workers in manufacturing.
> Layoff rate in manufacturing, inverted scale on a chart.
> Value of manufacturers' new orders for consumer goods and materials, expressed in 1972 dollars.
> Index of net business formation.
> Standard and Poor's index of 500 common stock prices.

Contracts and orders for plant and equipment, expressed in 1972 dollars.

Index of new private housing units authorized by local building permits.

Vendor performance, percentage of companies reporting slower deliveries.

Net change in inventories on hand and on order, expressed in 1972 dollars.

Change in sensitive prices, excluding foods, feeds, and fibers.

Change in total liquid assets.

Money supply, expressed in 1972 dollars.

SOURCE: *Business Conditions Digest*, monthly publication of the U.S. Department of Commerce.

The leading indicators are statistical measures that tend to foreshadow movements in the coinciding group. This is quite apparent in the indicators that report on new orders for consumer goods, on contracts and orders for plant and equipment, and in the index of housing permits. Movements in these indicators may be expected to be followed by movements in employment, production, incomes, and sales.

Other leading indicators generally have a rationale for their particular place in the timing sequence of economic measures. The stock market, for example, is sensitive to changes in the state of confidence concerning future business activity. Improved confidence about the future often leads to higher stock prices, and deteriorating confidence brings stock prices down.

Changes in sensitive prices of crude materials—excluding foods, feeds, and fibers—reflect variations in demand and supply pressures for particular raw commodities. Thus a rise in this index could reflect rising levels of demand and, hence, expectations of increased business activity, while a drop in the index could signal the reverse. However, if price declines reflect increased supplies, as they did in mid-1977 following an unusually cold winter, their decline doesn't necessarily reflect a softening of business.

The money supply, measuring the total of currency plus demand deposits and expressed in 1972 dollars, is another measure that often can be expected to precede, in its ups and downs, changes in the general level of business. Expansion of money tends to fuel expansion of business activity, while contraction of money tends to have a dampening effect on levels of such activity.

In recent years, investors, and especially stock market traders, have devoted a good deal of attention to short-term movements in the money supply (without adjustments for price level changes). The weekly money supply reports come out late in the afternoon every Thursday. Some observers interpret increases in money as signs that the Federal Reserve Board is likely to restrict monetary growth and thereby tighten credit. Thus stocks often drop on Friday when the Thursday report shows a higher money supply. If the report shows no gain or even a reduction in the money supply, the expectation sometimes develops that the Fed will ease the money supply and credit, and, accordingly, stocks may rise on Friday. This interpretation of money supply movements is short term. The role of the money supply in the leading indicator index depends on the actual movements of money rather than expectations of how money is going to move.

It is not generally a good idea to pay much attention to the movements of the leading indicator index for any single month. One reason for this caution is that movements of the index over short periods sometimes reflect the influence of random events, such as strikes or unusual weather patterns. For example, in January 1977 the index dropped (after three months of gains) as a result of unusual snows and cold weather. An extreme case of random performance was that of the housing permit index, which fell from 130.5 in December 1976 to 112.6 in January 1977, then rose sharply to 131.8 in February and to 147.5 in March. April then saw a fallback to 134.7.

The index of leading indicators dropped in May 1977 and again in June. This was probably a case of a slackening off after the rebound of late winter. From the depressed January figure of 126.5 the index rose to 130.8 in April. After a rise of that magnitude, an easing would not be unusual. Viewed from this perspective, the May-June drop was nothing to be excited about. Preliminary reports for July showed a further small easing, but later revision turned the small drop into a small gain for that month.

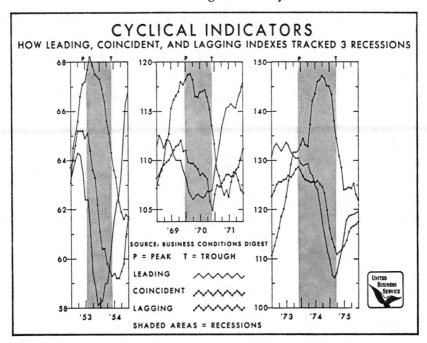

CYCLICAL INDICATORS
HOW LEADING, COINCIDENT, AND LAGGING INDEXES TRACKED 3 RECESSIONS

SOURCE: BUSINESS CONDITIONS DIGEST
P = PEAK   T = TROUGH

LEADING
COINCIDENT
LAGGING

SHADED AREAS = RECESSIONS

UNITED
BUSINESS
SERVICE

The leading indicators are actually part of a family of economic indicators. The two other branches of the family tree are the *coinciding indicators*, which are generally the economic measures being led by the leading indicators, and the *lagging indicators*, which tend to bring up the rear, but which also have an importance of their own.

Coinciding Indicators: Four Track Broad-Based Activities

The coinciding indicators are those that move with general business conditions, that is, those that move up and down with the swings that pervade most or all of the economy. In general, one would expect the coinciding indicators to encompass measures of employment, production, incomes, and sales on the basis that these activities reflect the broad movements of the economy. As it turns out, these four aspects of economic activity are exactly the components of the index of coinciding indicators.

The particular measure of employment used as a coinciding indicator is the monthly report on the number of employees on nonagricultural payrolls. This tests out better than other possible employment (or unemployment) measures as a reporter of the general ups and downs of business. One reason for this is that the payroll reports upon which this number is based reflect a markedly larger sample than does the household survey upon which the monthly labor force, total employment, and unemployment data are based.

The second coinciding indicator is the monthly index of industrial production prepared by the Federal Reserve Board. This index measures activity in manufacturing, mining, and electric and gas utilities. Manufacturing activity tends to be cyclical and represents a declining share of the gross national product. However, the industrial production index reflects important activities and is still worthy of inclusion in the index of coinciding indicators.

The income measure included is the monthly report on personal income. It is expressed in constant dollars and with transfer payments (Social Security benefits and other nonwage government "transfers" of funds into the hands of individuals) deducted. These adjustments improve upon the performance of the personal income figure as a measure of cyclical behavior, which is what is desired of a coinciding indicator.

The final coinciding indicator is a combined figure for manufacturing sales and wholesale and retail trade sales, expressed in constant dollars. This figure provides a comprehensive report on distribution and consumption activities and, like the personal income measure, is one from which the inflation influence has been removed.

A notable exclusion from the list of coinciding indicators is the most comprehensive of all measures. This is the gross national product, the total dollar volume of the nation's output of goods and services. It is not included because it is available only on a quarterly basis rather than monthly and is subject to rather frequent revision.

The four coinciding indicators are combined in a single index of coincident indicators, again using the year 1967 value of 100. The combined index tends to follow movements of general business quite closely, a result that is not surprising, given its broad composition. Although the combined index has a slight tendency to lead general downturns by a couple of months, its upward movements tend to coincide in timing with upswings in business.

The Coinciding Four

Number of employees on nonagricultural payrolls.
Index of industrial production.
Personal income, less transfer payments, in 1972 dollars.
Manufacturing and trade sales, in 1972 dollars.

SOURCE: *Business Conditions Digest,* U.S. Department of Commerce.

Lagging Indicators: Six Tend to Trail Behind

The third member of the indicator triad is the group of lagging indicators, those that rise or fall after the general upward or downward movements of the economy have appeared. In the period from 1947 to 1970, the index of lagging indicators turned down, on average, three months after the peaks in general business and turned upward, on average, five months after the low points.

The lagging indicators, however, are more than faithful followers. A sequence exists among the three groups of indicators, so that the lagging indicators turn down before the leading, and later the coinciding, indicators turn up.

Since the lagging indicators tend to make their moves before the leading indicators make theirs (in the reverse direction), this gives the group of lagging indicators a place in the forecasting scheme. Thus, one would not expect the leading indicators to signal an upward or downward move until the lagging indicators had made a downward or upward move.

Since World War II, the three groups of indicators have performed on track; after all, that is why they have been selected. Individual indicators, however, occasionally lead lives of their own, and this seems to be especially the case with some of the components of the lagging index. The following comments on those components explain the nature of their errant behavior.

The average duration of unemployment, measured in weeks, is used in an inverted manner, with its low values corresponding to business highs and its highs corresponding to business lows. In general, the average duration of unemployment tends to lengthen one month after business peaks and to shorten eight months after troughs.

The index of labor cost per unit of output tends to rise for an average of eight and a half months after a recession begins and to fall for eleven months after expansion begins. In recent years, inflation has reduced the reliability of this indicator.

Manufacturing and trade inventories expressed in constant dollars rise for an average of two and a half months after recessions start and fall for three months after expansions start. However, the recent inflation has also affected the reliability of this series.

Commercial and industrial loans follow a pattern somewhat similar to that of inventories, probably because such loans are frequently utilized in inventory financing.

The ratio of consumer installment debt to personal income tends to rise for an average of six and a half months after a business peak and to fall for seven months after a business trough. These lags in the total of consumer debt seem to reflect a tendency of consumer credit repayments to trail extensions of new credit.

The prime rate charged by banks tends to lag, on average, three and a half months behind business downturns before falling and to lag an average of fourteen months behind business upturns before rising. Sometimes, however, prime rates remain unchanged for long periods of time.

The Six Laggards

Average duration of unemployment in weeks, charted on inverted scale.

Index of labor cost per unit of output in manufacturing (1967 = 100).

Manufacturing and trade inventories, expressed in 1972 dollars.

Outstanding commercial and industrial loans of large commercial banks that report weekly.

Ratio of consumer installment debt to personal income.

Average prime rate charged by banks.

SOURCE: *Business Conditions Digest,* U.S. Department of Commerce.

The family of leading, coinciding, and lagging indicators forms a useful tool in the forecaster's kit. It is important, however, not to draw conclusions from observations pertaining to just one or two months. Unfortunately, the indicators don't foretell much about the severity or duration of business movements. Nor do they purport to forecast stock prices. But since the monthly reports on the leading indicators are widely published, it is easy for the general reader to follow them and thereby get an indication of where the economy is headed.

Chapter 20 Measuring the Market's Ups and Downs

THE MARKET is "up." The market is "down." The market is in a sustained "rally." It is moving "sideways." The daily stock market reports make it sound as if all 1,500 companies listed on the New York Stock Exchange, plus the 800 or so on the American Stock Exchange, and the 25,000 others that are traded on the regional exchanges and off the regular exchanges, or over the counter, are all moving in lockstep up, down, and sideways.

Obviously that's not the case. Just as obviously it would be an impossible task to provide a daily analysis of the aggregate price movements of all stocks. Yet investors, corporate money managers, stockbrokers, economic forecasters, government policymakers, and others concerned with the pulse of investment and business must have some way of keeping a running check on the investment climate.

So they have devised various averages to keep tabs on both the general trend and the present status of the market. Since the "market" is such a huge and diverse agglomeration, even the averages frequently have difficulty in agreeing on precisely what the trend and status of the market are at any given moment. Furthermore, just as the presence of a television news team can sometimes affect the outcome of the event it is covering, the averages themselves can have an impact on the extent and duration of a market movement. If the averages, particularly the more widely followed averages, say the market is "rising," investors perk up and start buying. If the averages say the market is "declining," they start selling to nail down profits or to trim losses. Other elements play their parts, of course: the general strength or weakness of business, the availability of credit, the cost of borrowing money, the needs of corporate finance. The factors affecting stock market movement and the movement of individual stocks are virtually limitless and many of them defy analysis or rationality. Measurement of the stock market thus is an imprecise undertaking.

How to "Build" an Index

There are many ways to go about constructing an index of stock market activity. You could take a relatively small sampling of tried and true blue chip companies and compute a simple, arithmetic average of their stock price activity on a day-to-day basis. You would have something like the Dow Jones Industrial Average. You could take a larger group of what you consider to be representative stocks and apply the same simple arithmetic averaging. You'd have something like the Associated Press and *New York Times* averages.

If you decided that such a simple arithmetic average would not provide sufficient accuracy because it gave equal weight to each stock regardless of the impact of that stock on the total market volume, you could construct a so-called weighted average. You would factor in the differences in size among the components of your index by multiplying the price of each by the number of shares outstanding in each case. You would then average these resulting market-value figures and express them as a percentage of some base figure. You would then have something like the Standard & Poor's, the New York Stock Exchange, American Exchange, and the National Association of Securities Dealers Automated Quotation (NASDAQ) indexes.

This approach might not satisfy you either, because the largest components exert much more influence on the total than the smallest. You might regard this as a situation that unduly distorts the bottom line. So you would take still another tack. You would apply equal dollar investments to a fairly large group of stocks. You would need a firm grasp of mathematics, for you would then apply some rather complex geometric calculations to the daily price changes in order to come up with a result. Your index would resemble the composite index published by Value Line, an investment advisory company. It would also bear a resemblance to two indexes developed by Indicator Digest, Inc., another investment advisory publisher— the IDA, which covers all stocks traded on the New York Stock Exchange, and the AIDA, for those traded on the American Stock Exchange.

Different Indexes Yield Different Results

As you might suspect, these different approaches yield different results. For the most part, the differences are not so much in direction as in extent. The point is best demonstrated with a chart. As you study the chart below, you will notice that the divergence in volatility among the various averages is most prominent during the bull market that ended in late 1968 and the subsequent bear market. In the 1972 market rise, the weighted S&P 500 outdistanced the others, largely reflecting the 120-point rise in IBM, which accounts for about 7 percent of the average's total market value, and, to a lesser extent, Xerox, which doubled.

Perhaps the most interesting revelation is the performance of the Value Line Index since its high in 1968. Both the Dow and S&P had by the end of 1976 recovered to their highs reached in 1968. In contrast, the broad unweighted Value Line Index was still 50 percent below its 1968 high. One reason—probably the major reason—is that the secondary stocks that make up such a large part of the Index are usually slower to respond to a market upturn. But once the rise gets securely under way, they generally outperform the blue chips.

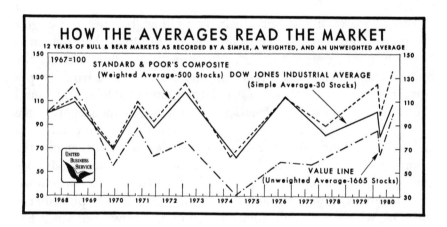

The "Dow"

The Dow Jones Industrial Average is the granddaddy of today's stock market measures. It's also probably the best-known and most widely quoted. The "Dow" dates back to 1896, when it contained an even dozen stocks, none of which remained on the list continuously. In 1916, another eight were added, bringing the total to twenty. It was not until 1928 that the average assumed its present shape. Not only were ten stocks added, but a new method of computation was adopted. It is still in use.

Before 1928, stocks which were split were adjusted by multiplying the split price by two or three or whatever the split was, to make the price consistent with the pre-split value. Adjustments made after 1928 take into account stock dividends, rights, and mergers, as well as splits.

Here are the thirty stocks that made up the Dow Jones Industrial Average in 1980. Dates in parentheses indicate the company's first appearance in the average. Only American Brands and General Electric were in the original average, though both have been in and out several times since.

Allied Chemical (1925)	General Foods (1928)	Minnesota Mining (1976)
Aluminum Company of America (1959)	General Motors (1915)	Owens-Illinois (1959)
American Brands (1897)	Goodyear (1930)	Procter & Gamble (1932)
American Can (1916)	INCO Ltd. (1928)	Sears, Roebuck (1924)
American Telephone & Telegraph (1916)	International Business Machines (1979)	Standard Oil of California (1924)
Bethlehem Steel (1928)	International Harvester (1925)	Texaco (1916)
Du Pont (1924)	International Paper (1901)	Union Carbide (1928)
Eastman Kodak (1928)	Johns-Manville (1930)	United Technologies (1933)
Exxon (1928)	Merck & Co. (1979)	U.S. Steel (1914)
General Electric (1897)		Westinghouse (1916)
		Woolworth (1924)

What is now known as the Dow Jones Transportation Average boasts an equally long history. Until 1970, it was known as the "Railroad" Average; the name was changed when other types of transportation companies were added to the list that year. The twenty stocks that were used originally were all rails, some with names that are still familiar. But many others have succumbed to mergers and bankruptcies. The Dow Jones Utility Average made its debut in 1929. The initial list of twenty utilities included both electric and gas companies, as well as American Telephone & Telegraph, International Telephone, and Western Union. Today the list has been whittled to fifteen electric and gas utilities. The Dow Jones Composite Average was begun in 1933 as a compilation of the stocks used in the three individual averages. All of these are computed essentially the same way as the industrial average.

For several reasons, the historical significance of the Dow industrial average is subject to question. Until 1928, no adjustments were made for stock splits of less than 100 percent. Furthermore, when the new issues were added, the continuity of the average was disrupted. Substitutions in the names of companies in the list were frequent in the early days; through 1939, more than sixty were made. While this probably made the list more representative of the current market, it also produced a historical bias.

Another complaint frequently lodged against the Dow, and one that has some justification, is that it is an elitist sampling of the market. Only 2 percent of the stocks listed on the New York Stock Exchange appear in it. Even when you consider that these 2 percent constitute 25 percent of the total market value of Big Board issues, they are still an extremely narrow representation of all the issues regularly traded on all the exchanges and over the counter.

Other critics of the Dow note that it is heavily loaded with cyclical stocks and includes few solid growth issues. Since price action of basic industry stocks is usually skewed by the ups and downs of the business cycle, these stocks are not necessarily representative of the market as a whole. Then, too, this venerable average completely ignores some of the most dynamic growth areas of today's market.

The S&P 500

Aside from the Dow, the most familiar average is the Standard & Poor's 500. This broad average is widely used by institutional investors and mutual fund managers as a yardstick against which to compare their own performance. In fact, some funds and institutions have adopted investment policies that restrict their holdings to those in the S&P 500 list, thereby giving up any attempt at outperforming this index.

Standard & Poor's also publishes separately the various component averages that make up the 500-stock composite. These are the 400 industrials, 40 utilities, 20 transportation companies, and 40 financial stocks. These new indexes were begun in 1957 to replace the original series started in the 1920s. As we noted above, the S&P averages are weighted. They are also expressed as a percentage of the base market value in 1941–43.

Other Indexes

The New York Stock Exchange Index uses as its base December 31, 1965 = 50, which approximated the average price of a share on the Big Board then. Thus, if the index stands at 60, it indicates that the market has advanced 20 percent above its value on December 31, 1965. The NYSE Index should not be confused with the figure cited by daily newscasters, the average price of a share on the New York Stock Exchange. This figure is simply the average price for all the stocks that traded on a particular day on the Big Board. There is no day-to-day continuity in this figure, for not all issues trade every session; neither is any attempt made to adjust for splits or other changes.

The American Stock Exchange Index is based on equal dollar investments in a list of 1,665 stocks—1,475 industrials, 19 rails, and 171 utilities. It uses June 30, 1961, as its base. The Indicator Digest indexes use 1964 as a starting point.

Indexes Are Useful—to a Point

Are market indexes useful tools for the average investor? Yes, up to a point. Certainly the person who plunges in and buys a stock with a high price-earnings ratio after the averages have recorded a steep and prolonged advance is asking for trouble. The investor who gets discouraged and sells stocks he has been holding through a protracted decline in the market is equally unwise. In other words, the averages are valuable as rough guidelines for timing your transactions.

Using the market averages as forecasting devices, although a favorite pastime of the technicians, can be tricky and unreliable. Complex formulas, involving virtually every conceivable variable, have been devised by serious students of the market, mathematical wizards, and charlatans. While some may prove accurate from time to time, no one has ever come up with a forecasting device of any kind that is always correct. If such an infallible formula exists, it is surely being kept under wraps by its originator, who is busy reaping his own fortune.

In trying to gauge market timing by consulting one of the market averages, you should use an average that represents the type of stocks you own or plan to purchase. The Dow industrials will be of little help if you are interested in utilities, glamour stocks, or rails. Junior growth stocks would more closely parallel the action tracked by the Value Line, IDA, or AMEX indexes.

By keeping in touch with the general trend of the stock market averages, you should develop a better understanding of the action of your own portfolio. Many investors operate in a vacuum. Their holdings are down, and they grow panicky, overlooking the fact that the entire market is in the doldrums. Then, too, keeping an eye on the market rather than on a few individual stocks helps you keep things in proper perspective. If one of your stocks diverges suddenly from the norm, you are more likely to spot this counter movement, investigate, and take the indicated action. Use the averages, by all means, but use them judiciously.

Chapter 21 Getting the Picture from Charts

CHARTS, QUITE simply, are devices which can be valuable aids to investors. They translate into graphic form—with bars or lines—information which could also be presented in tabular form. The basic usefulness of a chart is the picture presented, its conciseness, and the portrayal of relationships not possible in a table.

Here is a tabulation of information showing the daily high, low, and close of the Dow Jones Industrial Average over a two-month period:

		High	Low	Close			High	Low	Close
April	1	930.27	919.55	927.36	May	2	934.02	923.00	931.22
	4	926.70	913.48	915.56		3	939.70	929.27	934.19
	5	920.88	909.74	916.14		4	944.96	929.44	940.72
	6	922.12	910.07	914.73		5	949.46	934.53	943.44
	7	921.21	910.57	918.88		6	943.27	932.24	936.74
	11	928.85	916.47	924.10		9	938.52	928.77	933.09
	12	940.98	924.69	937.16		10	941.40	930.55	936.14
	13	942.76	927.49	938.18		11	937.84	923.85	926.90
	14	956.07	943.69	947.00		12	930.04	917.74	925.54
	15	953.10	941.74	947.76		13	932.58	923.17	928.34
	18	951.32	939.28	942.76		16	938.43	926.73	932.50
	19	944.28	934.79	938.77		17	939.45	925.20	936.48
	20	948.69	933.43	942.59		18	947.34	935.46	941.91
	21	949.37	933.43	935.80		19	945.13	933.34	936.48
	22	935.13	923.59	927.07		20	937.16	925.71	930.46
	25	924.02	910.45	914.60		23	928.17	915.03	917.06
	26	922.74	910.36	915.62		24	917.83	906.55	912.40
	27	928.34	913.08	923.76		25	916.72	901.46	903.24
	28	931.14	919.78	927.32		26	910.45	899.17	908.07
	29	931.99	922.32	926.90		27	909.60	896.29	898.83
						31	904.77	892.55	898.66

Just about any set of data can be depicted graphically, and the result is a "picture" that the eye can encompass quickly. The chart below shows the same information contained in the table, plotted on a simple arithmetic scale. This particular chart is a "bar chart," and its purpose is to show a range. In this case, the top of each bar represents the high price for the day, the bottom represents the low, and the cross line represents the close.

If the data to be plotted do not involve a range, the result would be a line connecting each of the points, like the chart on the next page. In that case, the line represents the daily closing price indicated in the table.

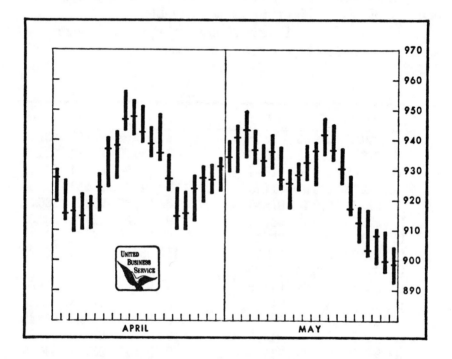

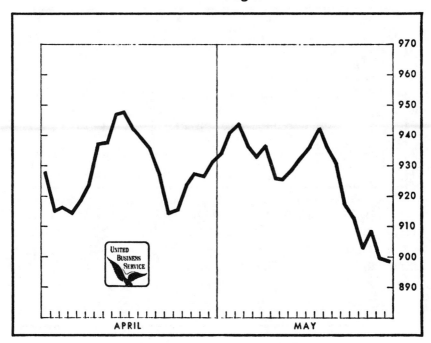

Practical Application

Here are some practical examples of how charts can be useful in conveying information. In the chart on the next page on price-earnings ratios, you can tell at a glance how the ratio for the stocks that make up the Dow Jones Industrial Average compares with the status of the Dow itself. You can see that during the height of the bull market of 1968 the ratio was likewise high. By 1977, the ratio was down substantially, in actual terms as well as in relation to the Dow, suggesting that stocks were cheap on fundamentals and that a buying opportunity might be present. (As things turned out, it wasn't. The main reason was not the fundamentals, but investor psychology, a quality chartists thus far have not been able to quantify.)

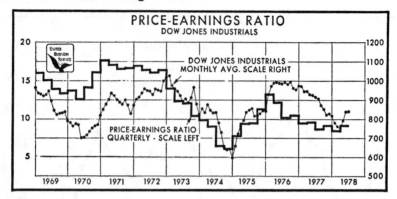

Or, take the chart on federal debt yields, a good barometer of interest rates in general. It shows that while long-term rates remained relatively stable during the period plotted, short-term rates jumped all over the lot. This is a typical circumstance, but the chart shows the relationship of long-term rates to short-term rates at any particular time.

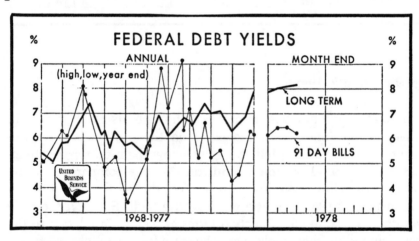

A chart can give you a quick indication of how a particular item is performing now in relation to its performance in past periods. From that picture, you can frequently draw some conclusions about the future. Take the next chart on retail sales. It shows a steadily rising trend, with somewhat slower growth in 1969 and 1970 compared with that of later years. Performance to the middle of 1977 suggested that another slowing might be in progress. Subsequent events, however, disproved it. Such examples could go on and on.

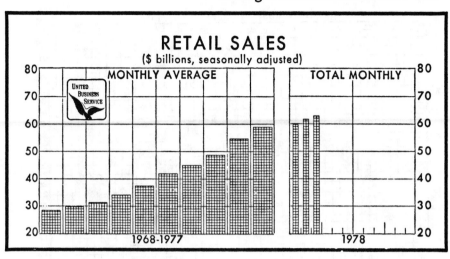

Charts and Your Investments

In the quarterly chart book *3-Trend Cycli-Graphs*, published by Securities Research Company (a division of United Business Service Company), there are 1,105 stock charts and 73 industry charts, as well as various business and market-average charts. The stock charts contain plottings of monthly price ranges, volumes, ratios, plus earnings and dividends over a twelve-year period. There are close to *one million* plotting points in one book of 272 pages. Much of the book may be scanned in a fairly short time, though a real study would take much longer. Imagine how many volumes would be required to show this information in tabular form, how long it would take to comprehend the material, and the difficulty that would be encountered in comparing one company with another.

A typical *Cycli-Graphs* chart is shown on the next page.

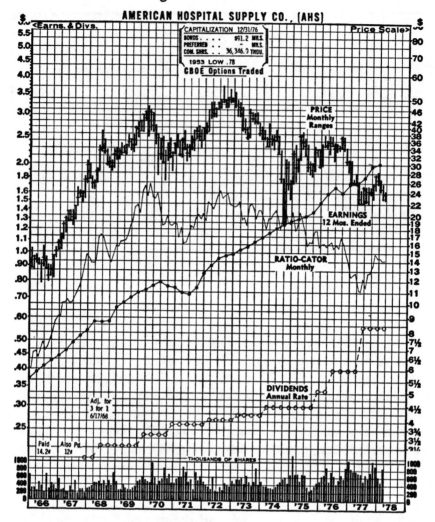

AMERICAN HOSPITAL SUPPLY CO., (AHS)

You don't have to possess a lot of investment expertise to draw some conclusions from this chart. It shows you that the price of American Hospital Supply Company stock rose steadily through the end of 1969, then fell back in 1970 before beginning to climb again to higher ground, eventually reaching a new high in 1972, only to retreat again by March 1977, when this chart stops.

But the chart tells more, too. It shows that earnings advanced at an almost constant pace, leveling for three quarters in 1968, dipping in 1970 and '71, and pausing a bit in 1976 and '77. Of more significance to the long-term investor, dividends rose at a steady pace throughout the period, taking a sharp jump in 1977.

If you were a regular reader of these charts, you would know that the "Ratio-Cator" line indicates a stock's performance in relation to the performance of the Dow Jones Industrial Average. You would see that American Hospital Supply performed significantly better than the Dow through 1969 and again in 1971 and '72, but since then its performance vis-à-vis the Dow has tracked a declining path. It is also worth noting that while the stock's price went to a new high in 1972, its relative performance line indicated weakness, since it failed to top the peak achieved in 1969 and '70. You can deduce something about investor confidence in the stock by examining the pattern of trading volume. If anything, it has trended higher, suggesting that investor interest in it remains high and shows no sign of drying up, despite its failure to keep up with the Dow. (Others would say this represents distribution of the stock as large holders sell.)

Plotting the Percentages

You have probably noticed that the *Cycli-Graphs* chart looks somewhat "different" in that the vertical scale figures are not evenly spaced. That is because it is a "semi-logarithmic" or "ratio-scale" chart. Its purpose is to present everything on the chart in proportion. If a stock moves from 2 to 4, it has appreciated two points, or 100 percent. If it rises another two points, from 4 to 6, the gain is 50 percent. Another 100 percent move would have required a gain to 8. Even though the number of dollars or points may be greater at higher levels, the principle remains the same—the stock must move from 20 to 40 or from 200 to 400 to achieve a doubling, or 100 percent rise. The logarithmic scale is formulated so that any move of a particular percent uses the same vertical linear distance on the chart, regardless of where it may occur. Thus, for example, a move of 10 percent takes the same amount of space on the chart regardless of whether it occurs in a stock selling at 60 or one selling at 6. Furthermore, the use of a standard logarithmic scale permits the comparison of any one chart with any other so that movements may be perfectly related without fear of distortion.

The arithmetic-scale chart with which most people are acquainted does not work in this manner. A move from 2 to 4 looks exactly the same on such a chart as a jump from 4 to 6, or even an edging up from 98 to 100. Obviously, two points have greater significance when a stock is selling at 2 than when it is selling at 98, but the arithmetic scale conceals this. The extent of a price movement, large or small, is easily hidden, and comparisons of one stock with another on such a chart are difficult to make and can be deceptive.

Charts can also be something of an eye-opener. Over a period of time, you might have become accustomed to the current price action of a certain stock, while losing sight of what happened in the past. A glance at a chart, particularly if the stock used to be a high-flyer, can be edifying and, sometimes, sobering. Similarly, when a stock is rising sharply, you might easily forget the base from which the rise was initiated, an important consideration in making an investment decision. A chart will furnish the relationship.

A good example of this "Gosh, I didn't realize that" reaction can be seen in the chart in Chapter 20 which shows the performance of three market averages. The Standard & Poor's 500 is a weighted average. The Dow Jones Industrial Average, a simple average of thirty different stocks, is heavily biased by industrial giants. The Value Line Composite Average, with 1,665 issues, is unweighted. As explained in Chapter 20, a weighted average gives particular importance to heavily capitalized companies, and while this may reflect total market *value*, it does not tell us what the total market of all *stocks* may be doing. That is what the unweighted averages try to correct. In effect, they give one unit of value to a stock, regardless of whether it is a General Motors or a small company which is a fraction of the size of that giant.

Furthermore, to show how tables and charts can be employed to complement each other, note the combination opposite. The statistics can be used to argue that the general price level of the market is down sharply from 1968, regardless of what the Dow Jones Industrial Average says. The charts provide a graphic picture of what the statistics purport to prove. (These figures show the closing prices of all common stocks traded on the days indicated on the New York and American Stock exchanges.) Note that at the high in 1968, 34 percent were selling at 25 or lower while at the bottom in 1974, that figure had risen to 90 percent.

GENERAL PRICE LEVEL OF THE MARKET

	DJIA	NYSE	Shares	% of Shares trading at			
				0–10	10%–25	25%–50	Over 50
December 3, 1968	985.21	61.27	2,241	5.40%	28.29%	45.42%	20.89%
May 26, 1970	631.16	37.69	2,338	41.40	41.19	14.72	2.69
January 11, 1973	1051.70	65.48	2,612	27.30	39.63	25.58	7.49
December 6, 1974	577.60	34.45	2,454	63.41	27.10	7.90	1.59
July 15, 1975	881.81	51.24	2,499	44.38	36.25	14.93	4.44
June 24, 1976	1003.77	55.35	2,294	37.97	38.97	18.13	4.93
October 20, 1977	814.80	50.78	2,320	36.04	43.36	18.49	2.11

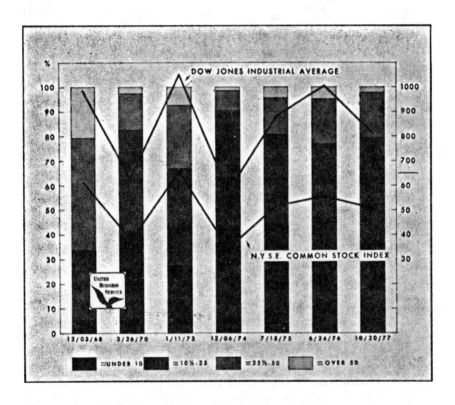

Since the price levels on the New York and American Stock exchanges vary considerably, the following is a breakdown for several days on each exchange.

Trading	NYSE			AMEX		
Range	12/3/68	12/6/74	10/20/77	12/3/68	12/6/74	10/20/77
0–10	.46%	48.62%	20.12%	12.31%	87.39%	66.62%
10½–25	16.83	36.82	50.85	44.33	11.33	28.97
25½–50	53.10	12.19	25.95	34.69	.96	7.49
Over 50	29.61	2.37	3.08	8.67	.32	.25

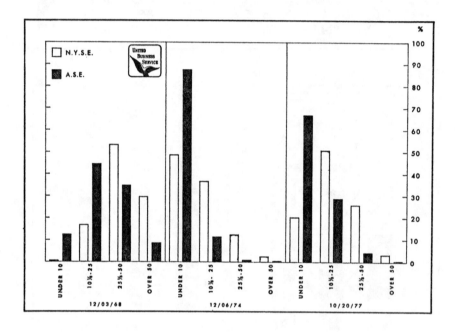

Not Only for Technicians

Charts are basically a tool, one of many, which the investor may use to determine his investment action. There are myriad charts available, showing not just a stock's price action, but market details, business statistics, interest rates, money supply—you name it. What a chart does is show the quantitative factors involved in the study of the market, a company, or an industry. It does not show the various qualitative considerations involved. In a manufacturing company, for example, these might concern management, product line, plant efficiency, labor relations, and many other items impossible to quantify, although they may be reflected to a certain extent in specific or general price action.

Many people tend to think that if someone uses stock charts in his investment decisions, he is a technician. Actually, the fundamentalist has just as much use for charts. The pictures they show and the amount of information they provide help to make the task of investment selection much easier for the busy person.

Chapter 22 Technical Analysis

Definitions:

Fundamentalist: One who bases his investment analysis and decisions primarily on basic factors such as economic conditions, supply and demand, labor, products, earnings, and dividends.

Technician: One who bases his investment actions and decisions upon a reading and interpretation of chart formations or compilations of statistics.

The discussions in this book are principally oriented toward the fundamentalist. This chapter is intended to furnish an introduction to the technician and some of his methods of analysis and must be very general in nature. To some, technical analysis is not a valid investment approach, perhaps because some of the technical theories seem too "far out." Yet technicians will argue that their record certainly is no worse than that of the fundamentalists, and, based upon the number of those attracted to technical analysis, it may possibly be better.

There is no one method of technical analysis. In fact, there are so many methods and interpretations and there is such a wide variety of data and relationships developed, that it is doubtful if any one person could become well versed in all. Certain methods utilize common data, but others are individual and unique. Some technicians base their market and investment decisions wholly or partly on the study of chart formations. Others may depend wholly or partly on statistical compilations and work relating one series of data to one or more other series. Based upon prior study and experience from which models of behavior are created, the technician derives from chart patterns and relationships and from statistics the material he needs to make his decisions.

Once the technican has created his models and his chart or statistical relationships, he must stick to them. He may refine them, but he cannot allow emotional considerations to influence his decisions.

That is where many technicians go wrong. They allow their technical findings to be swayed by other factors. Perhaps this is because
they are not completely convinced of the validity of their method,
or perhaps their signal has been received far ahead of others. Thus,
the technician may be alone and exposed with his findings. And that
solitary position makes him wonder whether he has made a correct
interpretation of his charts and data. He cannot entertain such
doubts. While his method may not always work out—none is infallible, after all—it faces a greater risk of failure if he is influenced
by exceptions, emotions, and outside considerations.

More Than Charts and Figures

People tend to think of technical analysis as meaning chart formations such as flags, pennants, channels, heads and shoulders, etc.,
but it involves much more. With the advent of computers, the technician may now tear apart stacks of statistics to obtain relationships,
actions, and reactions over long periods of time—material which
previously might have been too difficult to obtain. These studies
permit the technician to determine a series of likelihoods and proba-
bilities—of rises, declines, and side movements. They do not necessarily project the magnitude of the moves but only that a move will
take place. As with any other analyst or investor, the technician is
attempting to ascertain the optimum time to make his buys and sells.

The advantage of chart analysis over the fundamental approach is
in calling a turn. Often the basics of a situation may look good, but
for some unperceived reason the technical picture turns weak. It is
at this point that technical analysis does better than fundamental.
The lines often tell something more than the fundamentals may indicate, and it is this failure of the latter on many occasions which
has led more people into technical analysis, not just of stocks but
of all sorts of economic factors. Actually, fundamental and technical
analysis seem to be coming closer together in investment decision-
making. However, if the technical approach shows weakness in a
situation and the fundamental does not, the former should be followed, because the fundamental will confirm too late. For example,
look at this chart of International Paper:

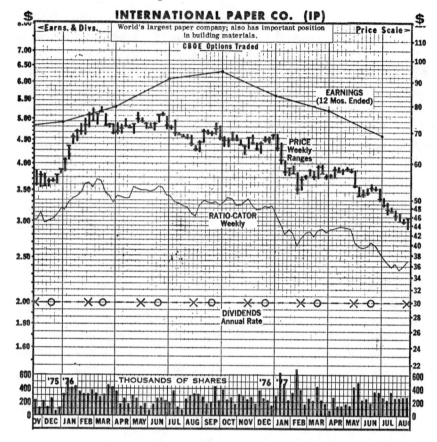

Note that despite **rising** earnings, the stock developed weakness in March 1976, stayed **level** for several months, and then broke out on the downside. At the **same time,** the Dow Jones Industrial Average recorded a basically **sideways** movement. The relative performance line (Ratio-Cator) demonstrates how weak IP was in relation to the Dow. In both March and June, the fundamentalist might have been saying that the earnings outlook was still favorable and therefore the stock should be held. The technician, however, seeing the March weakness and, by June, noting that the stock was unable to match the March high in either price or relative performance, would have said as he watched the downside breakout, "This is the time to sell, despite the rising earnings." Another clue which would have supported the technician's position is the decline in trading volume which occurred as the stock rose in January and February 1976.

Note also during this period how volume generally increased on the declines and decreased on the rallies, a pattern which persists during a downtrend.

The chart for Raytheon gives an example of a rising price trend. Here we have a picture of declines which are accompanied by reduced volume and where rallies occur with increased volume. In addition, the stock's performance indicates relative strength at three important highs. Accompanying this is the rising earnings trend and dividend increases, plus a stock split.

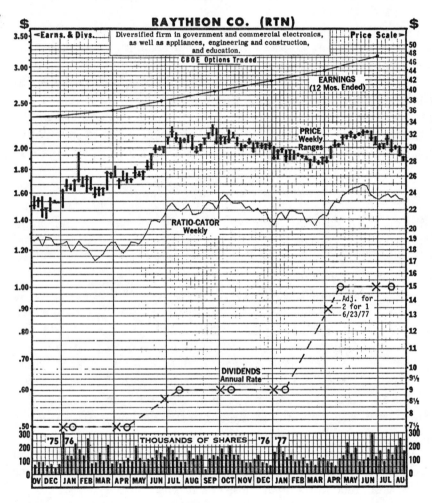

Some Technical Indicators

There are various popular indicators used in attempting to determine market direction. Some, which are best shown by charts, include (not necessarily in order of importance):

Market averages. The chart patterns of averages such as the Dow industrials, the Standard & Poor's 500, the New York Stock Exchange Composite, the Value Line Composite, etc., are studied for clues to future action.

Trading volume. This information, in figures or as plottings on charts, is important to determine whether strength or weakness accompanies various price movements.

Speculative index. This is the relationship of American Stock Exchange volume to New York Stock Exchange volume and is expressed as a percentage. The theory here is that since most of the issues listed on the AMEX tend to be of lower or more speculative quality than those on the NYSE, they will be slow to participate in the earlier stages of a bull market and will be very active in the later and declining phases. Thus, the lower the figure the closer the market presumably is to a bottom, and, conversely, the higher the figure the closer it is to a top. A low figure may also indicate a lack of public interest. In the past, this indicator has fluctuated within a 20 to 60 percent range. In more recent times, it has dropped to as low as 10 percent.

Advance-decline index. This index may be started at any point in time and is the net result of all the advances and declines which have occurred on the New York Stock Exchange since that starting point. The significance of this line is its comparison with the Dow industrials or other market averages to detect any divergence which may occur. Thus, in a bull market this line will often start down while the averages are still rising and, conversely, in a bear market will start to rise while the averages are still declining. It can be an early signal of a change in general market direction.

A ratio derived from relating advances to declines provides an overbought-oversold index which, when it is substantially above or below 1.00, indicates one of those conditions.

Upside-downside volume. This is a tabulation of the shares traded on the NYSE at prices higher or lower than the previous day's close. The trend of either line may be used to confirm the movement of a market average, and the crossing of the lines is interpreted as possibly indicating a change in market direction.

New high–new lows. This is another indicator of market strength or weakness. In a strong market, the new highs should greatly exceed the lows and follow the market averages. The converse is true in a weak market. It is when either line diverges from the averages and when the lines cross that an indication is given of a change in direction. A line representing the differential between these figures will perform similarly to the advance-decline index in peaking while the market averages continue to rise and in bottoming when the averages are continuing to decline.

Odd-lot trading. This is the buying and selling activity of the small investor who deals in units of less than 100 shares (round lots). The extent to which this investor buys or sells has been used to indicate turning points for "informed" selling or buying. To greatly simplify the theory, the small investor is said to buy or sell at the wrong time, and the extent to which he does so provides a signal to the smart investor to do the opposite. Thus, odd-lot selling may peak around the bottom of the market, and odd-lot buying may reach its maximum around the top. The odd-lot index is the relationship of sales to purchases, and the higher the percentage the more bullish the indicator. Thus goes the general theory.

A more recent study claims the odd-lotter has been maligned and has been more attuned to market action than generally believed. Thus, at major bottoms he is seen to have been a buyer and at major tops, he is often a seller.

To further refine odd-lot indicators, odd-lot *short* sales are related to odd-lot sales. The resultant figure is considered a significant indicator, since the small investor does not usually sell short, and when he does so it is under rather extreme conditions. Once again, he purportedly picks the wrong time. While there may be some difference of opinion concerning these figures, when the odd-lot short-sales figure is up around 10,000 and the ratio is in the 4 to 6 percent area, a major bottom may be signaled; on the other hand, when short selling is low and the ratio is around 0.5 to 1 percent, a top may be indicated.

Short interest. This is the total number of shares sold short. The higher this figure, the more bearish are investors (frequently at the wrong time). But since the stock which has been sold must be bought back, it provides a good cushion of buying power when the short sellers seek to cover their short contracts. When the market is at its top, short selling has usually diminished to a fairly low figure, reflecting the general optimism. Member and specialist short selling is also looked at for market signals.

Short interest ratio. This figure is obtained by relating the monthly short interest to the average daily trading volume in the period concerned. When the ratio moves up to 2 or more, it is generally considered a bullish sign; and when it declines to 1 or lower, the signal is bearish.

Barron's Confidence Index. This is a relationship between the yields of high-grade and intermediate-grade bonds on the theory that informed investors will put their money into the former during periods of market uncertainty and into the latter during better times. A decline in this index indicates that more investors are seeking refuge in high-grade issues, and a rise indicates a more optimistic attitude. The value of this index is that presumably the stock market will follow the same pattern, but usually at a somewhat later date.

An indication of how some of these data look when plotted and related to each other is shown in the charts that follow.

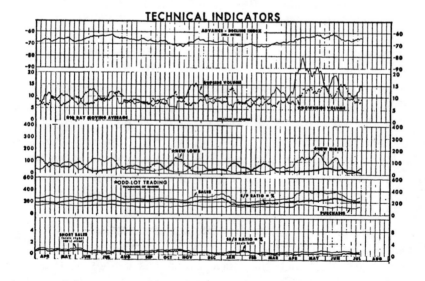

Irregular Forecasting Methods

There are many other methods of predicting market action. They are not especially technical but they are far from fundamental. Here are a few:

Years ending in 7 tend to have an upward trend.

National election years have certain patterns.

The first year of a new presidential administration is likely to be down or to be the worst of the four years of that administration.

An up or a down January sets the tone for the month and the year.

The first ten days of January set the tone for the month and the year.

There is usually a summer rally.

A poor July–August market is usually followed by a rally in September.

The direction of the market is indicated by whether General Motors makes a new high or new low within four months of a previous high or low.

Strength or weakness of sunspots will affect the market.

A strong indication of bearishness or bullishness by investment advisory services is a sign that the market will move in the opposite direction.

It is obvious there are nearly as many ways to "forecast" the market as there are those willing to express an opinion, and the variety seems limitless.

Interpreting Chart Patterns

When it comes to technical analysis of individual stocks, you will find a variety of formations and interpretations. While some of these formations are rather easy to identify, others tend to be more obscure. Sometimes the technician must strain to identify the pattern that makes his point. Also, formations vary with the type of chart used—daily, weekly, or monthly, arithmetic or logarithmic—so that what shows up on one chart will not necessarily appear on another for the same stock. The technician then must decide which charts make him most comfortable and confident, and then proceed accordingly.

The discussion of formations which follows is intended only as a brief explanation of the most common terms.

Support level. A price area in which the demand for a stock is sufficient to keep the price from dropping below it on repeated occasions. Once there is a breakout below the area, a new support level is created.

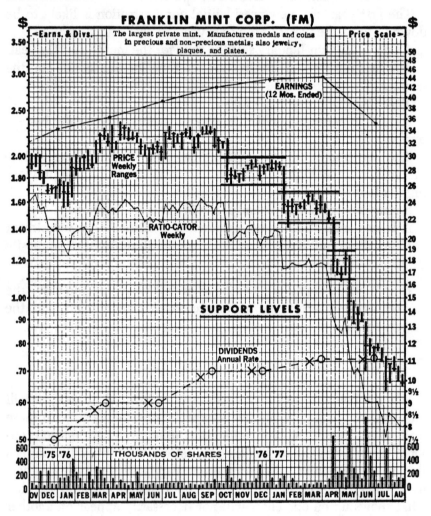

FRANKLIN MINT CORP. (FM)

The largest private mint. Manufactures medals and coins in precious and non-precious metals; also jewelry, plaques, and plates.

Resistance level. A price area which attracts selling sufficient to keep the price of a stock from rising above it on repeated occasions. However, once it has been broken through on the upside, the old resistance area becomes a new support level.

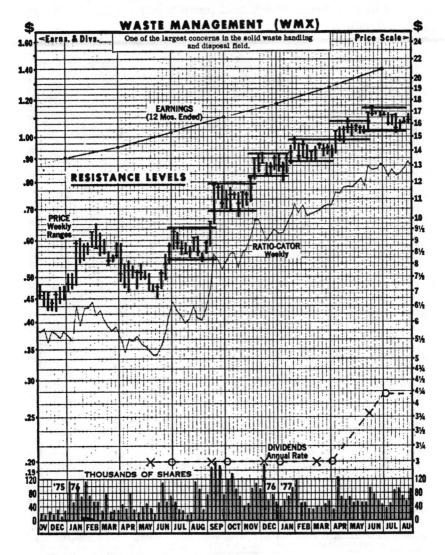

WASTE MANAGEMENT (WMX)

One of the largest concerns in the solid waste handling and disposal field.

Channels. These are drawn by connecting a series of highs and a series of lows to make parallel lines. Characteristically, the stock will trade within the ascending and descending channels, indicating a sell at the top of the channel and a buy at the bottom. A confirmed breakout in either direction would mean a buy on the upside and a sell on the down.

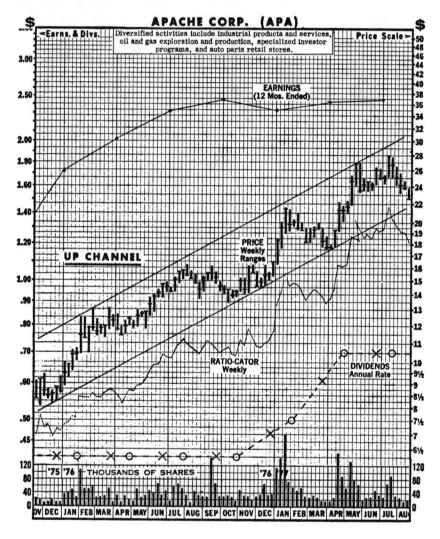

APACHE CORP. (APA)

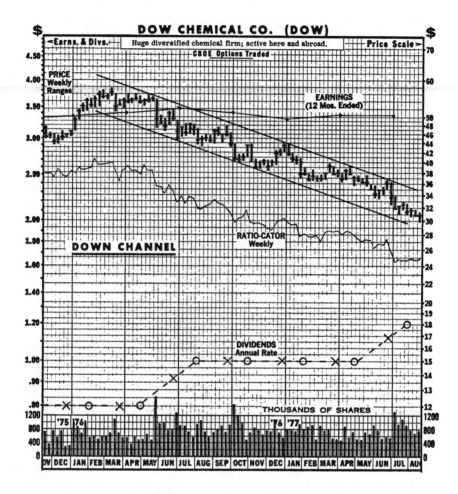

DOW CHEMICAL CO. (DOW)

Huge diversified chemical firm; active here and abroad.

CBOE Options Traded

PRICE Weekly Ranges

EARNINGS (12 Mos. Ended)

Price Scale

DOWN CHANNEL

RATIO-CATOR Weekly

DIVIDENDS Annual Rate

THOUSANDS OF SHARES

'75 '76   '76 '77

DV DEC JAN FEB MAR APR MAY JUN JUL AUG SEP OCT NOV DEC JAN FEB MAR APR MAY JUN JUL AU

Double tops and bottoms (M and W formations). These are formations in which the stock fluctuates, hitting the same top or bottom on two, and sometimes three or four, successive occasions. The breakout from such a pattern is the clue to the action to be taken. The chart of American Family which follows is an example of an upside breakout from the W formation. The chart for Denny's

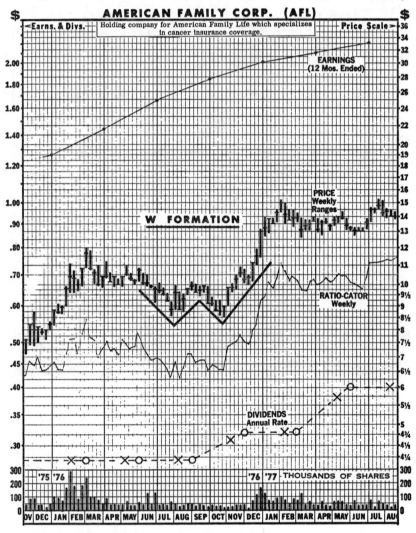

AMERICAN FAMILY CORP. (AFL)

Holding company for American Family Life which specializes in cancer insurance coverage.

W FORMATION

is an example of an indecisive triple top which might have been in the process of making a fourth top or breaking through to create an entirely different type of formation.

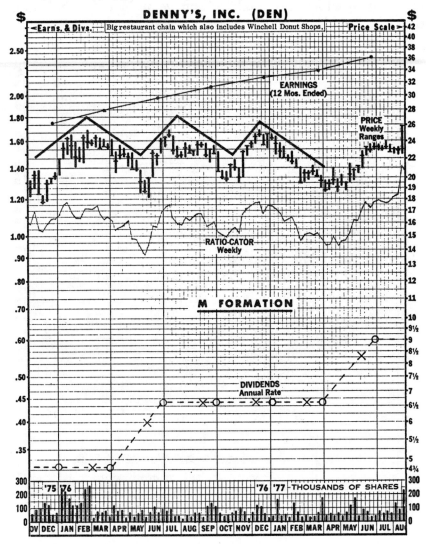

DENNY'S, INC. (DEN)

Big restaurant chain which also includes Winchell Donut Shops.

Head and shoulders. This formation's name is derived from the appearance given by the pattern of a head and right and left shoulders. The important thing here, if one has not previously sold on the higher head level, is to take advantage of the rally which forms the right shoulder, because price deterioration on reduced volume can set in very quickly.

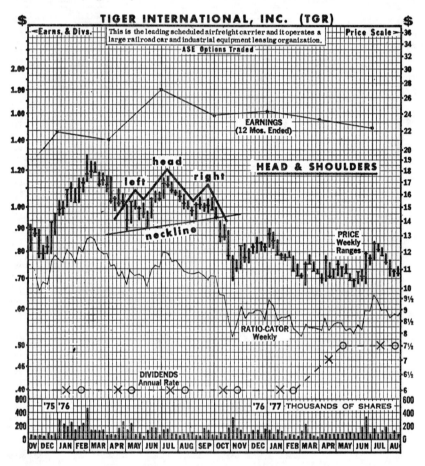

TIGER INTERNATIONAL, INC. (TGR)

Other patterns which may be drawn by connecting a series of highs and lows, usually during short time spans, include flags, pennants, triangles, wedges, and rectangles, all of which may give a message to the technician. And then there are bowls and saucers, and variations thereof, as well as trading volumes, which also tell a story. You must remember, however, that none of these patterns is exact and perfection is impossible. However, the astute and perceptive student may achieve a high percentage of successful interpretation.

Relative strength. This is the relationship of the price of a stock to the price of the Dow Jones Industrial Average or perhaps to one of the other major market averages. The resulting percentage, multiplied by a factor to bring the plotting closer to the price bars on the chart, shows by the direction of the curve whether the stock is performing better, worse, or the same as the market average used. The line is studied for trends as well as for variations of direction from that indicated by the price ranges. For example, the price of a stock may reach a new high but the relative performance line may not, a possible indication of weakness. Similarly, strength may be observed when the price drops to a new low but the relative strength line does not. The charts printed earlier in this chapter of International Paper and Raytheon provide good examples of how effective the relative performance line (Ratio-Cator) may be on the downside and the upside, respectively.

Moving averages. One of the popular indicators for determining market and individual stock strength or weakness is the moving average. This is obtained by adding up the prices for a certain number of days and dividing the total by the days involved to obtain an average. For the next figure, the price for the earliest day or week is dropped and the current one is added. A moving average rounds out the ups and downs, and the investor is then able to derive buying and selling signals from the action of the price in relation to the moving average curve. These figures are easily plotted, or they may be conveniently used in tabular form. The chart below plots moving averages for three different time periods and can be referred to for an indication of short- and long-term market direction.

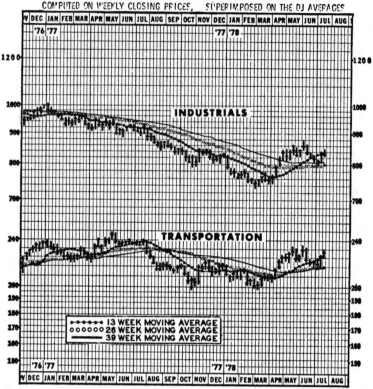

The most popular time period for individual stocks appears to be 200 days, or roughly 40 weeks. The moving average gives a quick indication of where strength or weakness may lie, but, as with all other formations, the user must develop certain rules to avoid false moves. The chart on the next page provides an example of the moving average–price range relationship.

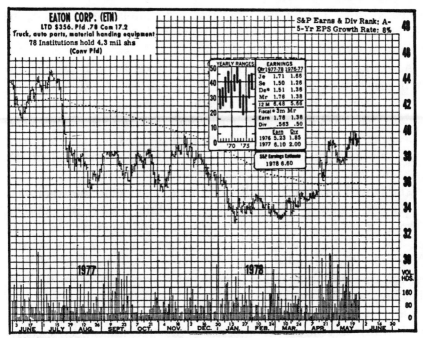

Chart courtesy of Trendline, a division of Standard & Poor's Corp.

Point and figure analysis. This method of interpretation of price movement has its own dedicated devotees. Basically, these charts are designed to show strength of price movement and to emphasize changes in direction. Just as with bar charts, formations are created by the plottings, and these form the basis for interpretation and analysis.

The Dow Theory

Most of the foregoing approaches to technical analysis involve the use of charts. One that does not, and one that certainly should be included in any compendium of technical analysis, is the Dow Theory, if for no other reason than its wide following.

The Dow Theory was developed around the turn of this century by the editors of the *Wall Street Journal.* It was never clearly stated in its original form, and it has been bent, twisted, distorted, and elaborated on for most of its existence by those who seek to apply it in their own fashion. But its basic tenet is that a trend should be expected to continue until a reversal is definitely signaled. For investors, this means that profits will be made by taking advantage of the primary trend, not by resisting it.

According to the Dow Theory, a bull market trend is assumed to be in progress as long as each successive market advance continues to a higher peak than the one preceding it, and each successive secondary reaction stops at a higher bottom than the last. Conversely, a bear market trend is defined when each successive decline carries to a new low and each interim rally ends at a point below the previous one.

The Dow Theory also holds that these moves must be confirmed by similar action in different averages within a short period. The averages most frequently used as reference and confirmation points are the Dow Jones industrial and transportation averages. If the Dow industrials signal the start of a bull market, the faithful wait for the transportation index to move similarly; and when it does, they begin buying stocks.

On paper, the Dow Theory allows profits to continue indefinitely while it restricts the extent of losses. In practice, it has been successful only some of the time. One reason is the wide divergence in interpretation of the same signals by Dow theorists. Another reason is the great difficulty in pinpointing the moves that are indeed the true turning points of the market. Finally, the effectiveness of the Dow Theory has been diminished somewhat by its wide following.

In Conclusion

The analysis of the stock market as a whole or of individual stocks, whether by the technician or the fundamentalist, is not an easy task. You must endure a good deal of trial and error as you build up your own background and experience and as you develop the methods that make you most comfortable. It is often a slow and painstaking process. Except for the very lucky or those who are highly intuitive, success can come in no other way.

Chapter 23 How to Read an Annual Report

SHAREHOLDERS AND prospective shareholders can increase their knowledge of companies if they know how to read and analyze an annual report. In recent years, these reports have become much more informative than they used to be, thanks to pressure from the Securities and Exchange Commission, the Financial Accounting Standards Board, auditors, and securities analysts.

Annual reports are easy to obtain. A company listed on the New York Stock Exchange, for example, is required to send one to each shareholder every year. In addition, many companies will send them to anyone who asks.

An even more detailed and comprehensive document is the 10-K statement that large, publicly owned companies are required to submit each year to the SEC. Some companies will send copies of the 10-K to shareholders and others on request. The 10-K's are also available in many large public and business school libraries.

But most annual reports contain sufficient information to give you a good basis for analyzing a company. You'll have to devote considerable time and thought to the task at hand to understand an annual report. It will help if you have some knowledge of the basics of accounting and financial statement analysis. But even if you don't, you should still be able to draw several valuable insights out of such a document, with a little coaching and guidance—the kind we're about to give you in this chapter.

What Is in an Annual Report

Since the annual report is not an official SEC filing, companies have considerable leeway in determining what the report will contain. Some give it to you in a straightforward, simple form, the figures juxtaposed between workaday text. But the trend in recent years has been toward typographical extravaganzas heavy on graphics, full-color photography, and art work.

Whether the report is the former, the latter, or, as is more likely the case, falls somewhere between, it will typically begin with a letter to shareholders. This epistle is generally written by one or more of the company's top executives. It will usually summarize the highlights of the year and, possibly, offer some commentary on the business outlook for the firm. Because of this, we caution you to regard this letter with some skepticism. It is not subjected to the auditing process, and in a good many cases its authors have succumbed to the temptation to tout.

The letter is usually followed by a more detailed description of the company's various products or services, the recent performance of its operations, and perhaps the outlook for each sector. Here again you must keep in mind that the company is talking about itself, and a certain amount of puffery is likely to be present.

As your eyes pass by the list of company officers, pay particular attention to the names and affiliations of outside directors. Their stature, experience, and fields of interest can yield clues to the ultimate success and possibly even the directions the company is likely to take.

But the real meat of the annual report will come out of the figures. Here again, the pattern is basically the same for all annual reports within an industry. And the information presented will be "consistent with generally accepted accounting principles," as the trade jargon puts it.

An annual report for a manufacturing or merchandising company must include a balance sheet, an income statement, a statement of accumulated retained earnings, a source and application of funds statement, an analysis of changes in working capital, and footnotes. We will discuss each of these areas in some detail. For illustrative purposes, we will use a mythical manufacturing company, which we will call TCA Industries.

The Balance Sheet

The balance sheet shows the financial condition of the company on the last day of its fiscal year. Normally, the figures for the previous year are also included to facilitate comparisons. Note that in

BALANCE SHEET

Assets	Year Ending Dec. 31 (000 Omitted)	
	1977	1976
Current Assets:		
Cash	$ 11,000	$ 8,000
Marketable Securities at Cost (market value: 1977, 6000; 1976, 5400)	7,000	6,000
Accounts Receivable (less allowance for bad debts: 1977, 200; 1976, 150)	114,000	90,000
Inventories	163,000	145,000
Total Current Assets	$295,000	$249,000
Fixed Assets		
Land, Plant & Equipment	$195,000	$168,000
(less accumulated depreciation)	68,000	65,000
Net Land, Plant & Equipment	$127,000	$103,000
Intangibles	25,000	13,000
Prepaid Expenses & Deferred Charges	6,000	5,000
Total Fixed Assets	$158,000	$121,000
Total Assets	$453,000	$370,000

Liabilities	Year Ending Dec. 31 (000 Omitted)	
	1977	1976
Current Liabilities		
Accounts Payable	$101,000	$ 77,000
Notes, Loans, etc. Payable	25,000	14,000
Long-Term Debt Due within One Year	5,000	4,000
Accrued Income Taxes	13,000	17,000
Total Current Liabilities	$144,000	$112,000
Long-Term Debt	98,000	80,000
Stockholders' Equity		
Preferred Stock,$2.50 cum. $50 Par Value (authorized and outstanding shares, 60,000)	$3,000	$3,000
Common Stock $10 Par Value (authorized 10,000,000 shares; outstanding 1977 and 1976, 5,000,000)	50,000	50,000
Capital in Excess of Par Value	8,000	7,000
Retained Earnings	150,000	118,000
Total Stockholders' Equity	$211,000	$178,000
Total Liabilities and Stockholders' Equity	$453,000	$370,000

the balance sheet for TCA Industries, our manufacturing company, the assets of the company are listed on the left-hand side and the liabilities and stockholders' equity, or capital of the corporation, are listed on the right-hand side. Note also that the totals for each side are in balance—that total assets equal total liabilities plus stockholders' equity. Another way to look at it is to subtract liabilities from assets, the difference being the stockholders' equity or ownership interest. More about that later.

The balance sheet will also yield the company's *book value*. Book value merely represents common stockholders' equity less goodwill, all other intangible assets, and preferred stock. In effect, then, book value is the amount of money stockholders originally invested in the company, plus profits the company has retained from year to year, subsequent equity offerings, and acquisitions.

Now let's go over the various categories of the balance sheet. *Current assets* are items that normally can be converted into cash within a year. *Cash* itself would include petty cash, checking accounts, and other demand or short-term bank deposits. *Marketable securities*, which are usually listed at cost, would be principally confined to short-term U.S. Treasury securities or commercial paper. *Accounts receivable* are amounts owed by customers for goods delivered or services rendered. Presumably, these are collectible within a year. But note that the figure is net after an allowance for bad debts. *Inventories* consist of raw materials, partially finished goods, and finished products. The method of evaluating inventories is usually described in the footnotes of the balance sheet.

Fixed assets are items needed for carrying out the company's business and might include factory buildings, machinery, offices, and land. Traditionally, these items have been shown on the balance sheet at their original acquisition cost. Now some of the largest companies are required to show in their 10-K statements the estimated replacement cost of these assets.

Accumulated depreciation is deducted from *gross plant and equipment* to reflect the fact that these assets have been declining in their useful value each year. Land, though, is never depreciated. Its balance sheet value doesn't change. Several depreciation methods for plant and equipment are available, and the footnotes will indicate which one has been used.

Intangibles usually refer to patents, franchises, or goodwill. While these assets may have a very real value, some companies follow conservative accounting practices and assign them only a nominal value. A *goodwill* value results when one company acquires another for a price exceeding its book value. The difference (goodwill) becomes an intangible asset which must be written off within forty years.

Prepaid expenses refer to items that have been paid for but have a useful life beyond the next twelve months. *Deferred charges* refer to items the company has chosen to add to the balance sheet (capitalize) rather than treat as expenses that are shown only on the income statement. Some questions might arise if the deferred charge account has been increasing rapidly and is now shown as a substantial asset. Under new accounting procedures, research and development costs must now be expensed annually against income. Formerly, they could be capitalized and written off over a period of years.

Current liabilities are items payable within a year. *Accounts payable* are sums owed to the company's regular vendors and suppliers. *Accrued expenses* refer to unpaid wages, insurance premiums, etc. *Notes* and *loans payable* refer to short-term money owed to banks and other creditors. *Long-term debt due within one year* is self-explanatory.

Accrued income taxes are federal, state, local, and foreign income taxes, also due within one year. Sometimes a deferred tax account is set up as a short-term, long-term, or other liability that may be due in future years. These deferred taxes arise from the fact that companies can employ different accounting procedures for shareholder and for Internal Revenue Service purposes. Thus they may report and pay less tax to the government than is reflected in the income statement for shareholders. There is nothing illegal about this, and the company, in fact, may never actually have to pay these additional taxes. But the quality of *earnings* would be diminished for a company with a large tax deferral account.

What is referred to as the capital structure or capitalization of a company will include such different securities as straight and convertible bonds, straight and convertible preferred stocks, common stocks, and warrants. *Long-term debt* usually consists of bonds and bank debt due more than one year from the date on the balance sheet. The interest rates and payment schedules for debt securities can be found in the footnotes.

Stockholders' equity includes preferred stock, so to compute book value or earnings on shareholders' equity the preferred stock should be subtracted. The principal categories under common stockholders' equity are *common stock, capital surplus,* and *retained earnings.* These three items in total show the amount of equity or ownership that the common stockholder has in a corporation. *Common stock* is shown on the balance sheet at *par value.* But this is an arbitrary figure having no relation to market or liquidation value. *Capital in excess of par value* is what it says—the amount in excess of par value that shareholders have paid for their stock. This account would be set up when shares were initially sold. It would be increased after any subsequent new issues of stock. *Retained earnings,* also sometimes referred to as *earned surplus,* is the accumulation of profits remaining after payment of dividends on all outstanding securities.

Analyzing a Balance Sheet

Many investment analysts maintain that the balance sheet is more important than the income statement in assessing a company's prospects. Yearly increases in certain balance sheet items are good indicators of the company's growth potential.

There are a number of rather simple calculations you can make to help determine the financial strength of a company. Let's first consider the ability of a company to liquidate its debts and other obligations. This would logically come from current assets. Hence, to relate these two items, we employ the *current* (or *working capital*) *ratio.* This is computed by dividing current assets by current liabilities. A ratio showing current assets in excess of current liabilities by two to one is generally considered quite acceptable for the typical manufacturing company. But for certain other industries it might either be unnecessarily high or unacceptably low. Businesses require different amounts of working capital and liquidity. But where a company does have current assets in excess of current liabilities, that difference is available to reduce long-term debt or help finance growth.

It is also worth noting if working capital is expanding from year to year. A growing corporation probably needs expanding working capital.

A more exacting test for liquidity is the *quick ratio*, which is also called the *liquidity ratio* or *acid test*. This is figured the same way as the current ratio, omitting the inventory from the asset side. The rationale for this is that inventories may not be easily liquidated except at a discount. A one-to-one liquidity ratio is reasonable.

To further test financial strength, long-term debt and preferred stock outstanding should be related to stockholders' equity. Creditors' and preferred stockholders' claims on assets in liquidation and on earnings for interest and preferred dividend payments have priority to those of common shareholders. Then, too, a relatively large amount of long-term debt or preferred stock may mean the company is burdened by these fixed charges. This may help to leverage the company's earnings upward in years when there is rapid growth, but it works on the downside, too.

Capital structure varies from industry to industry. Utilities usually carry larger amounts of debt than manufacturing companies because of the stability of the former's operations. But generally speaking, shareholders' capital should total substantially more than long-term debt and preferred stock combined.

To help measure these relationships, you could compute a *common stock ratio* or a *debt to equity ratio*. The common stock ratio is derived by totaling all items in shareholders' equity except preferred stock and dividing by the total capitalization. The *debt to equity ratio* merely relates long-term and other liabilities to the common shareholders' equity.

Some analysts in making these same calculations deduct intangibles from stockholders' equity because of what may be their "uncertain" worth. Also, in computing the preferred stock's worth, the liquidation value of the preferred is sometimes substituted for the generally lower par value figure that is shown on the balance sheet.

The Income Statement

The *income statement*, sometimes called the *profit and loss statement*, is intended to describe the performance of the company's operations during the year. Again, the figures for the two most recent fiscal years are generally given. We will now discuss each of the categories in the income statement shown here.

INCOME STATEMENT (OR STATEMENT OF PROFIT AND LOSS)

	Year Ending Dec. 31	
	(000 Omitted)	
	1977	1976
Net Sales	$554,000	$478,000
Less:		
Cost of Goods Sold	(389,000)	(346,000)
Selling, General, and Administrative Expenses	(68,000)	(55,000)
Depreciation	(11,000)	(10,000)
Interest Expense	(5,000)	(7,000)
Income Before Taxes	$ 81,000	$ 60,000
Income Taxes	(39,000)	(29,000)
Net Income	$ 42,000	$ 31,000
Net Income Per Common Share	$ 8.40	$ 6.20

Net sales, in the case of our model firm, TCA Industries, represent money received by the company from the sale of its goods, minus an allowance for returned goods. *Cost of goods sold* includes raw materials, plant wages and salaries, utilities, maintenance, and other factory overhead costs. These expenses are directly related to the company's manufacturing operations. *Depreciation,* you will remember, was included on the balance sheet. Each year, a certain amount of depreciation is charged as an expense, and this figure is added to the accumulated depreciation figure on the balance sheet. Please note that while this is shown as an expense on the income statement, it is a noncash expense because no cash actually leaves the company. Here again, companies have considerable leeway in choosing the rate at which they will depreciate their assets, and this can have a substantial impact on earnings. In our section on footnotes, we'll comment specifically on permissible depreciation methods.

Selling, general, and administrative expenses cover certain costs not involved directly in production and thus not shown under cost of goods sold. The expenses in this account would include such things as executive salaries, rent, miscellaneous office expenses, advertising, and travel. *Interest expense* is the amount paid in the latest fiscal year to bondholders and other creditors. Unlike dividends on preferred and common stocks, interest is a deductible expense and, therefore, is shown before income taxes.

We can now determine pre-tax income by subtracting these various expenses from net sales. We then subtract income taxes, which are all U.S., foreign, state, and local taxes. What remains is the *net income* or *net operating income* figure. Some companies set up a net operating income figure and below that an account to cover income and expense items which are essentially nonrecurring. These are items that would not be part of the company's normal business operations, such as the sale of a plant, the discontinuance of certain operations, the collection of insurance proceeds, and foreign expropriations.

The calculation for *net income per common share* involves subtracting from the net income figure any dividends paid on preferred stock during the year and dividing the result by either the number of shares outstanding at the end of the year or a weighted average of the number of shares outstanding during the year. If companies have sufficient convertible bonds, convertible preferred stocks, warrants, or options outstanding to dilute per-share earnings by more than 3 percent, they must also show *primary earnings per share* and *fully diluted earnings per share*. The primary earnings per share figure is arrived at by dividing net income after preferred dividends by common shares outstanding plus dilutive common share equivalents. The latter are those securities whose dividend or coupon rate at the time of issue was less than two thirds the prime rate at that time. Since options and warrants have no payment, they are regarded as common stock equivalents at all times. The *fully diluted earnings per share* figure assumes the conversion of all outstanding securities that would reduce earnings per share.

Analyzing the Income Statement

There are a number of ratios you can use to derive information from the income statement. Some of these involve determining profitability, such as the amount of each dollar of sales the company is able to bring down to net or pre-tax income, or how much the company is able to earn on stockholders' equity.

In establishing the return on sales, you could calculate a *pre-tax profit margin*, a *net income profit margin*, an *operating profit margin*, and a *gross profit margin*. The pre-tax profit margin is computed by dividing pre-tax income by net sales. This may be a more significant number than the net income profit margin, because the latter can be distorted by sharp changes in the tax rate. The operating profit margin would be operating profit before interest expenses, and sometimes depreciation, divided by net sales. The gross profit margin is the income that remains only after cost of goods sold is deducted from net sales and again this figure is divided by net sales.

There is likely to be a sharp increase in profit margins in the years when sales have risen markedly. Also, industry leaders tend to have higher profit margins than their smaller competitors. A deterioration in profit margins might reflect more severe price competition or certain expenses temporarily running out of control. Some industries or businesses are inherently more profitable than others, so the ratios you calculate for the company you are examining should be compared with those of firms in similar fields.

A common stockholder also should be concerned about how much money the company is able to earn on his investment. The return should be much better than that which he could obtain from a bank savings account, for example. So the *return on equity* is an important ratio. This figure is calculated by dividing net income for the common stockholder (what's left after preferred dividends have been paid) by the previous year's common stockholders' equity. You use that figure to see what the company was able to earn on the stockholders' equity available to it at the beginning of the year.

If return on equity seems high it might mean that the company was using substantial amounts of borrowed funds (so-called leverage) and preferred stock instead of common stock. So check back in your analysis of the balance sheet to see what the common stock or debt to equity ratio was.

Some other items worth checking are the *tax rate* and the *inventory turnover* and *accounts receivable turnover*. The tax rate is taxes paid as a percentage of pre-tax income. These rates vary considerably. Most U.S. corporations are subject to a 48 percent federal statutory tax rate. So if the tax rate you have computed is not roughly 50 percent, you should find out why. There may be some satisfactory reasons. A good portion of the company's income might be taxed at only capital gains rates. Earnings from foreign operations are usually subject to a much lower tax rate, and the company might have substantial overseas business. The investment tax credit which is available to corporations could temporarily reduce taxes in a year of heavy buying of equipment. Also, a much lower tax rate might reflect the presence in a particular year of tax-loss carry-forwards stemming from some earlier deficit years. That credit may not be available in subsequent years, either.

The *inventory* and *accounts receivable turnover* ratios are meant to show how liquid the company's inventory and accounts receivables are. The inventory turnover ratio is usually derived by dividing net sales by the year-end inventory figure shown on the balance sheet. A high ratio would suggest strong demand for the company's products. A low ratio might indicate either severe competition or inventory obsolescence. These ratios, though, will depend on the business. A food chain is likely to have a much faster inventory turnover rate than a heavy machinery company. The *accounts receivable turnover* ratio is net sales divided by receivables. A low ratio might indicate that the company has poor collection procedures.

Other Lodes to Mine

After you have gained an understanding of a balance sheet and an income statement, you would do well to examine three other related financial statements in the annual report.

The first of these is the *statement of retained earnings*. An example is shown below. The purpose, quite obviously, is to show changes in retained earnings from one year to the next. Net income is normally the principal contributor to retained earnings. But this account could also be affected by an acquisition or merger. The growth of retained earnings is important. It affects book value and the company's ability to pay dividends on the common stock.

Another statement that is closely related to both the balance sheet and the income statement is the *source and application of funds statement*. It shows the sources of a company's money or working capital and where it goes. Depreciation is an addition to working

STATEMENT OF RETAINED EARNINGS

	Year Ending Dec. 31	
	(000 Omitted)	
	1977	1976
Retained Earnings at Beginning of Year	$118,000	$ 95,000
Net Income for the Year	42,000	31,000
Less Dividends Paid	(10,000)	(8,000)
Retained Earnings at End of Year	$150,000	$118,000

capital because, you will remember, this is treated as an expense on the income statement when it is really a noncash charge. In addition to dividends and capital expenditures, debt repayments would be an example of the uses of working capital. For a company in healthy circumstances, the bottom line figure will usually show a year-to-year increase in working capital, and not just because of a heavy reliance on long-term borrowings.

SOURCE AND APPLICATION OF FUNDS STATEMENT

	Year Ending Dec. 31	
	(000 Omitted)	
	1977	1976
Working Capital Provided by:		
Net Income	$ 42,000	$ 31,000
Depreciation	11,000	10,000
Proceeds from Long-Term Borrowings	48,000	12,000
Sales of Plant & Equipment, Deferred Income Taxes, etc.	11,000	19,000
	$112,000	$ 72,000
Working Capital Used for:		
Dividends	$ 10,000	$ 8,000
Additions to Plant & Equipment	14,000	18,000
Reductions of Long-Term Debt	35,000	4,000
Acquisitions	34,000	—
Other	3,000	13,000
	$ 96,000	$ 43,000
Increase in Working Capital	$ 16,000	$ 29,000

The third document is the *analysis of changes in working capital.* Its purpose is to disclose how the various changes in working capital actually showed up in the balance sheet in terms of current assets and current liabilities. A substantial increase in working capital might not seem quite as appealing if it resulted from an increase in inventories or receivables rather than an increase in cash or marketable securities.

ANALYSIS OF CHANGES IN WORKING CAPITAL

	Year Ending Dec. 31	
	(000 Omitted)	
	1977	1976
Increase (Decrease) in Current Assets		
Cash	$ 3,000	$ 2,000
Marketable Securities	1,000	2,000
Accounts Receivable	24,000	15,000
Inventories	18,000	25,000
Other	2,000	1,000
	$48,000	$45,000
(Increase) Decrease in Current Liabilities		
Accounts Payable	$(24,000)	$(14,000)
Accrued Income Taxes	4,000	(10,000)
Notes, Loans Payable	(11,000)	9,000
Long-Term Debt Due within One Year	(1,000)	(1,000)
	(32,000)	(16,000)
Increase in Working Capital	$16,000	$29,000

Let us now turn to some of the other sections of the annual report that are mandated by the SEC. One of these is *management's analysis of operating results.* The SEC requires that material developments during the last two fiscal years, particularly those relating to the income statement, be discussed in considerable detail. Some corporations might extend the discussion back over the past five years. The SEC expects companies to be more factual and objective in this section than they might typically be in their letter to shareholders. However, this section likewise is unaudited, so it, too, should be read with some degree of skepticism.

The SEC also requires an unaudited five-year *statistical summary.* The summary normally will carry key items from the income statement and balance sheet, as well as some of the important ratios we have already discussed. This helps to establish significant trends in the company's fortunes. But, as an actual or potential investor, you're primarily interested in trying to predict the company's future.

Let us suggest here some of the trends you might look for. Have sales shown a sharp increase over the past five (or ten) years? If so, have the sales gains been consistent or erratic? Have earnings generally moved in line with sales? If not, can you find the reason in various expense items or the tax rate? Do the sales and earnings trends seem consistent with the general business picture and industry performance in that same time period?

You might also look to see if earnings per share have matched the improvement in net income. If not, it may mean the company has been "buying" earnings (through acquisitions) for stock and the effect has been dilutive. Have dividends ever been omitted or reduced? Have there been increases in the total dividend payments every year?

As far as the balance sheet items are concerned, we have already noted the importance of increases in working capital. But has long-term debt also increased substantially? Has long-term debt risen more than shareholders' equity? Has book value risen markedly? Other items worth looking at are changes in the number of employees and capital spending trends.

The push by the SEC and the Financial Accounting Standards Board for fuller corporate disclosure in annual reports has resulted in companies being required to include (1) a breakdown of sales and earnings for at least five different product lines if there are that many; (2) a price range of securities; (3) dividends, if any, paid during each quarter of the two most recent fiscal years. The product line breakdown can be helpful in revealing that some operations are considerably more important to earnings than they are to sales, or vice versa, than one might expect after reading the earlier textual material.

Analyzing a Common Stock

There are still other ratios with which you should be familiar. (Is there no end to these? you may well be starting to wonder.)

The *price-earnings ratio* is the market price of the common stock divided by earnings per share for that stock. You are likely to find some variation in price-earnings ratios for the same company's stock, because newspapers tend to use the latest twelve-month earnings figures that are available, whereas investment analysts generally prefer estimated current year results. Also remember that price-earnings ratios will fluctuate over time, with the general psychology of the market, anticipated earnings growth, dividend yield, marketability, volatility, and the quality of the earnings per share.

The *dividend yield* is the indicated annual dividend rate divided by the current market price. By relating this return to a bank savings rate or the yield on AA or AAA corporate bonds, you can get some indication of the stock's appeal for income purposes. On the other hand, too high a yield may indicate that the dividend is shaky.

The *dividend payout ratio* is arrived at by dividing indicated dividends per share by the latest available annual earnings per share. This shows what percent of earnings is paid out in dividends. The *earnings retention rate* is found by subtracting the dividend payout ratio from 100 percent. If the payout ratio is 40 percent, the retention rate would be about 60 percent. That is, the company is reinvesting about 60 percent of its earnings. Some analysts suggest that if you multiply the retention rate by the percentage amount that the company returns on stockholders' equity, you get a good indicator of the future earnings growth for the company. What they are saying is that the company's growth will be determined by what it is able to earn on the new money it is retaining. So if the rate of return on stockholders' equity is 10 percent and the retention rate is 60 percent, future income growth might be about 6 percent. While some companies obviously are interested in pleasing their stockholders by boosting dividends, many do wish to retain as much of their earnings as they can in order to facilitate the corporation's growth.

The Footnotes Are Important

The footnotes undoubtedly constitute the most yawn-inspiring reading in the annual report. But they shouldn't be skipped. Fortunately, SEC rules require their type size to be at least as large as

the numbers in the financial statement. The footnotes are important
for several reasons. For one thing, they often explain the accounting
methods used. There are a number of methods available that would
meet an auditor's approval, each of which produces a different bottom line result. Furthermore, most companies employ one accounting procedure for stockholders and another for Internal Revenue
Service purposes. This point is generally elaborated upon in the
footnotes.

Here are some of the other items frequently covered in the footnotes:

Inventories, as computed for cost of goods sold and carried in the
asset section of the balance sheet, can be assigned widely different
values. Many analysts believe that in a period of rising prices the
most conservative accounting treatment for inventories is LIFO
(last in, first out) as opposed to FIFO (first in, first out). In figuring
the cost of goods sold, LIFO assumes that the latest items added to
inventory, which should be the most expensive in a period of inflation, are sold first. That means assigning a higher value to inventories in cost of goods sold. The effect is to increase expenses and
reduce income. Lower income means lower taxes. It also means,
though, that in expensing the latest inventory figures, the corporation will be carrying a lower inventory value on the balance sheet
than the real figure.

Various acceptable methods are also available to compute depreciation. Straight-line depreciation means depreciating a fixed asset
at the same rate each year over its useful life. The sum of the year's
digits and the double declining balance methods employ accelerated
depreciation, which means writing off more of an asset's worth in its
earlier years than in later years. Most companies use straight-line
depreciation for stockholder purposes because it tends to reduce
income less, and accelerated depreciation for tax purposes in order
to reduce the amount of income subject to a tax bite. A more conservative accounting practice is to use accelerated depreciation for
both stockholder purposes and tax purposes.

Companies are now required to state in the annual report their
pension accounting and funding policy, as well as the pension charge
for the preceding year and the unfunded vested liabilities. For some
corporations, these numbers are already large, and for others they
are increasing rapidly. Some companies even have unfunded pension

liabilities that represent a substantial percentage of stockholders' equity—or may even exceed stockholders' equity.

The annual report also must disclose any potential legal problems. You should be somewhat wary of these even though the company might indicate that in its opinion a suit against the corporation is "without merit." Adverse settlements in an era of growing "consumerism" have proved expensive for many companies.

As a rule, the footnotes contain a detailed breakdown of long-term debt by type of security and schedule of maturity.

Many companies lease rather than own equipment, and these leases can then become a substitute for longer-term debt incurred to purchase that equipment. Use of leases is sometimes referred to as *off balance sheet financing*. But under new regulations of the Financial Accounting Standards Board, these leases must be capitalized and shown as a liability on the lessee's balance sheet, albeit on a phase-in basis. FASB rules prohibit a company from capitalizing research and development outlays on the balance sheet and writing them off gradually against income over a period of years. Instead they must be expensed in the year incurred.

Some annual reports reveal in the footnotes stock options granted officers and other employees plus intercompany transactions. Whether the company takes all of its available investment tax credit directly into earnings each year or amortizes it over a period of years may be revealed. Also detailed in the reports of multinational companies is the impact of certain currency changes.

Companies are also now required to carry in their annual reports a statement reconciling any differences between a tax rate for stockholder purposes and the statutory U.S. tax rate. Foreign taxes, state and local taxes, and the investment tax credit are some of the items that might account for such a difference.

The SEC now requires about a thousand of the largest nonfinancial corporations to include in their 10-K statements the cost at current prices of replacing their inventory and productive capacity (plant and equipment). The 10-K also must show how depreciation and the cost of goods sold would be affected if the balance sheet were recalculated on a replacement cost basis. In doing this, however, companies are permitted to show cost savings that might result from replacing old equipment with more modern technology.

The Accountants' Report

Every public company must have its accounting records reviewed and audited by a firm of certified public accountants. That firm will also issue an opinion regarding the veracity of the financial statements in the annual report. The accountants' report is definitely worth reading, if only to see whether the auditors include some qualifications or exceptions or note changes in accounting procedures that are material. The investor should be concerned about any departures from what is normally a routinely worded statement. The corporate examination by the auditors will generally include a review of bank statements, a physical counting of the inventory and an estimate as to its salability, and a confirmation of receivables.

As you can see, if you've only been looking at an annual report's photographs you haven't been getting half the picture. The text can tell you a lot about the companies you own or contemplate owning—if you take the time to read it right.

Chapter 24 Analyzing Specific Industries

UNTIL NOW, we have been discussing in general terms how to go about analyzing a company as a potential investment. Obviously, certain tests will be more important for companies in one industry than for those in another. Some industries by nature are cyclical. The ebbs and flows of their fortunes are tied closely to the ups and downs of the economy. Others are more stable. They follow the same path regardless of what business in general is doing. Still others are mature. They have grown just about as much as they ever will and, in fact, may even be declining. Others are emerging. New technology and changing lifestyles are bringing them into prominence.

How do you know what tests to apply to which industries? Common sense is a good starting point. It is often easy to surmise which industries will be affected by rises and falls of the economy and which will not be. Then there is performance. There's a good chance that patterns occurring in the past will be repeated in the future. Finally, there is awareness. Careful study depends on keeping up with events and trends that might affect an industry. These broad categories, of course, embrace the many finer points of the financial analyst's art and science.

Financial analysts, in fact, spend most of their time poring over figures, reading extensively in the various industries they cover, and talking with key executives in those industries. Because of the vast amount of material which they must keep under surveillance, most analysts confine their efforts to a limited number of industries. Indeed, some devote their entire careers to a single industry, becoming more knowledgeable than many in the industry itself.

To give you an idea of what you should be looking for in the industries that interest most investors, the analysts on our staff at United Business Service have provided the commentary that appears in this chapter and the next. They won't get into the fine details, but they'll tell you the important things they themselves look for as they analyze their industries and the companies in them.

The Basic Industries

Automotive, chemical, coal, construction, machinery, metals, oil and gas, paper, textiles. These are the basic industries—"Smokestack America," as it were. Without these industries, our way of life would be primitive indeed. For all the abuse that is heaped upon the steel-makers, the oil moguls, and the auto producers, theirs is no bed of roses. Between the demands of labor, the restrictions of government, the protests of environmentalists, and the exigencies of business, they do well to keep their heads above water, let alone turn a profit for their shareholders.

All these industries suffer to some extent from the cyclical nature of their markets. Some lead the economy, others follow it, and the rest move in close conjunction with the ups and downs in the business cycle. The ability to fine-tune capacity and output to demand is an important aspect of a company's profit record. These are capital-intensive companies, but some groups have less trouble generating sufficient cash flow to meet their capital needs than others.

While the investor can reap long-range profits from investments in basic industries, he must be willing to sit through the dry spells or be able to jump in and out with facility.

Automobiles and trucks. This industry, which includes manufacturers of parts and components, is one of the most pervasive influences in our lives. Not only is it the nation's single largest employer after the federal government, but it affects the prosperity of such giant industries as steel, nonferrous metals, chemicals, tires, and glass. When consumers are in a car-buying mood, the economy prospers; when demand for new cars ebbs, the entire economy suffers. Because the automobile has become such a necessity in the lives of most of us, it would be easy to conclude that demand is always high. The truth is, this is a highly cyclical industry, studded with peaks and riven with valleys. Personal income trends, the jobless rate, and consumer sentiment in general play major roles in the strength or weakness of auto sales.

Because theirs is, in the final analysis, a consumer industry, auto manufacturers must be able to anticipate taste trends, buying fads, and domestic and foreign competition. Then they must market products that will fulfill the fantasies and needs of their customers. Poor judgment or a misreading of the public's tastes can spell disaster, since model changes are not easily made. A manufacturer also must be able to gauge accurately the level of sales for a model year. Overproduction can be nearly as disastrous as misjudging style preferences. So can underproduction, for that matter.

Factors affecting sales also include used car trends, credit availability and cost, consumer confidence, foreign demand, and scrappage levels. Tied closely to sales are the costs of production. Are raw-material prices rising? Is a union contract about to be renegotiated? When rising costs are coupled with sluggish sales, the industry usually is headed for hard times.

With federal regulation assuming ever greater proportions, this is an area that will have to be watched closely in the future. Stricter rules on emissions, energy consumption, and safety—and the added cost burdens they imply—are likely to inhibit the level of profits possible over the next few decades. Then, too, the whole question of energy availability will be of overriding significance. Finally, the effect of trade with major auto-exporting nations has become a crucial factor for domestic producers as imports capture an increasing share of the U.S. market.

Thus, with all of these major problem areas hanging over the industry, investment in auto companies is now more appropriately suited to those willing to assume some risk in return for longer term capital gains. This is in contrast to earlier years when investors seeking secure and steady income could turn with confidence to the major auto makers.

Chemicals. This industry is more truly an aggregation of many subindustries—organic and inorganic commodity chemicals, intermediates, functional specialties, and various product groups not strictly classified as chemicals, such as plastics, fertilizers, industrial gases, synthetic fibers, minerals, carbon black, etc. Within each of these subgroups, different forces are at work. The supply-demand balance, competition, price-cost differentials, geographic advantages, and alternative processes vary from one product area to another. Thus, the product mix of an individual company must be studied before assessing other information bearing on its prospects for the future. The subindustries vary widely in cyclicality, from the sustained growth of specialty chemicals or industrial gases to the feast-or-famine swings of fertilizers.

Once the analyst has determined a company's product mix, he can see what portion of the business is in mature product lines and what portion is concentrated in expanding fields. Ideally, while a company should have a sizable stake in growth areas, its more mature business areas are likely to produce a substantial cash flow, not only for current income but also for investment in the growth ventures. However, a company must be willing to recognize and phase out those weaker lines which are no longer generating sufficient cash flow. A key consideration is the company's market share in each subgroup, since market leadership is the prime determinant of profitability and growth for a chemical company.

A highly important factor for many firms today is the status of their fuel supplies and raw-material feedstocks. How a company handles long-term supply contracts, process changes, and conservation requirements is a clue to the ability of its management. How well it manages captive resources and moves to alternative resources is also vital. Other considerations include environmental legislation, research, technical services, pricing strategy, foreign currency devaluations, cash flow versus capital requirements, and the upgrading of returns on investment.

Chemical stocks can be profitable investments if caught at the low end of a cycle. Yields are reasonable and price-earnings ratios usually below average.

Coal. Approximately 80 percent of the coal produced in this country annually is consumed by steelmakers and electric utilities; another 10 percent is exported. The needs of all other manufacturers, households, etc., are satisfied with the remaining 10 percent. This underutilized fuel constitutes 88 percent of our energy resources but only 20 percent of actual fuel consumption. There are stumbling blocks which must be surmounted before this nation begins to fully use this abundant energy resource. They include labor problems, environmental concerns, reduced worker productivity, government regulation, transportation, and more efficient and widespread use of automation.

Of the two major consumers of coal, utilities are the larger users, accounting for about two thirds of production. Yet, coal is used to produce less than 45 percent of all electric power generated each year. This proportion is expected to shift, with coal assuming another 5 percent of the total within a decade. In addition to the growth inherent in this larger share of the market, demand for electricity is expected to continue growing by 4 to 5 percent a year. New coal production will come primarily from the Western states, where the bulk of coal is stripped from surface mines.

The steel industry uses metallurgical coal, which has the ability to coke when burned in the absence of oxygen. Most of the reserves of premium low-volatile coking coal are located in West Virginia, with Virginia and Kentucky accounting for less than 40 percent of medium and high-volatile coking coal reserves. Growth prospects in this end of the coal business are less robust than for steam coal, reflecting the reduced demand forecast for steel.

Among the 35 largest coal producers, only six derive 40 percent or more of their earnings from this product. The others are divisions of companies whose main thrust is in other industries. A number are "captive" coal producers, owned by steel or utility companies intent on assuring a dependable and less costly source of fuel. Those few companies which derive the bulk of their earnings from coal mine either steam coal or a mix of both types.

In looking at individual companies, you should determine whether steam or high- or low-sulfur metallurgical coal is mined. If the company mines metallurgical coal, the bulk of it is probably exported, and the company's record of earnings will likely be spotty. Another important factor is the type of contracts that have been negotiated with consumers. If most are long term, do they provide adequate escalation clauses? Labor relations are a vital factor in this industry, which has been beset by wildcat strikes and showdowns with militant and unpredictable unions.

For investors, there are only a few companies from which to choose. Some of these have long-term potential for growth, both from the increasing value of their reserves and from such areas as coal gasification. (See Chapter 27 for more on this subject.) Investment timing is important, since the coal industry reflects fluctuations in the business cycle.

Construction. Although this is a cyclical industry, it generally moves prior to business in general. When the economy is running full steam and interest rates are high and savings are depleted, mortgage money is costly and in short supply, and housing begins to suffer. Conversely, toward the end of a downturn, interest rates reach more attractive levels, savings rise, the Federal Reserve Board increases the money supply, and building loans become easier to obtain. Building activity turns the corner as a result and signals a turn in the economy. Thus, this money supply–interest rate sensitive group should be watched closely as an indicator of economic cycles.

Some 10 percent of gross national product comes from construction spending, making the industry one of the economy's most important sectors. Because stimulation from Washington may create an artificial swing in the housing-start figures, the analyst must be aware of pump-priming programs. Any shift in housing trends— from suburb to city or from single-unit to multiple-dwelling housing—also must be watched. These trends will have a significant impact on the types of building materials that are in demand. Population shifts, such as the rush to the Sun Belt, also can make or break regional companies.

Remodeling and renovation of older homes are key segments of the building industry. It is from this sector that the industry derives a stable and continuing revenue base. Those firms which supply the remodeling market have generally better records of consistent growth, while the home building companies are historically volatile.

The suppliers of building materials such as lumber, plywood, cement, gypsum, glass, and paint have varied outlooks. Their potential depends on their market mix, new housing versus renovation, on their proximity to their market, and the adaptability of the product to new construction methods and requirements. Those companies which specialize in retailing building supplies, particularly to the do-it-yourself market, have compiled especially impressive records of growth. Makers of products which have application in energy conservation should be in an excellent position in the future. These could include the manufacturers of insulation, storm doors and windows, thermal glass, weather stripping, and thermostats.

Machinery and machine tools. While these two allied industries are cyclical, their cycles are dissimilar. Machine tool orders are often used as a bellwether of business upswings. Conversely, orders for the machinery industry lag behind in an upturn, sometimes by as much as six months. The key to this dichotomous behavior lies in the nature of their respective markets. Hard-goods manufacturers in anticipation of better times must tool up to meet the expected increase in demand; hence machine tool orders rise even though business in general may still be in the doldrums. Machinery makers serve the heavy industries—auto and truck, oil, coal, construction, utility. The huge outlays required for this type of equipment can be postponed until a recovery is well under way, creating a lag in orders for machinery.

Prosperity for tool and machinery manufacturers is dependent on real growth in gross national product, a good level of capital spending, and customer confidence in the direction the government is steering the country. Order levels can swing by 50 percent or more in one year. Within the industry itself, capital spending plans hinge on long-range economic forecasts. If these prove too optimistic, machinery and tool makers are left with excess capacity, which can play havoc with profits.

The machinery industry has benefited from the government's requirements on air and water pollution control and safe working conditions. The energy shortage has created a surge in orders for coal-fired electric generating equipment, construction machinery for new coal mines, coal mining equipment, equipment for oil and gas exploration, and pipeline construction machinery. The machine tool makers have had a share in this windfall as auto manufacturers have downsized and restyled cars in order to meet more stringent fuel economy standards.

In analyzing an individual company, you should determine whether it is a market leader in its specialized line, if its research program has been productive, its sales and marketing efforts effective, its service organization strong, and its markets expanding. A company should be geographically diversified, with worldwide sales, and it should be vertically integrated. In looking at order backlog figures, you should note, if possible, whether order levels are up across the board or only in certain segments of the company's operations.

Selective investments made with attention to timing can prove rewarding within this industry group. Tax incentives to spur the economy frequently take the form of credits for capital equipment. If you can time your investments to coincide with this type of legislation, all the better.

Metals. This is another lagging industry; it picks up steam only after the economy is well on its way to recovery. But unless economic conditions are sufficiently robust to support the industry at near peak capacity, these companies get caught in a squeeze between rising costs and dropping product prices. As a whole, the industry operates on razor-thin profit margins. Government pricing restrictions and huge pollution control expenses have created further headaches for industry management.

With the exception of aluminum, demand for metals has not kept pace with gross national product growth in recent years. The outlook for steel is clouded by competition not only from Japanese imports but from other metals as well. Within the steel industry, the specialty producers have managed to counter the trend as they have carved out their individual niches. In terms of price and demand, copper companies have had the most volatile record. This group historically has raised capacity in the wake of demand increases and rising prices only to see that demand dry up, creating an inventory excess and sagging prices.

Aluminum should continue to enjoy fast-paced demand. The trend toward lighter and more fuel efficient cars has been a boon for the white metal. In fact, each year auto manufacturers use more aluminum to fabricate their products, to the detriment of the steel industry. Other areas where the use of aluminum is on the rise include home building, containers, aerospace, and electrical products.

The metals industry, and particularly the steel companies, have high labor costs. Union demands for higher pay and more benefits frequently cannot be fully passed along to customers, either because of government restrictions on price hikes or supply-demand conditions. Labor costs for steelmakers amounted to 37¢ per revenue dollar versus 23¢ for an average of all manufacturing industries in 1977.

Thus the analyst must keep close tabs on when labor contracts are due for renegotiation, and must be aware when rising demand reflects pre-strike stockpiling rather than normal business requirements.

Over the long run, metals stocks sell at a discount to the market, a concession to their many problems. Although yields on steels are usually higher than on aluminum stocks, the latter group has greater growth potential. However, dividend cuts under adverse conditions are not unusual. Several companies are broadly diversified within the metals industry, which helps spread investment risk.

Oil and Natural Gas. Getting oil and gas from deep inside the earth into our homes, cars, and factories requires the efforts of many hundreds of companies. Some of these are giant international corporations involved in every aspect of the business from wellhead to gas pump. An even greater number concentrate in only one area, such as producing, drilling, marketing, or equipment. Because petroleum is the most widely used industrial fuel, its consumption closely parallels the curve of the gross national product. But this may change as manufacturers turn to less costly or more plentiful alternative fuels.

The fact that five of the nation's ten largest corporations are oil companies is not surprising in view of their enormous capital needs. Estimates of annual industry capital requirements to develop oil productive capacity exceed $20 billion. Despite technological advances, about one third of all wells drilled are dry holes. Building new refineries or upgrading, modernizing, and expanding capacity at existing plants likewise requires huge infusions of cash. Thus, the ability to finance this process is critical. Historically, internally generated cash flow has funded the bulk of the industry's operations. A glance at a few balance sheets will show that the group is not heavily laden with debt (generally less than one third of capital).

Increasing government regulation has become a major force with which the industry must contend. The natural gas industry in this country is only now recovering from a 1954 Federal Power Commission decision that has held natural gas prices below free market levels. The ruling was changed in 1976, allowing higher prices for so-called new gas, and that liberalization resulted in increased drilling. In 1978, Congress passed legislation that gradually lifts controls on newly discovered natural gas, with full deregulation scheduled for 1985. The benefit to producers of the gradual phasing out of oil price controls over the period ending October 1981 will be at least partially offset by the effects of the windfall profit tax enacted in 1980. Rulings by the Environmental Protection Agency, the Energy Department, federal courts, and Congress can and do have a vital impact on the industry. Thus the analyst must carefully and constantly monitor them.

The geographic location of reserves or exploratory acreage has a bearing on the market's evaluation of an individual company's shares. First, there is the political standpoint; many international oil companies have lost ownership or control of large chunks of their foreign reserves in recent years. The market thus gives little weight to the existence of long-term contracts with foreign governments, even though in many cases fees and crude oil received in payment of services rendered are an important source of the company's revenue. Second, geography plays a role in the company's drilling and transportation costs. For example, the cost of drilling a well in Alaska is substantially more than the cost in California.

The future of an oil or gas company in the long run may depend on how well it has diversified into alternative energy areas like synthetic fuels, shale, oil sands, and solar. (See Chapter 27 for more in this area.)

Paper and forest products. This is a relatively concentrated industry, with the top ten companies accounting for about one third of industry production. Some companies are pure paper producers, while many are diversified, growing and processing trees and turning out finished products ranging from computer printouts to disposable diapers. In addition, they may produce lumber and plywood for the building and remodeling markets. The product mix can vary widely from company to company and should be examined closely.

Paper and related product shipments have traditionally closely followed general economic trends. A deterioration in this relationship in the mid-1970s, however, bears close observation, as it may be signifying some loss of market share—or possibly greater substitution of lower-grade paper products for higher-priced lines. Still, an accurate forecast of the economy is essential to judge industry growth potential. Lumber and plywood shipments more closely approximate cyclical building industry patterns. In the past few years, the paper and forest product companies have been cross-integrating.

The entire industry is heavily capital-intensive, requiring huge expenditures on new plants and more modern equipment. Expenses for the control of air and water pollution are particularly burdensome for the paper companies. A firm's unfilled spending requirements and its financing ability require close assessment. Growing capital needs, in fact, forced these companies to be more stingy with dividends in the 1970s than in the previous decade.

Capacity utilization of plant and equipment is watched closely as a clue to the industry's pricing flexibility. When operating at about 92 percent of capacity or more, the paper companies are better able to raise prices to meet higher operating expenses. During such times, industry profits as well as the group's stock price action can be quite favorable.

The degree to which a company is integrated and can supply end products through its own timber is important. Substantial timber holdings, in fact, have proved to be a valuable inflation hedge. For the past few decades, timber values have increased more rapidly than the rate of inflation. Furthermore, in contrast to most other inflation hedges, trees are self-renewing, with much of the care and feeding performed by Mother Nature.

Location is another important factor. A company's proximity to major markets has a bearing on its prospects. For instance, the United States as the world's low-cost timber producer should derive long-term growth from export markets. Those companies nearer seaports should be particularly favored. Similarly, owners of large tracts of Southern timber should do well as a result of that region's fast growth. Many forest product companies already have shifted operations to the South, where timber growth exceeds harvest levels.

In the past, the industry has benefited from increasing per capita consumption of paper. However, continuation of this favorable situation will hinge on the outcome of developing trends. For example, plastic could well be substituted for paper in packaging if paper prices rise too high. Increasing use of electronics in the transmittal and storage of information might make obsolete important markets for paper.

Despite its many problems, the forest products industry represents an important sector of the economy, one that should grow in importance as other resources become scarcer. But because of the cyclical nature of many of its components, the potential investor should look for companies that have well-diversified positions within the industry, those that command sizable market shares within several of these areas, and those that have demonstrated creative management and pursued aggressive marketing strategies. Such companies can provide attractive rewards for the careful investor.

Textiles. While this industry remains fairly fragmented, a considerable amount of consolidation has taken place. Of the approximately 5,500 textile companies, the five largest concerns capture about 25 percent of total industry sales. Serving as it does such cyclically sensitive markets as apparel, home furnishings, and industrial fabrics, the textile industry tends to be pretty much feast or famine. To help reduce this inherent vulnerability to overall economic conditions, the industry has undergone a considerable technological, managerial, and marketing face-lifting in recent years.

Along with the trend toward consolidation, textile manufacturers have been placing increasing emphasis on cost control, with particular attention being given to all-important inventory controls. When heavy inventory accumulation occurs along with sluggish business activity, the result is product markdowns and reduced profits. Research and development has also become a top priority as companies search for new technologies to increase productivity, reduce costs, and meet constantly changing fashion trends.

Raw-material costs account for more than 50 percent of the value of all textile shipments. Synthetics are a good deal more price stable than cottons and wools and have gained good consumer acceptance for their durability and easy care. Manufacturers are diversifying both inside and outside the textile area. So, when choosing a textile issue, the analyst must be particularly alert to such items as cost control, use of advanced technology, product mix, and diversification. Some of the major difficulties facing the textile industry include competition from imports; skyrocketing energy and labor costs; and the growing need for capital to modernize facilities, finance research and development, and meet increasingly stringent environmental regulations. It is most important to keep these in mind when analyzing individual companies.

The textile group historically has moved in line with the industrial averages. Growing in importance is the individual company's dividend policy. Since the textile group's profits can be volatile, the analyst should look closely at the company's record of consistency of dividend payments. In view of the low price-earnings multiples as well as high yields which pervade the group, selected textile issues have above-average investment value.

Science and Technology

Aerospace, data processing, electronics, and health care. The industries in this segment have several characteristics in common. Their shares usually trade at a premium over the market, dividend payouts tend to be modest, research and development expenditures large, and earnings growth rates well above average. New-product development costs are huge yet necessary, as product obsolescence is a constant threat. However, the rewards for technological breakthroughs are sufficiently large to offset these risks.

The long arm of the federal government reaches into almost every facet of operations in the form of product, price, and advertising regulation, safety and environmental standards, and funding. The DOD, FCC, FDA, FTC, GSA, NASA, USAF, and USN are more than alphabet soup to these companies. Cyclical influences are less apparent in technology companies than in the basic industry group. In some areas, in fact, members may move in a countercyclical pattern.

Investors willing to take on a degree of risk with these stocks are often rewarded by an above-average return. At the same time, more than the usual degree of selectivity is essential when investing in this premium-priced group of industries.

Aerospace. The aerospace industry frequently moves counter to the prevailing business cycle, a phenomenon that has its roots in government funding. As an employer of 5 percent of all manufacturing workers and as the source of equipment vital to the nation's defense, the aerospace industry encounters little resistance from Congress in obtaining huge fund allocations, particularly in bad times. In recent years, sales of military equipment to foreign nations, most notably the Arab bloc, have been a significant factor in supporting the industry through economic downturns. Aerospace exports doubled between 1972 and 1977.

Military spending accounts for 60 percent of total aerospace revenues. Six major companies control the bulk of this business. Defense spending began to accelerate in the mid-1960s and picked up momentum in the mid-1970s. However, it should level off through the 1980s. Foreign sales, which account for about a quarter of aerospace billings, will probably not move much above that proportionate share. Conversely, commercial sales should be in high gear as the airlines replace uneconomical equipment and try to comply with federal noise standards. Of course, it is always problematical whether the transport industry will be able to fund another equipment-buying round.

In looking at individual companies in the industry, the analyst must always keep in mind the possibility of a major new military contract award or cancellation. Product diversification as well as the military-commercial balance are areas he should study. Also important in this industry is the amount of aggressiveness a company displays in pursuing new contracts, its research program, and its ability to finance new products.

Data processing. As an industry, data processing is a virtual infant compared with such graybeards as shipbuilding and railroading. Mushrooming growth in the 1960s saw one technological breakthrough after another as applications and utilization expanded hand in hand with declining product prices. Computer usage has become so prevalent today that even the possibility of home computers is no longer in the realm of science fiction.

The industry is divided into four major segments, but there is considerable overlapping from one area to another. The mainframe market is dominated by a few large companies, with International Business Machines doing two thirds of the business. Softwear is marketed by all the majors, by a number of publicly owned smaller companies, as well as myriad privately and individually owned enterprises. Add-ons, or peripheral equipment, are packaged and sold by the mainframe manufacturers and also by numerous others, large and small, some concentrating in this one area and others having it as part of a widely diversified product line. Minicomputers, the newest segment of the business, were made possible by developments in microminiaturization. Again, some of the majors have reached down to expand the bottom end of their lines into the fast-growing minicomputer field. Although a few minicomputer specialists control this end of the business, competition from the other entrants is intense and will probably heat up, squeezing out the weaker, undercapitalized companies.

Cyclical influences such as capital spending have the biggest impact at the heavy end of the business—large mainframes. Manufacturers operating in this area spend heavily for product development; IBM alone expends $1 billion annually on research and development. Foreign operations also bulk large, often accounting for nearly half of a company's sales. However, currency fluctuations, governmental restrictions, and labor relations can affect profits from overseas operations.

In line with other high-technology stocks, computer issues have long commanded a premium. Similarly the bulk of earnings have been plowed back rather than being distributed to shareholders. But market conditions and industry maturity have wrought changes so that price-earnings ratios have worked down as payouts have worked up. New products and record backlogs and profits, along with improved yields and lower earnings multiples, make this an attractive investment area.

Electronics and electrical equipment. In discussing this industry, it is difficult to generalize, since it covers manufacturers of such diverse products as citizen band radios, television sets, massive generating equipment, semiconductors, and highly sophisticated scientific instruments. While one segment may be seriously hurt by a business downturn, another won't be. Some areas may require large infusions of capital to stay afloat; others are characterized by the ease of entry for new companies. Those companies that primarily produce household appliances and home entertainment equipment will be subject to the same influences as other consumer product companies, while those fabricating expensive capital equipment will move in line with the cyclical basic industries. Of course, the larger companies have a stake in both ends.

The future health of these producers is assured by the massive sums that will have to be spent by industry and government to reduce the nation's dependence on oil, to improve mass transportation, to develop alternative energy sources, to automate manufacturing, to explore the universe, and to advance our technological applications. The government is also pouring billions into electronic warfare devices, intelligence and surveillance equipment, and improving the nation's retaliation capabilities.

In analyzing individual companies, you should look at the competitive position, marketing expertise, patent position, product diversification, government-commercial product mix, and research leadership. Many of the larger firms in this industry are multinational and subject to the usual considerations of currency stability, regulation, and political climate. As a whole, these issues are attractive investments.

Health care. Key factors in the appraisal of health care securities include federal regulation, research, and marketing strength. For some companies, especially the major drug firms, international business also involves significant considerations. Actually, more than half of the health care dollar goes to nonprofit hospitals and to doctors. But investor-owned businesses also bulk large; here is a partial listing: ethical pharmaceuticals (with promotion directed toward the medical profession), proprietary drugs (consumer advertised), medical supplies and equipment, diagnostic products, and health care services (investor-owned hospitals and diagnostic labs being notable areas). Diversification is another aspect of investment appraisal, since many companies cover a broad range of health care fields.

A common denominator for appraising companies in this industry is federal regulation. Even the merest rumor of Congressional committee hearings can have a marked impact on the price of their stocks. Although the government underwrites a sizable chunk of our medical bills, soaring costs to some extent have been fostered by Washington's efforts to improve the quality of health care and the safety and efficacy of health care products. These costly standards are forcing smaller companies out of business and concentrating activities into fewer, stronger companies. At the same time, ironically, Congress is enacting antitrust legislation aimed at preventing such concentration.

The key regulatory agency is the Food and Drug Administration (FDA), which has unusually strict standards for new drug clearance.

Several years and millions of dollars must be expended to bring a new drug from its initial research stage, through animal and human testing, to final FDA clearance. The clearance of new medical devices is much less difficult, but still more costly than small companies can generally afford. Hence, an analyst is essentially concerned with tracking the research progress of the larger companies, including the cost-effectiveness of the research approach and the progress of products through the various test stages. Moreover, he must keep abreast of the technological competition among the companies in every major health care field.

Marketing strength is another important facet. In ethical drugs, a company's basic marketing force is its detail staff, people who keep physicians and pharmacists informed on products and their usage. In proprietary drugs, the marketing effort is centered in advertising and promotion directed to the consumer. Another government watchdog, the Federal Trade Commission (FTC), steps in here to see that advertising doesn't get out of bounds.

International business plays an important role in the operations of health care companies, particularly for the major drug manufacturers. Because Japan is second to the United States in total health care expenditures, it is an especially significant market. Analysts consider a drug company's handling of currency fluctuations a telling clue to its management. They also like to see effective use of tax havens like Puerto Rico. The resultant cash resources that are tied up in Puerto Rico should also be managed effectively so they contribute to corporate profits.

Thus far, we have touched on a few of the general considerations which apply to the appraisal of several segments of the health care industry. In weighing the specifics of a given company within that industry, the analyst must start by knowing how the business is divided. What are the company's major products? What services does it provide? Where are its geographical markets?

Then each of these factors is appraised with regard to competitive strengths, basic earning power, and potential for future growth.

As in other industries, ultimate considerations include the quality of earnings, the overall growth trend in terms of profits and dividends, and the relative price-earnings ratio of each individual stock of the companies within that industry.

For the investor, health care stocks have above-average long-term potential.

Transportation Industries

Airlines, intermodal shipping, railroads, and trucking. The movement of goods and people is big business, but it also is a business which has been and will continue to be in a state of flux. The trucking industry has significantly increased its share of the freight hauling market, to the detriment of the rails. The airlines have made major inroads into the passenger hauling market, once dominated by the railroads. In recent years, another contender for freight revenues has come into its own, intermodal shipping or container leasing. Demand for these shipping containers is growing at about 20 percent per year.

In general, the transportation industries are cyclical, reflecting changes in the level of freight being moved and in the amounts being spent for travel. All are capital-intensive, while most are also labor-intensive. The public outcry for less government in the private sector is having its greatest impact on the transportation industries as the airlines, rails, and truckers all witness an ongoing reduction in federal regulatory constraints.

Airlines. This capital-intensive industry's sensitivity to economic conditions has produced a boom-and-bust earnings pattern over the years. That volatility is clearly exhibited in the industry's 1979 profits nosedive to about $200 million versus $1.4 billion just one year earlier. Scheduled air carriers dominate intercity public transportation and held about 85 percent of that market in 1979. That dominance is not likely to be challenged in the foreseeable future.

A relatively short equipment-replacement cycle, combined with the high cost of new aircraft, produces highly leveraged balance sheets among the airlines. The early 1980s will mark a major initiative to upgrade fleets as the industry expends more than $4 billion annually for a new generation of modern fuel-efficient aircraft. Procurement of those planes is strategic to most carriers since fuel costs have spiraled; in 1979 fuel was a hefty 30 percent of operating expenses versus just 12 percent in 1973.

Potential investors should seek information on a carrier's overall financial strength, as debt ratios vary widely. Planned equipment purchases and options to buy new planes are also valuable indicators of future financing needs. Equipment utilization rates, load factors, passenger yields, and degree of exposure to business and tourist markets are also important tools in the investment selection process.

Passage of deregulation legislation in 1978 gave airlines greater rate-setting flexibility while also easing entry requirements on new and existing routes. The Civil Aeronautics Board's authority over domestic rates, mergers, and acquisitions will terminate in 1981, while the CAB itself will be abolished in 1985. Deregulation evoked considerable changes in the operating environment, including intensified competition on lucrative routes and abandonment of marginal short-haul service by many of the trunk lines. Meanwhile, regional carriers are expanding into interstate markets.

Perhaps the most important long-term impact of deregulation on the investment decision regards the emerging importance of management. In a free-market environment the stakes are likely to be far greater than under a regulatory umbrella. Also, success or failure will increasingly stem from managerial decisions.

Historically, airline stocks begin to outperform the market prior to the trough of a recession in anticipation of renewed traffic growth. Investors are cautioned that stock action, like profits, tends to be volatile, with fast-paced movements on both the upside and the downside.

Intermodal shipping. Considerable efficiencies and cost savings are provided by packing cargo in sealed steel containers that are then easily transported on trailer chassis, railroad flatcars, ships, and airplanes. The adoption of uniform international standards and the rapid, if erratic, expansion in world trade have been mainly responsible for a boom in containerized shipping. Demand for cargo containers has been growing by around 20 percent a year, and prospects for continued high growth rates appear realistic. Meanwhile, container leasing companies are growing even faster because of improving fleet utilization and the capital savings they provide.

Because of their capital-intensive nature, container lessors are heavily leveraged. Debt-to-equity ratios of two or three to one are common. These levels appear to be manageable, however, since most leases are long term and obsolescence from technological changes is minimal. Moreover, where lessors enjoy high depreciation rates and are often chartered overseas, tax rates are low and returns on equity tend to be high. However, the stocks tend to be interest rate-sensitive, while economic contractions take their toll on profits.

Container leasing stocks are certainly not for widows and orphans, but can be considered by aggressive investors searching for above-average, yet cyclical, growth opportunities.

Railroads. Few industries are as closely linked to business cycles as the railroads. Fluctuations in such basic industries as autos, steel, mining, coal, and capital goods have a decided impact on carloadings. As the revenue ton-mile (movement of one ton of freight one mile) performance is the analyst's basic tool for measuring traffic growth, these variations are crucial. In one major business cycle of perhaps two years' duration, these figures can vary by 100 billion tons. Fixed costs are high, so profits are hard to come by in recessions. Thus, when reviewing this industry, current and projected economic trends are important factors.

Rails are among the most labor-intensive of industries. In 1979, wages accounted for more than 42 percent of revenues, an improvement over the figure in 1950, when labor represented more than 50 percent of revenues. Therefore it is important to keep tabs on the timing and content of union contracts. Other major costs include maintenance of way, structures, and equipment, and transportation accounts (fuel, loss, and damage). By measuring a carrier's transportation expenses against revenues, the analyst can compare the efficiency of one road with another. A similar comparison can be made with maintenance costs and revenues to get information on the condition of fleet and property.

Another important consideration is the railroad's geographical operating area. The industry is generally reviewed in three segments, Eastern, Western, and Southern. Operators in each area have many similarities, but they have important and distinct differences in weather conditions, types of freight hauled, and their areas' growth prospects.

Deregulation is also in the cards for the nation's rails, while the Interstate Commerce Commission is already moving to loosen the regulatory noose over the industry. The Railroad Revitalization and

Regulatory Reform Act of 1976 provided the initial catalyst to the ICC's increasingly constructive stance on questions of track abandonment, rate setting, and mergers.

The latter point has, in recent years, resulted in a flurry of proposed combinations, which adds a unique shading to rail investment decisions. Here, one must determine the outlook for the combined systems, resulting in individual stock valuations on the basis of the proposed entity, and in accordance with announced merger terms. Dividend restrictions also appear in formal agreements and must be weighed. Since consummation of a proposed merger can take up to three years, the possibility of the merger never reaching fruition must also be considered. In such instances, sharp stock price corrections can occur as investors reappraise the value of each firm.

Trucking. More than half of all the freight moved within the country is carried by truck. In view of the prominence of the trucking industry in transporting raw materials to manufacturers and manufactured products to the market, it is not surprising that the industry tends to be an economic bellwether. Changes in the weekly intercity truck tonnage figures, whether they are changes in direction or velocity, often signal a shift in the business climate. For this reason, the group is important to the analyst trying to ferret out clues to business trends.

The industry is labor-intensive, with personnel costs taking almost two thirds of every sales dollar. This is strong testimony to the effectiveness of the International Brotherhood of Teamsters in dealing with a fragmented industry to negotiate ever escalating labor contracts. Equipment and terminal maintenance, as well as fuel costs, have risen sharply in recent years and are significant expense items for the motor carriers.

The Motor Carrier Act of 1980 provided for significant changes in trucking regulations, including relaxed entry requirements, reduced operating restrictions, greater pricing flexibility and a phase-out of single-line collective ratemaking. That legislation, combined with the dynamic changes already taking place in other transportation sectors, suggests that realignment of the nation's transportation industries will continue in response to demands for maximum energy efficiency.

When the dust finally settles, many transportation specialists expect large intermodal companies—with important trucking components—to emerge as the most viable competitors in coming years. An investor considering trucking firms should therefore keep in mind the sweeping changes affecting the nation's transportation system and the likelihood of an acceleration of merger and acquisition activity within the trucking group in particular. Financial strength, professional management, and access to capital are the key elements to success in this industry for the 1980s.

For the investor, this industry can provide some exciting rides. The shares generally are volatile and, caught at the bottom of a cyclical swing, can be rewarding investments.

Chapter 25 More on Specific Industries

THE INDUSTRIES reviewed in the previous chapter were largely those that make the things we use and those that transport the goods to market. In this chapter, we shall look at the industries that most closely touch our own everyday lives—the consumer-oriented segment of the economy. It's a large segment; personal consumption expenditures make up nearly two thirds of our gross national product.

Consumer Products and Leisure Time

Food processing, lodging, the media, motion pictures, personal care, recreation equipment, and retailing. How each of us chooses to spend his disposable income has a strong influence on these industries. Thus, competition is intense and top profits go to those companies with the greatest marketing skill and highest advertising budgets.

A constant parade of new products designed to dazzle and bewitch the consumer into parting with his cash is a necessity for survival in these industry areas. To some of these companies, the energy shortage poses a major threat, and to others product obsolescence is a continuing specter. Shifting demographic patterns can have a pervasive influence on the entire group.

Food processing. Because of their relatively stable earnings growth and high dividend yields, food processing stocks historically have been attractive as both defensive and growth investments. With food literally being the world's most basic need, it stands to reason that this industry would enjoy rising demand for its products. Since the United States is the largest producer of foodstuffs, the long-range potential for domestic food processors is impressive.

While the overall industry outlook undeniably is favorable, the

269

rate of growth of any individual company hinges on several important factors. One of the most important considerations when analyzing a food stock is to determine the company's vulnerability to and ability in dealing with the volatile commodities markets. Since ingredients are a major consideration, knowledge of present and future commodities price projections and supply-demand prospects is important.

Profit margins can narrow if demand weakens in the face of growing supplies. The same is true when the supply is low, since higher prices often lead to consumer resistance. So a company's ability to keep tight control on ingredient costs is of the utmost importance in determining its earnings potential. A diversified product line helps protect a company from the risk of oversupply or undersupply of any one ingredient. Many of the larger companies have expanded into nonfood areas to further reduce their commodity-related risks.

Other major operational costs include energy, labor, packaging, research and development, advertising and promotion. The energy situation bears close watching, as, for the most part, the industry is heavily dependent on natural gas in its processing operations. Research and development, marketing, advertising and promotional capability are vitally important contributors to the success of companies operating in this highly competitive environment. A successful food processor is one that is able to identify growing markets, has the research and development skill to come up with products that will meet these new demands, and has the advertising and promotional expertise to gain an adequate market share.

Because of the stability of the group, the stocks of the top-quality multi-product diversified companies tend to be very attractive to conservative investors. On the whole, food company issues have limited downside risk even under adverse economic conditions and are appropriate defensive investments.

Lodging. The hotel and motel industry has undergone a metamorphosis in the last two decades. A field once controlled by the independent owner-operator is now dominated by a handful of large motel-hotel chains. Increased mobility, rising construction and real estate costs, and widespread acceptance of expensive computerized reservation systems and other equipment have placed demands on the industry that could only be met by large well-financed companies. Gone to seed by the roadside are most of the "Bide-a-Wee" and "Dew Drop Inn" cabins. Today's motorist bypasses these anachronisms on his way to a well-equipped up-to-date motel featuring two pools, four restaurants, and a sauna.

Economic cycles play a role in the fortunes of the innkeepers. The business traveler long has been their bread and butter. As corporate profits decline, business travel shifts from luxury class to economy. But helping to smooth out these ups and downs is the pleasure traveler. As disposable incomes have risen, pleasure travel has increased. Although individuals also feel the pinch in a recession, they give up their pleasures as a last resort and resume them at the first signs of an upturn.

The two most important factors affecting the profitability of an individual chain are occupancy levels and room rates. The analyst is concerned with any major trend changes in these figures. Room rates must adequately cover the cost of the building. However, competitive or other conditions can cause temporary reductions in rates.

Individual companies differ in terms of the kinds of services they provide, i.e., restaurants, large convention quarters, extensive recreation facilities, etc. The percentage of overall income which is derived from these facilities and the profitability of each should be determined. Some innkeepers have diversified into such areas as bus transportation, catering, and cruise ships. These nonlodging functions should be reviewed as separate entities. If an operator has significant foreign exposure, it should be studied in relation to the possible impact it could have on future profits.

Several uncertainties face the industry. Perhaps the most important is the impact of the energy shortage. The Arab oil embargo, coming at the peak of an expansion period, had a severe effect on many companies. While the subsequent shakeout trimmed much of the fat from motel operators, gas rationing in the future could be a major blow. Although not as serious a threat, boosts in the minimum wage rate are an inflationary influence on labor costs.

The media. Although the industry is made up of somewhat diverse segments—broadcasting and publishing—it has an underlying similarity of purpose, the dissemination of information and communication of ideas. But broadcasters and newspaper publishers depend more on their advertisers than on the public for their bread and butter. Readership and audience figures are vital to their marketing success, but revenues are derived largely from advertisers.

Both broadcasters and newspaper publishers enjoy high operating margins, leverage, and profits; small volume gains can generate significant profit increases. For publishers, the greater utilization of automation and photocomposition equipment has reduced labor costs. Because broadcasting time is limited, advertisers are reluctant to cut back on their TV and radio commercial messages even during recessions. Thus the broadcasters are not as subject to cyclical influences as are the large metropolitan newspapers. In good times, there is a mad scramble among advertisers to secure time slots on the highest-rated network programs. Quite the opposite is the case for newspaper ad linage, which is highly sensitive to business cycles.

A discussion of the media industry is incomplete without mention of the new developments taking place in television. Viewer choice is no longer limited to the fare of the three major networks. Satellites, cable television and pay cable, as well as video cassette recorders and videodisk players, are ushering in an era of "narrowcasting"— programming geared to the special interest of select audiences. Also, several major newspapers are experimenting with placing their publications on computer or television screens. Down the road, television will gain increasing interactive possibilities, permitting such activities as shopping from the home. Many media companies are now diversified so that representation in more than one area can be obtained in one stock.

This industry is generally an attractive one for the investor. There are companies appropriate for the speculator and others more suited to conservative tastes.

Motion pictures. Though the motion picture industry bears little resemblance to its former self, it is likely to be around for many years, despite continuing prophecies of doom. There will still be a demand for the type of entertainment that only the movies can satisfy. We suspect, too, that many people will continue to prefer seeing movies on a theater screen. Even with rising ticket prices, movies will probably be less expensive than many other forms of entertainment. Home entertainment equipment designed to show first-run films is a far more costly alternative now and will remain so into the forseeable future.

The movie stocks, however, almost defy analysis. In fact, there are few if any "pure" movie stocks. Gone are the days of the big studios and their stables of stars—their properties, as it were. Many of the major film companies are now divisions of conglomerates with far-flung interests ranging from airlines to zinc. Others have evolved into vast entertainment complexes with important stakes in recorded music, publishing, and cable television, and are now supplying the industry's old archenemy, television, with most of its prime-time product. Those remaining few movie companies with the least diversification seem eager to explore other growth avenues.

Even for the most diversified companies, individual motion pictures can have an enormous impact on earnings. With one major box office smash, a company's earnings can mushroom, its cash position improve significantly, and its stock price rise dramatically.

For every hit there are usually many misses, though the industry is trying to elevate its batting average by releasing fewer but bigger movies. In addition, the hefty guarantees that are demanded from exhibitors actually assure a profit for some films. The industry must anticipate what its public will want to see many months in the future. This is dangerous business—for the movie moguls themselves, for the analyst, and for the investor.

Personal care. The personal care industry is highly competitive, with a score of large firms vying for 75 percent of the total dollar volume. A company's success or failure is largely determined by its marketing and merchandising ability. Huge amounts are spent annually trying to capture consumers' dollars and product loyalty. Advertising, packaging, new-product development, and promotion are major expense items. Spending for personal care products has been on the rise in recent years, reflecting the increase in the number of women working outside the home, a bulge in the number of persons in the 25–35 age bracket (a prime age for this type of spending), and the rise in disposable incomes. These favorable demographic factors and market trends are expected to continue.

There is a wide difference between the world of cosmetics and that of toiletries. Each has its own distinctive characteristics. Channels of distribution, advertising methods, packaging, promotional expenses, and competitive climates are different, and the analyst must approach them separately. Sales and earnings should be studied on a division-by-division level so these differences can be taken into account. Cosmetics are at the top end of the industry with medium- to premium-priced products, high profit margins, and fashion-related product lines. The more mundane toiletry business includes such pedestrian products as shampoos, deodorants, toothpaste, shaving products, and hair dyes.

While the industry as a whole is fairly recession resistant, inflation does have a stifling effect on growth. Periods of high inflation necessitate increased consumer spending for food and shelter and reduce the demand for personal care items. At the same time, manufacturers are forced to pay higher prices for raw materials and supplies. The combination can seriously squeeze profit margins. Because so many of these companies are multinational, it is imperative to determine how much of a company's business comes from overseas.

New products are the lifeblood of this group's growth. A company's record of developing and marketing new products may be a clue to its future potential. A strong and creative management which recognizes new consumer trends and is willing to make the changes necessary to accommodate these new ideas is one key to success in this highly competitive industry. Diversification efforts have further enhanced the outlook for many personal care firms as maturation of the domestic market looms late in the 1980s. Health care firms have been favorite targets for acquisition, given the compatibility of their operating requirements with the personal care sector.

Recreation equipment. This fragmented group includes manufacturers of boats, bowling equipment, sporting goods, video games, snowmobiles, and camping equipment. Thus, conditions which might hurt one company might not hurt another. However, the industry as a whole is sensitive to changes in the economy and in the level of disposable income. In line with some other leisure-time groups, recreation product manufacturers are among the last to be hit in a recession and the first to recover as business heats up.

Demographic conditions favor this group for the next few decades. The 35–54 age group—where most of the big-ticket recreation equipment purchases originate—is expected to increase by more than 60 percent through the year 2000. Americans are enjoying rising discretionary incomes, longer vacations, shorter workweeks, a high level of employment, and excellent retirement benefits, all of which are spurs to recreational activities.

Important to the success—or failure—of a company are its product research and development, its ability as a marketer, its skill in keeping costs down in an inflationary climate, and its product reputation. Because recreation equipment often tends to be seasonal, oriented to a particular population segment, easily duplicated, and short-lived in popularity, a broadly diversified product line is vital to a company's stability.

Major concerns facing these manufacturers include inflation, possible gasoline rationing, product obsolescence—as a result of changing buying patterns or technological advances—and raw-material shortages.

Yet these stocks, bought in an up cycle, can be highly rewarding. Leisure is big business, and the choices for investments are varied. However, those companies with strong managements, broad product diversification, and products which can be used near the home seem to have the most attractive prospects.

Retailing. An overview of retailing involves considering the business cycle, inflation, unemployment, consumer disposable income, installment debt, and savings. This industry is affected by seasonal factors, regional weather conditions, fashion trends, the promotional environment, and consumer buying habits.

Retailing covers a wide range of merchandising which is generally separated into food and nonfood groups. In the latter group, general merchandisers are studied separately from the specialty stores. But even within these broad categories, there is considerable overlapping. Food supermarkets are adding more and more shelf space for nonfood items, specialty stores are dealing in health and beauty aids. These two types of stores are not only competing with each other, but are encroaching on the business of the general merchandisers.

Central to all retailing is the competitive position of the individual company in its given segment. The food supermarket seeks to balance low prices with quality and convenience. The convenience chains stress their round-the-clock neighborhood shopping convenience and underplay their higher prices. A specialty store may appeal to a shopper's desire for service, high fashion, and top quality. Some retailers ply both ends of the mass-class market, with boutiques and bargain basements. Important in a retailer's success is the competitive force of the company's image. Site selection is often the key to the store's ability to achieve this success.

In appraising managements, you must consider how well central control and local autonomy are balanced. Chain stores do their buying from a central location on information fed from decentralized outlets. Many of the major department store enterprises are known as "ownership groups," since each division has a high degree of autonomy. However, staff support functions—computer systems, strategic planning, and real estate development—are centralized. Whatever the organizational structure, management's effectiveness in monitoring information, measuring results, and taking corrective action is what counts.

One measure of a company's progress is sales growth, which may come through adding new stores, replacing outdated units, or through acquisitions. The yardstick here is the annual figure for square feet of retail floor space. Growth of space is somewhat meaningless by itself; productivity of that space should be examined by comparing annual changes in volume of sales per square foot.

In appraising retailers' earnings, look at gross margins. This figure is derived by subtracting the cost of goods sold from total sales volume. Inventory control is an important factor in maintaining a favorable level of gross margins. Frequently there is considerable shrinkage between the initial markup and gross margin, reflecting pilferage, errors, and markdowns. Food supermarkets and other self-service operations have limited personnel expenses and rapid inventory turnover, therefore low expense ratios and low gross margins. Effective expense control is also an important contributor to company profits.

Though retailing for the most part is a mature and intensely competitive field, the group offers some excellent growth selections for the judicious investor.

Financial Services

Banks, insurance companies, and savings and loan associations. For these companies that provide financial services, interest rate trends are an all important key to their fortunes. The spread between short-term and long-term rates or between the rate of interest earned and paid can make the difference between a profit or a loss.

Investments made by these financial companies turn the wheels of American industry, fund most of the housing, and keep the various levels of government operating. They tend to make stable, if unexciting, investments with both modest yield and modest growth potentials.

Banking. An understanding of the banking industry requires an in-depth study of balances—balances between loans and deposits, between interest rates paid and interest rates earned, between deposit inflows and disintermediation, between short-term loans and long-term loans, and so on. The prosperity of the industry can often swing in either direction on no more than a quarter-point change in the prime lending rate. Thus it is important for the analyst to understand the subtle nuances of these balance and ratio relationships.

To facilitate the study, banks are generally segregated into two groups—money market center banks and regional banks. Within these categories are banks whose business is wholesale, retail, domestic, or international—or any combination thereof. Money center banks react more rapidly and dramatically to changes in the business climate. Regional banks, with their longer-term portfolios, more stable deposit bases, and better-balanced customer mixes, are in a more advantageous position to withstand economic cycles. Not surprisingly, their stocks display a similar pattern, offering the investor stability, good yield, and modest appreciation potential.

Money center banks, which are heavily dependent on commercial and industrial loans, can be hard pressed when the demand for such loans dries up, reflecting increased use of cheaper money from commercial paper, notes, and the like. Banks in need of business are forced to accept less attractive alternatives where loan costs or risks tend to be higher. An example of this is the upsurge in high-risk loans to underdeveloped nations, which may create problems for some large international money center banks. Helping to fill the gap in recent years has been the fast-growing credit card business.

Banking is one of the few industries in which book value or net worth per share has any substantive meaning. This is because tangible assets are usually of a type that are easily turned into cash, unlike those of a manufacturer with large amounts tied up in inventory. Therefore, book value comes close to approximating the actual value per share of a bank's worth.

Banks report earnings on two different bases: net operating income, which includes profits from operations only; and net income, which includes operating income as well as gains or losses from portfolio transactions. The latter figure including portfolio results is the one generally used in comparing banks statistics.

Stocks in the larger banks can provide you with an equity position to cash in on upswings in interest rates. But, because these bank stocks tend to be more volatile than those of the regionals, you'll have to keep a closer eye on them. Regional banks provide an opportunity to include some close-to-home investments in your portfolio.

Insurance. There are two major categories in the insurance business, life and property-casualty. Life underwriters have enjoyed relatively consistent growth over the years, unlike the more volatile property-casualty insurers. One of the biggest boons for the life companies has been the improved life expectancy figures. Furthermore, demographic trends favor the industry. Most policyholders are in the 25–65 age group, which is expected to expand at a faster rate than other age brackets. Automation has helped life insurers establish and maintain low operating ratios.

In analyzing a life company, look at its premium growth, quality and type of risk, mortality experience, lapse rate, rate of earnings on investments, reserve position, and operating expenses. The policy mix—ordinary, credit, industrial, and group—is important, since each type has its own characteristics. The recent trend toward diversification into the health and accident, disability, and fire and casualty areas, which involve higher risk, is an important consideration as you look at a company.

Companies which operate in the property-casualty fields are more difficult to analyze. They include auto, workers' compensation, liability, homeowners, and commercial multiperil. The industry is highly cyclical and can swing from overall underwriting profits to underwriting losses in a twelve-month period. In an era of rising profitability, competition heats up, creating margin squeezes which turn the cycle. Inflation was a major industry problem in the mid-1970s as costs skyrocketed and fixed-premium coverages made recovery of those expenses impossible. The industry now utilizes shorter term contracts and built-in price escalators to mitigate inflation's impact.

Other things to look for are the rate structure, underwriting risks, reserve position, and investment income. The latter has become a major profit source as money managers invest their substantial cash assets in high-yielding money market instruments. Nevertheless, the susceptibility of these insurers to wide earnings swings makes investment timing important.

Insurance companies have two sources of income—premium income and income on invested reserves. The latter has contributed about 75 percent of total industry profits for the past three decades. These invested reserves are the funds set aside to cover current unpaid claims, future claims, and the expenses related to these payments. The larger the company's loss-reserve position the better the quality of its earnings.

Savings and loan associations. S&L's are a major source of home mortgage capital, supplying more than half the credit for housing in this country. Mortgage funding is generated primarily from the deposits of savers, but advances from the Federal Home Loan Bank are a secondary source. Earnings are derived from the spread between the interest costs on deposits and the return from mortgages outstanding. Origination fees on new mortgages are also a source of income. New funds are also raised by the sale of mortgages and participations in existing mortgage portfolios.

Because mortgages tend to be written for the long term and deposits are frequently short term, S&L's can be in the unenviable position, under certain interest rate conditions, of having to pay as much for borrowings as they are earning on portions of their loan portfolio. Short-term interest rates fluctuate more rapidly and more widely than long-term. The industry has a highly cyclical history, usually experiencing margin squeezes in the latter stages of the economic cycle, when interest rates and inflation begin to accelerate.

The trend of short-term interest rates is a key determinant of the fortunes of the industry. As rates move higher in other debt instruments such as Treasury bills, savings deposits are withdrawn in favor of these higher-yielding investments, a process known as disintermediation. This reduces the funds available for mortgage loans, which in turn hurts the building industry. However, in recent years, the popularity of long-term certificate accounts has been a stabilizing influence. Some 60 percent of accounts at insured associations now are in these certificate accounts.

Conditions in the industry can have a pronounced effect on housing and ultimately can alter key economic and social goals. Therefore, the industry is heavily regulated, as is banking. Regulation will continue to be a way of life and, for the most part, the industry has accommodated itself well to this presence. Other trends, though, will likely have a more significant impact on its future. These include variable rate mortgages, negotiable orders of withdrawal (NOW accounts), six-month Treasury bill-tied savings certificates, and increasing competition from other segments of the financial services industry.

Public Utilities

Electric power, natural gas pipelines, telephone companies. The tie that binds these three public utility groups together is regulation, at both federal and state levels. Indeed, for some companies in these industries, the only growth they can expect will come from rate increases granted by the regulating agencies that control them. This is particularly true for some of the more poorly situated electric power companies and for those pipeline companies that have failed to diversify. Of the three industry areas, the telephone companies have suffered the least from regulatory manipulation only because they require rate boosts less frequently.

In general, investors turn to these groups for generous yields, gradual growth, and better-than-average stability. The electric utilities are particularly liberal in their dividend payments; the integrated natural gas distributors are the least generous.

Electric utilities. As one of the most capital-intensive of industries, electric utility companies are vulnerable to interest rate swings, shifts in the money supply, and inflation. The industry has to combat such problems as fuel availability, rate regulations, and pressure from consumer and environmental groups. Because electric power companies all face these difficulties, there is a tendency to view them as a homogeneous unit. There is, however, a wide variation in the investment opportunities represented within the group.

One of the most important criteria in evaluating the group is the regulatory climate under which the company must operate. Is the regulatory agency sympathetic to the needs of the company, with decisions rendered promptly and a reasonable return on equity allowed? (A 13 percent return on equity is a workable figure.) If construction work in progress is included in the rate base, so much the better.

In comparing company earnings, an analyst must pay close attention to the quality of those figures. If a large percentage of profit comes from allowance for funds used during construction, the quality of these profits is questionable. If, in addition, a liberal accounting policy is used in treating depreciation, then the analyst can conclude that earnings quality likewise is poor. Normalizing depreciation, rather than flowing it through to earnings, is a more conservative accounting method.

A utility's financial position is particularly important, since the company's future depends heavily on its ability to raise new capital economically. Two important ratios are *fixed charges coverage* and *debt to equity*. A fixed charges ratio of two times is desirable—that is, earnings that are twice as great as total bond interest and preferred dividends. In the debt to equity ratio, when debt moves up to account for more than 60 percent of capitalization, the balance begins to get unhealthy and equity financing becomes the obvious alternative. If, however, the stock is selling below book value, equity financing will result in heavy earnings dilution. The greater the percentage of capital requirements that can be generated internally from cash flow, the healthier the utility.

The fuel used by an electric utility has an important bearing on its attractiveness. Hydropower, coal, and nuclear energy have been the more traditionally preferred generating fuels in this era of more costly oil and less abundant natural gas. However, the near-disastrous malfunction at the Three Mile Island nuclear plant in Pennsylvania in 1979 precipitated a controversy which cast a cloud over the future of nuclear power. Stringent safety guidelines have since been imposed on utilities with nuclear exposure. Thus, fuel risk has evolved as a significant criterion in evaluating securities within the utility group. A final measuring stick to apply to these companies is their comparative earnings and dividend growth rates.

As long as inflation remains within bounds and interest rates stable, electric utilities offer above-average current yield, reasonable dividend growth, and moderate price appreciation.

Natural gas distributors. Regulated pipeline and distribution companies stand to benefit from increased supplies which will result from higher prices. The industry received a shot in the arm with passage of the Natural Gas Policy Act of 1978, which will phase in full deregulation by 1985. The act also places controls on previously unregulated intrastate gas, and this allows interstate pipelines to compete for Texas and Oklahoma supplies.

In the mid-1970s, a number of natural gas distributors were forced to curtail service to customers because of insufficient supplies. But supply positions subsequently improved, and by 1979, most were able to take on new customers. Throughout the 1980s, good demand growth should be forthcoming in both the residential and industrial sectors. Also helping earnings should be reasonable regulation by most state bodies and the Federal Energy Regulatory Commission.

It is also important to mention the impressive diversification efforts of many leading pipeline and distribution companies. Most have expanded into oil and gas exploration and some have already had impressive results. Tenneco, for example, has had an enviable success ratio. Other diversified activities encompass such areas as savings and loans and trucking. Synthetic fuels also hold long range promise.

Most industry members appeal to the conservative investor seeking a reasonably high yield and rising dividend income. Past dividend growth should be examined as a partial clue to future growth of payments. As a general rule, the less diversified the company the higher the yield, and the lower the dividend growth.

Telephone companies. These utilities are in a better position than most of their regulated colleagues. Although they are not completely immune to inflationary cost pressures, future capital needs are manageable. Since telephone companies generate 75 percent of their capital needs internally, they are not as interest rate–sensitive as the electric utilities, which raise only 40 percent of their needs from cash flow. Furthermore, costly pollution controls, customer conservation measures, and soaring fuel prices have not affected the communication companies. Earnings quality is generally high, reflecting more conservative accounting, the normalization of tax benefits, and limited allowance for funds used during construction.

Although telephone companies are dependent on favorable treatment on rates, improved industry fundamentals should lessen the amount of rate assistance needed in the future. In general, costs have been well controlled in the industry, while direct distance dialing and electronic switching equipment have provided more efficient operations and lower maintenance costs. Revenue growth has been accelerated by the increase in household formations and the installation of second phones, which have outpaced population growth.

American Telephone & Telegraph and its Bell System dominate the industry, servicing 83 percent of domestic telephones. The remaining 17 percent, or one out of six phones, is parceled out among about 1,600 independents. However, the four largest—General Telephone & Electronics, United Telecommunications, Continental Telephone, and Central Telephone & Utilities—service 75 percent of the non-Bell phones.

The independents cover the smaller but more rapidly growing rural and suburban sections, where phones are being added and toll usage is rising at a faster clip. Unlike Ma Bell, the independents are still permitted to make acquisitions, an important source of growth. The majors have been bolstering their financial standing vis-à-vis AT&T.

Those telephone companies with manufacturing arms are more sensitive to economic slowdowns than are the straight utility firms. They are also in greater jeopardy from the interconnect companies (those that make equipment for private use) and the specialized common carriers (voice and data transmission companies). The latter have received widespread support from the Federal Communications Commissions (FCC) and Congress. In fact, the overall industry trend has been toward increased competition, notably fostered by the FCC's terminal equipment deregulation order. Regulatory uncertainties make it difficult to assess the eventual impact to the industry. Regulation is not expected to be excessively damaging, although the analyst is well advised to watch the direction of future regulatory decisions. For those investors seeking income or who may already hold several electrics in their portfolios, the telephone utilities offer an appropriate investment alternative.

Chapter 26 Cashing in on the Future

A MODERN industrial economy, Free World style, is a constantly changing body. New industries emerge, and old industries disappear. Some regions advance, while others fall behind. Cities decline, and suburbs grow. The crucial industries that provide power and transportation undergo transformations.

Some sources of change in the economy are the result of legislation. Others may reflect influences like wars or weather changes. Many major changes, however, are generated within the system itself.

Many years ago, the Austrian-born economist Joseph A. Schumpeter identified the process of innovation as the primary source of internally generated change. In furthering understanding of the complexities of a modern economic society, the work of Professor Schumpeter, probably the most neglected of the great twentieth-century economists, has major contributions to make.

Dr. Schumpeter's first writing on the subject of innovation was published in 1911 in Germany. This work was not translated into English until 1934. In 1939, while at Harvard, Dr. Schumpeter expanded upon and further developed the ideas of his youth in a two-volume work called *Business Cycles*.

Innovation, in Dr. Schumpeter's system, takes four forms: the introduction of a new product, the utilization of new methods of production, the opening up of new sources of supply, and the development of new forms of business organization. Examples abound.

New-product innovation may be illustrated by such diverse examples as the automobile, the development of photography, the introduction of antibiotics, and the microwave oven.

New methods of production may be illustrated by developments in the steel industry, from the Bessemer process through the open-hearth furnace to the modern basic oxygen process. The jet engine powers airplanes by means superior to the internal combustion engine. Nuclear energy offers an alternative to water, coal, and oil in producing electricity.

New sources of supply as innovations are illustrated by oil from offshore wells or from Alaska, iron ore from Labrador, the irrigation of desert areas, and the procurement of electronic products from the Far East.

Finally, new forms of business organization may be legal, as in the case of the limited-liability corporation and the one-bank holding company, or functional, as in the case of the supermarket, the "full-service" bank, and the fast-food emporium.

Innovation Versus Invention

The business innovator or entrepreneur should be distinguished from the inventor. First, many innovations, such as the supermarket or the medical clinic, have little or nothing to do with invention. Also, the inventor's skills are likely to be of a mechanical or scientific nature. The innovator's strengths lie in the area of business organization and management. The innovator may start a new business, select a site, obtain the capital, hire the people, provide the raw materials, and sell the product. Like many inventions, a particular innovation may come to nothing, but the hallmark of successful innovation is the earning of profits.

The profits of innovation will attract new entrants into the field. Sometimes the competitors have to circumvent patents or copyrights, or attempt to offer a superior product. In other cases, entry may be possible by duplicating the activity elsewhere, say, in some other part of the ore or oil field. The entry of competitors will stimulate plant and equipment spending and increase output and employment. The increase in output will bring down prices and reduce profits. Eventually, the innovating industry becomes mature. Firms in the industry may attempt to sustain themselves by superior management, by consolidation, and by making minor innovative adaptations of the basic product.

The Effects of "Future Shock"

Superimposed over Dr. Schumpeter's ideas is the acceleration of change that has now reached such proportions that there is hardly anyone in our midst who can escape its effects. "Future shock," Alvin Toffler calls it in his 1970 book by the same name. Mr. Toffler's claims are hardly an exaggeration. Think of all that has been discovered, invented, produced, and experienced in the brief span of years we have been around. Today's 25-year-old will see more changes by his fiftieth birthday than today's 50-year-old has experienced since he was 25.

While all this is apparent and interesting, what is more to the point is how we can profit by this acceleration of change. Perhaps those among us with the imagination of Jules Verne find it easy to envision a world a quarter century into the future. But most of us are not such visionaries. Our feet and minds are firmly planted in the here and now; we think we're doing well if we can anticipate a week, a month, or a year ahead.

Given the limitations of our prophetic powers, perhaps we should turn to the past for some clues. What were the conditions that fostered the growth of such an industrial giant as International Business Machines? From its humble beginnings as a manufacturer of scales and cash registers in St. Louis, Missouri, in 1911, who could have foreseen its rise to a behemoth grossing close to $20 billion a year?

By 1954, when IBM marketed its first large-scale stored-program computer, it already had achieved a commendable growth record, with annual sales well over $400 million and net income approaching $50 million. To some analysts, who failed to comprehend what the future held for the computer, IBM was already a maturing company. Anyone venturing to buy ten shares of stock at that time —which would have cost less than $3,000—would have owned 363 shares worth almost $100,000 at the close of 1977.

The advent of transistors enabled IBM to market solid-state computers in 1960. Between then and the end of 1977, the stock moved up 280 percent. A ten-share purchase in 1960 at a cost of $5,000 would have increased by 1977 to 70 shares worth $19,000. In 1965, the plug-in compatible 360 Series was introduced; the value of the stock doubled between then and 1977. As this is written, IBM is moving heavily into automated business systems. Who knows how much an investment in IBM today might be worth tomorrow?

This success story has less to do with technical leadership—Sperry Rand beat IBM to the market with a large-scale computer—than with recognizing the product potential and creatively moving to capitalize on it. The leadership of Thomas J. Watson, the development of an outstanding marketing organization, and access to adequate financing were also major factors in the company's growth.

Why Some Companies Succeed

A study of IBM's modus operandi reveals a number of factors that contributed to the company's success. Early on, it established a strong position in the computer industry; by 1964, it had sold 75 percent of all computers in place at the time. It worked hard to build a solid customer relationship, providing programs, hardware, peripheral equipment, installation, and services. It nurtured strong customer loyalty, effectively disarming the competition. It built up a large base of future revenue by renting as well as selling its equipment. It worked to make its customers "dependent" by generating a steady stream of new products and supplies to operate, expand, and upgrade the old.

Xerox and Polaroid are other examples of companies that have capitalized on the "captive customer" situation by coming up with new products that consume company-produced supplies. American Telephone & Telegraph is another past master of this technique, supplying first the apparatus required to use the service, then providing the service, and finally creating broader and broader applications of that service. The lesson, then, is that you must not only find companies capable of producing goods and services for the next new era, but you must find companies with the imagination to provide for and capture the markets for those goods and services.

Watch for Trends

In any search for future profit opportunities, then, you must give thought to the changing trends of our society. For example, there has been a shift toward later marriage, fewer babies, and single-parent households. The increase in demand for energy-saving devices and supplies has created new areas of opportunity. People are working fewer hours. Women are working away from their homes.

Which are the industries that will benefit from these shifts and which will be hurt?

A classic example of a company that has felt the pinch of later marriages and the declining birth rate is Gerber: "Babies are our business—our only business." In a series of defensive maneuvers, Gerber has branched out into other, more adult areas and has quietly retired its long-standing slogan. Conversely, delayed marriages and more single-parent homes have tended to increase the demand for apartments, furnishings, and other consumer products. The upsurge of women in the work force has had a noticeable impact on the sale of convenience foods and on the growth of the fast-food business.

Another demographic change that is being felt in sundry ways is the increase in the number of people among us who are 60 years old and older. The Sun Belt states were the first to feel the effects of the older people in their midst. The population explosion in these areas has far outpaced growth in the more northern states as retirees flocked there to escape the cold. Longer life spans have been a boon to the life insurance companies, the leisuretime industry, extended-care nursing facilities, the broad spectrum of health care services, travel-related companies, and consumer products firms.

Profits in "Cleaning Up"

If there has been a "graying of America," there has also been a "greening of America." We as a nation have become aware of the finiteness of our environment and at last have begun to take big steps toward restoring and preserving it. Pollution control and environmental protection efforts have provided major opportunities for many companies. They will provide even more opportunities in the future, and investors who assess the winners most accurately stand to profit most handsomely.

This country will continue to serve as the world's breadbasket. Companies involved in "agribusiness"—the seed hybridizers, the pesticide manufacturers, and agricultural equipment companies—will be direct beneficiaries of efforts to provide sufficient food for a growing global population.

The Age of Consumerism will have its effects on business and investments. Some companies will feel a pinch never before felt as governmental involvement at all levels on behalf of consumers becomes ever more common. Other companies will be born to provide services in this area. Some companies will meet the new challenges with creativity and will wax; others will ignore the trends and will wane.

We've already alluded to the prospects for health services in the Age of Ageism. But the area should be singled out for some special consideration, for it represents a field containing a potentially bountiful harvest for the canny investor. Not only must products and services be made available for a population that is growing older, but they must be provided for one that is bent on remaining as young and healthy as possible for as long as possible. Ethical drugs, hospital supplies, medical appliances, and electronic diagnostic equipment all provide potential avenues for profitable investment. Governmental involvement in health care is certain to burgeon in the years ahead and will provide further stimulus to growth and, consequently, profits.

Cashing in on "Getting There"

We talked of Jules Verne at the start of this chapter. We're already well along into the space age, so we shouldn't give his brand of vision short shrift as we explore future areas of investment opportunity. A space shuttle has moved from the drawing board to test-flight status. How long before it is in scheduled service? Who will provide the vehicles? Who will fly them? The obvious beneficiaries will be the major aerospace companies and airlines. But what about the small subcontractors that provide the "working parts" and the ancillary services?

"People movers" of a more earthly variety will be important in the future, too. Mass transit is in the early stages of a major comeback. Someone has to supply the vehicles, someone has to build the tracks and roadbeds. Someone has to provide the capital and, in turn, reap the rewards for undertaking the risks. Again, major governmental involvement will help provide a ready market for these "products."

If future investment opportunities lie with major changes in transportation, so do they lie with the development of new energy sources. In fact, the future of energy looms so large that we have devoted all of the next chapter to it. Even so, it does not touch on the broad area of energy conservation, and the opportunities that lie with investments in that sector.

Some Guidelines

So now we get down to the real nub of this chapter. How do you break out of the rush of today's events so you can cash in on tomorrow's investment winners? From the foregoing brew, let's distill a few guidelines.

First, look for companies in the process of developing new products or new ways of doing things. Look for companies on the ascendancy in their fields, not those that have matured or passed into a declining phase or those entrenched in a mature industry.

Second, look for companies that have the managerial expertise necessary to capitalize on their innovations.

Third, examine the basic trends in our society. Look for the real changes in direction that are already occurring and that are likely to occur in the years ahead, based on what is happening today. Then, look for companies already positioned to take advantage of the trend.

Fourth, don't confuse a fad with a trend. We've already cautioned you to exercise diligence in distinguishing between a substantive change in cultural or economic direction and a passing fancy. Sometimes it's not easy to tell the difference, particularly at the outset. Once you have discerned a bona fide trend, and invested accordingly, keep an eye on your investment to be sure that conditions do not develop to jeopardize the trend or the position you have staked out in it.

Chapter 27 Investing in Energy for Tomorrow

JUST AS an army marches on its stomach, a modern industrial economy "marches" on its energy supply. Since petroleum is today's predominant source of energy, the companies that explore for and produce oil and natural gas play an important role in a country's economic growth, national defense, and balance of international payments. As a result, they are closely scrutinized by governments whose control over their activities has grown in past decades.

In the United States, policies relating to the "oils" often walk a rather narrow path between consumer interests and a powerful petroleum lobby in Washington. Oil and gas exploration incentives and deterrents come and go. Tax breaks are granted, then taken away. Pricing or import controls are here one day and gone the next. The political winds must be tested regularly for keys to the future operating environment for the oil producers.

The oil companies cheered President Carter's April 1979 decision (under powers granted to him by the Energy Policy and Conservation Act of 1975) to gradually release domestic oil prices to uncontrolled levels by October 1981. But the potential benefits of decontrol were substantially reduced by the subsequent passage of a windfall profit tax, which became effective March 1, 1980. Decontrol without a windfall tax would have brought producers $1 trillion over the 1980–1990 period, with their net being $442 billion. The tax will take $227 billion of that amount.

Nonetheless, those companies with considerable domestic reserves will still benefit from decontrol. Spending on exploration in the United States is slated to rise dramatically in coming years. One area drawing considerable interest is the Overthrust Belt in the Rocky Mountains, where such companies as Standard Oil of Indiana and Standard Oil of California are active. Oil companies generally have sturdy financial conditions and despite government encroachment into their affairs, they should continue to prosper.

Is There Really an Energy Crisis?

Not long after the first commercial oil discovery in the United States in 1859, fear surfaced that the well would soon run dry. In 1914, the Bureau of Mines estimated that total U.S. oil reserves would last less than twelve years. Other estimates by "responsible" agencies over the years have been woefully off the mark. So you certainly cannot be faulted for being somewhat cynical about "scare" projections based on the past record.

But things were changing in the early years of the 1970s, and they would never be the same again. Between 1948 and 1969 the wholesale price of refined petroleum products advanced only modestly, actually recording no net increase through 1964. The era of inexpensive energy was coming to a close, however. In 1970, U.S. production of crude oil hit a peak, and in 1973, after nearly twenty years of government involvement in pricing, natural gas output made its high. Then in the fall of 1973 and in 1974, the Organization of Petroleum Exporting Countries drove the final nails into the coffin of cheap and abundant oil, first by imposing a politically inspired embargo and then by quadrupling the price. Imports of foreign oil, however, did not subside. In fact, foreign oil increased from 26 percent of total U.S. consumption before the embargo to 47 percent in 1979—an alarming trend indeed both for the security of the country and its balance of payments. Truly, an energy crisis exists in the United States; only its exact nature and degree of seriousness are debatable. The outlook for companies able to provide answers to the energy dilemma seems exceptionally promising over the long term.

The government has become more determined to promote conservation of fuel and accelerate the switch to alternative energy sources in greater abundance—with particular emphasis on coal. Americans have a robust appetite for material benefits, and they will not quietly tolerate slower economic growth over the long run. The country's gross national product over the twenty years between 1956 and 1976 nearly doubled in real terms. Oil consumption has closely, and not coincidentally, paralleled this trend. Despite increased emphasis on conservation, our energy appetite is likely to remain healthy. While oil and natural gas may well account for a diminishing share of our energy supply, greater amounts of total energy will probably be needed in the years ahead.

Oils as Long-Term Investments

Despite their popularity, the oils remain controversial investments as investors wonder whether we really are running out of petroleum and whether the companies will have to find other income sources in order to survive. It is absolutely impossible to assess just how much oil and natural gas actually lie beneath the earth's surface awaiting discovery. Part of the difficulty in finding these supplies has come because pricing controls have stifled the incentive to explore and develop healthy industry reserves. The drilling process becomes increasingly expensive as companies are forced to drill deeper and go to more forbidding regions to find these fuels. Still, based on estimates of already proven oil and gas reserves, there is certainly enough to last at least until the end of this century.

On a value basis, then, these companies remain attractive long-term investments. Based on the present worth of the future earnings and dividends that oil and gas companies can generate from already "proven" reserves, many are undervalued. Even when future earnings potential is adjusted for the erosive effects of inflation, stock values have been considerably higher than market prices in recent times. Realistically speaking, therefore, these companies have excellent potential for many years to come.

Oil companies, however, have not been content to sit on their reserves. Most have been preparing for the day when petroleum resources will be of declining importance on their balance sheets. They have also become frustrated with a growing involvement by Washington in their activities—involvement that they say threatens their profitability and predisposition to reinvest funds in risky exploration efforts. Thus, as a defensive maneuver, most of these companies have been actively diversifying into alternative fuel sources such as coal and uranium. Today, for example, eight of the twenty largest coal companies are owned by major oils. Gulf Oil and Kerr-McGee hold significant uranium reserves. Conoco, Inc. owns the nation's second largest coal producer. Still other oils are moving into nonenergy areas; for example Mobil (Montgomery Ward and Container Corporation) and Sun Company (health care, shipbuilding).

What do these trends mean for the future of oil stocks? Those companies tied too tightly to the old ways of doing business, those, for instance, with heavy commitments to refineries and gasoline products, may be penalized. Their overhead costs threaten to remain high; and as oil production declines, profit margins could easily be squeezed. This is already happening to a certain extent; but a saving grace is the oil companies' healthy cash positions, which make possible reinvestment in new activities possessing high returns on capital. Analysis in the future will more and more require an assessment of the outlook for more fuels and activities than petroleum alone.

Natural Gas—the Ideal Fuel

Natural gas provides more than a quarter of this country's energy. Despite talk of potential shortages, a government study in 1977 determined that under higher (but not unreasonably higher) prices the country has at least 55 years' worth of natural gas left. Even more gas exists that would become economically feasible to extract at higher prices. For instance, researchers are exploring the commercial possibilities of extracting significant amounts of natural gas trapped in sea water in geopressurized zones of the Gulf of Mexico. By one estimate, there may be as much as 1,000 years' worth waiting to be taken. It is not unreasonable to expect that at higher prices such supplies might add substantially to our natural gas reserves. In addition, few people are aware of the substantial amounts of methane gas trapped in coal seams in the Appalachian Mountains that might be sufficient to provide fifteen years' worth of natural gas supply.

If any one fuel could be classified as "ideal" for heating and power generation, it undoubtedly would be natural gas. It is clean burning, easy to transport, and has been inexpensive relative to other fuels. Government involvement in the pricing of natural gas has existed since the mid-1950s. Natural gas is normally found along with petroleum in the exploration process. Frequently in the past, because of poor prices, it was flared off into the air rather than being used.

With the less rigid pricing constraints allowed in 1978, incentives to explore for natural gas were spurred. In addition, recovery of natural gas that previously was burned off became more economically viable. The future for liquefied natural gas likewise looked bright as methods of transporting it were improved.

Coal: A Sleeping Giant Awakens

In 1900, coal powered about 90 percent of the factories, homes, and machinery in the United States. By the late 1970s, this fuel satisfied only about 18 percent of our power needs, while making up an estimated 88 percent of our domestic energy reserves. To be sure, coal has its drawbacks. It is difficult and often dangerous to mine, it throws off sulfur and other pollutants when burned, and it is often found far from the consuming market. But it is abundant, relatively inexpensive, and offers the most immediate answer to the country's energy problem.

Coal's immediate role is to bridge the gap between the conventional fuels of the 1970s and the more exotic ones that will power the economy of the next century. Its function, however, may turn out to be more than transitory. There already has been dramatic progress toward the development of successful commercial synthetic fuels from coal.

Coal production is expected to reach about one billion tons by 1985, versus 680 million in 1976. The strongest demand will come from electric utilities. They will require greater amounts of coal to meet an ever rising demand for energy and to service a growing number of newly constructed and planned coal-fired power plants, as well as plants converted from oil to coal.

Coal stocks are basically long-term investments. Their prices may experience ups and downs in the short run, but the basic trend should reward investors who are patient. For the most part, the coal held by these companies is valued at the low acquisition costs of many years ago. Book values thus are often substantially understated.

The composition of the industry makes pure investment in coal very difficult. Coal companies have been acquired in great numbers by larger companies, particularly oils, steels, and conglomerates, seeking to gain a foothold in an industry in which they see considerable potential. Carbon Industries, for instance, was purchased by International Telephone and Telegraph, and Utah International by General Electric. Still, there are independents that are certain to share in the long-term growth of the industry. Mapco owns and sells almost exclusively steam coal to utilities from its nonunion mines. Eastern Gas & Fuel and Westmoreland both produce about equal amounts of steam and metallurgical coal. They have huge reserves of generally good quality coal which is destined to become even more valuable in the years ahead.

Squeezing Oil from Rocks and Tar Sands

One source of oil that will become more economically feasible as the easily extracted supplies become even scarcer is shale. Geologists estimate that oil shale rocks in this country may hold 23 times the amount of regular crude oil now in proven reserves. Excellent progress has been made on various processes by which oil and gas are cooked out of the shale without removing the rock from the ground. Perfection of this technique would be a major step forward, for disposal of waste rock has been one of the biggest stumbling blocks to this type of extraction.

But there are other problems, too. Many of the most promising deposits are under land tied up by old disputed mining claims. Other delays will be encountered in obtaining leases from the federal government, which owns 75 percent of the shale oil lands. Lack of water for processing and for employee living quarters is yet another limiting factor. Despite these difficulties, oil shale holds great promise, so the problems should eventually be solved.

Another source of synthetic crude oil that we will be hearing more about in the future is oil from tar sands. This requires an even more difficult processing than the extraction from shale. One of the world's major secondary oil sources—considered only slightly smaller than the huge Mideast deposits—is the Athabasca tar sands in northwestern Canada. The processing of crude oil from these sands is expensive, though with world oil prices continuing to move higher, tar sand efforts should pay off much more satisfactorily. Companies like Cities Service, Imperial Oil, and Gulf Oil of Canada Ltd. think so. They have invested more than $2 billion in a tar sands plant that should eventually be producing 129,000 barrels of synthetic crude a day. While this is a minute portion of the world's energy consumption, it is a start.

Geothermal Interest Heats Up

Oil companies have been among those in the forefront of development of geothermal energy, the planet's inner heat. Huge reservoirs of steam deep under the earth's surface can generate power if properly tapped. Such a system is already in use on the West Coast, and geothermal power accounts for 6 percent of Pacific Gas & Electric's output. Energy derived from the project would be sufficient for a city the size of San Francisco, and power generation costs are expected to come in slightly below those of fossil fuels or nuclear power. Smaller, more speculative ventures are also being developed.

Energy from the Atom

In the early 1970s, nuclear power was being hailed as a major answer to our future energy needs. Since then, however, the nuclear industry has been stymied by environmental concerns, licensing delays, and utility plant construction cutbacks in the face of declining electricity demand.

The issue of nuclear-waste disposal is one of the thorniest problems confronting the industry. The Carter administration issued a prohibition on spent fuel reprocessing, since it would produce material that could be used to make atomic bombs. Currently, the fuel is accumulating in storage facilities at plant sites, but most of these pools will be filled by 1985. Storage facilities away from the reactor site are unpopular.

Sharply increasing the anti-nuclear sentiment in this country was the March 1979 accident at General Public Utilities' Three Mile Island plant in Pennsylvania. Shortly after the accident, the Nuclear Regulatory Commission placed a moratorium on the issuance of new licenses. A host of local organizations dedicated to preventing the spread of nuclear power sprang up across the country.

Nevertheless, nuclear power seems a necessary part of our energy future. Exxon estimates that this source will furnish 13 percent of our needs in the year 2000, versus 5 percent in 1980.

The Solar Age Is upon Us

It would be hard to deny that the solar age is here. More than 200 companies now have a stake in it. That the field is also in its infancy is equally apparent. More than 54 quadrillion BTUs of energy (excluding fuel used for transportation) are consumed in this country every year. Yet, more than 90 percent of them are generated by finite exhaustible fossil fuels. Although some experts predict that the sun will supply 7 percent of our needs by the year 2000, others say this is an optimistic estimate. But with our finite fuels fast vanishing, development of a new, inexhaustible energy source such as solar power becomes increasingly necessary.

The solar industry is attracting the capital of a number of large corporations. About half of the top 25 solar companies in the United States are currently owned or controlled by corporations with more than $1 billion in annual sales. Exxon, for example, has a subsidiary that makes solar water heaters, and another that accounts for about one fifth of the world's production of solar electric cells. General Electric is committing funds to such areas as solar heating systems for commercial and industrial uses, solar electric cells, and solar storage systems.

Other large companies with a stake in this area include Grumman Corporation, General Motors, and Westinghouse. Of course, it is unlikely that solar-related activities will have a significant impact on the earnings of these larger concerns in the foreseeable future.

Using solar cells to convert sunlight to electricity has been done commercially for many years. Cadmium sulfide cells that give off low energy impulses regulate street lights and other day-night lights. However, these cells have a low efficiency level, making electricity generated by them costly. Gallium arsenide and silicon are also being used to manufacture solar cells. Each has its proponents, but generating costs are still prohibitive.

Once the cost of solar cells and energy storage has been reduced, solar power generation will become more attractive than the conventional power plant on the basis of weight and structural costs.

Efficiency ratios and costs per watt generated are still major stumbling blocks.

For the present and the immediate future, probably the greatest profit center will be in the marketing of residential solar water heaters. A solar hot-water system costs about $1,800 to install. Both the Department of Energy and the Department of Housing and Urban Development are committed to promoting the installation of these systems, and tax credits are available to homeowners who install them. Solar heating systems are larger and more costly, and a conventional heating system is still needed for long periods of cloudy weather. Thus they will likely take longer to achieve widespread acceptance.

Summing Up

In general, American enterprise has responded to natural market forces as well as to policies emanating from Washington to begin changing the makeup of the total U.S. energy picture. In the last quarter of the twentieth century, the mix of fuels will clearly change. This is how Exxon Corporation projected that mix for the year 1990, compared with what it actually was in 1980:

Sources of U.S. Energy Supply

	1980	1990	Change
Oil	46%	39%	−7%
Gas	27	22	−5
Coal	19	26	+7
Nuclear	4	9	+5
Hydro/Geothermal	4	4	0
	100%	100%	

It seems quite likely that the major energy companies are capable of responding to the challenge while continuing to enjoy a worthwhile return on their investment. Patient investors who choose wisely should have no qualms about staking out a position in energy.

Chapter 28 Where to Get Advice

"WHERE DO I get investment advice?" That's a difficult question to answer, because the answer depends on what kind of advice you expect to get. If you want panaceas, secrets to sure-fire success, or that one key that unlocks all the mysteries of the stock market, you'll find them aplenty; they litter the road of broken investment dreams. You need but ask—friends, relatives, passersby in the street—and you will be deluged with all manner of theories, explanations, and "wisdom." It is no wonder that a new investor so often finds himself reeling under the barrage of information and opinion available. The intelligent and experienced investor who has delineated his investment objectives stands a better chance of obtaining usable advice. He has been around long enough to know the superficial, appreciate the possible, and recognize the charlatan. For the novice, this chapter attempts to highlight the major categories and sources of investment information.

Some investment sources present facts only and leave interpretation to the reader, while others provide an interpretation of the facts and specific advice. Most investors, without substantial time to devote to the formulation of their portfolios, prefer the latter. No matter what sources you choose, the most important prerequisite for successful investing is the formulation of a specific goal. The retiree, dependent on his dividends for "eating money," should think twice before acting on a speculative recommendation, no matter how reliable he perceives the source to be.

Your Broker and the Bank

Your broker can provide good information if he has a large research department to back him up. Many sizable houses publish market letters as well as company and industry studies. Much of the literature put out by investment houses is available to clients free of charge. Some will analyze a portfolio and make suggestions in line with a given investment objective. An important caveat to keep in mind, however, is that brokers survive on commissions, and thus are under pressure to advise change. If you are not an aggressive trader, watch out for excessive switch recommendations.

Many banks also offer a number of services. The simplest is a custodial arrangement under which the bank maintains physical care of the securities, keeps accounting records, and executes transactions at the owner's request. No advice is included. Some banks offer more extensive services, ranging from periodic portfolio reviews and recommendations to continuous supervision. Most banks tend to be conservative in their recommendations and thus are not really appropriate advisers for the aggressive speculator.

Standard & Poor's and Moody's

Two financial publishing firms, Standard & Poor's and Moody's, are in a class by themselves. Both offer a wide range of services. Standard & Poor's provides more than a dozen—from *Corporation Records*, which includes factual descriptions of all important corporate and many public issuers of both listed and unlisted securities, to *The Outlook*, a weekly advisory letter. Especially valuable services for the individual investor are the monthly paperback *Stock Guide* and *Bond Guide*. The *Stock Guide* shows earnings, dividends, yield, capital structure, working capital, and market price data. The *Bond Guide* gives ratings, interest dates, form (bearer or registered), redemption provisions, earnings, prices, and both current yields and yields to maturity. Occasionally brokers and dealers distribute these to active customers free of charge.

Moody's publishes large reference volumes on listed industrials, over-the-counter industrials, utilities, Governments, and financial companies. It also offers numerous other services, including a weekly *Bond Survey*. Moody's and S&P are the major rating agencies for corporate and municipal debt offerings. Most of their publications are relatively expensive but are available in major university and public libraries.

Advisory Services

Advisory services vary widely in their scope and slant. Some rely on technical factors and try to gauge the likely short-term movement of the market as a whole and of individual securities. Others recommend fundamentally strong companies with only secondary emphasis on the near-term outlook for the market. Some seem consistently to presage doom; others tend to look mainly on the bright side.

The *Value Line Investment Survey,* one of the larger and better-known advisory services, covers more than 1,600 stocks. Each stock in the list is reviewed comprehensively every three months, and each week the service covers four to six industries on a rotating basis. Stocks are rated for safety and expected performance. The service each week also covers the outlook for the stock market and the economy, and highlights certain individual stocks. Sometimes other special studies are included. The service is relatively expensive, and is available in many libraries.

The weekly *United Business & Investment Report* is among the oldest and largest of these services. It presents a concise summary of economic and business news, and includes a page about commodity price trends, as well as industry or topical studies and specific buying and selling advice on individual securities. In the first issue of each month, it publishes a supervised list of common stocks divided by investment objective. It is generally up-beat, and steers its clients toward quality and investment for the longer term. Consultation privileges are included in the cost of a subscription.

Standard & Poor's *Outlook,* which we mentioned earlier, is another of the larger and better-known investment letters. It plots an investment course similar to United's, though its content is more fully devoted to securities investment rather than including broader commentary on economic, business, and financial affairs, as does United's.

Countless other advisory publications are available, many of which are general in nature, such as *Indicator Digest.* Still others embrace particular investment philosophies. These include the *Dow Theory Forecasts,* which uses the Dow Theory as its springboard; *The Dines Letter,* which follows gold and gold-related securities closely; *The*

Speculator, which advises on stocks selling for $20 or less; and *Growth Stock Outlook,* which recommends stocks it thinks hold high appreciation prospects.

Many of the services on the market are one-person, one-typewriter affairs. The Investment Advisors Act of 1940 requires all such advisers to be registered with the Securities and Exchange Commission. However, the registration is designed to guard against fraud; it does not indicate any particular expertise or guarantee favorable results.

We should mention here another type of service available: chart books. Although their publishers generally do not provide specific investment advisories, their products can be useful in showing you past performances and price, earnings, and dividend trends of various stocks. Such charts are particularly helpful in discerning technical market trends. Securities Research Company, a division of United Business Service, publishes monthly security charts and quarterly *Cycli-Graphs,* as well as quarterly wall charts. Daily Graphs, R. W. Mansfield Company, and Trendline provide similar services.

Before leaving the realm of advisory services, some mention of the sources of information available to the mutual fund investor is in order. *The Wiesenberger Investment Company Service,* published by Warren, Gorham & Lamont, provides an annual compendium of information about mutual funds and investment companies, an explanation of their functions, and their various uses to the investor. Data are included on the background, management policy, and salient features of all leading companies, including income and dividend records, price ranges, and comparative operating details. Again, this publication is relatively expensive and often available at your library.

A valuable statistical source on the fund industry as a whole is the *Mutual Fund Fact Book,* updated annually by the Investment Company Institute, 1775 K Street, Northwest, Washington, D.C. 20006.

The *United Mutual Fund Selector* provides a wealth of information on mutual funds. Published twice monthly by United Business Service, the *Selector* in one issue provides comparative tables that track the recent and longer-term performance of more than four hundred funds. The other issue includes a supervised list of mutual funds and provides specific recommendations in line with different objectives. Every issue contains general features about the industry, detailed discussions of certain funds, and investors' questions and answers.

The Financial Press

The financial press is brimming with valuable information. Most daily newspapers provide some sort of financial section, which generally includes price quotations as well as business highlights and sometimes commentary. *The Wall Street Journal,* the only national daily business and financial newspaper, provides much more extensive coverage of financial news, including, in addition to comprehensive price quotations, news about companies, industries, commodities, financial affairs, taxes, labor, and public policy. *The New York Times* publishes a comprehensive business and financial section daily. *The Journal of Commerce* is an excellent resource for the commodity investor, and also includes extensive business news, with emphasis on national and international economic developments.

The Media General Financial Weekly Market Digest is a compendium of financial facts and statistics providing coverage of stocks, bonds, mutual funds, options, and commodities. Also included is a digest of major money market instruments. The stock and bond tables are especially helpful. The stock tables provide at-a-glance data on individual companies' price trends relative to the market, five-year compound-earnings-per-share growth, profit margins, price relative to industry, dividend data, the composition of shareholders, and pertinent data on the company's financial position. The bond tables provide S&P ratings, conversion terms (if applicable), current yields, and yields to maturity.

The weekly *Commercial and Financial Chronicle* is a combination magazine and newspaper. One section provides articles on business and financial affairs, with emphasis on public policy. The second provides extensive statistical information on the stock market and individual companies.

Barron's, published weekly by Dow Jones & Company, provides a good wrap-up of the preceding week's economic and stock market happenings. It includes an extensive section on stock and bond quotations and economic and market statistics, in addition to timely articles on various companies, current economic events, and a section on commodities. Editorial commentary is liberally interjected.

Magazines

Numerous magazines available on the newsstand or by subscription can provide up-to-date information. *Financial World, Forbes, Business Week, Fortune,* and *U.S. News & World Report* are examples. *Financial World* and *Forbes* are more heavily weighted with investment news; the others deal more with general business topics. For investors with a strong interest in a particular industry, there are trade journals such as *Supermarket News* and *Women's Wear Daily.*

Government Publications

U.S. government publications can yield clues to economic trends that might affect the investment climate. *Business Conditions Digest* provides data on the cyclical indicators—leading, coinciding, and lagging (see Chapter 19). *Economic Indicators* is a monthly compendium of statistics on gross national product, employment, production, prices, money and credit, federal finance, and international trade. The *Survey of Current Business* is another comprehensive statistical source that includes detailed commentary on various economic subjects. The Federal Reserve Bank of St. Louis publishes *Monetary Trends* and other excellent bulletins on the money supply and interest rates, available at no cost. For labor and employment trends and developments, there is the *Monthly Labor Review,* published by the Department of Labor. Many of these publications may be available at your local library.

Investment Counselors

For the well-to-do investor who wishes to leave the research and decision-making to someone else, there are investment counseling firms. Their annual fee, as a rule of thumb, will run 0.5 percent of the value of the portfolio being managed. Most firms handle large accounts only, those valued at $100,000 and up. They provide in-depth investment advice, watch your portfolio continuously, and notify you when they believe changes should be made. Major companies in this category include Scudder, Stevens & Clark; Loomis Sayles; and United Investment Counsel, a subsidiary of United Business Service.

A number of small investment counseling companies do handle accounts of less than $100,000, but they generally either pool funds or restrict portfolios to stocks on a master list. Thus, technically, their counsel is not individualized. The annual fee is usually 0.5 percent on the managed assets, with a minimum in the vicinity of $200. Danforth Associates is an example of a company providing such services.

There you have it, a sampling of the wide spectrum of investment advice and information available to you. With experience, you'll be able to tell how much digging you want to do on your own, how much you're willing to pay others to dig for you, and whose advice best suits your own investment needs and philosophy.

Part IV MASTERING THE STRATEGIES AND TACTICS

Chapter 29 **Five Rules for Investors**

UNTIL NOW, the focus of this book has largely been on the definition and analysis of various savings and investment vehicles. Now it's time to start applying this body of information to the construction and maintenance of your own program. As with any other undertaking, you will be well begun if you set down some rules ahead of time.

We have five that tend to crystallize the investment philosophy we at United Business Service have pursued for more than half a century. We believe they will serve you well, too. After reading our earlier chapters, you should find none of them surprising.

The thoughts have all been expressed at least once before in this book; some will be expressed again. By bringing them together here, we provide a yardstick against which you can measure future investment decisions. Read them carefully. Commit them to memory. Recite them whenever you have an investment decision to make. If you are a compulsive investor, tempted by every hot tip that comes your way, tattoo them to the back of your hand. Ignore them at your peril.

The five: Set your goals. Buy the best-known companies. Invest for the long term. Avoid fads. Diversify.

Set Your Goals

Rule number one. Decide what you want your savings to do for you. You wouldn't buy long underwear for a trip to the Bahamas; neither would you travel by way of the Yukon when you finally set out. But you'd be surprised at how many investors pack their portfolios with inappropriate garb and travel needlessly circuitous routes to their investment destinations.

Before you plunge into your savings and investment program, sit down and list your objectives on paper. College education for the children? How long before they'll need it? How much will they need? Retirement fund for yourself? When will you want to start drawing on it? Next year? Three years from now? Trip to Europe? New car? Emergency fund?

The answers to these questions are important, for they will determine whether you should invest for capital growth or current income. Most of the time you will have to accept one or the other. Rare indeed is the investment that offers a generous helping of both. The answers, too, will tell you how much risk you can reasonably assume—and which type of risk.

Suppose you're a mid-career salaried individual who can divert regular amounts of income from your family's spending stream to savings. Your aim is a retirement fund to supplement your company's pension. As with most of us who labor in the corporate vineyard, the Internal Revenue Service enjoys a generous share of your income. Since you're already earning enough so you can set some aside, and since your objective is relatively long term, there's no reason for you to shoot for investment income now. It would only have to be shared with Uncle Sam. What you want is capital growth and little or no current income.

Furthermore, since you have a secure job and considerable time before retirement, you're in a position to assume some market risk in the chance of making better-than-average capital gains. That's because if you should lose, you would still be in a good position to replace those lost dollars from regular earned income. So you concentrate your investment efforts on building a portfolio of growth stocks.

Now, suppose you have a maiden aunt in her middle years whose pay just barely covers her needs. Let's further suppose that she inherits or otherwise comes into a $25,000 windfall. Not only is this a sum larger than anything she had ever known before, but it is a bit of fortune that is not likely to be repeated.

What should she do? Her first objective would be to preserve that capital, since her ability to replace it is negligible. So she chooses investments that will provide the highest possible current return and the greatest possible "safety." Savings certificates and bonds, both corporate and government, spring immediately to mind. But there are common stocks that fit the description, too, that would provide some chance for dividend growth and capital appreciation at minimal risk to her nest egg, all the while giving her a substantial current return which, of course, she immediately reinvests.

Your uncle the doctor, his children through college, his retirement approaching, would take still another tack. He would have to re-evaluate his investment program, gradually shifting it from the growth orientation of earlier years to an income orientation to provide his "eating money" in retirement. Again, because his working years are drawing to a close, he would have to concentrate on preservation of principal, since his opportunities for replacing it are fast closing.

The doctor's case illustrates another point you should keep firmly in mind. Your investment goals can—and usually do—change as you proceed through life. Therefore, you should subject your program to periodic review to see that its objectives remain consistent with your needs.

Buy the Best-Known Companies

Rule number two. Buy the best-known companies. Stick with the tried and true. There is far too much risk in trying to unearth tomorrow's Xeroxes. The mortality rate of these ventures is staggering, and you'd do best to leave this kind of financial wildcatting to someone else.

There are plenty of firmly established companies around that offer attractive investment possibilities. American Hospital Supply, IBM, and Schlumberger still can add zip to a portfolio despite their maturity.

There are promising lesser lights like EG&G, Inc., MAPCO, Inc., and Warner Communications with good survival records despite the vagaries of the economy and the stock market. They have been in business for a long time, their products are well known, their markets firmly established, and their financial condition solid. They're not necessarily blue chips. Some, in fact, have a clearly speculative tint. But because they have demonstrated an ability to survive, they should not be overlooked.

Equally important, their stock prices are reasonable in relation to such fundamentals as assets, earnings, and dividends. In short, there are plenty of attractive, reasonable investments that offer the promise of real and substantial profit someday for the investor who can take the risk.

Invest for the Long Term

Rule number three. Invest for the long term. Patience with the stock market is more than a virtue. It is a must. Things rarely work out overnight on Wall Street; and when they do, almost everyone is taken by surprise. So, when you buy a good stock, buy it for the long pull. Consider yourself a part owner of the business. You have become one because you believe the business is fundamentally sound and the prospects excellent. Therefore, you don't have to watch the daily gyrations in your stock's price with fear in your throat when it is down and exultation in your soul when it is up.

Take Burroughs, which we mentioned earlier in the book. The investors who bought the stock in the late 1950s and early 1960s were motivated by the company's movement into the computer field. The stock had long been a so-so performer, reflecting quite accurately the humdrum existence of an adding machine maker. When Burroughs moved into computers for banks and other financial institutions, it was also hurtling headlong toward a clash with supergiant IBM. So there was considerable risk that it would not succeed in the venture.

The stock bumbled along for several years, and investors might have been excused if they had bailed out. But in the mid-1960s, earnings finally turned higher, and so did the stock. By the mid-1970s, a dozen or so years after its initial foray into computers, patient investors were enjoying a gain of 1,500 percent.

The key was patience. Those who waited prospered. Those who wanted instant rewards lost out, as they usually do in the stock market.

It might help you to develop patience if you think of your commitment in a stock as you do your investment in your own home. You bought your house to fill a specific need after applying certain qualifying tests. As long as your living requirements remain the same and nothing seriously wrong develops with the structure or the neighborhood, you stay put.

You don't regularly check with your real estate broker for the current value of your home, and you shouldn't need to be constantly concerned with the day-to-day price fluctuations of your stocks. Even if you read in the real estate section of the Sunday newspaper that "Home Values Slump as Mortgage Money Tightens," you don't rush out and sell. You realize any such slippage in price will be temporary. Think long term with your stocks just as you do with your home.

Avoid Fads

Rule number four. Avoid fads. Stay clear of the crowd, even when it looks right. This is one of the most important rules of successful investing—and one of the most frequently violated, to the ultimate chagrin of legions of hapless violators. If everyone seems to be rushing out to buy stocks in a particular industry group or company, let them. But don't do it yourself. If a particular stock seems to be the darling of the day, don't compete. Let the others have it.

Fads come and go on Wall Street just as they do on Madison Avenue or Seventh Avenue or Main Street U.S.A. One big trouble with fads is that it's sometimes hard to tell when something is just that—a passing fancy—or if it's truly a technological or sociological breakthrough and represents something that will become a fixture in our everyday lives. The distinction is particularly difficult to make in the early stages, when the temptation is greatest to "get in on the ground floor."

Who could have foretold, for instance, back in the 1950s that a photocopying device being toyed with by a little firm known as the Haloid Company out of Rochester, New York, would change the lives of nearly all of us and in the process firmly affix the word "Xerox" in our lexicon? The spectacular success of that xerographic photocopier made fortunes for its supporters, some of whom, corporate legend tells us, included cab drivers and bartenders.

Or, who could have known that an instant-picture camera developed by Dr. Edward Land would catapult a manufacturer of polarized-lens sunglasses to the forefront of American industry in the days following World War II? Investors in Polaroid in those days were surely involved in a gamble. They won, and some of them won big.

But for each of those two legendary corporate successes, how many "hot ideas" have failed, leaving their gamble-oriented investors holding the bag? More to the point, how can you—or anyone— separate the Xeroxes and Polaroids from the failures? The plain fact is that few can. And since your chances of riding a loser are tens or hundreds of times greater than climbing aboard a winner, you'd do best to let the out-and-out gamblers play those odds. There will be ample opportunity for reaping substantial returns from the winners once they have become established, as thousands of investors in Xerox and Polaroid have learned over the years.

Consider those who perceived a great new day as digital time- pieces began to replace the world's conventional wristwatches and invested accordingly. The watches caught on all right, but electron- ics companies thronged to that marketplace in such numbers that many fell helplessly aside and were trampled in the stampede, their backers with them. The industry is more stable now that the shake- out has occurred, and investors have a better chance to see which ones will provide the best long-term prospects. The same thing happened with pocket calculators, double knits, and citizens' band radios. It will happen again with something else. And again. And again.

It sometimes happens with the stock of an established company. A new product or new process is announced, and before its true market worth has been established, eager investors are beating a path to their brokers' offices to grab a piece of the action. Remember when Bausch & Lomb announced the soft plastic contact lens back in the early 1970s? The stock shot up in anticipation of a surge in sales. Complications set in and the "surge" was disappointing. The stock settled back into its previous mundane pattern.

When such a situation develops, the stock's price eventually rises above its intrinsic value and the "greater fool" theory takes over. Those who play that game purchase shares in the hope of eventually selling at a profit to a "greater fool." Pity the "greatest fool"—the one finally left holding the bag. That is not a risk with which you need burden yourself.

Diversify

Rule number five. Diversify. Spread your risks, for few "sure things" prove to be such. Someone once said that the way to make money is to put all your eggs in one basket and then watch that basket like a hawk. That's fine, as long as the stock you choose soars; as it does, so will your fortunes. The corollary, of course, is that if the stock plummets instead, your fortunes vanish. Even if you know a company intimately and its industry inside out, you still stand to lose, for luck is very much a part of the game. Too many things can happen that no amount of research will foretell.

Take the Equity Funding case. The best analysts in the investment business had not uncovered the fact that the company was manufacturing bogus insurance policies. After all, its financial reports had the seal of approval from one of the most respected accounting firms.

When it all unraveled after an insurance analyst named Raymond Dirks happened onto the situation in April 1973, stories abounded of people who had used Equity Funding as their basket. One was a 70-year-old New York woman, retired, living in a tiny apartment. She had put her all, $7,000, in the stock. When the company went down, so did her life's savings, the result of 55 years of hard work. Across the Hudson River, an elderly father refused to retire despite his failing health. His wife and son could not understand, and he could not bring himself to tell them that his retirement fund was gone. He had put his $25,000 into 9.5 percent Equity Funding bonds. A Nebraska couple had borrowed on their assets and bought Equity Funding common in the hope that the wonder stock's fast-rising price would turn their modest savings into a large enough sum to buy their son some badly needed medical attention. When the bubble burst, so did their hopes.

The lesson is clear. Even if you have only a little to invest, spread it around. Diversify your holdings to reduce the overall risk. If one element in your portfolio goes sour, the others should hold it up.

There are several ways to do it. One, of course, is to buy securities of a variety of companies. By choosing well-diversified firms you can spread the risk even further. Or you can buy mutual funds. Even here, you should diversify, buying several different funds.

Besides diversifying as to companies and funds, be sure to spread your investments over a number of different industries as well. Look for promising industries, though; don't buy into a dead-end field just for the sake of diversifying.

Your diversification will likely restrict your portfolio to an "average" or even "mediocre" performance. You will miss the thrill of instant riches. So also will you avoid sudden financial disaster. But you will sleep better at night.

So there you have the five key rules for successful investing. Here they are again, all in one place for your quick review:

1. Set your goals.
2. Buy the best-known companies.
3. Invest for the long term.
4. Avoid fads.
5. Diversify.

Chapter 30 How the "Stock Market" Works

ONCE YOU have set your investment objectives and promised yourself to stick with the best companies, be patient, avoid fads, and diversify your holdings—that is, to abide by the five rules outlined in the preceding chapter—you're ready to start polishing your investment techniques. An understanding of the basic workings of the stock market and of your buying and selling choices within that framework is essential to your mastery of successful investing.

To provide that background, we shall discuss briefly in this chapter the various securities markets, the major stock exchanges, the types of orders you can use in executing your buys and sells, and, finally, some important considerations regarding the timing of your buying and selling.

The Role of Investment Bankers

When a company originally offers new securities for sale, it does so through the *primary markets*. In recent times, the primary market has been largely a bond market, with relatively few new common stock issues being offered. Securities are sold in the primary market either through private placement or public offering. In either case, the details are usually handled by investment bankers. Private placement is a choice made by the company for a variety of reasons; privacy, economy, and circumvention of certain registration requirements are the most common. Since there is no public participation in private placement, nothing more need be said about it here.

On public issues, investment bankers use three basic methods of bringing the securities to market: standby agreements, agency marketings, and purchasing-distributions. *Standby agreements* are usually employed when companies seek to sell more stock or bonds to their own security holders by way of a "rights" offering. Since most

317

of the rights will be exercised, there is little market risk to the investment banker handling the details. But since the company wants all of the capital from the issue as soon as possible, it arranges with the banker to buy up any rights that are not exercised. The investment banker, in turn, will market those securities to the public.

The *agency marketing* procedure is used when the investment bankers perceive some difficulty in marketing an issue, either because of its size or because of its doubtful reception by the public. Or, it might be employed because the issuing company is confident that the issue will sell and there is little marketing risk involved. In this instance, the banker may take an issue on a "best effort" basis. The bank will receive a commission on that portion of the issue which it makes its "best effort" to sell, but it does not actually buy the issue itself for resale. In effect, the banker merely serves as the "broker," seeking to match buyer and seller.

However, most of an investment banker's business comes from *purchasing-distribution,* where the banker buys the entire issue outright and resells it to the public. The banker then assumes the marketing risk associated with the underwriting. Sometimes a syndicate of underwriters is formed so that no single firm assumes full risk on the issue.

When you as an individual investor buy original issue securities, you pay no commission on them; the fee has already been worked into the selling price. However, you are more likely to be buying "previously owned" securities than new issues. In that case, and likewise when you yourself sell any securities you hold, you'll be dealing in the *secondary market.* Trading in existing securities occurs in the organized exchanges and the over-the-counter markets.

The organized exchanges are actually auctions where traders and investors negotiate by setting "asking" prices and making "bids" on thousands of different securities. The New York Stock Exchange (NYSE) is by far the most important of these trading centers. It is followed in order of importance by the American Stock Exchange (AMEX), the Midwest Stock Exchange (MW), the Pacific Stock Exchange (PS), and the Philadelphia Stock Exchange (P).

The New York Stock Exchange

The New York Stock Exchange was formally established in 1792, though it was not known by its present name until 1863. Often called the "Big Board," it is a corporation with more than 1,200 members, each of whom has purchased a "seat" (membership) on the exchange. This membership gives its holder the privilege of trading on the floor of the exchange; no one else is allowed to do so. Members of the NYSE include member-firm corporations, specialists, floor brokers, and registered traders. Each type of membership is designed and regulated to assure the continuation of an efficient, liquid market.

Member firms are the various brokerage houses that do commission business with the public. Their seats are usually filled by general partners or holders of substantial amounts of common stock in the firm.

Specialists are the exchange members responsible for maintaining orderly markets in the stocks of specific companies. Each of the more than 1,500 stocks listed on the NYSE is assigned to a specialist. Each specialist rides herd on a number of these assigned stocks, making sure to avoid excessive spread in the bid and asked prices in the auctioning process. In maintaining an orderly market for their assigned securities, the specialists may buy and sell for their own accounts. Their operations are governed by the statutes and regulations of the Securities and Exchange Commission (SEC) and the exchange itself. In addition, specialists execute orders which other exchange members have left with them. In this capacity, they are acting as brokers or agents.

Floor brokers help commission brokers when they become swamped with orders to execute. In this way, they protect the customer against the possibility of missing a market because of an overburdened stockbroker.

Registered traders buy and sell stocks strictly for their own personal accounts. The activities of these traders are monitored by the exchange, which requires that their transactions contribute to the market's liquidity. As this is written, the SEC is considering the elimination of registered traders.

In order for a stock to be listed on the New York Stock Exchange, certain criteria must be met and maintained. Among them: a demonstrated earning power of at least $2.5 million annually before taxes for the most recent year and $2 million for each of the two preceding years under competitive conditions; net tangible assets of $16 million, though greater emphasis will be placed upon the aggregate market value of the common stock; at least $16 million in market value of publicly held common stock; at least one million common shares publicly held; at least 2,000 holders of 100 shares or more.

The listing agreement between the New York Stock Exchange and the company is designed to assure timely disclosure to the public of earnings statements, dividend notices, and other data which can affect security values and hence investment decisions. A company is not guaranteed continued listing on the exchange.

AMEX and the Regional Exchanges

The American Stock Exchange had its start in the 1850s, though it was not known by its present name until 1953. Before that, its name was the New York Curb Exchange, reflecting its earlier history, when trading was done outdoors at a number of New York City street corners. The Curb Market moved indoors at Trinity Place in 1921.

The AMEX follows procedures much like the New York Stock Exchange, although listing requirements are not as stringent as those of the NYSE. As a general statement, it can be said that companies traded on the AMEX are less mature and seasoned than those on the NYSE.

The principal regional exchanges are the Midwest Stock Exchange, the Pacific Stock Exchange, and the Philadelphia Stock Exchange. Altogether, there are nine domestic stock exchanges outside of New York City. In addition to the three already noted, there are exchanges in Boston, Cincinnati, Honolulu, Chicago (the Board of Trade), Salt Lake City (Intermountain), and Spokane. Besides these, five Canadian exchanges actively trade mining, uranium, and oil stocks, as well as industrial issues.

In addition to these organized exchanges, there is a huge and active over-the-counter market. It consists of various brokers and dealers who make markets in securities not listed on the exchanges. In recent times a growing number of securities listed on the organized exchanges have been trading in the over-the-counter markets as well. This development has come to be known as the "Third Market." When securities trade in the over-the-counter market, they are bought and sold on a negotiated price basis rather than in an auction market.

Coming: A Central Securities Market

Since the early 1970s, the Securities and Exchange Commission has been moving toward the formation of a central marketplace. In 1975, Congress, by amending the securities laws, provided the SEC with the power to take the necessary steps to implement such a market. The SEC's general objective is to establish a nationwide system so all investors will have their orders executed in whichever market provides the best price for a particular stock.

The SEC envisions a nationwide system electronically linking all existing markets. This would enable broker-dealers to route orders to all markets trading the stock to obtain the most favorable execution. Finally, a central file would be established for storage of all limit orders, again to provide best execution. The NYSE-sponsored Intermarket Trading System is one step toward a central market. This electronic system links most of the regional exchanges with the New York and American exchanges. Certain over-the-counter issues are also part of ITS.

Setting up such a system means tearing down old and protected institutions. It will be a slow process, but in the end will mean that individual investors will be on an equal footing with institutions regarding where and when the best price on a stock is available.

Types of Orders

Investors have at their disposal several types of orders they can use in executing their purchases and sales of securities. A full understanding of the uses and advantages of these various orders can help you become a more successful investor.

The most frequently used orders are the market order and the limit order. When you place a *market order,* you are instructing your broker to execute the desired transaction at the prevailing market price. He is obliged to consummate the trade at the most advantageous price to you. This means that in the case of a buy order he seeks the lowest price, while in the case of a sell order he seeks the highest price.

Market orders are particularly valuable in that they are executed rapidly at a price close to the last sale price. This characteristic is particularly desirable in a rising or declining market. In effect, this order protects you against the possibility of missing a market. The obvious disadvantage of a market order is that you cannot be certain of the exact price at which your order will be executed. This factor can be crucial in an erratic market, because you cannot be certain that your order will be executed anywhere near the most recent sale price.

Limit orders are used when you indicate to your broker the price at which you wish the order executed. These orders are placed "away from the market," in that the broker leaves the order with the specialist assigned to the particular stock. The specialist enters your limit order in his books, according to the time he receives it, along with others left with him. If the stock reaches the limit price, the specialist will execute the order according to when it was received. Obviously, some limit orders are never executed. If and when the limit order is executed, the specialist informs your broker, who in turn relays that information to you.

A limit order is useful because you can specify the price "or better" at which you wish the transaction to occur. Issues with limited markets and wide price spreads are the most appropriate candidates for limit orders. Over-the-counter stocks frequently display these characteristics.

The principal disadvantage of a limit order is that you can miss a market completely over a fraction of a point. For instance, an investor buys a cyclical stock such as Ford Motor Company at $40 a share. At the same time he places a limit order to sell at $50. That order might never be executed, although the stock could sell at 49½ or 49¾. On the other hand, the stock could reach the $50 limit price, but there could be insufficient buyers to cover all the limit orders on the books at that price.

A limit on the buy side is always placed at a price below the current market. A sell limit is above the current price. When buying a stock that is moving down, you place the limit in hopes of a better price. If the stock is moving up, you use a market order.

When selling a stock that is declining rapidly, you would sell at the market. But in selling a stock that is rising, a limit order might get you a better price.

Several other types of orders are available, too. Although they are more valuable to those who trade frequently or tend to tinker with their portfolios than to those who choose good stocks and hold them for the long term, you should have some passing acquaintance with them.

Stop orders, or *stop loss orders,* specify a particular price at which a stock should be bought or sold. A buy stop is always above the current market and a sell stop is below. The buy stop—at a price above current market—limits the loss or protects a gain on a short sale. The sell stop—below market—protects a gain or limits a loss on a long position. When the issue reaches the specified price, the stop order automatically becomes a market order and is executed. But, as we said earlier, a market order is executed at the most favorable price near the last sale price, and there is a chance that when execution occurs, there will be a substantial spread between the execution price and the last sale price. A large backlog of stop sell orders can touch off a price break sharp enough for trading to be suspended.

Stop limit orders are a hybrid form of stop and limit orders. A specified limit is indicated that the buyer or seller will accept, should the stock reach the stop price. For instance, an investor wishes to sell 100 shares of Falcon Seaboard at 25 stop, limit 24½. In other words, if the price of Falcon Seaboard falls to $25 per share his stop order becomes a market order to sell. But, if the order is not executed by the time the stock reaches $24.50, the limit order takes effect and no transaction occurs.

Day orders are orders which are only good for one day. Hence, if it has not been executed, the order expires at the end of the day on which it was placed. All market orders, obviously, are day orders. Limit orders are also day orders unless the customer places them as open orders, which is usually the case.

Fill or kill (*FOK*) orders are price as well as time limited; if they cannot be filled immediately at the set price, they are killed and the current price level of the stock is reported to the buyer for reconsideration.

Open orders can be placed for a specified period or can remain effective until executed or canceled.

GTC orders (*good until canceled*) run indefinitely. However, the NYSE requires that all GTC orders be confirmed with the floor specialist on a semiannnual basis. GTC orders pose certain risks, in that an investor could forget that he has them outstanding or they could be executed at a time the investor finds unsatisfactory.

Finally, an investor can place a *discretionary order*. In this case, the broker determines the timing for buying and selling as well as the selections and number of shares to be bought and sold. Under these circumstances, the investor is utilizing a complete discretionary order. This order must be given in writing to the broker and then must be approved by an officer of the broker's firm. A limited discretionary order allows the broker to decide only the price and timing. In using discretionary orders, it is absolutely essential that the investor have an established and trusting relationship with his broker.

Special Timing Situations

There are times when the price of a stock is affected by the impending distribution of a dividend or stock right. Buying or selling at these times requires the consideration of information an investor does not usually have to evaluate. Take *ex-dividend,* a term we discussed in Chapter 5. Recalling that earlier discussion, the declaration is the date a company's directors vote on the dividend. The date the checks will be mailed to shareholders is the payment date. The date a shareholder's name must be on the corporation's record books to receive a dividend is the record date. Finally, the ex-dividend date is the date that determines whether the buyer or the seller receives the dividend.

The exchanges and the over-the-counter markets have determined that investors must purchase a stock five business days before the record date to be eligible for the dividend payment. In other words, a purchaser of stock must buy before the stock trades ex-dividend in order to receive the dividend payment. Otherwise, the previous owner will receive the dividend.

When a stock sells ex-dividend, the market price will drop by an amount approximating the dividend. Hence a buyer will pay less for the stock but will not receive the dividend. Once the stock comes out of ex-dividend, the market price will rise to its prior level, other things being equal.

Should the investor buy or sell during ex-dividend trading? As an overall rule, it is best to execute purchases before ex-dividend trading begins. That way, you are entitled to the dividend payment. While the price will decline during ex-dividend trading, it will probably return to its former level shortly after ex-dividend trading stops. An exception is the investor in a high tax bracket. The lower price level of the stock trading in ex-dividend is preferable to receiving the dividend on which a high income tax will have to be paid.

Sales are best executed after ex-dividend trading, since the stock probably will recover the amount it declined during ex-dividend and in addition you will receive the dividend payment.

When a company decides to issue new securities through a rights offering to its shareholders, it issues *stock rights*, also known as *pre-emptive rights*. These are short-term options granted to shareholders to purchase new stock issues, generally at reduced price levels. Stock rights are distributed to shareholders in certificate form. The shareholder can either exercise the rights and purchase the stock at the designated price or he can sell the rights in the open market. Rights are issued for common stock and debentures (especially convertibles). You can determine the market value of the rights with this formula:

$$\frac{\text{Stock Market Price} - \text{Subscription Price}}{\substack{\text{Number of shares required to buy one} \\ \text{share at subscription price} + 1.}}$$

Hence, a stock selling at $30 per share, with rights to purchase one share at $20 for every three shares owned means that the rights themselves are worth $2.50 each, or:

$$\frac{\$30 - \$20}{3 + 1} = \frac{10}{4} = \$2.50$$

An investor should exercise rights to purchase stocks solely on the basis of the prospects for the stock generally. The attitude that rights should be exercised because they offer a "bargain" is not valid, since the rights themselves can be sold.

The term *ex-rights* denotes when a stock is selling without rights, the rights having been retained or exercised by the seller. As with dividends, you must own the common stock before it trades "ex-rights" to be entitled to the rights. The price of a stock will also decline by the value of the rights on the day the stock trades ex-rights. Once a stock trades ex-rights, the amount of the decline is determined by the following formula:

$$\frac{\text{Stock Market Price} - \text{Subscription Price}}{\substack{\text{Number of shares required to buy one} \\ \text{share at subscription price.}}}$$

Hence, in the situation already described, the stocks decline by a value of $3.33 when ex-rights trading begins. According to the formula:

$$\frac{\$30 - \$20}{3} = \frac{10}{3} = 3\frac{1}{3} = \$3.33$$

A stock might sell at depressed levels throughout a rights offering, but normally it will recover after expiration of the rights. This period can be regarded as an attractive purchasing opportunity, providing overall prospects are sound.

Buying Low and "Taking Profits"

Fortuitous investment timing is probably an even more difficult endeavor than deciding what securities to buy. The most naive investor recognizes that the fastest route to stock market success is to "buy low and sell high." But even the most seasoned professional is hard pressed to pick market tops and bottoms with any degree of consistency. Experienced hands don't even try; they leave that game to novices driven more by greed than common sense.

They also know that when the market in general is down, even the bluest of the blue chips will likely go down, too. But because the decline is the result of a general market drop and not due to any fundamental changes in the individual company's stock, experienced investors recognize this as a buying opportunity, and they add to their portfolios accordingly. They know that once the market starts back up, the quality issues will probably bounce back faster than others.

So much for buying "low." What about selling "high"? If it is considered advantageous to put money into a good stock when it is down, then shouldn't it be sold when the market is up? Generally, we would say no. In stock market parlance, this is called "taking profits." Presumably, the reason you want to do so is to allow you to reinvest the proceeds in another stock, which you hope you'll be able to run up into a similar profit. How will you do this? If the market is "high," so then are most quality stocks. Putting the money into anything less would be like gambling. Putting the money into the bank while you wait for the market to go down again into a "buying range" would foreclose the opportunity for further capital gains should the market continue to rise. Not only that, in your profit taking you would incur a capital gains tax liability, thus eroding the real size of the gain.

If you want to sell a stock, do so because you question its long-term prospects, not simply because you have a profit. Or because you have an overconcentration in a certain area and wish to diversify your holdings. Or because you have some capital losses against which you can offset these gains and thus upgrade your portfolio.

Dollar Cost Averaging

You don't have to wait for the market to hit its low before adding to your investments. There is an investment strategy that will give you good results over a long period of time. It is called dollar cost averaging and it is a simple technique that sidesteps altogether the issue of market timing. All it requires is that at regular intervals you make investments of a constant dollar amount in a stock or a variety of stocks that have generally favorable long-term prospects. Your dollars purchase fewer shares when the market is up, but they buy more when it is down. Because the market is fluctuating a certain amount even during a period of relatively flat price movement, this technique can bring a profit. For instance, if you had put $1,000 each into shares of Dresser Industries and Hewlett-Packard in January of every year from 1971 to 1980, your equity position would have been about $15,577 ahead after making your 1978 investment. You'd have had dividends to reinvest on top of that, of course.

DRESSER INDUSTRIES

	Amount	Price (Adjusted)	No. Shares Bought
January 1971	$ 1,000	17	58.82
January 1972	1,000	17	58.82
January 1973	1,000	24	41.66
January 1974	1,000	33	30.30
January 1975	1,000	22	45.45
January 1976	1,000	32	31.25
January 1977	1,000	42	23.80
January 1978	1,000	44	22.72
January 1979	1,000	38	26.31
January 1980	1,000	51	19.60
	$10,000		358.73

358.73 shares bought times 51 (Jan. 2, '80 price) = $18,295

HEWLETT-PACKARD

	Amount	Price (Adjusted)	No. Shares Bought
January 1971	$ 1,000	15	66.66
January 1972	1,000	24	41.66
January 1973	1,000	44	22.72
January 1974	1,000	41	24.39
January 1975	1,000	31	32.25
January 1976	1,000	48	20.83
January 1977	1,000	44	22.72
January 1978	1,000	36	27.77
January 1979	1,000	46	21.73
January 1980	1,000	58	17.24
	$10,000		297.97

297.97 shares bought times 58 (Jan. 2, '80 price) = $17,282

In Conclusion

Proper timing of your buys and sells can get to be a complicated matter, if you let yourself become preoccupied with it. Obviously, you should give it some thought as you adjust your portfolio, but in general you should place greater emphasis on sound values. When you do that, it is almost impossible to lose over the long term. Good stocks go down with everything else in bear markets, but they tend to bounce back faster. We don't believe you will profit in the long run by jumping from stocks to cash and back to stocks again with the ups and downs of the market. The experience of mutual funds and major banking trust departments confirms the assertion that investors with the most money and experience tend to remain fully invested in the best stocks most of the time.

While you might be advised to lighten up your portfolio at critical junctures in the stock market, you'll find that if you stick with the best stocks they will rise more often than they will fall. This, over the long pull, is where your brightest profit opportunities lie.

Chapter 31 Capitalizing on Special Situations

BACK IN the free-wheeling days before erection of the federal regulatory superstructure, fortunes were made by taking advantage of "inside information." Deals were struck, stock prices manipulated, mergers consummated, securities bought in advance of public knowledge of favorable developments, or sold in advance of adverse publicity. The trouble was, those fortunes were made at the expense of investors not privy to the information. That meant the investing public was often left holding the bag after the execution of such schemes.

It's much harder to do such things today, and those who even inadvertently tread into this forbidden territory can pay mightily. An example is Raymond Dirks, the insurance analyst we mentioned in Chapter 29 who blew the whistle on the Equity Funding phony life insurance caper. Dirks got into a peck of trouble with the Securities and Exchange Commission because he informed his own company's clients of the situation before making it public, thereby giving them the chance to bail out before the massive rush to the exits. He argued in his own defense later that his primary obligation lay with his clients; after all, they were the ones paying for his advice, and they had first rights to whatever his analysis yielded. We won't argue the merits of either side here; we merely want to point out how thin the line sometimes can be between legitimate "inside information" and the public's "right to know."

Corporate officers and directors are required to make "full disclosure" of anything that might affect the price of their company's securities. This includes filing intentions of their personal sale or purchase of large blocks of the company's stocks or bonds. It also includes making known more basic information regarding the company, such as an impending legal judgment, merger possibilities, major diversification intentions, the advent of new products, and the like.

You might wonder, then, whether any "special situations" can yet exist. The fact is, they do, and they often can reap handsome rewards for the alert investor. The major point is that you have as much chance as the company's key officers to share in these developments. What, then, is a special situation?

It is any unusual opportunity for profit which the market as a whole has failed to recognize. It might be a merger or acquisition or the introduction of a new product, as we mentioned above. It might be a hidden asset value. It might be a new management policy. Or new management. Although companies are required to make full disclosure of their intentions, they are not required to broadcast them. Ferreting out a special situation frequently takes a good deal of detective work that goes above and beyond routine analysis of a company.

Mergers, Acquisitions, and Takeovers

Mergers, acquisitions, and takeovers are among the more common forms of special situations. Many companies today are seeking capital expansion not only through internal growth but also externally. They can achieve this by acquiring companies that complement their existing operations. Frequently, because a company's stock is selling well below the cost of replacing its fixed assets, it is less expensive for an acquisition-minded company to buy a sufficient amount of the stock of an undervalued company to obtain control of it.

A special situation exists for shareholders of both the acquiring company and the company that is a candidate for takeover. Almost always, once it sets its sights on acquiring a company, a corporation will offer a premium price for outstanding shares to entice shareholders to sell. In other words, it will make a tender offer to buy stock of another company at a stated price for a stated period. The holder of such shares must then decide whether his best long-term interests lie in selling or in holding out for a better deal later. That deal might come in yet another tender offer by yet another acquisition-minded company seeking to outbid the first. Or it might come with an attractive conversion arrangement of his stock for that in the parent company once the acquisition is completed.

It's one thing to be the holder of such stock in a company that is being taken over. It's yet another to be able to "discover" such companies, then buy their stock before such tender offers are made. This is where the real profits lie in such a special situation—finding takeover candidates, buying their stock, and waiting. Of course, this won't work for every company whose stock is selling below book value. Some of them will be bridesmaids but never brides; others will be perennial wallflowers.

Perceptive investors may also profit by buying stock in companies that are doing the acquiring. Such companies abounded in the late 1960s and early 1970s, when the investment community witnessed the epidemic of acquisitions that spawned the conglomerates. The fever ran so high in those days that companies were stumbling all over each other to outbid on available takeover candidates. The bidding became so fierce and the pace of takeover so pell-mell that many conglomerates found after their buying spree was over that they had not purchased good value. Indeed, many had purchased major headaches and had dashed into industries they knew little about. There was a substantial shakeout during the market declines and straitened business climate of the mid-1970s, and this tended to break the fever.

By buying shares of a company that is pursuing a rational and studied acquisition program, you will be able to share in its growth. Not only will it acquire valuable assets at bargain prices, it will have the advantage of leverage, for it will be able to pledge its own assets to help finance the takeover. As the company increases its market share by acquiring companies in the same industry, and adds profit centers by acquiring companies in other areas, its shares become more valuable, and this value will be translated into higher prices on the stock market as more investors come to recognize it.

Spin-Offs and Turnarounds

Sometimes, instead of adding to its whole, a company will subtract. It will "spin off" a certain segment of its operations into a separate company. This, too, presents special-situation opportunities for investors. Take the case of Georgia-Pacific which in 1972 was forced to divest itself of a sizable part of its timber and manufacturing assets. It did so by creating a new company, Louisiana-Pacific. In this case, the spin-off was a virtual clone of the original.

Prior to the announcement of the intended spin-off, Georgia-Pacific stock was selling at about 36. When the news broke in mid-October, it promptly moved to 40, and by the end of November the shares closed at 43, representing a gain of some 20 percent in a matter of six weeks.

About a year later, Georgia-Pacific was trading at 40, while Louisiana-Pacific was trading at 42. The original buyer of Georgia-Pacific at 36 in October 1972, as a result, was holding a combined value (one share of Georgia-Pacific, one fifth of a share of Louisiana-Pacific) a year later of 49, for a profit of 35 percent. Even more convincing was the fact that this occurred at a time when the Dow Jones Industrial Average did not budge. Here clearly was a case where one plus one equaled more than two.

Another form of special situation is the turnaround. A company in decline suddenly springs back to life. Take the case of Memorex, which challenged International Business Machines in the computer business in 1973. A flex of the IBM muscle sent Memorex tumbling. It soon teetered on the brink of bankruptcy. The New York Stock Exchange delisted its shares. Employees fled for more secure positions elsewhere. It reported a loss of $119 million, and it owed a staggering $150 million to BankAmerica.

Sensing a potentially disastrous write-off, the bank took steps to effect a turnaround. A highly regarded executive named Robert C. Wilson was persuaded to accept the challenge of rescuing Memorex. When he signed on in 1974, he immediately took some drastic measures. With the cooperation of BankAmerica, he arranged a refinancing of debt, converting most of it to preferred stock. He reorganized operations, changing a loosely structured product line into five autonomous units. He brought in new engineers and recruited a vigorous new sales force. He shifted emphasis from leasing to direct sale of computers. He raised prices and instituted stringent cost-cutting measures.

By early 1975, earnings once again were in an uptrend and the company was well on its way toward a strong turnaround. Shareholders were among the major beneficiaries as stock that was selling at a low of 1½ in 1975 zoomed to nearly 34 a year later.

The results of a turnaround are not always so dramatic, but solid improvements in a seemingly hopeless situation can and do frequently occur when strong and creative management is brought in to mount a rescue operation.

New Products

Special situations may also originate through introduction of new products. A notable case was Syntex, whose early development of the birth control pill gave it a commanding lead in this market in the early 1960s. By 1965, "the pill" had brought a 1,000 percent gain in the stock's price. SmithKline experienced a similar, though not nearly as spectacular, result when it introduced a new ulcer therapy drug, Tagamet, in 1977. Indeed, the drug firms are good places to look for such special situations, since they have a serious commitment to research.

Companies in other industries that spend heavily on research and development bear exploration, too, especially where a good record already has been established in the creation of new products. Aerospace, chemicals, and electronics have provided their share of special situations via new products.

But the laboratory is not the only place where new products are born. The marketing department can spawn its share. Hanes, a staid and unspectacular manufacturer of underwear, suddenly exploded into nearly every feminine wardrobe in the country after its introduction of L'eggs pantyhose in 1970. On the other end of the sartorial spectrum, Levi Strauss tripled its sales and quintupled its earnings between 1972 and 1977 producing blue jeans to fill a seemingly insatiable market.

Entertainment has profited from new "products." In the case of Twentieth Century–Fox, that "product" was a film called *Star Wars*. For MCA, it was *Jaws*. For Warner Communications, the "product" is home entertainment in all its forms. These special situations have reaped good rewards for investors, but they are not easy to capitalize on, because of the virtual impossibility of predetermining what will capture the moviegoing public's fancy.

Investing "At Home"

Beyond these special-situation profit opportunities are those afforded by companies in your own geographical region. They are special situations in the sense that you as a "neighbor" often have a unique opportunity to understand their problems and their possibilities.

You should remember, though, that investment decisions should always be made on the basis of objective facts rather than on subjective or emotional interpretations of facts. The latter, whether applied to investing "at home" or anywhere else, will only multiply your potential for making sour investments. Keeping a logical mind regarding your investment decisions does not mean that regional or local investment vehicles should be avoided. It only means that these opportunities should be examined with a more careful eye, lest your regional chauvinism be allowed undue weight in the final decision.

The first step in considering local investment is to determine what kind of investment is available. Utilities and banks spring immediately to mind. However, you should not buy stock in them at random, any more than you would with any other kind of investment. You have to examine their individual strengths and weaknesses and evaluate their long-term prospects. You have to look at the effectiveness of their management, their pattern of earnings and dividend growth, and the regulatory and economic climate in which they will be operating in the future.

Obviously, you need not confine your search for home-grown investments to banks and utilities. Perhaps your area is noted for some particular product or industry. You would be in a good position to judge the leading companies in it. Perhaps you work for a local investor-owned company, or you have friends or relatives who do. Even lower-echelon employees frequently can sense what is happening in the company and are in a position to say whether it is expanding, contracting, or holding its own.

If you're employed by a company that offers an employee stock purchase plan, you are eligible for one of the most assured special situations—the opportunity to buy stock that is in some way subsidized by the company, either through a share-price discount or a matching funds program. These are opportunities that should not be allowed to pass by.

Besides home-grown equity investment possibilities, you should not overlook the opportunities presented by bonds issued by your own state or its municipalities, particularly if you are in an income tax bracket that would make their tax-free status attractive. Besides being exempt from federal income taxes, their income generally is also exempt from state and local taxation, another special situation that can mean additional profits for you.

Chapter 32 How to Use Options in Trading

REGARDLESS OF what may be written to the contrary, options trading is not an exact science. No amount of studying, charting, planning, or figuring will guarantee favorable results. By planning a carefully programmed strategy and observing a few rules, you can reduce your losses, and increase your chances for gains. Options trading is less costly but more risky than investing in the underlying equities. The mathematically inclined may derive much comfort from setting up elaborate systems of charting and calculating options trades. For others, a more simplified approach should produce satisfactory results.

A few rules which apply to all types of options trades should be adhered to. First, diversify. Start out by limiting yourself to only one option on any one expiration date. Second, before making any commitment, set upper and lower limits at which you will cover. This will limit gains but, more importantly, will limit losses. Third, if you are a buy-'em-and-forget-'em type, go no further—options are not for you. Fourth, buy calls or sell puts only after several days of down markets. Conversely, buy puts and sell calls only after several rising trading sessions.

Buying Calls

The simplest option transaction to understand is the purchase of a call. Say, for one reason or another, you expect International Business Machines to rise in price. Your capital is limited, but you still want to get in on the act, so you decide to buy a call. The stock is trading at 65, but there are calls available at premiums of 6¢ a share ($\frac{1}{16}$) up to $15. Striking prices range from 50 to 90, and expiration dates are October, January, and April. (For a review of the mechanics of options, see Chapter 14.)

CALL OPTIONS ON IBM SELLING AT 65

	Premiums on Options Expiring in:			
Striking Price	*October*	*January*	*April*	
50	14⅞	15⅜	–	In the money
55	10⅜	11⅛	–	In the money
60	6¼	7⅜	8	In the money
65	3¼	4½	5⅜	At the money
70	1½	2½	3½	Out of the money
75	⅜	–	–	Out of the money

This set of quotations presents a wide range of choices. How should you decide where to put your money? There are rules which help narrow the choices. First, don't buy a call that is far "out of the money" (striking price above trading price). In the example, the price of IBM stock would have to rise 15 percent to reach the 75 striking price. Second, take advantage of time to reduce your risk by choosing the middle expiration date. Third, limit your risk by buying an option with a striking price close to the stock price. In the example, the selection rules narrow the choice to the January 65 or 70 options. In the case of the January 65 call, the premium of 4½ represents time, and is a pretty steep price to pay. The January 70 call will participate fully in any rise in IBM shares at a lower cost.

By reducing the premium to a cost-per-week basis, you will have a better idea of the time value. Rather than reaching for the moon, you should decide beforehand that you will sell once you have a reasonable profit on the call. On the loss side, you should also make a decision to close out the trade when the premium drops below a preset level. In any case, it is always good policy to be out of the position at least a month prior to expiration. Remember that 70 percent of options expire worthless, so buying calls in expectation of a short-term profit is risky business.

Selling Calls

Why do investors sell calls? To maximize their return. In addition to obtaining dividend income, the writer pockets the call premium. Unlike the buyer, who usually buys calls on high-volatility issues, the seller writes options on low volatility—high yield stocks. He is willing to settle for the smaller premium this type of stock commands in order to increase his return.

Since your objective as a writer is to increase income while retaining your stock, you will choose to write the option with the highest striking price if you expect your stock to rise in price. Your premium may be only $100 on 100 shares of $30 stock, but on an annual basis your income has been increased by $400, for a 13.3 percent return. Should you anticipate a drop in the stock price, you would get greater protection by writing the in-the-money option with the highest premium. A price reversal would mean you would lose your stock yet still make a profit.

An investor who does not actually own the underlying stock may write what is known as a "naked call option." This strategy takes courage, for the downside risk is potentially unlimited. The speculator in naked calls writes an option on stock he doesn't own but which he may have to deliver at a price well below the market. For example, a call writer of stock selling at 48 receives a $300 premium for a 50 striking price. The stock rises sharply to 58 and he is called on to deliver. He must purchase shares for $5,800 to deliver at $5,000. His loss is $800, minus the $300 premium, or $500. To prevent this type of squeeze, a simultaneous GTC (good until canceled) order is placed to cover the option if the premium rises to $600, limiting his loss to $300, the amount of the premium received when the call was written.

Another means of reducing risk is to write only calls that are out of the money, where the stock is trading below the striking price. Since only 3 percent of all stocks rise or fall as much as 20 percent in a year, the odds favor the writer of calls with far-out-of-the-money striking prices. The speculator in naked calls reduces his risk by settling for smaller premiums and trading frequently.

Trading Puts

The put buyer expects to profit by a drop in the trading price of the underlying stock. He may make his profit by delivering his shares at a price above market or by covering the put. And, he may be either long or short in the shares, since the choice of whether or not to exercise is his. If he is short the shares, he will probably elect to cover, as it is generally more profitable. The long buyer is protecting his shares against a drop in price. If the market moves up, the put buyer's loss is limited to the premium paid for the option. This loss may be reduced by selling a covering put prior to expiration.

The put buyer has effectively locked in a profit—or limited a loss—at the exercise price. Unlike a stop-loss order, which may be executed at a price lower than specified on the order, a put buyer is guaranteed receipt of the striking price at exercise.

The put writer agrees to accept delivery of shares at the striking price and receives the option premium in return. For an investor interested in acquiring a particular stock which he considers too high priced, selling a below-market put may accomplish his purpose. Suppose you like the long-term prospects of Revlon, but at 48½ think it is currently overpriced. You can write a put at 45, receive $200 in premium income, and if the option is exercised your shares will have cost you $4,300, plus commission. The shares will have been acquired at 10 percent below current market. Should the stock fail to drop below the striking price, you would not acquire them but would be ahead by the $200 premium income.

As a put writer, you should observe some very basic rules. First, be sure the stock is one you wish to own—and at that striking price. Second, be certain you have the cash or the buying power in your account to take delivery on the shares. Third, remember that if the stock drops in price and you have only the minimum collateral required, you could be faced with a margin call for additional capital.

Hedging with Options

One of the most frequently employed strategies is the "straddle," the purchase of a put and a call on the same underlying stock having identical striking prices and expiration dates. In an uncertain market, this tactic allows the trader greater latitude for error. If the stock rises or drops substantially, he will be a winner. Sideways price action, of course, would mean a loss on both options. For example, you would buy a November 30 call on McDonnell Douglas (market price 33 at 5 and a November 30 put at 1¼, spending $625 plus transaction costs. A rise in the stock's trading price to above 36¼ or a decline to below 23¾ would produce profit. In either case, one option would expire worthless, the other would generate the profit. Obviously, in actual practice the losing side (leg) could be cut short by the sale of a covering option.

In trading straddles, you should choose stocks with a high "beta" coefficient—that is, one whose price tends to be volatile. These issues have a greater probability of moving far enough and fast enough to make a straddle profitable. Choose options with striking prices close to the trading price of the underlying issue. Also select higher-priced issues, since the premiums on these usually represent a smaller percentage of the stock's trading price. You will also add to your chance for success if you place your straddle on an issue that has an established price range. For example, on a stock trading in a channel between 80 and 100, the options would be at a 90 striking price. An issue with a clearly defined resistance and support level gives you better odds for success.

Because stocks fluctuate, the straddler will generally have ample opportunity to cover both options at small profits before expiration date, particularly if the underlying security has a high beta. As a trader in straddles, you must keep on top of your investment at all times, making new moves as indicated by market conditions. At the point where the premium on either the put or the call leg is sufficient to make the entire straddle profitable, that leg should be sold out and the proceeds reinvested. This procedure is known as "leg lifting."

On the opposite side is a straddle writer, an investor who anticipates only a narrow movement in the chosen stock over the life of the straddle. As a straddle writer, you wish to enlarge on the premium you would receive by writing only a call or a put. Concurrently, you subject yourself to the risks of both positions. Should the stock break out of its trading channel, you will be forced to deliver your shares at the lower-than-market exercise price. However, since you retain premiums from both the call and the put (which has expired worthless), you have a greater margin for profit than with either option alone. If the stock drops, the call expires unexercised. But you will have to take delivery on stock put to you at the above-market strike price. Again, downside protection from a straddle is greater than from the put alone, reflecting the premiums from both options.

The further a stock moves in either direction from the striking price the greater the amount of equity required in the margin account. A good financial backlog is a must for dabblers in straddles.

Spreads—Bullish and Bearish

Spreads may be accomplished using either put or call options. As a spreader, you would buy a call (or a put) and simultaneously write a call (or a put) on the same stock, using options with the same exercise date and different striking prices to transact a price spread. For a calendar spread, you buy and sell options with the same striking price but different exercise dates. A bullish spread using calls might entail buying an at-the-money call (strike and trading price similar) and simultaneously writing a call that is out of the money. Should the stock advance as anticipated, a profit is made on the buy side, and the call which was sold is covered, leaving a limited profit. If the market drops, the call which was written expires worthless, and the call which was bought may be covered to limit the loss, for a smaller loss on balance.

A bullish put spread requires buying a put with a striking price below trading price while selling one with a higher strike price and the same expiration date. When the premium on the long put (the one purchased) exceeds the proceeds from the one written (short), the spread is termed a "credit"; the reverse situation results in a debit spread.

Price spreads which use options bought and sold with the same expiration dates and different striking prices are also referred to as "vertical" or "perpendicular" spreads. When the expiration dates differ, the spread is a "calendar," "horizontal," or "time" spread.

Bearish investors wishing to spread may do so with either puts or calls. Using calls, the trader inverts the technique used by the bull, by buying an out-of-the-money call and selling an in-the-money call. Should the stock drop as expected, the call which was bought expires worthless and its cost is deducted from the proceeds of the call which was sold. While this limits the profit when the market price of the stock moves as anticipated, it also limits the loss if the stock rises counter to expectations. A bearish put spread involves writing a put with a lower striking price than the one on the put which is purchased.

Since margin rules relating to puts and put spreads are complex, you should become well versed in them before using these strategies. A long put (one which is purchased) must be paid for in full and has no loan value in a margin account. Furthermore, to qualify for put-spread margin treatment, the long side must not expire before the short side of a spread. These and other special margin rules are explained in the prospectus of the Options Clearing Corporation, a document which your broker will furnish. One of the main advantages in using options is the additional leverage they provide the trader, so understanding the margin rules is a must.

Still another technique, called "ratio writing" or "variable hedging," involves writing calls on more shares than are actually owned. A ratio writer holding 100 shares of IBM trading at 65 would write one covered and two naked calls to gain greater income as well as greater downside protection. For example, he could write three January 70 calls on his IBM to receive a premium of $750 ($250 per call). This gives him downside protection to 57½ rather than to 62½ with one call. But a rise in the stock to above 70 leaves him vulnerable to three exercise notices and the need to satisfy them with 200 shares bought at the market. Even though his break-even point is 77½ on the IBM, he would still face having to raise the capital to deliver the shares. The trader, of course, would cover before getting into this situation.

Risk Versus Reward

The use of any combination strategy such as straddles, spreads, variable hedges, or the like increases the cost of the transaction, thereby reducing profits. Furthermore, there are possible tax implications that should be taken into account before plunging. For example, buying a put in a stock you already own might change the long-term status of that issue. If the stock has not been owned long enough to qualify as a long-term holding, the purchase of a put would wipe out the time previously accrued toward that qualification. Until the put is liquidated, a new holding period will not begin. Conversely, calls may be used to turn a short position into a long position.

It is possible to provide considerable protection against investment risks through the informed use of options. But this is possible only if you have a complete understanding of the subject or have an investment adviser willing and able to guide you through the intricacies of the various maneuvers.

Chapter 33 Investing in Commodity Futures

THE SEARCH for profits in the commodity futures markets is not one that is generally pursued by the conservative investor. If he considers "playing the commodities markets" at all, his thoughts are just that—entertainment, a divertissement from more conventional investment avenues. More adventuresome investors pursue futures with greater seriousness, their eyes always on that chance to maneuver their stake into a killing.

That's fine if you're psychologically up to it, and if you fully understand the rules of the game. In this chapter, we'll introduce you to some of the basics needed for trading in futures contracts. However, because it is impossible to cover all of the topics adequately in a single chapter—or, indeed, in a single book—we strongly recommend that if you are serious in your intent to participate in this investment area you expand your knowledge before starting to trade.

You'll recall from Chapter 15 that the clearing house always breaks even. Everything it takes in it pays out, less commissions and fees. The same concept is a fair description of commodities futures trading in general. It is a zero sum game, with the participants swapping money among themselves, the only attrition coming from those clearing house expenses. That being the case, in order to win you must take money from another player, who, in turn, is attempting to take money from you. Theoretically, your odds of winning should be fifty-fifty, and they are—on a single trade. In the aggregate, however, the odds are much less favorable that you will win; indeed, some observers claim they are nonexistent. Unfortunately, there is no reliable body of information on the success rate of commodity traders. The consensus among people in the business, though, is that most speculators lose, and the lion's share of profits goes to a relatively few professional traders. You can make money in the futures markets, but the competition is keen and success does not come easily or without cost.

Should You Speculate?

Whether participation in the futures markets constitutes out-and-out gambling or whether it is a valuable and necessary part of our economic structure has been vigorously debated by moralists. We will not proffer a judgment on the question here. However, we will make this assertion: Successful commodity speculation demands the acquisition of price forecasting skills and the mental discipline to manage money in high-risk situations. The latter is the more difficult to master and probably is the principal reason the average trader loses over the long run. But price forecasting is only a little less demanding.

Choosing a Broker and Account Executive

As a beginning trader, your first decision would come in the choice of a brokerage house and an account executive within that firm to handle your orders. Basically, two types of brokerage houses are available to you. The more familiar is the wire or commission house that deals in almost any type of investment medium. The primary business of such firms is usually stocks and bonds, but many maintain separate commodity departments. The second type is the specialty brokerage house that restricts itself to transactions in only a few commodities. These firms are offshoots of cash or trade houses. In the past, the latter would have provided the better service; but in recent years, many of the wire houses have built their commodity departments to the point where they are equally capable of providing efficient handling of orders.

As for your choice of an account executive, if you feel you need specific trading advice, you probably will be more comfortable with someone who has experience in trading and is knowledgeable about the kinds of things important to your trading system. Conversely, if you like to plan your own trades, you may not like having someone fill your ear with advice. Whoever you choose, you should remember that all account executives are salesmen first and traders second. They make their living from commissions, not from successful trading of their own accounts. It is to their benefit, of course, if you win, and they will make every effort to assist you in that regard.

Opening a commodity trading account is a fairly simple procedure. The account executive will send a form called a margin or customer's agreement. It details the obligations you share with the brokerage firm when trading. Most firms also require personal and credit information to satisfy themselves that the prospective client can afford to speculate. You may have to sign a statement of risk as well. This is primarily for the protection of the salesman and the firm. It is their proof that you were informed and presumably understood that commodity trading is more risky than placing your money in a savings bank.

You will have to deposit some cash when opening the account. The amount will vary from firm to firm, but it generally runs from $2,000 to $5,000. On the whole, specialty commodity firms will require less up-front money, but all firms will expect you to meet the margin requirement in whatever commodity you have chosen to speculate.

Keeping Things Straight

Once the account is open, you will receive a variety of forms to alert you to what entries are being made in the broker's computer. Thus, if errors are detected, they should be called to the account executive's attention and corrected. The following list represents the basic correspondence nearly every commission house or specialty firm sends out.

Statement of account. When the account is opened and a margin deposit made, a statement of account showing the balance is sent to you. Thereafter, you will receive one at the end of each monthly trading period, listing the credits (winning trades, new money added, or favorable adjustments), the debits (losses, cash withdrawals, and unfavorable adjustments), and the end-of-month balance.

Trade confirmation. This is a record of a sale or purchase of a commodity futures position for the stated price and number of contracts. You'll have two confirmations for each completed trade, one for the entry price and one for the exit price.

Purchase and sale. When a trade is completed, that is, when a purchase is offset with a sale or a sale offset with a purchase, the broker will tally up the results, subtract the commission, and debit or credit the account accordingly. All the details of the trade appear on the purchase and sales slip, plus the *closed out* account balance. The latter figure does not include any gains or losses you might have outstanding in open or uncompleted trades. The net debit or credit for each trade is what appears on the monthly statement of account.

Open trades. When a new trade is entered but not offset, you will receive along with the confirmation slip a statement of open trades. This form shows a listing of all your open positions (including the new trade), their respective gains or losses, and the total account equity balance as of the close on the day the new positions were taken.

Because of the high leverage and rapid equity changes that can occur in a commodity account, a trader must be aware of his cash position on a daily basis. The statement of open trades does serve this purpose, but since it is sent only when a trade is actually made or offset, its usefulness is limited. To augment the statement of account, you should maintain a record of your daily account equity. This can be made as comprehensive as you like, but it should include at a minimum the daily profit and loss position on all open trades, the commission costs, and the net account balance. The net account balance is the amount of money that would be left in your account if all open positions were closed out at the day's settlement prices, and all commissions paid. That figure is your account's real net worth at any one time.

The Kinds of Orders

With the account open and margin money posted, getting into the battle requires only a call to your account executive, plus a little knowledge of orders. The following list covers the basic information you will need in order to properly convey your order to the salesman.

At the market. Buying or selling a commodity "at the market" is the quickest and surest way to enter or exit from a commodity market. A floor broker who receives this order will immediately execute it at the most favorable prices available at that moment. This is a "must fill" type of order.

Limit order. If you issue the instruction, "Buy at 45 or better" (the "or better" is understood and need not be given), you have posted a limit order. The floor broker will buy at your specified price or lower, but not higher. Unlike market orders, limits are not "must fill" orders, and a broker will not guarantee completion even if the market should go through your limit price. All you are assured is that if the broker can fill the order, he will do so at your price or better.

Stops or stop-loss orders. Stop-loss or stops are orders placed above or below the current market prices to protect a profit or limit a loss in an open position. When the stop price is reached, the order is executed "at the market."

Stops can also be used to enter a new position. If your price analysis indicates that a commodity must advance to a certain level before it is a good buy, you could use a buy stop; until it reaches that price no execution will take place.

Buy stops are always written at prices above the prevailing market, while sell stops are always below the market. When entering a market using stops, you must remember that stops become market orders when reached. Fills, therefore, can become unpredictable. However, by using stop-limit orders, you can control, or at least limit, the price which you are willing to pay for the new position. You would not want to use a stop-loss limit for a position that is being protected, because, like any limit order, there is no guarantee the broker can fill the order even if the market trades at your price. Assume you want to buy a commodity at 45 but do not want to pay more than 45¼. Your instruction would be: "Buy at 45, stop-limit 45¼."

On close and *on open* orders are executed, as the terms imply, during the commodity's opening or closing range, or not at all. Both of these orders are attached to either a market or a stop instruction.

One cancels the other (OCO). Like the preceding instruction, an OCO order is a contingency order. Something else has to occur before the floor broker can execute. In this case, you have placed two conflicting orders on the same contract (it can be used on differing commodities, as well), but only want one filled. You might do this if a commodity is in a trading range and you want to go with the breakout, but you aren't sure which way that will be. The solution is to use an OCO order. The instruction is to buy at 46 stop or sell at 44 stop, OCO. Whichever side is reached first will be filled, the other end will be canceled.

Good until canceled (GTC). Ordinarily, if an order is not filled during a day's trading, it is considered canceled automatically. It is possible, however, to instruct the broker to keep the order open by adding a GTC notation. The floor broker will keep this order in his deck of resting orders and will execute it at the first opportunity. The danger with this type of order lies in the ease with which it can be forgotten.

This catalogue of orders is by no means complete. It represents the most commonly given trading instructions, and the ones most likely to be accepted on an exchange. But even in this modest list will be found a few orders not accepted on some exchanges. Any type of contingency order is particularly vulnerable to being turned down by a floor broker. The market often moves so quickly that instructions weighted down with many options are too difficult to handle. As a rule, the more complicated you make the order, the less likely is the floor broker to accept it. It is usually best to keep your instructions as simple as possible.

Buying, Selling, and Delivery

There are two methods of selling commodity contracts. Either you make or accept delivery of the actual commodity or you offset the contract by taking an equal but opposite position in the same commodity. Offsetting is a fairly straightforward and simple process. Most futures contracts are settled in this manner; and for individuals not actually involved in the cash commodity, offsetting is the most practical way to meet a contract obligation. But delivery is an alternative, and one with which the speculator should be familiar. Ordinarily, it is the speculator who has bought a contract who is the most concerned with delivery. Short sellers must notify the clearing house when and where delivery is to be made, and this notice of delivery is passed along to the buyers. As a result, the seller has control of the delivery process. Since speculators do not usually have the product, speculative sellers are rarely concerned with making delivery. On the other hand, the long holder stands a good chance of receiving a seller's "notice to deliver" if he keeps the contract into the delivery month.

Some clearing house operations pass delivery notices to the buyers with the oldest position; others send delivery notices to the broker-age house with the oldest net positions. In most commodities, how-ever, the exchanges allow the long holder receiving a delivery notice the option of redelivering, for a fee, the notice back to the clearing house or brokerage firm for delivery to the next oldest long. The rules and procedures of delivery and redelivery vary with each commodity exchange, and the speculator should be aware of the specifics in the market in which he is trading. This is doubly im-portant if the particular commodity has no redelivery provision or if the provisions are exceedingly difficult to meet. Your broker should be able to provide you with the details, but if he does not have the information, you can write or call the exchange. Your best bet, of course, is to be out of the contract well before delivery time.

Other considerations relating to commodity contracts include margin requirements, daily price range limits, and commissions. We have not included margin requirements here because they fre-quently differ from firm to firm, and because the exchanges them-selves routinely raise or lower margins to counteract changes in volatility.

Each commodity has a specific maximum amount by which it is allowed to move either up or down from the previous day's settle-ment price. This is known as the daily limit. The limits are intended to prevent unusual circumstances from causing extreme one-day price changes. If the price does go up or down "the limit," trading is not necessarily stopped. It means no orders will be filled beyond the limit prices. Trading often continues to take place at the limit, but usually those traders wanting to take up the disadvantaged side disappear, and trading dries up.

Three Classes of Commissions

There are three classes of commissions: regular, day, and spread. A *regular commission* is what a brokerage firm charges for a com-modity transaction that takes more than one day to complete. The *day rate* is for a position entered and exited within a single day. A *spread commission* refers to a type of trading in commodities called "spreading." It is similar to hedging except that the cash position is replaced with another futures position. In effect, with spreading you get two positions for slightly more than the price of one.

When you pay a commodity commission, you pay your in-and-out charges at once—the equivalent of a "round trade" in stock market parlance. You don't pay for each leg of the trade separately as you do in a stock. Furthermore, you don't pay the commission until you terminate your position in the contract. Each commodity has its own commission structure, and commissions on each type of commodity contract will vary from broker to broker.

Market Quotes and Price Forecasting

To follow what is happening in a commodity and to determine your financial health at any given moment, you must be familiar with commodity quotes. Where do the quotes come from? In each exchange, market observers are posted on the outskirts of the pit, their function to report price changes to the various ticker services. The services, in turn, send the information to brokerage house clients.

Your account executive will have access to these quotes and can keep you informed of intra-day changes. A more complete record of overall commodity trading will appear in the following day's newspapers. If you live in a sizable city, it is possible that your daily newspaper will carry a fairly complete listing of commodity quotes on its financial pages. If not, you might want to subscribe to *The Journal of Commerce, The Wall Street Journal,* or *The New York Times,* all of which carry extensive listings.

Keeping tabs on these price changes after the fact is one thing. The real key to success is in being able to judge the movements beforehand. This is one of the most complicated and diverse aspects of trading, because there is no *best way* to forecast prices. There is even some argument that prices are random and cannot be forecast at all. However, short of darts, coin flipping, or moon phases, there are two general approaches to forecasting that lie at the foundation of nearly every commodity trading method you will likely encounter. They are, as in stock market analysis, *fundamental* and *technical*.

Traders generally have strong opinions on whether the fundamental or technical approach is the better. There really is no clear-cut answer, because what works well for one individual may not work at all for another. But you should become familiar with both methods of analysis, for they are the tools of the trade. In theory, the fundamental approach seems to appeal to most beginning traders because they feel better about basing buying and selling decisions on supply and demand factors than they do on a series of lines drawn on a piece of paper. The majority of traders, though they may lean heavily toward one discipline or the other, use both methods to some degree.

A fundamentalist operates on the principle that prices will rise if supply is short relative to demand and will fall if it is abundant. Fundamental analysis is an attempt by the trader to figure out what the supply and demand balance will be for a given commodity over a given period of time. Once this set of figures is divined, the fundamentalist then must decide what they mean in relation to current prices and whether the market has erred in interpreting the facts.

For the fundamentalist to trade, the market forces setting the futures prices must be in error, or there would be no reason to trade. For example, if the market price today for a hog contract deliverable six months in the future is quoted at 46¢ a pound, that is what the market, based on all the current trading and statistical input, believes hogs will be selling for six months from now. Through statistical analysis, the fundamentalist seeks to justify or disprove the market's judgment. If, in his opinion, the market forces are wrong, he will buy or sell accordingly.

While the fundamentalist is submerging himself in myriad statistical data relevant to supply and demand, the technician is content to view price, volume, and open interest as the true measures of the market. To him, fundamentals are irrelevant. He is interested in market action as it is reflected in changing prices, not external data that are difficult to determine, overwhelming in volume, and more often than not inaccurate or old.

The technician assumes that price changes are not without pattern, and that by studying past action it is possible to predict the direction of future market movement. Moreover, he believes markets act irrationally at times as the result of unpredictable changes in the mood of the trading public. A fundamentally strong market, for example, can easily collapse for no more apparent economic reason than a hard-to-measure change in public confidence. A technician feels he is better able to detect psychological or irrational shifts and act on them than the fundamentalist, who needs statistical input to justify a position change. Two of the more popular technical methods traders use are price charts and moving averages.

The Role of Price Charts

The success a chartist enjoys rests largely on his ability to recognize patterns that are developing on price charts. The most common method of price information storage—or charting—is the simple bar chart, described in Chapter 21. When using charts, the technician looks for patterns that in the past have preceded certain types of price behavior. The formations he looks most closely for are trend lines, channels, reversals, head-and-shoulders movements, triangles, double tops and bottoms, and gaps. The significance of these was discussed in Chapter 22.

Charting is highly subjective, and recognizing tradable patterns can be difficult. It doesn't take much to turn one pattern into another. Moreover, many traders follow charts, and this in turn can influence the price of the commodity in the direction the chartist thinks it will turn. However, that can frequently lead to false breakouts and costly traps once the chartist's buying or selling is completed. Nevertheless, there is ample evidence that traders using chart study can provide the trader with information on the relative merits of one trade over another, and can help the fundamentalist in timing entry into or exit from a market position.

Technicians using the trend-following discipline are operating on the assumption that a price trend, once begun, is more likely to continue than to reverse. The trick is in finding a method that can get you into the market as close as possible to the start of the move, keep you in when the market corrects, and take you out before the correction turns into a trend reversal. There are several general methods in use, but the most popular is a moving average, which we discussed in Chapter 22.

Spreads

As defined earlier, spreading is the taking of two equal but opposite positions in the futures market. Basically, a spread is a hedge with the cash position replaced by a futures contract. As in a hedge, spread traders are not interested in outright price changes; they are concerned with the price relationship between two commodity contracts and how that difference widens or narrows.

A brief example will illustrate the principle. If a trader were to buy a 30,000-pound June hog contract at 46¢ a pound and sell a December hog at 47¢ a pound, he would have a spread difference between the two contracts of 100 points (1¢ a pound). To make money on this particular spread, the trader would need the front month, June, to gain relative to the back month, December. Ordinarily, this would happen if the hog market were in a bull trend; hence this type of spread (long the front, short the back) is called a "bull spread." However, in actual practice, bull spreaders can make money in bear markets and lose in bull markets.

In any event, if the June hog should go to 47½¢ a pound while December were able to reach only 48¢, the spread trader would have gained a half cent per pound, or $150 profit less commissions.

Spread trading, involving as it does two or more commodity contracts, is a fairly complicated variation of futures trading, and certainly not as easy as some brokers would have you believe. Indeed, it is not unusual for spreading to be touted as a safe and almost risk-free venture. The truth is that spreads run the gamut from almost-risk-free carrying-charge spreads (with little or no profit potential) to those that are probably more dangerous, as a result of lower margins and higher leverage, than open positions.

Your Trading Plan

It should be clear by now that a trader can devote a considerable amount of time to the development of a trading system. But no matter how meticulously he constructs his system, it will not be perfect; and he would be foolish indeed to proceed as if it were. Even the professionals expect to lose on a large percentage of their trades. At best, the trader hopes his plan will succeed more often than it fails, and that it will return him a profit over the long term.

As you devise your own plan, keep these thoughts in mind. Also heed our earlier comments on the importance of devising some sort of price forecasting system. Without one, you will be at a serious disadvantage. Then you should draft a realistic trading plan—and develop the discipline to exercise that plan properly. The need for discipline cannot be overemphasized. Fear and greed are the commodity trader's worst enemies and they can cause even the best traders using superior price forecasting systems to make costly errors. Indeed, one of the lures of a mechanical trading system is that buying and selling signals are given mathematically, thereby eliminating much of the human element.

In its simplest form, a trading plan defines the criteria for entering a trade and specifies the point at which the position should be terminated. The latter is the more difficult, and where the greatest discipline is needed. A market can do one of three things: it can go with your position, it can go against your position, or it can do nothing. A trading plan must consider, *in advance*, the alternatives, and provide a course of action for each of the three possibilities. Failure to do this leaves the speculator at the mercy of his emotions and makes commodity trading far more difficult—and more risky— than it need be.

Another important part of your trading plan is money management. Unfortunately, there is no formula that can be set forth to tell you how you should manage an account's capital resources. Trading and financial conditions are different for each individual, and money matters must be handled on a personal basis. But keep in mind that capital protection is the key segment in any money managing effort. How well you succeed at this effort, in fact, is probably the single most important element in whether you win or lose in the long run, since the game ends immediately when the chips are gone. That suggests, at the very least, that overtrading in all its forms should be studiously avoided. If there is a mistake in judgment to be made—and all traders make plenty—let it be on the conservative side.

Part V TAKING CARE OF THE HOUSEKEEPING

Chapter 34 **Choosing a Broker**

BACK IN the good old days, the broker you started with would probably still be handling your investments on the day you retired. It was a lifetime decision, like choosing a family doctor, and one that could have a considerable impact on your financial health. Today this decision is not likely to be as final. With brokerage company mergers and hard times causing staff cutbacks, you might go through two or three or more account executives in a single year. A lifelong association with one firm and one representative is now a rarity. As a result, the criteria for selecting a broker have also shifted.

If you are starting your investment career from scratch, having never invested or had a brokerage account, you probably would like some guidelines to help you in making a selection. You should start by deciding just what you want, or expect, from a broker. Do you need someone who will give you investment advice and financial guidance? Do you want a company that will safeguard your certificates, forward dividend checks, and execute specialized transactions? Do you want a firm that can provide financial services and products other than stocks and bonds, such as tax shelters, Keogh, IRA, and employee benefit plans, insurance programs, and the like? If these are your needs, then you probably should select an old-line full-service brokerage company.

But if you are planning to do your own research and require only efficient and economical execution of your orders, you may want to consider a discount brokerage firm. These "plain pipe rack" companies offer no hand-holding, no purveying of advice, no ancillary services. Some even charge extra for special executions like limit and GTC orders. They all discourage personal involvement in their clients' financial affairs.

Full-Service Houses

Obviously, there are still legions of investors who are looking for service, the staple of the conventional brokerage firm. If this is your choice, select a New York Stock Exchange member firm, one that offers not only the $100,000 minimum account protection insurance required by law, but additional coverage as well. When you deal with such a firm, you can expect your account representative to call you from time to time to offer investment "suggestions." More stocks are "sold" to investors than are "bought" by them. Before acting on any of his recommendations, you should be sure the stock he suggests fits your investment goals. Don't be sidetracked from your particular financial needs by the tempting visions of a quick profit, for these are few and far between and are seldom shared.

Speculation is no substitute for investment, and you should view with suspicion any broker who tries too hard or too often to get you to accept his profferings. Always keep firmly in mind that his motivation in persuading you to buy is not his desire to be a nice guy, but a piece of the commission you'd pay. On the other hand, a smart account executive is one who realizes he'll do best in the long run by giving his clients good advice and the kind of service they want.

Discount Brokers

Discount brokers came along when the Securities and Exchange Commission began putting on the pressure for negotiated commission rates. Until the mid-1970s, all brokers used a fixed schedule of rates, a situation the SEC regarded as a hindrance to free enterprise. It reasoned that if rates were unplugged from the schedule, competition among brokers would result in lower commissions. Despite its actual and philosophical proximity to the center of the free-enterprise system, the brokerage industry objected strenuously. The SEC proceeded in spite of the protests. Its first step was to rule that the commission on the portion of all trades above $500,000 could be negotiated. The limit was later dropped to $300,000. This did not help small investors, whose flight from the stock market had been a major factor in the financial straits that had beset many brokerage houses. So on April 1, 1974, the SEC started freeing up the other end. Trades of $2,000 or less were taken off the fixed schedule. Finally, as of May 1, 1975, the vast bulk of trades between these limits were included, and the move to fully negotiated rates was completed.

Did it help? Not much. In fact, in many instances, investors found themselves paying more in commissions, as a percentage of the transaction, than they had under the fixed rates. Here is where the discounters began making hay. By cutting out all extra services and by running tight no-frills offices, they were able to offer substantial savings to investors seeking straight no-nonsense transactions. Eventually, the full-service houses, which had been scorning small individual accounts as unprofitable, began to see that there was indeed a dollar to be made in that area. They started challenging the discounters. Free enterprise at last was beginning to work in the brokerage industry.

How Much Should You Pay?

This development is good news for you, for it places you in a better bargaining position. Because of a little-discussed but often-practiced discounting of rates, active investors now may be able to bring some pressure to bear in "negotiating" their commission rates. No one in the industry will volunteer to give you a break on the fee, but if pressed, some yield. So by all means ask. A 15 percent rake-off is fairly standard now.

Rake-off from what? That's a legitimate question. Before fixed commissions were abolished, there was no mystery as to the cost of a transaction. The broker looked at the schedule and computed your charge. Even today some conventional brokerage houses use the old schedule for setting the fee on smaller orders. Where the traffic will bear, many charge higher rates. Many discounters use the old fixed rates as a base from which they discount. Thus, the rake-off generally is from the old fixed rates. If an account representative tells you you're getting 15 percent off, or 80 percent, you can safely assume that it's off the old schedule. Thus, the old table (on page 362) is still important. Use it for comparison when you are quoted a commission.

If the discounter does not use a certain percentage of the old

MINIMUM FIXED COMMISSION RATES PRIOR TO MAY 1, 1975

Share Price	Number of Shares				
	25	50	100	200	500
$ 5	$ 7.59	$10.34	$18.04	$ 36.08	$ 81.95
10	10.34	15.84	27.50	55.00	106.70
15	13.09	21.34	34.65	67.10	148.41
20	15.84	25.30	41.80	77.00	176.36
25	18.59	28.88	48.95	86.90	204.30
30	21.34	32.45	53.90	109.29	232.25
35	23.52	36.02	58.85	120.47	260.19
40	25.30	39.60	63.80	131.64	288.14
45	27.09	43.17	68.75	145.06	306.76
50	28.88	46.75	71.50	154.00	325.39
75	37.81	64.62	80.75	161.46	399.91

rate as his basis for computing the fee, he will quote you a fixed charge plus a certain number of cents per share, generally 5¢ to 8½¢. To encourage larger and more active accounts, discounts are calculated on a sliding scale with the largest breaks going to the bigger traders. Some discounters will advertise 80 percent off, but upon careful investigation this turns out to be the maximum break on the largest orders. Then, too, you must be sure to look for hidden costs, such as added fees for limit orders or GTC orders. Or you may be required to pay for the transaction in full or in part before execution of an order. On the plus side, some discount brokers pay interest on cash balances in an account.

Since there can be a considerable variation both in the size of the discounts and in the services offered by the no-frills brokers, you should do some shopping around before deciding on one. More and more are cropping up all over the country, and since most have toll-free 800 telephone numbers, their physical location matters little.

Special Programs Available

If you don't have access to a discount broker or if you simply wouldn't be comfortable in dealing with one, you might find some opportunities for reduced commissions with a conventional firm.

Perhaps the best known of the brokers' specialized plans is Merrill Lynch, Pierce, Fenner & Smith's "Sharebuilder Program." Bache & Company's "Stock-Invest" is similar, as are those of other, smaller firms. These plans feature discounts of 15 to 35 percent for purchases from a selected list of stocks in transactions of $5,000 or less. Dividends may be reinvested automatically, as well. Some companies have reductions on commissions for "round-trip" trades; that is, on a stock bought and sold within 45 days, the fee for the sell side is cut in half. For an active trader, this type of account offers big savings, but for the long-term investor it is useless.

Here is another important point in considering the choice of a broker. While the major firms are members of the New York Stock Exchange, most of the discount brokers are not. That means that when you deal with the NYSE member firm you are buying and selling directly into the auction market; whereas, when you deal with a discounter you may be dealing secondhand, for, as a nonmember firm, it must in turn run the executions through a member firm. This might mean a higher transaction price when you buy and a lower one when you sell. Thus, dollars you might save on commissions are thrown away if you are penalized a half point per share in the process. Once the Central Securities Market is in operation this will of course change. (See Chapter 30.)

Making the Choice

If you live in or near a large urban area, you probably have access to offices of several of the major firms, plus some local firms. In deciding upon one, you can canvass friends and business associates who have had dealings with them. Your lawyer and banker might be able to help, too, particularly in providing insights as to the quality and extent of services offered.

It is not imperative that you live close to your broker's office, particularly if you are a long-term investor who will not be placing frequent orders. In fact, some distance might prove useful, since it will tend to reduce the number of overtures from your account representative seeking to persuade you to take advantage of his hot tips.

Once you have made the choice of a brokerage firm and an account representative, you should take time to acquaint him with your investment goals. It is the only way he has of knowing your needs and how he can help you implement them. Don't hesitate to let him know exactly what you expect—and don't expect—of him.

Your next step will be to open an account. This involves filling out some forms, and there is not a great deal of difference from one firm to the next as to what type of questions you'll be asked. But it's a simple process; opening a charge account at a department store is probably more complicated.

Besides supplying basic information such as full name and address, you will be required to give your Social Security or tax identification number. You will also need to instruct the broker as to how you wish him to handle your dividends and certificates and what type of account you are opening—joint, margin, etc. You'll have to provide the name of your bank and employer, too. For a margin account, you will have to complete and sign a customer's agreement and loan consent. Once these forms have been completed, you will be ready to start on a new adventure in investing.

Chapter 35 Safeguarding Your Securities

IMPORTANT AS it is to select the right investments to meet your financial needs, the protection of these assets once they have been acquired is equally vital. The safeguarding process should begin even earlier, before any money has ever been invested. Your choice of brokerage firm, how you elect to have your securities held, and what records you keep are all factors crucial to the safety of your investments. These are also matters which can and should be attended to before embarking on an investment program.

Holding Your Securities

There are four basic ways you can hold your securities. You can obtain and safeguard the certificates yourself. You can have them registered in your own name and have them held by a bank, a lawyer, or someone else as custodian. You can register them in your own name and keep them on deposit with your broker in a custodian account. Or, you can keep them in street name—this means leaving your certificates in your broker's name and in his possession.

Which way is best? The answer depends on your own psychological makeup, and the way you plan to operate your brokerage account. If you prefer to keep a firm grip on your possessions, you'll probably want to take delivery of the certificates and see to their safekeeping yourself. This means you will have immediate access if you need them for such things as loan collateral. It also means some inconvenience, for you must be sure to keep them safe, preferably in a safe deposit box at the bank. It means you must go down to the bank and remove them when you sell, then be sure they are safely delivered to the broker for transfer.

If you do a good bit of traveling or are away from home much of the time, you might wish to place them in your own name but have your bank or lawyer hold them for you. You might make such an arrangement temporarily if you go away on an extended trip. While you are away, you may effect a transfer merely by signing a stock power and sending it to the custodian. Or you may sign a power of appointment beforehand.

Alternatively, you can have them registered in your own name but held by your broker. That way a sale can be executed by sending him a signed stock power. But in recent years, some brokers have experienced back-office logjams that have resulted in delays in obtaining certificates and even in lost certificates. Even though shares held by your broker in your name eventually would be returned to you in a brokerage house bankruptcy, there inevitably would be a delay. This could result in a loss of capital if the stock began dropping in price and you were unable to sell.

Street name accounts are popular with investors who trade their securities frequently. Shares held this way can change hands without being endorsed by the owner. However, besides running the risk of lost or mislaid certificates or bookkeeping mixups, in some cases you have no direct control over your securities. You would lose this control if you signed a hypothecation agreement, a document that gives the broker the right to pledge his customers' securities as collateral for loans the broker himself takes out. You need not sign such an agreement if you have a strictly cash account, but you must do so in order to open a margin account. Normally, such an arrangement would not cause any problems, but it could in a brokerage house bankruptcy. Thus, even with insurance against brokerage house failures, your street name investments could be tied up for a long time if something went wrong.

How SIPC Protects You

Creation of the Securities Investor Protection Corporation (SIPC) by Congress in 1970 was a boon to investors. Until then, when a broker went bankrupt it was catch-as-catch-can for the investor whose securities were held in street name at that house. Under SIPC, brokerage accounts are insured for up to $100,000, of which $40,000 can be cash. SIPC does not protect customers against market losses from price declines.

An individual having several accounts with the same brokerage firm may or may not be covered separately for each account. For example, if you had an account in your own name, another as a trustee, and a third held jointly with your spouse, you would be covered to $100,000 in each. But if you merely had three different types of account in your own name only—cash, margin, bond, etc.—coverage would be limited to a total of $100,000.

With the exception of those firms engaged solely in the distribution of mutual funds, variable annuities, insurance, or investment advice, all broker-dealers registered with the Securities and Exchange Commission must be members of SIPC. Funding for SIPC comes from assessments on member firms. The agency does have access to additional funds in emergencies; it may borrow up to $1 billion from the U.S. Treasury through the SEC. Once the insurance corporation determines that a brokerage firm should be liquidated, application is made to the federal district court for appointment of a trustee. The trustee, in turn, notifies all customers of the firm. Claims against the broker should be submitted directly and promptly to the trustee.

How well has SIPC worked? It was created at a time when a major shakeout was occurring in the brokerage industry. In the first five years, it handled thousands of liquidations, most of them relatively smoothly, most of them involving small regional firms. Experience shows that in segregated accounts, where the shares are fully paid and held in the customer's own name, restitution has been prompt. In margin accounts, the experience has not been as favorable. Margined shares are held in street name and may be held by a bank against a broker's loan. Thus, they might be sold off during a market decline to maintain the required collateral to cover the loan. This means that in a brokerage house liquidation, customers with margin accounts could be paid off in cash rather than securities. This, in turn, means they might have to accept a sizable loss. In addition, it sometimes takes considerable time to sort out the failing firm's affairs, and in a liquidation that occurs during a down or falling market— when most of them do occur—this can mean even deeper losses for the holder of a margin account.

Besides carrying the required basic protection, some brokerage houses carry supplementary insurance protection, often up to $500,000 per customer. This would be a point to check out during your selection of a broker, if the size of your account warrants it.

Good Records Are Important

Whether you hold your own certificates or they are held for you by your broker, it is important that you keep accurate records of what securities you own and where they are located. For each transaction you make you receive a confirmation slip, which carries all the information needed for your records and for filing your income tax return. The confirmation slip shows the number of shares bought or sold, the trade and settlement dates, price per share, total amount of the transaction, and the net amount. Because confirmation slips may get misplaced over the years, you should keep a chronological record of all your transactions. Certainly this record should list the number and cost of the shares held, the trade date, and the net received in a sale or the gross paid on a buy. If you hold your own securities, you should be sure to record the certificate number in case of loss.

Your broker will send you monthly or quarterly statements indicating the status of your account. These statements should be retained for a reasonable period of time, because they provide good records of your transactions. Another reason you should keep them is to provide you with corroborating evidence of a claim against the firm, either in a bookkeeping slip-up or in the event of the firm's bankruptcy. Some firms include on the year-end statement the total margin interest charged to the account during the year.

If you have taken possession of your own stock or bond certificates, you have the problem of delivering them to the broker when you make a sale. But you can safely do this by mail, using certain precautions. One way is to execute a power of substitution—a stock or bond power. Your broker, bank, or stationery store should be able to provide the necessary form. The power should be endorsed with your name appearing exactly as it appears on the face of the stock or bond certificates. No other information need be filled in on the power; your broker will complete it. After signing it, you will mail the power and the unendorsed certificate to the broker in *separate* envelopes. Another way is to endorse the certificate itself. You do this by affixing your signature and the brokerage firm's name in the appropriate places on the back of the certificate. An endorsed certificate should only be sent by *registered mail*. This is also true of bearer bonds—those that can be cashed in by anyone bearing them.

Most corporate bonds today are issued in registered form. The cartoon of the rich old man sitting in a bank vault clipping his coupons is all but an anachronism these days. Even tax-exempts and Treasury debt issues, about the only remaining bastions of coupon bonds, allow you to choose registered bonds as an alternative. Treasury bills, however, are available only as bookkeeping entities. There are several advantages of registered bonds. For one thing, the bondholder's name is registered on the company's books, so interest checks are mailed directly to him. Notifications of calls, redemptions, and the like also are mailed directly to the holder. On the other hand, with coupon bonds he must watch for notices of such events in the financial press, since the issuing company has no other way of notifying him. However, if a bank or other institution is acting as trustee, custodian, or investment manager for him, they are responsible for keeping abreast of such developments. Registered bonds are not transferrable to another party unless they are endorsed. Bearer bonds, because they are so readily turned into cash, require special care in safekeeping.

If Certificates Are Lost or Destroyed

Replacing lost bond or stock certificates is a costly and time-consuming process, so a thorough and determined search should be made before initiating replacement proceedings. If certificates are destroyed in a fire or are stolen, it is possible that your insurance carrier may be responsible for underwriting some of the costs involved in getting them reissued. Be sure to check into this if you ever lose any this way.

Once you have ascertained that the certificates really are missing, you should notify either the bond trustee or the stock transfer agent. The trustee or agent will place a stop on the security to prevent its sale. If you have been assiduous in your record keeping, you will have noted the certificate numbers, which you should pass along to the trustee or agent. Then you will be required to furnish a perpetual indemnity bond to protect the company from any losses it might incur should the lost securities turn up later. Such surety bonds are expensive—they typically cost around 4 percent of the certificate's current value. Then you will have to meet certain conditions established by the company, and they vary in strictness from firm to firm. No corporation likes to reissue, and some do their best to discourage replacement until absolutely sure the certificate is lost. If the original should turn up within a year of buying the surety bond, you can get back only part of the premium; after a year, you will get nothing back.

There are times when you must reregister a certificate. Again, it is the bond trustee or stock transfer agent who will make the change. The agent generally is a bank, but in some cases the issuing company acts as its own agent. The bond trustee will always be someone other than the company. In any case, the name and address of the agent appears in the company's annual report, and this would be another useful piece of information to add to your record book.

If your shares are held jointly as joint tenants with rights of survivorship, the survivor receives full title on death of the co-owner. Shares held as tenants in common have no such survivorship rights; the decedent's share goes into his estate. When held with survivorship rights, the survivor can have the securities reissued in his own name merely by forwarding a certified copy of the death certificate to the transfer agent. In some cases the transfer agent may require a residence certificate for tax purposes. It makes no difference whether the conjunction "and" or "or" is used between the joint owners' names, as long as the shares are held as joint tenants with rights of survivorship.

Are Old Certificates Valuable?

According to those who keep track of such things, five out of every hundred old stock certificates traced have some value. In 2 percent of the cases, the obsolete certificates have a worth of $1,000 or more. With odds like these, time spent doing some digging on your own or money spent on experts to do the digging for you can be well invested. There are at least three firms that specialize in tracing old certificates: R. M. Smythe & Company, 170 Broadway, New York, New York 10038, B. S. Lichtenstein & Company, 101 Maiden Lane, New York, New York 10038 and Tracers Company of America, 509 Madison Avenue, New York, New York 10022. If the shares turn out to have any value, you will receive information on how to collect.

These companies are also useful if you should need to establish the date a security became worthless for tax-loss purposes. In the past, the Internal Revenue Service has considered them sufficiently authoritative to accept their information without challenge.

If you want to pursue the investigation on your own, your local library may be an invaluable source of information. Not all small libraries have an extensive business and financial section, but they might have arrangements with state libraries that can obtain books for you. Here are some books to look for: *Robert D. Fisher Manual of Valuable and Worthless Securities, Directory of Obsolete Securities,* and *Capital Changes Reporter.* An older volume might also be in stock—*Valuable Extinct Securities,* published by R. M. Smythe in 1934.

Determining their value is only the first step in receiving such windfalls. Not infrequently, these old stock certificates turn up in Great-Aunt Bessie's trunk, made out in her first husband's name. Before you can collect, you will have to establish your right to them. Of course, if they were issued in bearer form, it's finders keepers. If, in the long run, they turn out to be worthless, you can always frame them and hang them on the wall as curiosities.

Minority Shareholder Rights

Normally, a shareholder has the right to vote, to receive a portion of the profits, to inspect company books, to share corporate property, and to subscribe to subsequent stock issues. When a company goes private by buying up a majority of its outstanding shares or merges with another company in an exchange of its stock for that of the acquiring company, usually 3 percent or less of its common stock remains outstanding. Owners of this remaining portion are known as minority shareholders and have forfeited virtually all of their rights. Numbers alone have silenced their voices. The best way to protect yourself and your investment against this problem is to avoid getting boxed into the position in the first place.

The most frequently given reason for getting into the position is that the tender price of the stock was unfair. Yet, the alternative to accepting the offer is equally unattractive—ownership of a batch of unmarketable shares. Attempts to obtain judicial redress are almost always unsuccessful. The usual court response to aggrieved share-holders is that they go through the appraisal system in effect in their state. This is frequently a complex procedure that yields varying results.

Just plain ignorance is another factor contributing to a sharehold-er's finding himself in a minority position. He received the tender offer but did not know what to do with it, so he ignored it. Most cor-porations make a concerted effort to buy back small batches of stock in such cases, so several offers are made before they close the books on such conversions. Once the major part of the stock has been ten-dered, the minority shareholder might as well face the facts—he is not going to get any more for his shares than the tendering holders received. If he continues to hold out, he might as well forget about dividends, too.

Shareholders occasionally have an opportunity to join in a settle-ment on a class action suit. If they held the stock during the critical time period, they should receive an application to participate in the settlement. However, this is not always the case, and unless they return the application by the stated date, with the required docu-ments of proof, they will not share in the settlement.

Unless your investments are in a trusteed account or otherwise supervised, it is your responsibility to safeguard them, physically and otherwise. Although most publicly owned corporations will extend themselves within reason to protect and inform shareholders, it is up to you as an individual investor to read all company communications and take action when required. The small amount of time, care, and intelligence you must spend on your investments will pay off in the long run.

Chapter 36 Running Your Investment Program

NOT EVERYONE is financially able to invest a few thousand dollars at a time to buy securities in round lots. Fortunately, that isn't the only way they can be purchased. Several alternatives are available for the periodic investment of smaller amounts of money. Among the choices are monthly investment plans offered by brokerage houses, dividend reinvestment plans operated by individual companies, and mutual fund accumulation plans.

Besides these rather formally structured programs, you can, of course, design your own plan for making regular additions to your savings and investment program. You can have funds deducted from your salary and set aside for periodic investment. The bond-a-month payroll savings plan has proved a boon to millions in building a financial reserve of U.S. Savings Bonds. You can pick stocks in three or four—or a half dozen—different well-diversified companies and by investing a predetermined monthly amount on a rotating basis build yourself a mini mutual fund of respectable size in fairly short order.

The possibilities are endless, bounded only by your own imagination and desire to accumulate a savings and investment portfolio. We will discuss several alternatives in this chapter. One of these is the monthly investment plan offered by many brokerage houses. These plans vary from one firm to another, but the concept is the same—to provide a systematic periodic method of building a stock portfolio. Generally, you're allowed to invest a regular monthly or quarterly amount in one or more stocks chosen from a list of thirty or forty Big Board issues. Although there may be a discount of up to 25 percent from standard commission rates on these trades, the expenses can prove costly on small transactions. In addition, a small service fee may be charged. Usually a minimum of $20 can be invested.

Dividend Reinvestment Plans

Upwards of 1,000 companies offer their shareholders the choice of having dividends automatically reinvested in stock instead of being paid directly to them. In addition, the plans allow cash to be added to the dividend to purchase more shares and to build the pot faster. Many of the companies with such plans pay all or part of the commissions and bank fees involved. A few will reinvest the dividends in shares at a 5 percent discount from the market price. With a small initial investment to acquire a few shares through the customary channels, you can then enroll in the company's dividend reinvestment plan, add small cash infusions, and acquire additional shares at a reasonable fee and perhaps with no fee at all.

Here's how the plans work. Enclosed with your first dividend check should be application forms and information about the company's plan. Once you're enrolled, your dividends will be reinvested automatically in shares and fractions of shares (computed to three decimal places). Cash additions are generally limited to $12,000 a year, with a minimum addition of $10. If a pro rata commission is charged, your share probably will not amount to more than 1 percent of the amount invested. The bank fee is charged at a rate of 4 to 5 percent of the invested amount, but only to a maximum of $2.50 to $3 per transaction. If you plan only small cash additions, it would save on the bank fee to lump these annually or quarterly. Even after paying the bank fee and commission, your cost will be only about $4 per $100 invested, compared with the $7 or so it would cost by going through a broker.

To find out which companies offer such plans, you can check with a broker or with the Standard & Poor's Stock Reports, if your local library subscribes. Once you've zeroed in on a few companies that offer the plans, you can get the full details about each by writing the corporate secretary for a booklet. Your broker or the Stock Reports will provide the address.

Aside from being a painless and economical way to build a portfolio, dividend reinvestment plans offer the additional advantage of growth through compounding. From the initial investment forward, the reinvested dividends themselves are earning more dividends.

This means that even if you do not add any more cash as you go along, your investment works harder for you with each passing quarter.

Participants in dividend reinvestment plans receive a detailed statement of their account after each investment is made. If you decide to make voluntary cash additions, you should send them shortly before each dividend payment. Most companies accumulate participants' cash additions until collectively there is enough to purchase a round lot. That means your cash could sit around for a month or more without earning any interest.

Bank service charges are deductible for tax purposes. Commission costs are handled in the usual manner by adding them to your cost basis, and even though the dividends are reinvested they are taxable as income in the year received.

Mutual Fund Programs

Most mutual funds, loads and no-loads alike, offer some kind of systematic investing program. In general, these fall into two types— contractual and voluntary. Contractual plans have earned a bad name with their front-end load. But some of the worst aspects were reduced with the 1970 revisions in the Investment Company Act. The plans work by committing an investor to pay a predetermined amount into the fund over a period of ten to fifteen years. Before the reforms were instituted, the unwary investor found that the lion's share of the load fee for the entire plan was skimmed off the first year's investment. While this was wonderful for the salesman, it did little for the investor. Even with the 1970 revisions, the load is fairly heavy—as much as 20 percent of the first year's contribution can be allocated to sales charges, as long as it is 9 percent or less of the total investment. In a 150-payment plan, more than half the load fee is collected in the first 36 payments.

Operators of the plans point out that the penalty serves to encourage people to complete the programs. Furthermore, because a contractual plan is, in effect, "a letter of intent," the load fee could be at a lower rate than on a voluntary plan, if the total investment was large enough. The contractual plan offers the person who has trouble disciplining himself a form of forced investment program. Of course, there is nothing in the contract that requires him to complete the plan, except for the threat of forfeiting the large up-front sales fee.

Voluntary or systematic investing programs are looser. Often they are without any specified number of payments or amount to be paid. A simple notice is sent as a reminder at the appointed time. Terms and conditions of the various programs offered by a particular fund are set out in that fund's prospectus.

Stock Dividends and Rights

Another way to build your portfolio is to choose companies that regularly pay stock dividends. By limiting your choices to such issues, you could build a sizable portfolio in just a decade. For example, Georgia-Pacific has paid one or more small stock dividends annually for many years. Had an investor purchased 100 shares of this stock in January 1967, he would have had 404 shares ten years later— plus 122 shares of Louisiana-Pacific obtained in a spin-off. His cash would have doubled. By the simple expedient of putting up the $20 or so required to round out the fractional share at each distribution, he would have held 458 shares of Georgia-Pacific and 135 shares of Louisiana-Pacific at the end of the decade.

Adding the small amount of cash required to exercise rights is another means of increasing your holdings. Rights offerings are a common method of raising capital in the utility industry. In the last few years, American Electric Power has offered shareholders rights on a one-for-ten, one-for-nine, and one-for-eleven basis. Shares acquired through rights are free of commissions, and prices are under the market. In a six-year period, the owner of 100 shares of American Electric Power would have added 60 more shares if all rights had been exercised.

U.S. Savings Bonds

Until now, this chapter has discussed alternative methods of acquiring and building assets with marketable securities. However, as a supplement to stocks, bonds, and mutual funds, most well-rounded financial plans include nonmarketable investments such as U.S. Savings Bonds, savings time deposits (time certificates), and annuities (which we discuss in detail in Chapter 43). While it is not always possible to adhere to a program of regular investment, serial purchase has the advantage of producing income on a monthly or quarterly basis at retirement. We provide an example, using Savings Bonds, in Chapter 44.

U.S. Savings Bonds, in fact, should not be overlooked as you consider investment alternatives. Though snubbed by "sophisticated" investors, more than $70 billion worth are owned by millions of Americans. In fact, about $10 of every $100 saved in this country is invested in Savings Bonds. Their popularity lies in their safety, convenience, low denominations, and ease of purchase and redemption. More than two thirds of Savings Bond sales come in the form of payroll deductions, with close to 10 million workers enrolled in this periodic savings plan.

Series E Bonds, which have not been sold since 1979, have been superseded by Series EE Bonds. The latter are priced at 50 percent of their face value. The length to maturity varies according to what interest rate the government wishes to pay. In mid-1980, maturity was eleven years, giving them an effective interest rate of 7 percent. Series EE bonds are issued in denominations from $50 to $10,000.

You need not redeem Series E or EE Bonds at maturity; they shift automatically into an extension period. However, they reach final maturity after forty years. The Treasury has already announced final maturity for those issued between 1941 and 1952. Even then, you don't have to redeem them. They simply stop paying interest. You may always cash them in or exchange them for Series HH Bonds at their value at final maturity.

The stated return on Series E and EE Bonds is an average return; in the early years it works out to considerably less than that, providing an incentive to hold them at least to maturity. The income generated by Savings Bonds is subject to federal income taxes, but not to state and local taxes. On Series E and EE Bonds, interest is compounded semiannually but is not actually paid until the bond is redeemed. Likewise, tax on that interest need not be paid until it is actually received. Hence, a Series E or EE Bond is a means of deferring income taxes and qualifies as a "tax shelter."

However, if you desire, you may pay the tax on the interest annually as it accrues. This election is useful in buying bonds for persons in low tax brackets, particularly children, whose income is lower than the individual exemption, where the effect can be the same as holding a tax-free bond. See Chapter 39 for a detailed description of the maneuver.

The tax liability is an important factor in deciding what to do with bonds you have held for a number of years. By cashing them in, you would subject yourself to a large tax bite, particularly if you are in a high bracket. By waiting until after retirement, when you will likely be in a lower bracket, the tax impact would be reduced. There's another way to do it and continue to defer the tax on your stored up interest. That is to exchange the E-type Bonds for H-type Bonds.

The main difference between E-type Bonds and H-type Bonds is that the latter pay interest currently, rather than compounding it. They don't necessarily pay the same amount of interest, either. In mid-1980, when E-type Bonds were paying 7 percent, H-type Bonds paid only 6.5 percent. As with Series EE Bonds, the new HH Bonds carry penalties if redeemed early; they must be held for at least five years to escape such penalties. H and HH Bonds mature in ten years. Interest on them is paid by check semiannually and is taxable in the year paid. However, the tax on the accrued interest of any E-type Bonds exchanged for H-type Bonds is not payable until the latter are sold, disposed of, or reach final maturity.

Series H and HH Bonds are available in minimum denominations of $500. Thus, any shift of E or EE Bonds to H-type Bonds must be in multiples of $500.

Since Savings Bonds are registered securities, no one but the actual owner may cash them. This also means they can be replaced if lost or destroyed. To replace bonds, write the Bureau of the Public Debt, 200 Third Street, Parkersburg, West Virginia 26101. Provide as much information as possible about the missing bonds—their registration numbers, date and place of purchase, names and addresses of owners, and the like.

Savings Bonds are not transferrable or acceptable as collateral on loans. Partial redemption of E Bonds of over $25 face value, EE Bonds of over $50, or H-type Bonds of over $500 is allowed; the reissued portion will carry the original issue date. Likewise, smaller denominations may be exchanged for bonds of larger denominations. Again, the original issue date is applied to the reissued bonds.

Redeeming a bond you own is almost as easy as buying one. All you need is your signature and proper identification. On an E or EE Bond, you will get your proceeds on the spot. However, on an H or HH Bond, the proceeds will be sent to you by the Treasury Department.

When a more complicated transaction is involved, as when you wish to change the name of a beneficiary, add the name of a co-owner, or if you inherit bonds issued in the decedent's name, you will have to furnish certain documents. When this occurs, the change cannot be made on the spot. Instead, the bond must be sent to a Federal Reserve Bank for payment or reissue.

Other U.S. Obligations

Other U.S. Treasury and agency securities are not as elaborately packaged for consumption by the general public. In fact, most members of that public rarely trade them, even though they almost always yield a higher return than Savings Bonds. However, if you do decide that your program could use some "Governments," there are four ways you can buy them and three ways you can sell them.

For most investors, the most convenient channel for buying and selling is through a local bank. Bank fees vary, but generally amount to a flat charge of $20 or $30 plus mailing expenses per transaction for amounts up to $100,000 and an added fee of around $5 per $100,000 above that.

Alternatively, your broker can handle the business for you. Here again, the expenses vary widely, so it's best to inquire beforehand. Some brokers will fill the order on a net basis, that is, charge the asked price and derive the "commission" from the spread between the bid and asked price. Others charge a flat fee of, say, $25 plus another $25 if you want the bonds delivered to you rather than being kept by the broker.

For the investor who buys in round lots ($100,000 or more), a dealer in government bonds will charge the asked price and receive as his compensation the spread between the bid and asked price, just as is done by some brokers.

On new issues, you can buy directly from the Federal Reserve Bank in your district. Your order must be received by the stated deadline accompanied by certified or cashier's check (or cash, if you go in person) to cover the amount of the offering price. There is no commission involved and the transaction can be handled entirely by mail. Contact your nearest Federal Reserve Bank for the necessary forms and information.

Thus, you can buy government securities from a bank, a broker, a bond dealer, and the Federal Reserve Bank. You can sell or redeem them through a bank, broker, or dealer, but not through the Federal Reserve Bank. However, you can "roll over" maturing Treasury securities into newly issued ones through the Federal Reserve Bank.

Time Deposits and Term Certificates

Just as savings institutions charge different rates of interest to different types of borrower, so do they pay interest according to the type of savings account involved. They pay for the largest deposits or for the highest money left longest on deposit. Forced by competition, consumerism, and the regulatory structure, the industry has grudgingly moved toward paying interest on checking accounts and escrow accounts where money is held for payment of taxes and insurance premiums on mortgaged property.

Although maximum interest rates for various savings vehicles are regulated by the Federal Reserve Board and the Federal Home Loan Bank Board, savings institutions are not obliged to pay that maximum, nor are they obliged to offer every type of account. The lesson is clear: you should check around before committing your cash.

Because there is a substantial penalty for early withdrawal from a time deposit, you should be reasonably sure the money will not be needed before maturity. Federal regulations require forfeiture of three months' interest on the amount withdrawn, plus reduction to passbook rate of any interest due above the amount forfeited.

Here's a catchy sales pitch one bank used that you could adopt for yourself. "Give us $100 a month for twelve years," the bank's ads read, "and we'll give you $100 a month for your lifetime—and your children's, and their children's." The fine print stipulated that the offer was valid only as long as 6 percent interest rates prevailed. While the ad was an attention grabber, the scheme involved no giveaway. A monthly deposit of $100 over twelve years amounts to $14,400 in deposits which, at 6 percent interest, would be worth

$20,000 at the end of the period. With this capital invested serially at 6 percent interest, you would earn the $100 a month forever—as long as your assets were earning at a 6 percent rate. There is no reason why, with some self-discipline, you couldn't set up the same kind of program for yourself.

Self-discipline, in fact, is the real key to any successful savings and investment program. Another is regularity. Resolve to put something away on a regular basis, then see to it that you keep up the "payments." By using some combination of the methods outlined in this chapter, you should be able to draft a plan that suits your needs and objectives.

Chapter 37 Tax Pointers for Investors

WHEN IT comes to tax laws, Congress is an inveterate tinkerer. It is constantly adjusting, dismantling, and reassembling, adding new gadgets, altering old ones, and "reforming" rules that are "unfair." Yet it rarely seems to succeed in simplifying, even when it deliberately sets out to do so. The result is a burgeoning compendium of regulations that change from year to year. Therefore, any discussion such as this can only give you some general guidelines.

Seasoned watchers of the shifting sands of tax law only half jestingly refer to the legislation as the Federal Attorneys' and Accountants' Welfare Program. Congress does indeed keep a good many lawyers and CPA's busy untangling the continuing flow of laws, rules, and regulations for their corporate and individual clients.

All humor aside, unless you're willing to tackle the job yourself or unless yours is the very simplest of investment programs, you would be well served to seek the advice of qualified counsel to help you map the tax strategies that go along with your investment and personal financial planning program. However, to get you started, here are five basic rules.

Don't Let the Tax Tail Wag the Investment Dog

The cardinal rule for investing is to let the basic validity of the investment itself be the deciding factor in whether to acquire, hold, or sell it. Thus, tax considerations should always play a secondary role in your decision. But once a decision has been made, the way in which you implement it frequently can make a difference in your profit (or loss).

For instance, if a security which you want to sell for a loss will change from a short-term holding (held one year or less) to long term during the current tax year, you'd be better off to sell it while it's still short term. On the other hand, if you want to sell for a gain, you'd be better off to wait until it qualifies as a long-term holding.

That's because net short-term losses may be offset dollar for dollar against ordinary income up to a maximum of $3,000 a year, while it takes $2 of long-term losses to offset $1 of ordinary income. Only 40 percent of net long-term gains is included in taxable income. Special rules apply to large gains under the alternative minimum tax. Short-term gains are taxed at ordinary rates.

Give Uncle Sam His Due

Don't cut off your nose to spite Uncle Sam's face. Many investors who have enjoyed substantial capital appreciation on well-chosen securities are reluctant to cash in on these profits because of the capital gains taxes involved.

That can be a costly mistake. If good judgment dictates that the time has come to unload, then the investment should be sold. A large profit—even one which Uncle Sam shares—is better than a smaller profit later (he'd get a piece of that, too), and infinitely preferable to a long-term loss (which, remember, Uncle Sam makes you write off at $2 for $1). When it's time to sell, sell—and give Uncle Sam his due.

But there are times when you can blunt the tax effects of a substantial gain. Any capital losses you take in the same tax year or carry over from previous years are offset dollar for dollar against capital gains before any of the gains go onto your Form 1040 as income. Thus, you can use the capital gains as an opportunity to weed out your portfolio by selling off investments in which you're showing losses and which should be unloaded anyway. Conversely, if you've had to take some losses, you can use them to liberate some capital gains on which you'd otherwise be taxed.

The last maneuver, by the way, can have some beneficial long-term implications for you. Suppose you have some IBM that you bought way back during the torrid 1960s, and it's done so well for you that you'd never think of selling it out of your portfolio. On the other hand, you took a flyer a couple of years back on what looked like the next Xerox. It's turned out to be anything but, and you think you'd be best off if you dumped it. Go ahead and sell it to establish your loss. But at the same time, sell an amount of IBM shares so that the gain on the IBM sale equals the loss on your bummer. While you're still talking with your broker, buy as many new IBM shares as you sold. This will maintain your position in that stock. Presto! No net capital gains or losses. Not only that, you've raised the tax basis on your newly acquired IBM shares, reducing the amount of capital gain you'll be liable for when you dispose of them at some future time.

Don't Go to the Showers on a "Wash Sale"

Many investors play losses against gains by selling a position to establish an appropriate loss, then buying it back because they believe in the long-term soundness of the investment. That's OK, as long as you don't run afoul of the 30-day repurchase limitation, the so-called wash sale rule. That rule prohibits you from claiming a loss on any security that you've replaced with a substantially identical security within 30 calendar days before or after selling your original holding. The wash sale rule applies only to losses; you can repurchase immediately before or after establishing a gain.

Remember, the wash sale rule applies on either side of a loss sale. You may sell your holding first, then wait the 30 days and buy the replacements, or you may buy the replacements first, and then sell the holding after the appropriate period has passed. The date of sale is the date the loss is established. The wash sale rule applies even though the maneuver spills over from one tax year to another. This has useful connotations, for it means that with proper forethought you can establish a loss toward the end of one year or delay taking it until the start of the next, depending on which would be more advantageous for tax purposes.

Another point that's important to remember about the wash sale rule is that it may apply to more than the common stock itself. The rule says "substantially identical" securities, and this can mean the common stock and warrants or options on it. It can mean bonds sold by the same company with similar yields and maturity dates, even though they are of different issues. However, you probably would not run afoul of the wash sale rule if you sold common stock and bought bonds or preferred stock in the same company within the 30-day period, as long as these were not convertible into the common.

In fact, that's one way of getting around the wash sale rule if you want to establish a loss yet retain a position in the company. Another way is to sell the securities to establish the loss, then buy a similar position in another company within the same industry group and possessing similar investment attributes as the one you sold.

Don't Trip over the Calendar

Much portfolio adjusting is done toward the end of the year as investors obtain a clearer picture of their gain-loss situation. If you do this, keep one eye on the calendar.

If you're a cash basis taxpayer, as most individuals are, you can sell a stock any time up to the last day of the year to establish a loss. But to establish a gain, you have to sell at least five business days before the end of the year to allow the transaction to clear. You have to watch the calendar, too, to avoid problems with the wash sale rule discussed above.

Don't Compare Stock Loss Apples with Tax Saving Oranges

Remember, a $1,000 loss does not mean a $1,000 saving on your income tax. If you're in the 50 percent bracket, it means a $500 saving; in the 25 percent bracket, $250. What's more, these "savings" are cut in half if the loss is long term and applied $2 for $1 against ordinary income.

The Art of Creative Giving

How would you like to have Uncle Sam as a partner in your charitable giving? He can be, and he won't even claim any of the credit for the gift. He gets involved because you can take tax deductions on gifts to domestic nonprofit organizations of a religious, charitable, scientific, literary, or educational nature. You don't have to pay gift taxes, either.

Deductions for gifts to organized charities are restricted generally to 50 percent of your adjusted gross income. In the case of appreciated property which if sold would have brought long-term capital gains, you can deduct the market value, as long as it amounts to less than 30 percent of adjusted gross income. In the case of appreciated property which if sold would have brought ordinary income, the deduction is limited to your basis rather than market value.

So, you see that with gifts of stocks or other securities, you can get a tax deduction for the full current value of the property, while your actual cost might be much lower. Uncle Sam absorbs the cost of your capital gain. He already is a partner in your charitable giving, since a portion of the gift would have gone for federal income taxes had you not made the gift and thus qualified for the tax deduction.

Suppose you have some highly appreciated property and you'd like to give away the gain as a gift while retaining your original capital. You can do that, too, with Uncle Sam's help, by selling the property to the charity at your cost. In turn, it can sell your property at the higher market value, keeping the difference as your "gift." However, your tax deduction is limited to the gain on the sale. You must also report as capital gain the portion of sale proceeds attributed to your cost.

If you have property on which you have a loss, it's better to sell the property, establish the loss, and give the proceeds to the charity, than to give the property outright. Otherwise, no one would be able to claim the loss, and it would be "lost" for tax purposes.

There are other, much more sophisticated, vehicles for making charitable contributions and obtaining tax deductions. One example is a charitable remainder trust. Such a trust can be set up to give you or someone you designate the lifetime use of property, with the property going to charity upon your death or the death of your beneficiary. The advantage of doing this is that you get a large charitable deduction right away, while still enjoying the use of your property. Similar benefits can be obtained with unit trusts and charitable annuities.

Since these and other less-than-routine charitable gifts can be complicated and should be undertaken only with your total financial picture in mind, you should have the help of qualified legal and tax counsel when contemplating such large gifts.

Other Strategies

Sometimes you can use the tax laws to advantage by transferring assets to other family members. By doing so, you can frequently shift income-producing property to someone in a much lower tax bracket, thus achieving total tax savings. See the discussion of "Clifford trusts" in Chapter 39.

However, there is a strategy involving securities of highly appreciated value that will substantially ease the capital gains tax bite. It is called an "installment sale." Instead of giving the securities away, sell them to a family member, say your daughter, in a lower tax bracket. She, in turn, will pay you for them over an extended period, rather than right away. Since your daughter purchased the securities, her cost basis is what she paid for them, their current market value. She can sell the securities right away and incur no capital gain, hence no capital gains tax liability.

You will not escape capital gains taxes on shares that appreciated while you owned them. But you'll be able to spread them out over the period your daughter is paying you for the securities. In addition, you'll be receiving interest from your daughter on the balance outstanding (you have to charge interest to make the deal legitimate). She, in turn, will be able to deduct the interest payments from her income taxes. She'll also have immediate use of the full value of the securities. Had you sold them all at once, you'd have forked over a sizable chunk in taxes to Uncle Sam. To make sure such a deal meets all the legal requirements, be sure to have an attorney work out the details for you.

There are times when even the most astute investors are caught holding securities in companies that go down the drain. Who would ever have thought such venerable temples of American free enterprise as Penn Central or W. T. Grant would ever fall? Yet, for a variety of reasons, they did, leaving thousands of trusting investors holding the bag. Countless other companies, riding the crest of the torrid stock market of the 1960s, were broached and swamped in the economic trough of the 1970s. About the only recourse for their common stockholders was to claim a loss deduction on their income taxes.

It's not always as easy as it sounds. The tax people say you can't claim a loss until the securities are deemed completely worthless, that is, when there is absolutely no chance that the company will ever do business again. We talked about obsolete, "worthless" securities in Chapter 35.

But here's a point you have to watch when claiming a tax loss on a "worthless" security. If you've used it to offset capital gains and it's later disallowed, you'll be hit with some capital gains taxes—adding insult to the injury incurred by the sour investment.

We said it at the outset, but it bears repeating in concluding this discussion about taxes and your investments: Don't hesitate to get professional help with anything that goes beyond the most routine investment maneuver. The tax laws have become so complex that even the experts have trouble keeping things straight. The money you pay for qualified guidance in most cases will be among your most worthwhile investments, and frequently will represent only a fraction of the cost of do-it-yourself tax counseling.

Part VI INVESTMENTS AND YOUR FINANCIAL PLAN

Chapter 38 Are Your Affairs in Order?

WHEN WAS the last time you gave your family's financial situation a thorough going-over? In the rush of everyday living, it's easy to let these things slip. Yet, when you stop to think about it, in the process of managing your income and outgo, you're running a sizable "business." How well or poorly you do it depends in large part on how thoroughly you have organized the job.

When you first started out, it was an easy task, and you could handle it efficiently on a week-to-week, month-to-month basis. Then came a house, with a mortgage running twenty years or so. And children. And the start of a nest egg for the future. The management task has become considerably greater as you have added more places for your money to go, and as you have moved up the income scale.

Your acquisitions quite likely have come gradually—so gradually that you may not have recognized just how complex your affairs have become. No longer can the week-to-week, month-to-month approach suffice.

Then, too, there is the concern that your family might have to get along without you at some point. How well have you prepared for that possibility? If you were to duck out for good tomorrow, would you leave behind a jumble of records, some here, some there, for your survivors to try to find as best they might?

If you are the well-ordered type, you probably have things well in hand. Even so, you might profitably run through this chapter in the event you have overlooked some point worth reviewing or reworking. If you feel your family's financial program needs some organization, you can use what follows as a starting point.

Finding Your Net Worth

The first thing to do is to find out where you stand. How much are you worth? Take a stab at the answer before you write anything down. Chances are, when you do the arithmetic, you'll find that your guess was on the low side.

"Well, let's see," you say. "I have some life insurance, we're buying a house, the car's almost paid for, we have a few stocks and bonds. That's about all. Guess I'm not worth much, am I?"

Guess again. Better yet, take a few minutes to compile a balance sheet. It might be very pleasing to your ego.

The reason you might mislead yourself into believing you don't have much material worth is the state of your wallet. It's pretty flat most of the time for a good many of us. But think of what you're buying with what comes out of it. Sure, there are the necessities—food, heat, clothing, contributions, a night out once in a while. You don't have much to show for the shelling out on these items.

But what about the mortgage payment? A portion of that goes each month toward paying off the principal, and increasing your equity in the property. This is like a savings account. The same is true, though to a lesser degree, of your automobile. Your life insurance policy, too, might be building some cash value each year, yet another form of "enforced" savings not immediately visible.

In fact, most of your net worth is "invisible." Or it's so visible that you don't really see it. Take your furniture. You probably don't think of that in terms of its material value. Yet, you laid out cash for it; it represents an investment. You'd have to lay out more cash to replace it if it were lost. Same thing for your home appliances. Add up their value—the refrigerator, dishwasher, clothes washer, dryer—just these major items represent a sizable sum in themselves. Of course, their value diminishes each year with their use, but as long as they are of use they have value. They are part of your assets.

Almost anything you own can be included among your assets. This includes sporting goods, jewelry, cameras, your boat, home workshops, garden tools, snowblowers, bicycles, and art. Of course, you wouldn't forget to include the value of your vacation home. As you work up an inventory of such things you can see just how much you have accumulated along the way.

Another "invisible" asset might be your interest in your company's pension or profit-sharing program. Some companies have group life insurance policies, and you might be contributing to one that will return these contributions when you leave the company or retire. You should check up on the status of your company benefits from time to time and add their value to your assets.

Don't forget to add in savings and checking accounts and the current worth of your stocks and bonds. Since your house has probably increased in value since you bought it, include the full current market value on the asset side of your ledger. Now add everything up.

Chances are, you owe money, too. Get this all together. The balance due on your mortgage. On your car loan. On any other loans outstanding. Insurance premiums. Current household bills.

Subtract the total of these liabilities from the total value of your assets and you'll have your net worth. Not bad, you might conclude. By making an accounting at about the same time each year, you'll get an idea of how well you're progressing. You'll also have an idea of what your goals should be, where you should be devoting more or less emphasis. This provides an excellent chart of the family's financial progress.

Where Does the Money Go?

Great. But where does all your money go each month and each year? Find out by drawing up an income statement. Your checkbook is probably as good a data source as you can get, particularly if you write checks for most of your bills. If you don't pay by check, by the way, you ought to consider doing it, because it serves as an excellent record, and it can provide proof of payment if you're ever challenged on that score. Taking your most recent full year period, go through your records and write down all expenses, putting them into such general categories as mortgage, auto loan, heat, lights, phone, food, clothing entertainment, and so on.

Next, jot down your total income, making note on the expense side of the amount taken out for taxes and Social Security. Work your figures over until the "income" and "outgo" sides of the ledger balance. This income statement gives you an idea of how much you're paying for what. It makes a good starting point for drawing a budget.

Controlling the Outgo

A budget is needed to keep future spending under control. It need not be cast in concrete at the start of the year; in fact, it should not be so rigid that it allows no flexibility. Your budget shouldn't run your life, but instead it should serve as a map of your financial trip through the upcoming year and as a chart to keep you on course.

Once you have these three basic tools—a balance sheet, an income statement, and a budget—you're well on the way to getting your family finances under control. A couple of other things might be worth mentioning at this point. One is a household inventory. The other is an insurance checkup.

As you probably discovered when you added up your possessions for your net worth tally, you own a lot more than you realized. Should you be hit with a burglary or fire, it might be difficult to remember the specifics in placing an insurance claim or filing a loss deduction on your income tax return. It would be a lot easier to have a list made ahead of time. It wouldn't be a bad idea to keep a copy of that list somewhere other than in the house; say, in your safe deposit box at the bank or perhaps in your insurance agent's file. You ought to update the list from time to time. Include specifics as to brand and style, your cost, date acquired, and estimated replacement cost.

In this inflationary period, you are at risk, too, with your homeowner's insurance coverage if you don't add to it from time to time. One reason is obvious: if you have a total loss, you wouldn't be fully covered on replacement costs. The other isn't so obvious; if you're not covered to within 80 percent of the value of the property, your coverage for any partial loss will be reduced to the extent that full coverage falls short. To make sure that your coverage is up to snuff, you should give it a yearly checkup. You can also ask your insurance agent to write an inflation escalator clause into your policy, and coverage will be automatically increased each year in line with the rise in prices. You should be certain your other casualty and liability coverage, such as that on your automobile, is periodically upgraded, as well.

Providing for Illness, Disability, and Death

While you're thinking about insurance, you should give your health and life insurance programs a going-over. Since it is not the purpose of this book to educate you on that score, we'll only mention in passing the need to take a look at them from time to time to make sure they still meet your needs, both immediate and long term. With medical bills rising constantly, only one hospital stay would put you behind unless you're adequately covered.

If your family insurance program doesn't include disability coverage for the principal breadwinner, you ought to consider taking some on, to provide continuation of income in the event of his incapacitation. This protection, frequently overlooked because of its expense, in some ways is more important for younger families than life insurance, since disabling illness and accidents are more likely prospects than death.

That does not mean life insurance should be ignored, either. How much coverage you carry depends on how you regard such protection, how much you think the family will need to function comfortably in the absence of the principal wage earner, and how much you can afford to lay out for premiums.

Again, without getting into an involved discussion, we believe that, in general, term insurance buys you more protection for your dollar than whole life, which shunts a portion of the annual premium into a "savings" program that builds up cash value. We believe that by investing the difference yourself you can do much better over the long run—providing you discipline yourself to put that money aside each year. Your term policies should have a guarantee that they will be renewable at the end of each term regardless of your health at the time, and you might do well to pay a bit extra for a guarantee that the premiums will be paid if you become disabled.

A Record-Keeping Checklist

So, now that you have your income and outgo under control and your insurance coverage checked, what other records need to be assembled? Here's a list to get you started.

Will. Note where copies are filed, when it was last drawn, and when any changes were made.

Safe deposit boxes. Note where they are located and list their contents as of a certain date. Note where keys are kept.

Insurance. List all policies, their numbers, and note where they are located and whom to contact if needed.

Bank accounts. Note account numbers, location of passbooks, and other pertinent information on all family accounts.

Securities. Provide a complete current listing, including costs, and note where certificates are located.

Real estate. Maintain a list of capital improvements with supporting invoices for tax purposes; note basic expenses such as property taxes, utilities, etc., as well as mortgage data.

Income taxes. Retain copies of final returns for past several years and keep complete data for the current year.

Professional advisers. List names of attorney, trustee, and executor of the estate, insurance agents, stockbrokers, tax counsel, physicians, etc.

Requests and recommendations. Provide notes on disposition of personal effects after death for sentimental or other reasons not specifically mentioned in the will; provide suggestions for survivors on how best to make sure of the resources and advisers; list obituary material.

Once these records have been assembled, don't keep them a secret. If you are married, go over them with your spouse, explaining each item and its significance.

But contemplation of death shouldn't be the only motivating force behind establishing a good record-keeping system. If you sell your house, it can help you establish costs so you can reduce capital gains tax liability on appreciated value. If the IRS challenges your tax return, you have your defense readily at hand. You can tell at a glance how your investment portfolio is performing. You can detect potential financial problems ahead of time and take remedial measures before they become expensive crises.

The earlier you start such a system the more help it can be to you in preserving your hard-earned assets and making them work more efficiently for you. Now is the time to get on with it.

Chapter 39 Investing for a College Education

IF YOU have children, chances are that one of your primary financial objectives is to provide college educations for them. If you haven't priced a college education lately, you're in for a shock. And if you have some years to go yet before the youngsters are ready for college, your shock will be compounded by the ravages of inflation if you don't start setting something aside now.

The sooner you begin your college fund, the easier your task will be. It will be a twofold job: first, to provide the assets; second, to make sure these assets work as hard as they possibly can while they're waiting to pay the college bills.

If you have a chunk of cash you are able to salt away immediately, all to the good. A portfolio of good-quality growth stocks should appreciate sufficiently over the next decade to give you a solid start toward paying the bills.

Or you might have to set aside funds a little at a time. The secret to success is to do it on a regular basis. Such a program takes discipline, but it can pay off handsomely. For instance, if you had invested as little as $200 each birthday, since your child was one year old in 1960, in a growth stock like Abbott and plowed back all dividends, the $3,600 cost would have been worth about $12,000 in 1978 when he or she was ready to go off to school. By increasing the yearly contribution as your earnings rose, you could have accumulated enough to pay the entire cost of college.

It is well to keep firmly in mind as you start planning for your children's educations the importance of protecting your fund from inflation, because college costs are rising faster than prices in general and the trend is likely to continue for the foreseeable future. That's why we have placed emphasis on common stocks. The earlier you begin your college investment program the greater will be the benefits from capital appreciation of good investments.

Keeping the Tax Man at Bay

Whether you invest in a portfolio of growth stocks or prefer the comfort of investments that provide greater "safety" of principal, you must consider the potential effect of taxes on the nest egg. With growth stocks, the big bite comes when they're sold—as capital gains. With income securities, the bite is more gradual, a year at a time as the income is earned. But it is larger, because you lose the advantage of compounding as you draw off dollars to pay taxes and because you pay at ordinary income rates, rather than the more favorable capital gains rates. There are ways to reduce the impact of erosion from taxes. The most effective methods involve getting the assets out of your high tax bracket and into a lower one. Here are some ways to do it.

U.S. Savings Bonds. As noted in Chapter 36, one of the features of Series E Bonds is that interest is not paid as it is accrued but left in and compounded semiannually. Bondholders do not have to pay income taxes on this accrued interest until they redeem or otherwise dispose of the bonds, and they generally do choose to defer the taxes. However, if they wish they may pay the taxes annually. You can use this feature to good advantage in building a college education fund.

By buying Series EE Savings Bonds in your child's name, they will be taxable to him. You may name yourself as beneficiary, but not co-owner, or you'll also be liable for taxes and thus defeat the purpose of the maneuver. You then file a tax return the first year the child holds the bonds, signifying that he intends to pay taxes annually instead of deferring them. Unless he has a substantial amount of other income, income from the bonds will be less than his personal exemptions, and he will owe no taxes. If you're in the 40 percent tax bracket, the effective yield of a 7 percent Savings Bond will be the same as if you had invested in securities with a 12 percent return and held them yourself. (For more about U.S. Savings Bonds, see Chapters 36 and 44.)

Custodian accounts. Another easy way to get assets out of your high tax bracket is to establish a custodian account for your child under the Uniform Gifts to Minors Act. Setting one up is as easy as opening up an account for yourself at a savings institution or brokerage house. Beyond that simple paperwork, you need only to name a custodian.

Your contributions to the account are regarded as gifts and as such are subject to federal gift taxes. However, as the rules are presently written, they allow you and your spouse to give up to $6,000 a year to as many individuals as you wish without incurring any gift tax obligation. You may also utilize your combined gift and estate tax credit to make larger gifts if you wish.

Income earned by the assets in the custodian account is taxable to the child, and not to you. In most cases, this means a substantially lower tax bracket, as well as the opportunity to utilize the child's personal tax exemption.

However, there are some other things you should know about using custodial accounts. The first is that the assets automatically go to the child, no strings attached, when he or she reaches legal age. In some states, that is eighteen, and if that's the case in your state and you have any qualms about your ability to keep your child persuaded not to blow the wad on something other than college at that point, you might better consider another approach (see below).

Another important point is that you should name someone other than yourself as custodian. That's because if you are both the chief donor of assets and the custodian, and you should die while the account is still in force, the assets will be counted in your estate.

Finally, you should be careful not to use any of the account's income to provide support for your child. If you do, that income will be taxable to you.

Doing It with Trusts

Most of the characteristics of custodial accounts can also be true of trusts. The major difference is that a trust can be drawn up to deal with a situation in a particular and specific way. For instance, you can specify in a trust that assets will not go to the child until he reaches a certain age, even though that age is beyond the "legal" age.

If the trust is irrevocable, that is, if assets are placed in it with no strings attached and so that you cannot remove them at your own discretion, will, or whim, those assets will not be counted in your estate if you should die while the trust is in force. As with custodian accounts, income generated by the trust assets is taxable to the child. Again, to be sure that the irrevocably given assets are not tossed back into your estate, you should name someone other than yourself as trustee.

To establish a trust, you'll need the help of an attorney. Unless there are some compelling considerations you want clearly spelled out, there is little need to establish such a trust instead of the simpler—and less expensive—custodian account.

Short-term trust. One way to have your cake and eat it too is to establish a short-term trust, also known as a "reversionary trust" or a "Clifford trust." Under this arrangement, assets placed in the trust return to the donor after a specified period, as long as that period extends at least ten years and one day, or upon the death of the beneficiary. Meanwhile, income earned by the assets is taxable to the beneficiary.

But because the trust is revocable—its assets ultimately return to you—those assets would be counted in your estate if you should die while the trust is in force. Thus it provides no estate tax advantage, and is of no value as an estate planning device.

A short-term trust works best when it works longest, because it delivers its clout by compounding the dollars saved in income taxes that you otherwise would have had to pay. Ideally, it should be started when your child is age six or younger; if your child is within three or four years of college, you might as well forget about it as a tax-saving device, unless you're in a position to plunk down a very large amount into the trust, enough to earn a substantial portion of the child's annual college expense.

As long as the trust is building up funds, there is no problem with your claiming the dependency exemption on your child. However, once the trust begins paying out for college expenses, that exemption might be lost, though there are ways of preserving it; a couple of years before you need it for college, consult a tax adviser to show you how. At any rate, the only cost would be the tax on the amount of that exemption, and that would be a small price to pay for the tax savings achieved over the years.

The drawing of trusts is clearly a job for a qualified tax and legal adviser. He can steer you away from shoals that might be present in your own state's statutory structure.

Chapter 40 Countdown to Retirement

RETIREMENT EVE is no time to start wondering what you'll have for "eating money" once you bid your fond adieus to your job. Five to ten years ahead is not any too soon to begin figuring. Probably you have a pension plan where you work. But do you really understand how it operates—and how much you are likely to get out of it once you hang up your tools? You're pretty sure to be eligible for Social Security when you retire. But do you have any idea how large the monthly checks will be?

If you're like the vast majority of workers, these two items will provide the lion's share of your retirement income. To make any kind of realistic projections about your financial needs in retirement you'll have to have a rough idea of how much they will give you. You'll also have to know early enough so you can start laying away some savings to provide extra income.

A ball park figure is sufficient. It's impossible to get a precise fix anyway, because of the changes that will occur in your income and in the Social Security rules during your remaining years on the job.

The quickest way to estimate your potential retirement income situation is to assume you're retiring right now and compute your benefits on that basis. Ask your company what the pension plan would pay someone who retires this year at your income level and with the number of years' service you'll have at retirement age. Then estimate the Social Security benefit you'd receive if you retired this year. Your nearest Social Security office can give you the figure.

Add the two together. In all probability, that's pretty close to what you'll get in dollars of equivalent buying power when you do retire. Could you live on that sum? Make a quick calculation of your living costs in today's dollars under circumstances approximating those that will exist when you do reach retirement age. Remember, in retirement your income needs will be more modest than they are while you're working. No more expensive business lunches, not as many new clothes, no commuting costs, etc. If your mortgage is paid off at retirement age, your housing costs will be lower. With the children grown and gone, there will be fewer mouths to feed, no more college tuition bills to pay. Do the projected expenses fall within the projected income?

If not, you'll have to get cracking and (a) build some savings and/or (b) develop some ways of earning money in retirement.

How Much to Save?

Because conditions may change drastically between now and the time you retire, particularly if you are relatively young, it is difficult to judge with any degree of accuracy how much you'll have to save to provide an adequate retirement nest egg. But remember, inflation will play havoc with the figures both during your saving period and during the period you'll be drawing upon the account.

Just to give you an idea of what you're up against, let's assume a 5 percent inflation rate, probably a conservative estimate. At that rate, prices double in roughly fourteen years. (Based on the consumer price index, they doubled from 1958 to 1976, an eighteen-year period.) To provide the same buying power as $1,000 today, you'll have to have $1,276 if you retire in five years, $1,629 in ten, $2,079 in fifteen, and $2,653 in twenty. Remember, too, that during retirement that same process will continue; think what the effects will be on a nest egg that has to last three decades or so. Or what will happen to your lifestyle over that period if you don't have such a reserve.

Obviously, the earlier you start saving, the easier the task will be. Suppose you decide you'll need $200,000 on which to retire comfortably at age 65. If you're 30 now, assuming an 8 percent compounded growth rate for your assets, you'll need to save $1,160 a year between now and retirement, or $97 a month. If you're 55 now, you'll have to sock away $1,150 a month to meet your goal. The moral is obvious.

Savings Alternatives

After you've estimated how much retirement income you'll need and how much you must save to get it, you have to draft a retirement program.

It's stating the obvious to say your aim in providing a retirement nest egg is to build your assets as large as possible within reasonable bounds of risk. It's something else again to come up with a program that meets this goal.

The list of alternatives is well known, and we won't belabor it here. Basically, your choices divide into three general categories: *savings* (bank accounts, cash value life insurance, annuities, bonds, etc.); *equities* (business ownership, real estate, and common stocks); *speculations* (oil-drilling participations, commodity trading, options trading, etc.).

Weighing the obvious risks, you can quickly trim the list substantially at the outset. Unless you have funds you can really afford to lose, we'd suggest you leave the speculations to wealthier investors. Unless you're ready and able to undertake management of a business or real estate, we suggest likewise for these. That leaves stocks, bonds, bank accounts, insurance, and annuities for most.

By limiting your choices to these, you have substantially reduced, but not eliminated, the risk factor. Let's review our earlier comments on risk. Most likely your first thought is of the risk that your assets will shrink in the face of a decline in the securities markets just when you need to liquidate. That's a valid concern, and it should not be overlooked.

But there are other kinds of risk, and they are as important to consider. We have just demonstrated the risk of lost buying power of your savings. Then there is the risk that you'll get yourself locked into some investment to the extent that you can't easily or economically shift into a more lucrative one should the opportunity arise. Finally, there is the risk that the investment to which you entrust your savings will turn sour and fail altogether.

Ideally, you'd like an investment that would keep your capital intact, that would grow sufficiently fast to overcome inflation, that would be flexible, and that would not go down the tubes. Unfortunately, no single investment or savings vehicle exists that can guarantee all these goals at once. There will always be some element of risk involved. The trick is to get that risk under reasonable control and to spread it out to minimize its effects on your total program.

How do you do this? First, you determine which risks you can most easily live with. If you're nervous about putting your capital on the line, you'll have to live with the risk of shrinking buying power as you indulge in the "safety" of fixed-income investments. If you're more aggressive, you'll have to face the risk that your capital might possibly vanish in equity investments.

Isn't there some happy medium? We believe there is, and we've been preaching it for a good many years. It's called diversification. Don't put all of your retirement nest egg savings into the same investment basket. Your "mix" will be largely determined by the length of time you have before retirement and the amount of risk you're willing to undertake in relation to your expected return.

What kind of mix do you need to yield the desired results? If you have ten to fifteen years before retirement, we'd suggest you go heavily on the side of common stocks, to minimize the risk of buying power erosion. By choosing from among the strongest and best companies, you can select a portfolio of stocks that is highly resistant to market risk as well.

Don't make the list of stocks too long; keep it within manageable bounds. A half dozen to a dozen companies should provide sufficient diversification.

How much of your savings should you devote to equities? We would say 80 percent and still feel conservative, dividing the remaining 20 percent among bonds and savings certificates.

To retain flexibility, select bonds with maturities five or six years out, rather than those of longer term. This will minimize market risk should you wish to shift investments along the way.

As you move to within five years or so of retirement, you could begin to tilt portfolio acquisitions more toward fixed-income securities. You shouldn't start any wholesale shifting of equities already in your portfolio, though; there might be tax consequences that could be reduced if action is delayed until after retirement.

As you make the transition into retirement, you might have a portfolio consisting of 60 percent equities and 40 percent fixed income assets. Because the inflation risk is likely to be present during all of your retirement years, you should think seriously about retaining a solid position in equities to help offset the constant rise in cost of living.

Making Savings Grow

There's more to the creation of a nest egg than just putting funds aside. You must make them work as hard as possible while they wait for you to retire.

We've talked about determining how much savings you'll need for retirement and the various savings options open to you. Now let's look at some ways to make the retirement fund grow.

The first, and most obvious, way is to make regular additions to it. You've got to discipline yourself to do this, or your plan is doomed from the start. Play tricks on yourself, if you must. Have pay deducted from your salary so you never "see" it. Write yourself a check each month and deposit it to your retirement account. Start a regular investment program with your broker or with a mutual fund.

Another way to make savings grow is via compounding. Be sure all of your assets—including the income generated by them—are working for you all of the time. Keep dividends reinvested, rather than cashing and spending the checks. Pay any taxes out of pocket rather than out of the fund. Choose savings accounts that offer the most attractive compounding.

A third way is to defer taxes wherever you can. By putting off tax obligations until you pass into a lower tax bracket, you'll obviously have a lower tax bill. Not only that, you'll have the advantage of compounding with the earnings that otherwise would have gone to pay current taxes.

There are several ways of deferring taxes. If you are self-employed, you can start a Keogh plan. Current rules allow you to shelter up to 15 percent of your earned income to a $7,500 annual limit. If you work for someone else but don't participate in a qualified retirement plan, you can start an individual retirement account (IRA) and shelter up to 15 percent to a $1,500 annual limit. You can buy an annuity, where tax on the income generated by your contributions is deferred until you begin to draw benefits out. By choosing the right option on your ordinary life insurance policy, the dividends it earns may accumulate without any current tax liability.

But perhaps the greatest potential available to you for deferment of taxes lies with equities. The most convenient way to establish an equity position is through common stocks, and the best way to defer taxes via stocks is to choose those which emphasize capital growth. You pay taxes on dividends as received, but you don't have to pay any tax on appreciated value of the stocks until you sell them. Not only that, if you hold them until they qualify as long-term investments, you'll pay a tax on only part of the gain.

If you want to go whole hog and you're up to it, you can establish an equity position via outright ownership of a business. If you possess the necessary know-how and talents and if you do your homework properly, this could provide you not only with an appreciating asset but with a continuing source of income in retirement and a new "career" in the bargain. But it's risky, and not something that you should plunge into with all of your resources, for a loss could be disastrous and your time for recouping is severely limited.

Supplementing Retirement Income

If you think you'll need to generate extra cash to make ends meet in retirement, you should lay the groundwork before you get your gold watch. Whatever your motives for pursuing a post-retirement career, the earlier you start preparing for it before you actually step down from your primary job the better are the chances for its success.

For one thing, you might have valuable contacts in your profession that will not be as readily available once you retire. For another, there might be some resources at hand; more and more companies are helping their older employees prepare for second careers. Sometimes these can constitute major incentives for stepping down early to clear the decks for younger managers on the way up. At any rate, an early start can give you the chance to work out a lot of the kinks before you actually have to start depending on the income from the new career. And you should count on plenty of kinks.

The first step, naturally, is to decide what you'll do. Explore the possibilities carefully. Check your potential market—be sure there's really one out there for whatever it is you consider, be it as modest as a garage fix-it shop or as ambitious as a globe-girdling consultant practice.

As you do your planning, don't forget to take the Social Security rules into account, particularly the earnings limitation. There are indications that this ceiling is on the way out, but it hasn't happened yet and Congress is leaning toward a gradual phaseout.

Choose a business in which you have some demonstrated expertise—either professionally or via a well-developed avocation. Remember, the odds of failure of small businesses are very high. The more savvy and management skill you can bring to the job the better the chances of making a go of it.

Guard your resources. Don't forget the high failure rate of small businesses. Zero in on something you can try in a small way first, so if it doesn't work you won't have lost all your savings. Remember, your ability to replace lost wealth after retirement will be severely limited, if not nonexistent.

If you don't like the idea of putting your savings on the line, you might consider working for someone else instead. You might find your expertise affordable to a small business on the less than full-time basis you'd be able to provide.

But remember, you'll be "retired." Unless it's really what you want, be careful not to replace one all-consuming career with another. By shaking things down before retirement, you can get an idea of how to pace yourself, what kind of time the new venture will take.

Chapter 41 Keogh Plans

Until 1962, self-employed individuals enjoyed none of the retirement savings tax breaks available to their corporate peers. As a result, corporate pension and retirement programs waxed into extremely lucrative fringe benefits with the blessings—and indeed the tax-subsidized dollars—of Uncle Sam. Meanwhile, the retirement savings of persons who worked for themselves waned, laboriously financed as they were with after-tax dollars.

Representative Eugene J. Keogh, Democrat of New York, took up the cudgel in Congress for the self-employed with his sponsorship and active support of legislation that would at least partially remedy the situation. His bill was assigned the number HR-10 in the 87th Congress, and it ultimately became the Self-Employed Individuals Tax Retirement Act of 1962. As with so many other pieces of legislation, its ponderously formal name has been obscured by history, and it is commonly known as the Keogh Act or, simply, HR-10. Retirement programs established by self-employed individuals under the act—and its subsequent amendments—are known as Keogh plans or HR-10 plans.

In its original form back in 1962, the Keogh Act did not provide much of any tax incentive. It allowed a self-employed person to set aside the lesser of $2,500 or 10 percent of his earned income each year, and to deduct from current taxes half that amount, or $1,250 on a maximum contribution. Furthermore, it provided penalties—stiff to the point of being confiscatory—for excess contributions and premature withdrawals. The stringency of the rules is a mark of the political price the opponents exacted before agreeing to let the legislation pass.

As might be expected with such modest incentives, Keogh plans did not exactly spread like brushfire. But the law did provide a breakthrough in tax legislation, and it did allow holders of Keogh plans the benefit of compounding. The income generated by tax-sheltered retirement funds was likewise excused from current taxation. Even with such limited ceilings, some canny investors were able to fan their Keogh assets to fantastic heights in the rampaging bull market of the early 1960s.

The benefits were liberalized in 1968. Thenceforth, participants were allowed to shelter the entire contribution, which remained at 10 percent of earned income to a maximum of $2,500. This liberalization, plus the general feeling that eventually the boundaries would be widened even more, stirred up more interest in Keogh plans, and their numbers began increasing. That liberalization did indeed come.

In 1974, the tax-sheltered deduction was increased to 15 percent of earned income to a $7,500 annual maximum. The penalties for excess contributions and premature withdrawals were eased, and other liberalizations were provided. Keogh plans have become retirement savings vehicles that no self-employed individual can afford to overlook in the formulation of a sound financial program.

How Keogh Plans Work

So much for the evolution of Keogh plans. How can you, as a self-employed individual, use them? First, let's examine some of the specifics. How you determine eligibility and deduction limits. What your investment options are. How much flexibility you have in managing your plan. A review of the penalties and how they can be avoided. When you can start drawing benefits.

As all tax laws have a way of doing, the Keogh rules we review below could very likely change at any time. So, be sure to check on the current provisions if you pursue a Keogh program.

Who qualifies? Basically, if you pay your own Social Security tax in full, you qualify. But if you establish a plan for yourself, you also must establish similar ones for any employees 25 years old or older with three or more years of full-time service. Provisions must not give you more generous advantages than your employees. Contributions you make for employees (but not for yourself) are 100 percent tax deductible as a business expense. Employees must get full vested rights in pension funds.

As we said before, you can set aside up to 15 percent of your earned income to a $7,500 annual limit. Besides that, all accumulated earnings of the growing fund can be reinvested without paying current income taxes on them. Any taxes due are paid on assets as they are withdrawn; more on that in a moment.

Under certain circumstances, you may make voluntary contributions to your plan. If your employees are included and the plan allows them to make such contributions for themselves, then you can, too, within certain limits—up to 10 percent of earned income to a $2,500 annual limit, depending on the specific provisions of your own plan. The rate of such contributions cannot exceed the rate permitted for your employees. However, if you are the only one covered by a plan, you are not allowed to make voluntary nondeductible additions to the fund. In fact, you can be penalized for so-called excess contributions.

Since 1976, self-employed individuals have been able to initiate defined benefit plans that allow them to shelter more than the 15 percent–$7,500 limit under a formula based on earned income and age at entry in the defined benefit plan. Essentially, what the feature does is to allow a participant to make annual payments to a straight life annuity to the same extent he could if he were doing it under a corporate defined benefit plan, even if payments exceed Keogh limits.

As we indicated earlier, there are some penalties against which you must guard. You can be penalized for making excessive contributions. The penalty is a straight 6 percent a year levied on the amount of the excess as long as it remains in the fund. However, that excess can be counted toward current-year contributions, thus reducing or eliminating it. You can also be penalized for making early withdrawals. That penalty is an extra 10 percent added to the tax levied on the premature distribution. However, if you have made voluntary contributions to your plan, you may withdraw those assets at any time without incurring any penalty.

To make it easier and less expensive for you to begin a Keogh program, "master plans" and "prototype plans" have evolved. Under a master plan, several individual plans are grouped together, funded, and administered in common by a bank or insurance company. A prototype plan is individually administered under sponsorship of a professional association or a regulated investment company. A much more expensive alternative would be to have your advisers draft your own individual plan, which then would have to obtain

Internal Revenue Service approval before your contributions could qualify for deduction.

Investment Alternatives

There are, basically, five investment alternatives available to you. You can join a qualified bank trust, which might include pooled pension funds by a professional or business group, or an individual qualified bank custodial account can be set up. You can take out a qualified annuity plan with an insurance company. You can invest in mutual funds. You can purchase special nonmarketable Treasury retirement bonds. You can purchase IRS-approved face-amount certificates, which are somewhat like annuities.

Can these options be changed? Yes, for the most part. If you are in a mutual fund program, it is no problem to shift assets from one fund to another. You can also shift them into a trusteed account with a bank for investment in common stocks or other securities. Likewise, these assets can be shifted into mutual funds. In any switch it's safest to establish the new fund before making the transfer, and then transfer assets directly from one fund to the other to avoid premature distribution claims. If you have bought those special Treasury bonds, you must wait until you reach age 59½ to liberate the assets. However, you can "freeze" any plan that includes these bonds and start a new one. The greatest difficulty arises in trying to exit from an insurance program. About the only way you can do it is to end the plan by taking out a paid-up policy—usually at something of a loss.

If you're of a mind, you may manage your own Keogh plan. First you must find a trustee or custodian that the IRS feels confident will hold assets as prescribed by law. Banks have been traditional repositories for Keogh assets of this type, but under liberalized rules, such institutions as insurance companies, savings and loan associations, and credit unions have jumped into the act. Not all banks will allow you to retain such individual control, but there are some that do, and you can set up a qualified directed-trustee plan through them. Some brokerage houses have arrangements with such banks, and you can work through them.

When may benefits begin? Keogh assets cannot be withdrawn

before age 59½ without incurring penalties unless you become severely disabled or die. If your plan allows you to make voluntary contributions, you may withdraw them at any time without penalty. When you reach age 70½ you must start withdrawing benefits, though you may continue to make tax-sheltered contributions if you keep on working.

"Mini-Keogh" for Moonlighters

Before we discuss how benefits are taxed, let's consider another kind of Keogh plan. A provision in the law allows persons who are not essentially self-employed, but who earn income on the side, to shelter some of this income in a "mini-Keogh." This extra income must be from self-employment sources, such as consulting or free-lancing; if the "moonlighting" job involves being employed by someone else, you don't qualify. But if you do qualify, you may start and maintain a Keogh plan even though you are a participant in a pension program at your principal job.

Furthermore, in any year that your adjusted gross income from all sources is $15,000 or less, you are allowed to shelter up to $750 of self-employment income without regard to the 15 percent earned income ceiling. It works like this. Henry Jones is an engineer for a major aerospace company. On the side, he repairs foreign sports cars. The first year with the aerospace firm, his income was $12,500. He earned $600 as a self-employed mechanic. He started a mini-Keogh plan and put the entire $600 into it. The next year, his company paid him $20,000 (it got a fat government contract) and he earned $2,500 fixing sports cars. Since his adjusted gross was more than $15,000, he was able to contribute only $375 (15 percent of $2,500) to his Keogh fund.

Collecting Your "Benefits"

Now, what happens to the benefits you have built up over the years when the time comes to convert them into a retirement income program? Uncle Sam did not "excuse" the taxes you avoided during the contribution years, you can be sure of that. What he did was to allow you to defer them until you start using the assets you salted away. Besides the advantage of compounding we mentioned earlier, this also means that when you start drawing out the "benefits" you're generally in a lower tax bracket. Thus, the bite is not as great as it would have been had you had to pay during your earning years.

Withdrawal Options

Once you are eligible to begin withdrawing Keogh assets, you have several choices as to how you do it. You may take a lump sum distribution or, under annuity arrangements, you may choose to withdraw them over your own lifetime, over your lifetime and that of your spouse, or over a period not extending beyond the life expectancy of you and your spouse.

If you opt for a lump sum distribution, capital gains attributable to contributions made before 1974 will be taxed at the more favorable capital gains rate. Gains attributable to contributions made after 1973 will be taxed as ordinary income. However, a new ten-year averaging rule can be applied to them. You pay the tax all at once, but you compute it as if you had spread it over ten years. This will result in a lower tax than if you had had to count all of it in a single year's income. You must compute the tax separately from your regular income tax and use the schedule for single taxpayers, regardless of your own filing status. You may use this averaging device only if you choose to receive all of your Keogh assets in a lump sum. Furthermore, you may use averaging only once. Finally, you must have been a Keogh plan participant for at least five years prior to the taxable year of distribution.

Under the annuity arrangements, distributions are subject to taxation only as received, not on the value of the contract. If, however, you receive an amount equal to your investment within three years after the annuity payments start, you exclude from gross income everything you receive until you have recovered the full amount of any contributions that were not sheltered when they were put into the plan. After that, you must include in your gross income the full amount of each installment. If you receive the entire amount of the annuity investment within one taxable year, you are subject to the rules governing lump sum distributions.

Death Benefits

There are some tax implications on Keogh benefits left behind when a plan participant dies. In plans using retirement income, endowment, or other life insurance contracts, beneficiaries do not pay any income taxes on that portion of proceeds that exceed the cash surrender value of the policy at the time of death. The assets are considered under the same rules that govern life insurance proceeds. On cash surrender value, beneficiaries are taxed only on the portion that exceeds the nondeductible contributions made by the plan's participant.

If a distribution is made within a year of the participant's death, the rules governing lump sum distributions apply. If the assets are used instead to buy an annuity, the beneficiary is taxed at regular rates, just as with any annuity. Assets must either be distributed or used to provide annuity income for beneficiaries within five years of a participant's death.

Summing Up

There you have the basics of Keogh plans—how they originated, where they are now, and what you can and can't do with them. Given the current trend in pension legislation to equalize the tax breaks and benefit rules for all workers, whether they toil for themselves or for someone else, it is easy to foresee even more liberalization in contribution ceilings in the future.

By the same token, for self-employed persons with employees, this same trend is already proving somewhat expensive, as they must provide for their workers in the same proportion as they provide for themselves.

For the self-employed employer who either cannot afford or is not inclined to make such contributions for his employees and still provide a worthwhile pension plan for himself, an alternative is emerging in the much newer individual retirement accounts, which we discuss in the next chapter.

Chapter 42 Individual Retirement Accounts

WHEN KEOGH plans were introduced, banks, stockbrokers, and mutual funds offered them with indifference, because the modest annual contribution ceilings did not seem to indicate much potential business. For that reason, and because self-employed taxpayers themselves regarded them as more bother than help, they were slow to catch on.

Individual retirement accounts, on the other hand, spread like wildfire when they were introduced a dozen years later. In 1975, the first year they were available, nearly 1.3 million taxpayers established them. Suddenly IRA was a firm fixture in the financial lexicon and no longer meant "Irish Republican Army" to most Americans.

Their instant popularity demonstrated workers' hunger for a vehicle by which to build retirement nest eggs of their own. IRA's were introduced as part of the Employee Retirement Income Security Act of 1974, which itself has entered the language in its acronymic form of ERISA. The act's primary intent was to institute reforms in private pension plans to assure that workers would have easier access to retirement benefits and that the benefits would be there when they retired.

Recognizing the reality that many employers did not have plans and that even more would drop their plans when tougher rules were instituted, the lawmakers created a Keogh-type program for workers not otherwise covered. Because Keogh had broken the political ground, IRA's were not encumbered with the restrictions that accompanied Keoghs in their first form.

Although IRA annual contributions are considerably more modest than those of Keogh, they are more generous than the ones allowed at Keogh's inception. Furthermore, the pattern of rapid and generous increases in Keogh ceilings is quite likely to be repeated for IRA's. Financial institutions were quick to recognize the potential business that IRA's represented, and they jumped into the market with vigor.

How IRA's Work

First, a discussion of how IRA's work. Any worker who is not a participant in any qualified retirement plan may establish an individual retirement account or buy an individual retirement annuity. To this account or annuity he may contribute up to 15 percent of his earned income to a $1,500 annual limit. That ceiling can go as high as $1,750 in cases where a worker wishes to contribute on behalf of a nonworking spouse. The contribution may be deducted from his gross income before figuring his federal income tax. Most states also allow such a deduction before computing the state income tax. As with Keogh plans, income generated by IRA assets is likewise free of current income tax liability, the assets being taxed as they are withdrawn at retirement. Also, as with Keogh plans, there are penalties for making excess contributions or premature withdrawals from an IRA.

The rules are sticky about participation in any other plan. During any calendar year in which you do participate in a qualified plan where you work, you are not allowed to make contributions to an IRA. This does not mean that if you have a vested interest in a pension plan you cannot begin an IRA or that if you have an IRA you must give it up if you elect to participate in a plan where you work. They just say you can't contribute to an IRA in any year you are a participating member of such a qualified plan.

These plans include qualified pension, profit-sharing, or stock bonus plans of an employer, qualified annuity plans of an employer, qualified bond purchase plans of an employer, retirement plans established by a government for its employees, annuity contracts purchased by certain tax-exempt organizations or public schools, or Keogh plans.

Flexible Investment Options

How can you invest your IRA funds? There are four basic types of individual retirement savings programs—individual retirement accounts, individual retirement annuities, special retirement bonds issued by the federal government, and trust accounts established by employers or employee associations.

An individual retirement account must be a domestic trust or a custodial account created for the exclusive benefit of an individual or his beneficiaries. The trustee or custodian must be a bank, a savings and loan association, an insurance company, a federally insured credit union, a mutual fund, or any other person who can demonstrate to the satisfaction of the Internal Revenue Service the ability to administer the account in full accordance with the law.

To make it easier and more economical to establish an IRA, the Internal Revenue Service has created model trust and custodial agreements. By using Form 5305 (Individual Retirement Trust Account) or Form 5305-A (Individual Retirement Custodial Account), you can establish an IRA almost as easily as opening a bank account.

Depending on whom you use as a trustee or custodian, you have a wide degree of flexibility in choosing the investments that fund your IRA. Most banks will set up an IRA using savings certificates. Most mutual funds will set them up using shares in the fund as assets. Some stockbrokers, working with banks, can set up an account funded with stocks and bonds. These can be arranged so you can have an active hand in choosing the securities that fund the account.

No part of a trust or custodial fund can be invested in life insurance contracts. However, such an account may invest in annuity contracts, providing the contract's death benefit, if it has one, is not tied to mortality assumptions. Your interest in the account must be nonforfeitable, and the account's assets may not be commingled with other property except in a common trust fund or common investment fund.

An individual retirement annuity is an annuity or endowment contract issued by a life insurance company in your name for your exclusive benefit or that of your beneficiaries. As with custodial or trust accounts, your interest in a retirement annuity must be nonforfeitable.

Furthermore, the terms of the contract must provide that the contract is not transferable and cannot be used as security for a loan. This is to assure that payments will be used for your retirement. The annual premium under the contract cannot exceed 15 percent of your earned income or $1,500, and any refund of premium must be applied toward the payment of future premiums or toward the purchase of further benefits.

If you purchase an endowment contract, you can deduct only that portion of the premium allocable to retirement savings; any portion of the premium that pays for current life insurance is not deductible. However, if there is a difference between the premium and your maximum allowable deduction, you may invest the excess in a separate IRA or in retirement bonds. The insurance company that issues the endowment contract will provide you with an annual statement indicating the portion of the premium allocated to life insurance and therefore not deductible.

Group IRA's Possible

Another possibility that might be available to you is participation in a group retirement annuity. In such a case, the group annuity contract will be treated as an individual retirement annuity, providing it meets all the requirements of such an individual annuity.

Government retirement bonds are a special series of U.S. Individual Retirement Bonds issued by the federal government under the provisions of the Second Liberty Bond Act. The bonds come in $50, $100, $500 and $1,000 denominations and pay interest at the rate of 6 percent compounded semiannually.

The interest earned by the bonds will be paid only on redemption; none will be paid if they are redeemed within 12 months after purchase. Purchases are generally limited to a maximum $1,500 a year. The bonds are not transferable, nor may they be sold, discounted, or used as collateral on a loan.

No written agreement is necessary if you purchase U.S. Retirement Bonds for your individual retirement savings program. They will be issued in your name as the registered owner, and you may designate a beneficiary. The bonds may be purchased over the counter or by mail from the Federal Reserve banks and branches or the Bureau of the Public Debt.

IRA's can be used by self-employed professionals who wish to set up retirement plans for themselves but not for their employees, as they would have to do under Keogh.

Employers May Sponsor IRA's

To encourage employers to sponsor IRA's for their employees, the Revenue Act of 1978 created Simplified Employee Pensions (SEP's) under the IRA umbrella. Using an SEP, an employer need not set up a special plan or draft a trust agreement as with other retirement programs. All he must do is prepare a written allocation formula—or use the prototype formula prepared by the Internal Revenue Service —and follow some simple disclosure and administrative procedures.

In fact, what the employer does is set up a separate IRA for each participating employee. The employer then may contribute up to $7,500 a year for each employee, providing the contribution falls within the 15 percent annual limit on earnings. Conversely, if the employer does not contribute the full 15 percent, the employee may make up the difference to the $1,500 annual limit.

Employer-sponsored plans may not discriminate against any class of employee. In fact, if the employer sponsors an SEP, every employee must participate—with three exceptions—and that participation can be a condition of employment. The exceptions: Employees under age 25 and those with fewer than three years of service within the past five; employees covered under collective bargaining agreements if retirement benefits were the subject of good faith bargaining; and nonresident aliens who receive no earned income from within the United States.

In most other respects, the same rules that govern individual retirement accounts in general apply to SEP's.

Note the Penalties

As with Keogh plans, you are subject to penalties for making excess contributions to or for taking premature distributions from an IRA. Excess contributions are those made in any year that are greater than what you're entitled to—15 percent of earned income but not more than $1,500. Premature distributions are removals of funds from the account before you're entitled to receive them. As with Keogh plans, the minimum age for starting to receive IRA funds is 59½. Exceptions: total disability or death before that age.

You must begin withdrawing benefits by the time you reach age 70½. If you don't, you get penalized for that, too.

You may not take a current income tax deduction on excess contributions. Furthermore, you are charged an excise tax on them at the rate of 6 percent a year (which is not deductible on your income tax, either), for each year the excess remains in the account.

You can avoid the penalty tax by removing the excess contributions from the fund before the due date of that year's tax return. As the rules were originally written, you would incur further penalties for premature distributions by withdrawing excess contributions after your tax return due date. However, in 1978, Congress eased that provision, and you may now remove any excess at any time with no penalty other than the 6 percent excise tax. Excess contributions left in the fund may be applied toward future years' contributions, thus reducing the impact of the penalty tax.

The rules are equally explicit on premature distributions. If you receive a payment from your individual retirement savings program before you reach age 59½ or become disabled, the payment is considered to be a premature distribution. The amount of the distribution is included in your gross income for that year. In addition, your income tax liability for that tax year is increased by an amount equal to 10 percent of the premature distribution.

As we mentioned earlier, you can be penalized for not taking enough out of your IRA, too. Once you reach age 70½, you can make no more deductible contributions to your account and you must either take all remaining funds out at once or on a regular basis at a rate based on IRS life expectancy tables. If you don't, you'll be hit with a 50 percent excise tax on the underdistribution, representing the difference between the minimum payout required for the tax year in question and the amount actually paid out. For example, if you should have received $1,000 but you only took out $600, you'll be socked with a $200 "tax" (50 percent of the extra $400 you should have taken out).

Until 1978, there were no exceptions to that requirement. But liberalized rules adopted that year allow the stiff penalty to be waived if you can show that the deficit in the distributed amount occurred because of reasonable error or that you are taking reasonable steps to remedy the problem.

The rationale behind these tough rules is that since the whole idea of IRA's is to get you to put aside funds for your retirement, it would be defeated if it were too easy to withdraw them once they were committed. Besides, since Uncle Sam is providing a tax break to encourage participation, he wants to be sure no one takes unfair advantage.

You'll Pay Taxes—Eventually

Uncle Sam's "generosity" has other limits, too. When he lets you set up an IRA, he does not forgive the taxes that you otherwise would have to pay, he merely allows you to defer the payment of them. That deferral is operative until you start taking "benefits" out of your plan. Generally you do this when your earnings are substantially reduced from their peak, so you are in the lowest tax brackets. This, plus the benefit of compounding those tax-deferred earnings, constitutes the extent of his largesse.

There are some other clinkers in the rules that you should be aware of as well. One is that if you take all of your funds out of the IRA at once when eligible, you'll be hit with a whopping tax. You'll be allowed to cut the impact somewhat by using the regular income averaging provisions that allow you to spread the tax over the present year and the prior four years. But you won't have the benefit of the special ten-year forward averaging provisions available under Keogh.

Another thing you can't take advantage of is the tax break on long-term capital gains. They're taxed at 40 percent of your regular rate; when you take them out of an IRA, they're taxed as regular income. This could make a big difference in the size of your retirement nest egg, should you opt for a lump sum distribution.

These drawbacks shouldn't have much of a negative impact where you take your benefits out gradually. Besides a lump sum distribution, what are your options? You can simply withdraw a portion of the assets as you need them. They'll be taxed in the year the withdrawal is made.

You can set up a regular withdrawal program, based on the number of years you expect to need them. You can buy an annuity—see Chapters 43 and 44. If you do buy an annuity, the value of the contract will not be included in your income all at once, only the amount of annuity payments made in each tax year will be taxable in that year.

If you bought those special government retirement bonds, you'll count the proceeds as ordinary income in the year you cash them in. However, if you're still holding any when you reach age 70½, their value will be included in your taxable income that year, even if they have not been tendered for redemption.

Any other assets remaining in an individual retirement program after age 70½ must be entirely withdrawn or, as we said above, taken out at a predetermined rate. That rate must be at least as fast as it would be if based on your life expectancy or the life expectancy of you and your spouse.

If you should die leaving behind assets in your IRA, they will be included in your estate and taxed thus—unless your beneficiary or beneficiaries elect to receive them in installments extending over at least three years.

Using Tax-Free "Rollovers"

So far, we have discussed what might be regarded as "conventional" individual retirement accounts, those whose primary aim is to serve as repositories for regular annual contributions. But the law allows them to serve another—and, as it turns out, extremely popular—function. IRA's may be used to channel retirement funds from one qualified pension program to another, with no immediate tax consequences to the employee. This is what has come to be known as a tax-free "rollover." There are several ways you can use a tax-free rollover. You can use one, say, if you change jobs and want to take your built-up retirement benefits with you. You can use a rollover to shift funds into an individual retirement account and leave them there to continue building up under your direction and management. As long as you add no more contributions to the IRA account, you are free to participate in a qualified plan at your new job. If you wish, and if your new employer has a plan that can accept them, you may place the assets into his plan, where they will be handled as if they had been there all along.

You can also use a tax-free rollover to change your IRA investment vehicle. Say you have an IRA with a mutual fund and you're not satisfied with the fund's performance. You can roll the assets over into another mutual fund or a custodial or trusteed plan where they're invested in something else.

You can also use a rollover to shift benefits into an IRA if your employer terminates his qualified plan.

Rollovers and Your Retirement Fund

These were the basic concepts envisioned by lawmakers when they wrote the pension reform legislation. But retirement age workers have found that the rules allow them to take control of their pension benefits built up in an employer's plan without getting hit with a lump sum distribution tax. They simply transfer the benefits into an IRA rollover account, where they can invest them as they choose and withdraw them at their own pace.

This alternative has an attractive ring to it, but there are some things to consider if you contemplate trying it. First, remember that all funds withdrawn from an IRA are taxed at regular income rates. If the assets of your pension plan consist of a large proportion of capital gains, you might have a substantially higher tax burden under the rollover. Another thing, instead of having a regular pension check rolling in for life, you might find that you had worked yourself into quite a management chore in keeping tabs on your retirement assets.

On the other hand, you would have the chance to obtain a higher yield on the assets by assuming more investment risk. (And more chance to lose the bundle via ill-considered or unfortunate investments.) You would also have considerably more financial flexibility in that you could get your hands on the assets if you needed to, or slow down the payout (at least until you reached age 70½).

Some Rules on Rollovers

Whether you use a tax-free rollover to shift assets from one plan to another, to shift them into your control, or to take charge of your own retirement income program, you must observe certain rules. Here they are. First, you must transfer the funds distributed from the old plan into the new one within 60 days of the distribution. Second, if property other than money is distributed, you must transfer that same property (usually stocks or bonds) or proceeds from the bona fide sale of that property to the new plan. Third, you may use the tax-free rollover provision only once a year.

If you reinvest your retirement assets in your own IRA from a qualified plan, you have to have terminated employment with the company operating the qualified plan. In other words, while you may stop participating in a company plan where you work and start your own IRA, you cannot shift any benefits built up in the company plan into your IRA until you reach normal retirement age, which is the age at which the company plan regularly allows workers to retire and start drawing benefits. Furthermore, if you have made any after-tax contributions to the plan, those contributions may not be rolled over into an IRA.

As you have perceived by now, the rules surrounding IRAs are far from simple. What's more, they tend to change with considerable frequency. So, when you're ready to think seriously about an individual retirement account, you should check with your nearest Internal Revenue Service office for the latest rules. Ask for the most recent edition of IRS Publication No. 590, "Tax Information on Individual Retirement Savings Programs."

Chapter 43 Annuities as Retirement Fund Vehicles

THE MAIN purpose of an annuity program is to eliminate the gamble that your retirement funds and life span will come out even. A secondary purpose—particularly for those still some distance from retirement—is to provide a vehicle for creating these retirement funds and for protecting them as much as possible against the ravages of inflation and taxes.

In this chapter, we will define annuities, explain how they work, and discuss the different types available. In the following chapter we'll include some pros and cons regarding their use, both as to retirement and estate planning and as a continuing source of income after retirement.

Since annuities are tied closely to the concept of life insurance, they are sold primarily by insurance companies. In fact, insurance companies are the only ones legally permitted to vend commercial annuities. Mutual funds and stock brokerage houses that have begun in recent years to market annuities with special "investment" twists do so through tie-ins with life insurance companies.

You can purchase an annuity all at once with a relatively large chunk of cash (called a "single premium annuity") or a little at a time through regular installment payments (called an "annual premium annuity").

An immediate annuity is a single premium annuity that starts to provide income at once. (Payments must begin within a year of inception.) A deferred annuity is one you purchase, either as a single premium or annual premium annuity, on which income distributions begin at some future date as specified in the contract.

The period during which you are paying into the annuity but are not drawing income, or the period your lump sum payment is not being returned as income to you, is called the "deferral period," or "accumulation period." During this deferral period, your principal may be invested in a variety of ways. In a fixed annuity, the insurance company invests it in securities, such as bonds, that return a fixed amount. It can therefore guarantee you both safety of principal and the amount of return. However, this guaranteed result quite likely will fall below the rate of inflation and even below the rate of return your capital could generate elsewhere.

In a variable annuity the company invests a specified portion of the principal in securities providing some growth potential, such as common stocks. Since this portion is subject to the vicissitudes of the equity markets, the results cannot be guaranteed. You're trading a guaranteed result for the chance to obtain a better inflation hedge. A variation of this is the switch-fund annuity, which allows you to shift the assets at will among a number of mutual funds within a "family" of funds of the participating investment company.

Individual annuities can be purchased on one life or two. In recent years the growth of group annuities has been rapid as a means of providing company-sponsored employee retirement benefits.

How an Annuity "Pays" You

Once the annuity begins making regular payments to you it becomes an income annuity. At the point where you shift from a deferred annuity to an income annuity, you must take care to choose the desired income option. Once income payments begin, you generally are not able to change options.

There are several options. A *straight life annuity* provides a predetermined amount of income for the life of the annuitant. Period. When he or she dies, all payments stop—even if they fall far short of the amount paid into the annuity.

A *joint and survivor annuity* is one that provides income for the lifetime of two persons, generally a husband and wife. It may continue income at the same level until the second one dies, or it may provide larger payments while both are alive and reduced payments after one dies.

A *life annuity with installments certain* provides income for the lifetime of the annuitant. In addition, it guarantees to make these regular payments for a specified number of years, paying them to a designated beneficiary if the annuitant should die within that period.

An *installment refund annuity* pays income for life to the annuitant. But if he should die before receiving as much money as he paid in, the payments will go to a beneficiary until that amount has been reached. A *cash refund annuity* does the same thing, except that instead of continuing regular payments to the beneficiary, it provides a lump sum equal to the amount of undistributed principal.

An important point to remember is that these various options do not provide the same amount of income. The more guarantees the annuity has, the lower the payments to you. Thus, in making the proper choice, your main task is to determine what your present and future needs are likely to be.

Annuities as Savings Vehicles

Deferred annuities, whether single premium or annual premium, have long been popular repositories for savings that someday will be used to provide retirement income. One reason for this popularity is that an annuity program provides a discipline for regular savings. Another is that, in general, the assets thus set aside may be confidently regarded as "safe."

Because of their safety, the government has encouraged through its tax laws their use in personal retirement savings programs. It allows employees of charitable and educational organizations to salt away generous portions of income in tax-sheltered annuities. It includes annuities among the investment options for Keogh and IRA plans. It allows annuity users to defer income taxes on earnings of annuity principal during the accumulation period.

This tax-deferral feature, in fact, is one of the greatest selling points for annuities. Not only do you avoid current taxes on annuity interest, but those untaxed savings keep on earning for you, too.

What's wrong with that? Great idea, in principle, but the biggest drawback is that annuities earn so little. In traditional fixed annuities, the issuing company guarantees you a stated return on your principal. To do this, it must invest the principal in fixed-income securities such as bonds. The return thus frequently falls below the rate of inflation, and even in the best of times barely keeps ahead of it—even with the tax-deferral feature.

To overcome this, the insurance companies several years ago began offering variable annuities. These commit a certain portion of the principal to "safe" securities such as bonds, on which a guaranteed return is provided. The rest is invested by the issuing company in a portfolio of common stocks, à la mutual funds. The principal thus committed enjoys the benefits—and pays the consequences—of ups and downs in the stock market. You have no control over the choice of these investments.

The history of variable annuities over the past several years has not been noteworthy, reflecting in large part, of course, the performance of the stock market in general. Over the long haul, in a rising market period, they should do better. But you're still at the mercy of the company's investment managers, and it's sometimes hard to judge how good their track record is—or will be.

One way to beat that limitation is to take management of the assets into your own hands. Some insurance companies thought they had the ultimate answer to variable annuities with the so-called investment annuity. The idea was to allow you as the annuity buyer to retain control over the investments. You could fund the policy with securities you already held or with others, and you reserved the right to change your holdings at will, all the while sheltering any gains under the annuity rules. Not surprisingly, the Internal Revenue Service thought this was too generous and ruled them out.

Then, in 1980, came the switch-fund annuities noted on page 426. Instead of the investor's retaining control over the actual shares, he is given credits against the shares of mutual funds held by the insurance company. The funds are those in the "family" of the participating investment company. The investor is allowed to shift his credits at will among the funds in the family and retain the tax shelter provided by the annuity unless, of course, he withdraws his assets. This arrangement seems to be acceptable to the IRS, which has approved several such programs.

Should You Use Annuities?

We've discussed the various options open to you as a potential annuity buyer. What should you do? We're not convinced that you should do anything. We have never been enthusiastic about annuities as savings vehicles. They just don't grow fast enough even with the deferred tax break. A portfolio of good growth stocks that appreciates in value at an average of 9 percent or so a year should do much better, particularly if you have a relatively long way to go before retirement.

Another reason to be wary of becoming locked into an annuity program is that the very tax-deferral feature that attracts you to it could later work against you. That's because the only way you can escape a hefty tax on the accumulated earnings of the annuity is to take them out on an annuitized basis, that is, at a regular rate based on your life expectancy at the time you begin withdrawing them. As we noted earlier, this decision is an irrevocable one; once you've made it, you're stuck with it. You can no longer get your hands on the assets you've committed to this program, regardless of how desperately you may need them later.

If you decide that, instead of choosing an annuity payout, you'll take your assets and run, you'll have to pay a tax all at once on the accumulated income. You may be able to cut the tax impact of such a lump sum distribution with income averaging, but you also could find that in the long run you might have been better off to have paid the tax in the first place and placed your savings elsewhere where they would have grown faster.

But, suppose you have invested in annuities and it is now time to choose your payment method. As we said before, the amount of income you derive from an annuity depends on the way you choose to receive it. Again, the right choice is important, because once made, you don't have another crack at it.

Historically—and annuities date back at least to the ancient Phoenicians—sellers of annuities agreed to pay buyers a predetermined amount periodically for life. No more, no less. But along the line, various payment options have been woven into the annuity fabric. These have evolved largely because of the quirk in human nature that resists giving away assets irrevocably, and out of the strong desire of one spouse to assure continued financial security for the surviving spouse as long as she (usually) should live.

Thus, refund annuities and joint and survivor annuities have joined straight life annuities as available options. While each may have a place in your own financial planning, you should understand the differences and their possible consequences before making your choice. That's especially important, because, as we have said before, once you make your commitment on how you'll receive payments, the decision generally cannot be changed.

How Much Will It Pay?

Your health plays no part in your ability to purchase an annuity—unless the annuity has some life insurance aspects tied to it. The amount of income an annuity provides is determined by your age at the time the income payments begin, and by the type of annuity you choose. Since the life expectancy of women is higher than that of men, in general the payment schedule for a woman is about the same as that for a man five years younger.

The extent of the guarantees provided by the insurance company will also affect the payment level. The more guarantees, the lower the benefits.

Thus, straight life annuities, which guarantee nothing beyond a steady income as long as you live, yield the highest return. But when you die, the payments stop, and your estate receives nothing, even if the payments fall far short of the amount you paid in. They go instead into the pool to provide benefits for those who live beyond the life expectancy of the age group. Simple enough logic.

But many individuals, it seems, cannot live with the thought that their estates will receive nothing at their demise, or they want the guaranteed income from an annuity but wish also to provide survivors with some assets after death. So a variety of refund annuities were invented; we defined and described them at the beginning of this chapter.

A more common situation involves a husband and wife who desire to assure lifetime income for both. A joint and survivor annuity, which is simply a straight life annuity on two lives, answers this need for many.

Which annuity is best?

No single answer is possible, of course, because of the multitude of individual variables involved. However, you should keep these considerations in mind as you pick your way to a decision:

Since an annuity's main purpose is to deliver the highest income possible, you should look for the one that does this best. Straight life will usually win.

If you want to leave assets behind for your heirs, you can generally do it more profitably both for them and for yourself by means other than annuities. Divide your assets accordingly between annuity and estate.

Don't automatically assume a joint and survivor annuity would be best for you and your spouse. When determining the income payments of a joint and survivor annuity, greater weight is generally placed upon the wife's age than the husband's, since she is likely to live the longer. In the usual case where the wife is younger, the effects can be substantial. But even if she is two or three years older than her husband, the income level will probably be lower than that of a similar annuity for the husband alone. As you shop around, then, compare the income of a joint and survivor policy against the combined incomes of annuities purchased separately by husband and wife.

If you do choose a joint and survivor policy, consider taking one that reduces payments after the death of one spouse. Since living costs generally decline when one spouse dies, this arrangement would provide more income for both during their lifetime together.

Consider a "Private Annuity"

You don't always have to get an annuity from an insurance company. "Buying" one "privately" has much to commend it. When they think of annuities, most people think of the type purchased from an insurance company, so-called commercial annuities—those we have been discussing heretofore in this chapter. However, it is possible to enter into an annuity agreement quite independent of an insurance company contract.

Such "private annuities" have several advantages, most of which are generally associated with estate planning. The provision of a lifetime income for the annuitant is only one of them, and frequently is not the one that motivates the maneuver.

Because of these various benefits, you might find a private annuity a valuable tool in your own financial planning program. However, you should likewise be aware of certain disadvantages and potential pitfalls.

To create a private annuity, you (the annuitant) agree to turn over certain assets to another party (the obligator) in return for a promise to pay you a certain amount of money at regular intervals over your lifetime or for a set number of years. This payback must have a direct bearing on your life expectancy and it must include payment of a "reasonable" rate of interest in order to avoid being considered a "gift" by the IRS.

Private annuities are frequently undertaken within families, with the obligator generally someone younger than the annuitant, say, a son or daughter. Sometimes they are used as a method for an employer to pass on his small business to his employees. The business itself, whether it is to be kept in the family or passed to someone else, is often the asset used to finance the annuity. A family residence and other real estate are other types of property frequently used. A major advantage of employing a private annuity when dealing with highly appreciated property is that capital gains can continue to be deferred—taxes are paid on them gradually as capital is returned. (In buying a commercial annuity, you must first sell the funding assets and pay gains taxes on them "up front.")

Besides the deferral of capital gains and the prospect of having regular income over your remaining years, you can have these other advantages by using a private annuity:

The assets can be removed from your estate and thus reduce potential estate taxes and administration costs.

As long as the "present value" of the annuity equals the value of the property transferred, there will be no gift tax.

The transfer of the property frees you of investment and management responsibilities.

Where the obligator is a relative and is in a lower tax bracket than yours, you can lower the family's total tax liability with regard to income generated by the property.

The obligator, too, can reap benefit from such a transaction:

He assumes ownership of the assets and thus can take any tax deductions available on the property (but no deductions for payments to the annuitant).

He can use the assets to provide financial leverage.

He can sell or exchange transferred property without incurring any capital gains.

Proceed Carefully

There are, as we said, some potential disadvantages and opportunities for slip-ups that must be given consideration before committing your assets to a private annuity.

Foremost, the agreement must be carefully and expertly drafted in order to withstand a challenge by IRS. Because of the complexity of private annuities and this need for careful drafting, you should only undertake them with the advice and help of competent legal and tax counselors.

It is also important for you to realize that you must choose an obligator in whom you have complete trust and confidence. The same rationale that allows you to defer capital gains also results in an unsecured promise on the part of the obligator. If he should go bust or otherwise renege on his promise to repay you, you would have no way to protect yourself or your investment. (You can, however, cover yourself against his untimely death with a life insurance policy separate and apart from the annuity agreement.)

There are ways to avoid or minimize the drawbacks of private annuities, and your counsel can help you incorporate them into your program. In many cases the potential benefits of such private annuities far outweigh the hazards and make them worth the care and effort needed to create them.

Chapter 44 After Retirement

As you approach retirement, you must begin implementing the plans described in Chapter 40 to provide for sufficient income. About a year ahead is not too soon to start making specific arrangements. You're close enough so you can get a fairly accurate reading on how much Social Security income you'll be getting. The same goes for your company's pension plan, if you're included in one. Those two items are pretty much fixed by rules and policies beyond your direct control. In deploying the assets you've built up in your own private retirement nest egg, you'll need to exercise much more judgment.

Social Security

But before we get into that, let's talk a bit about Social Security. It forms the backbone of the retirement programs of nearly all working Americans. It is frequently the largest single source of retirement income. Company pension plans are often tied directly to it.

For those receiving its retirement benefits, Social Security provides a basic monthly payment for life. It provides extra for a qualifying spouse, and it provides for that spouse in widowhood. It meets certain medical expenses under its Medicare program. It reduces the benefits of recipients who retire early and those who earn more than a certain amount in retirement.

That much is generally understood. But beyond that, most people's knowledge begins to get hazy. Here is a nutshell description of how your individual benefit level is determined. To qualify for full benefits, you must have at least forty quarters of "covered" service; that means you have to have worked the equivalent of at least ten years in a job where Social Security taxes were deducted from your pay. These days, that means just about everyone except certain public school teachers and civil servants, who are covered by other plans.

Having thus qualified, you are then subjected to certain rules to determine the amount of benefits to which you are entitled. Your *primary benefit level* is based on your "best" forty quarters. For most of us, that means the most recent ones, because of rising income patterns and a rising wage base on which the Social Security taxes are computed. From these best forty quarters, your individual average monthly wage is computed, and once this has been determined, henceforth and forevermore your Social Security benefits will revolve around this figure. If you choose to retire before the normal retirement age of 65—the rules allow you to start drawing retirement benefits at age 62—your benefits will be set at a lower rate than if you wait until age 65. If you work beyond 65, you can earn higher benefits.

Because the rules and benefit tables are constantly changing, it is impossible here to get very specific about how much your benefit payments will be. So, about a year before your projected retirement date, contact your nearest Social Security office and ask for the appropriate pamphlets that show you how to determine your basic monthly benefit. (You should start the actual paperwork involved in getting signed up about three months before retirement.)

Then sit down with the people who manage your company's pension program and get a line on what to expect from that source. If you've been keeping tabs over the years, you'll have some general idea, and there should be no shocks or surprises there.

Next, take a pencil and calculator to the family budget to see where and how it will change after your retirement. If you're typical, you should be able to shave between a quarter and a third from your present living expenses. Now, put your expected retirement income figure next to your projected operating budget. You'll probably find a gap. As we mentioned in Chapter 40, it's a gap that's likely to widen with the years, too, because of the persistent rises in prices.

The wherewithal to fill that gap will come from the savings program you have been building and nurturing during your working years. The size of your nest egg will depend largely upon how conscientious you have been in adding to it and making it grow for you. The size of the nest egg in relation to the size of the gap will be a major factor in determining how best to deploy it.

What are your options? Annuities. Bank savings accounts. U.S. Savings Bonds. Bonds and other fixed-income securities. Real estate. Common stocks. Let's take a look, one by one.

Annuities

As you probably detected in Chapter 43, we take a generally cautionary stance on the use of annuities in a retirement program. The main reason is because you must commit those resources irrevocably to the annuity, and therefore you strip yourself of a considerable amount of financial flexibility. You restrict your opportunities to juggle your assets around to meet changes in your situation. Furthermore, we don't believe you get a particularly good return on your investment, at least not if you take out an annuity while still relatively young.

Nevertheless, we do concede that there are certain instances where annuities can serve well. So, we offer here some guidance on when and how to choose them. First, when might you consider the use of annuities?

When you want an assured income for life.

When you don't want to or don't feel you can manage your own investments—or if you seek such security for an heir.

When annuity "income" earns more than other investments in the marketplace.

When your health and condition make it likely that you'll live longer than the annuity tables.

Second, when should you not consider annuities?

When your age and other factors make the return on your annuity lower than those available from other securities.

When times are particularly inflationary—as now.

When it appears likely that you won't outlive the annuity tables.

Generally speaking, the older you are when you take out an annuity, the higher the yield will be. That's because the insurance company writing the policy is taking less of a gamble as you advance in age. The return on a policy taken out at age 55 would probably be lower than that which those same assets could earn in a bank account or with U.S. Savings Bonds. However, if you hold out until age 70, you could get an annuity yielding in the 10 percent area from principal and interest.

That meshes well with the idea that during your younger retirement years, when you are still physically active and mentally alert, you should retain all the flexibility and control that you can over your assets. Then, as you grow older and less able to perform these tasks, consider placing some emphasis on annuities for your income.

But always remember: Once you have committed your assets to annuities and income payments begin, you cannot change your mind. Unless there is some refund feature, your heirs will receive nothing when you die. All too many annuitants—and heirs—fail to realize this, to their ultimate woe.

One other caution: Because annuities so severely limit your financial flexibility once you're committed to them, we firmly recommend that under virtually no circumstances should you convert all of your available assets to them. They should be regarded only as partial answers to your income needs.

Because we do not regard annuities as good vehicles for building a retirement fund, we confine our commentary here solely to their purchase as sources of guaranteed income. In shopping for an annuity, do not assume that they all pay about the same. In one list of 39 different companies' straight life annuities,* the income per $1,000 per month ranged from $8.98 to $7.67—with the lowest more than 15 percent below the highest. A substantial difference. As you compare, you should also determine whether the companies charge a fee and, if so, how much it is. An unusually large one can significantly affect your return. Check, too, to see which companies offer discounts on larger annuities.

It may seem basic, but be sure that you compare the same type of annuity as you investigate each company. The straight life annuity generally offers the best income return, so that's a good place to begin. But if you feel another type better suits your needs, obtain comparisons on them.

Savings Accounts

Bank savings accounts can play a useful function in your retirement program. They can serve as repositories for funds on their way

---

* The list is contained in the booklet *Annuities from the Buyer's Point of View,* published by American Institute for Economic Research, Great Barrington, Mass. 01230.

from one investment to another. They can provide a fund from which you can draw to meet financial emergencies. They can even be used to provide long-term income.

Let's turn our attention for a moment to the latter function. The longer you promise to keep your money in a bank account or term certificate, the higher the interest rate you can receive. Federal regulations place a ceiling on how much a bank or savings institution may pay you. Furthermore, savings institutions—savings banks and savings and loan associations—are allowed to pay a quarter of a percentage point higher interest than commercial banks. However, there is nothing in the rules that says an institution *must* pay you the ceiling. So it's always best to shop around for the one that will pay you the most. While you're shopping, note how the institution compounds its interest. The effective rate is substantially higher where interest is compounded on a daily rate basis than it is when compounded monthly, quarterly or semiannually.

There are certain advantages to keeping your money in a savings account. Foremost is safety. The deposits are fully insured, thus there is no loss if the institution should go broke. Second, savings accounts are simple to open—and to close—and there are no sales commissions or other expenses involved when making deposits or withdrawals, as there are when buying and selling securities.

But there are some drawbacks, too. We think the most serious is the limitation on earning potential of the assets. At best, they barely keep even with inflation; at worst, they actually represent an erosion of buying power of the dollars on deposit.

Another drawback is the rule that requires savings institutions to impose a penalty on any deposits withdrawn before the time specified in the deposit agreement. The penalty is a forfeiture of three months' interest and a recomputation of any remaining interest due at the lowest savings (passbook) rate. The "penalty" has no stigma attached to it; the money is yours to withdraw at any time, no questions asked. It just means that if you take it out before the agreed-upon interim, you don't get the agreed-upon rate, and you're assessed something for the bank's trouble.

When deciding whether to use savings accounts or term certificates, you must compare this return against what you would be able to get elsewhere. Sometimes corporate bonds will pay more than the maximum savings rate and provide virtually the same safety of capital. Sometimes you'll want to link some prospects for capital growth to the income return on your assets, so you'll look at common stocks. Sometimes you'll have an opportunity to reap greater rewards with a real estate investment. We'll examine some of these below.

U.S. Savings Bonds

We discussed the savings aspects of U.S. Savings Bonds in Chapter 36. Now, suppose you had been salting away a $50 E Bond each month for the past twenty years or so. As you make plans for your retirement, you'll want to consider the alternatives for turning this substantial savings bundle into a source of continuing income.

For purposes of illustration, suppose by the time you retire you have an even twenty years' worth of bonds purchased monthly—240 of them. At a cost of $37.50 each, your total cash outlay was $9,000. At retirement, with the accumulated interest, your bonds are worth somewhere in the neighborhood of $15,000. Here are four alternatives. Although we use E Bonds in this example, the same principles apply to the Series EE Bonds issued after 1979. The new EE and HH Bonds are basically the same as the old E and H Bonds, though there are some differences worth noting. For a discussion of the similarities and differences, see pages 377–379.

Plan one. Cash in a bond each month for the next twenty years. You'd cash the longest-held bonds first, and in the first year, your "income" would amount to about $1,000. About $600 would represent tax-deferred interest, on which you'd have to pay federal income taxes. (Note that on Savings Bonds, as with most other U.S. Treasury and agency bonds, earnings are exempt from state and local taxation.) The annual income figures would rise somewhat in subsequent years as a result of the higher interest paid on newer bonds. All told, by the time you cashed in your last bond, you would have taken out some $25,000.

Plan two. Convert the E Bonds to H-type Bonds. The tax deferment on the accumulated E Bond interest would continue but the semiannual interest payments from the H or HH Bonds would be taxable as received. In converting the entire nest egg, you might have to add some cash in order to make an even exchange (H-type Bonds come in $500 minimum denominations).

Plan three. Cash in the E Bonds and reinvest the proceeds in bonds more lucrative than the 6 percent provided by Savings Bonds. You'd immediately be liable for income taxes on the $6,000 or so in deferred interest earned by the E Bonds. Assuming a 20 percent tax bracket, this would cost you about $1,200 (you might be able to cut the bite somewhat through the income averaging provisions of the tax law). Now suppose Treasury bonds (not Savings Bonds) were then yielding around 8 percent. By adding a few hundred dollars in cash, you could purchase $14,000 worth of 20-year Treasury bonds. These would yield you about $1,100 a year (all subject to federal taxes), but you'd still have your $14,000 when you cashed in your matured Treasury bonds two decades hence.

Plan four. Cash in the E Bonds and reinvest the proceeds in a common stock portfolio. As in plan three, you'd have an immediate tax liability. So, as above, assume you have $14,000 to invest. Further assume that the stocks you choose provide an average annual total return of 9 percent, a performance widely regarded as realistically attainable for well-chosen common stocks held over the long term. By tilting your portfolio toward income stocks, you could obtain, say, 7½ percent in dividend yield, with the remaining 1½ percent representing capital growth. This would give you on average, $1,050 in annual income. But at the end of twenty years, your $14,000 investment would have grown by about $5,000 to just under $19,000, nicely hedging you against inflation. To do this, you must be aware that you entail some risk, though that risk is minimized if you stick with investments in the highest-quality companies.

There can be variations of these plans, of course, or they can be employed in some combination. Then, too, the capital need not remain untouched under plans two, three, and four. It can be withdrawn gradually to provide steady income (see table on page 446) or it can be reserved to meet financial emergencies.

Here is a point to note when redeeming or exchanging E-type Bonds. Proper timing of the redemption or exchange can prevent lost income. Unlike daily interest savings accounts, Savings Bonds do not accrue interest between payment dates. Interest for the previous six months is earned and reckoned on the bonds' anniversary dates and midway between.

Thus, on a $25 E Bond which has been held for twenty years or so, poorly timed redemptions could reduce earned income by as much as $2. Careful planning, especially when a large number of bonds are being cashed or exchanged, can pay off.

Say you have bought an E or EE Bond each month over the past several years and now want to swap them for H-type Bonds to provide retirement income. You can do this most profitably by staggering the exchange over a six-month period. In January, exchange the bonds acquired in January and July of each of the past years; in February, the February and August bonds, etc.

By starting this exchange program six months before you retire, you'll begin receiving interest checks immediately after retirement, thus providing something to help fill the earnings gap right away and not six months down the road.

There's another benefit to employing this gradual exchange tactic. Since H-type Bond interest is paid semiannually, you not only avoid lost interest by using this serial redemption program but you also establish a schedule that provides you with an income check each month instead of only twice a year.

Corporate Bonds

We discussed corporate bonds extensively in Chapter 8, so by now you're familiar with how they work. But during the years you were building up your retirement fund, you probably did not give them much thought. Now, when income will become your primary investment concern, you may want to add some to your portfolio to provide assured income as well as safety of capital.

That's fine; and as we noted in the earlier chapter, you might even be able to build in some inflation protection by acquiring some deeply discounted bonds that you can redeem at par when they mature.

As you consider bonds, look at those with "medium" maturities—those whose maturities aren't too far into the distant future. As we said earlier, bonds trade on the market near their par as they approach maturity. If you should have to liquidate some along the way, you'll want to do so at par or as close to it as possible.

But because of their limited potential for capital growth, you probably won't want to commit all of your retirement funds to bonds. It depends on what your income needs are, of course, but we tend to believe that a limit of 20 percent or so in bonds is about right in most cases.

If you want instant diversification in the bond portion of your retirement portfolio, you can consider some bond funds; we discussed them in Chapter 13.

If you want more opportunity to provide capital growth but you still like the idea of bonds' safety and assured income, you can look at some convertible bonds. They were discussed in Chapter 9. They provide somewhat less yield than straight corporates, and somewhat less opportunity for capital appreciation than common stocks. But that's all part of the trade-offs we've been discussing throughout this book.

Real Estate

Unless you're looking for a new "job," or are willing to lay out money to a manager, the eve of retirement is hardly the time to start thinking about real estate as an investment. But there is this aspect: Rental income is not regarded as "earned" income as far as the Social Security rules are concerned, so no matter how much rental income you earn, it will not reduce your Social Security benefit.

What about the situation where you already hold real estate? Should you sell and reinvest the proceeds? Or should you keep the property, live off the income, and use its appreciating value as your inflation hedge? Several important factors will enter into your decision.

The best starting point would be to determine the true net yield on your investment—the amount realized after paying all expenses and taking into consideration the amount of your own efforts expended in management, etc. Then, compare that yield with the kind of yield the same assets would generate if diverted to other investments. (Remember, there would be some erosion of assets in making any switch—commissions, other sales expenses, etc.—and probably some capital gains taxes.)

Next you must determine the future prospects of continued ownership. Will the property continue to gain in value at least as fast as other comparable real estate? Will rent increases likewise keep pace with inflation? Is there a chance the property could decline in value? Factors such as location, condition of property, and development trends of the community and neighborhood must be studied.

Then you must consider the personal aspects of continued management. Would it tie you down more than you wish? Would the management become too much of a burden as you grow older? Does ownership tie up too much of your wealth, creating the risk of losses in a "distress sale" should you suddenly need to liquidate to obtain funds? Does the real estate constitute too heavy a proportion of your investment portfolio to afford good balance?

Having considered these factors, you then must choose from several alternatives:

Retain the real estate and continue to collect rent.

Sell it all now and reinvest the proceeds in stocks and bonds.

Hold the real estate until after retirement, when you'll be in a lower tax bracket, easing the effects of capital gains.

Gradually divest yourself of the property, selling first the least desirable pieces, reinvesting proceeds as received.

Sell the real estate, but write the mortgage yourself. This would give you income as well as a gradual return of capital, while freeing you of the burdens of management and ownership. (Be sure if you choose this option to have the help of competent legal counsel to safeguard your interests.)

Obviously, there is no "right" answer. In general, though, it is our feeling that retirees should make their financial affairs as trouble-free as possible, within the bounds of good sense and sound judgment. It has been our experience that carefully chosen common stocks and bonds go a long way toward providing the sort of returns needed for current income and protection against inflation's ravages, while at the same time minimizing the management effort.

Common Stocks

Now you come to your common stock portfolio. During its accumulation years, you have been concentrating on growth, on building its value as much as possible, with little concern for how much income it was generating—or even making a studied effort to avoid income while your salary was keeping you in a high tax bracket. Now, on the verge of retirement, you suddenly have to shift gears, to find investments that will provide income to fill that "gap."

Because it takes time to make an orderly transition, we urge you to move slowly in this regard, as in all other investment decisions. In the first place, a wholesale shifting of "growth" stocks for "income" securities could entail a large capital gains tax that would eat heavily into your assets. In the second place, some of your "growth" stocks might also be perfectly good "income" securities, and therefore should be wisely retained.

As you have done over the years, make the tax laws work for you, not against you. Use any "paper" losses you might be carrying to offset gains on the stocks you think are the best candidates for shifting. That way, you'll minimize the impact of capital gains taxes at the outset. Then, if possible, wait until the tax year following your retirement, when your tax bracket should be considerably lower, before you begin any wholesale shifting around.

If the sale of real estate is part of your retirement picture, be sure to take into account the tax impact of the gains on its appreciated value and mesh that sale with the sale of any heavily appreciated stocks. Don't let an oversight in this regard deal you a double tax whammy.

Don't feel that because you are retiring you must completely divest yourself of common stocks and go entirely into "safe" fixed-income investments. When you think of the impact inflation has on the assets thus deployed, you have to wonder just how "safe" they really are.

On the other hand, wisely chosen common stocks, because they are equity investments, will tend to rise in value right along with—or even well ahead of—the rise in prices. Not only will their asset value rise, but so also should their dividends. Therefore, common stocks should play an important role in your investment picture after retirement, just as they did before.

How, then, does a retiree's investment portfolio look? It will depend, of course, on your own particular situation, but for the purposes of example, here is a fairly conservative approach to deploying a $100,000 nest egg for a couple retiring at age 65:

Amount Invested		Annual Income
$ 5,000	Bank accounts and term certificates for immediate needs and minor emergencies. Average yield, 6%.	$ 300
75,000	Common stocks. A portfolio with somewhat less emphasis on growth than during the accumulation period, but not entirely committed to income. A representative income yield would be about 6½%.	4,875
20,000	Corporate and government bonds and/or bond funds. Yields will vary according to current market activity, but a representative expectation would be around 8%.	1,600
$100,000	.... TOTALS	$6,775

Consuming Your Capital

Contrary to the old Yankee axiom that it's sinful to dip into principal, it sometimes makes very good sense to do so. The trick is to make the available capital last as long as you'll need it. There's no sure way of foretelling this, of course, but there are some rules of thumb that you can apply to the task. More on them in a moment.

First, some ways you can consume your capital in a rational fashion. One way is linked to the discussion of common stocks above. Instead of taking your tax lumps to switch a growth stock to an income issue and then paying taxes on the income generated by the new stock to boot (not to mention the in-and-out brokerage commissions), why not sell off a few shares of the appreciated stock as you need the cash? You'll raise the income you require, you'll pay less than your regular tax rate on the long-term capital gain, and you'll still have a good part, if not all, of your original stake left to continue growing. In terms of the number of dollars invested, you might well stay ahead.

Another way you can do the same thing is to invest in a mutual fund that has a cash withdrawal program. They'll send you a regular amount each month, making up the required sum either from earnings on the assets or from the assets themselves. The rate at which the fund is growing and at which you withdraw from it will determine how long your assets will last.

If the combined earnings and appreciation of your stocks or mutual fund equal or exceed the rate at which you're withdrawing, your assets will last forever, of course. But what if you must consume your capital faster than it's growing? To get an idea of how long your capital should last, consult the longevity tables.

Age	Male	Female	Age	Male	Female	Age	Male	Female
50	23.6	29.5	62	15.0	19.6	74	8.5	11.0
51	22.8	28.6	63	14.3	18.8	75	8.1	10.4
52	22.0	27.7	64	13.7	18.0	76	7.7	9.9
53	21.2	26.9	65	13.2	17.3	77	7.3	9.3
54	20.5	26.0	66	12.6	16.5	78	6.9	8.8
55	19.7	25.2	67	12.0	15.8	79	6.6	8.3
56	19.0	24.4	68	11.5	15.1	80	6.3	7.9
57	18.3	23.5	69	10.9	14.4	81	5.9	7.4
58	17.6	22.7	70	10.4	13.7	82	5.6	7.0
59	16.9	21.9	71	9.9	13.0	83	5.3	6.5
60	16.2	21.1	72	9.4	12.3	84	5.0	6.1
61	15.6	20.3	73	9.0	11.7	85	4.7	5.7

SOURCES: National Center for Health Statistics and the Metropolitan Life Insurance Company (1973)

As a safe rule of thumb, about one and a half times the indicated life expectancy should be enough of a cushion for estimating your own longevity. Then, using the table below, determine the number

Withdrawal Rate	Annual Growth Rate of Funds									
	5%	6%	7%	8%	9%	10%	11%	12%	13%	14%
6%	36						number of years			
7%	25	33					principal should			
8%	20	23	30				last			
9%	16	18	22	28						
10%	14	15	17	20	26					
11%	12	13	14	16	19	25				
12%	11	11	12	14	15	18	23			
13%	9	10	11	12	13	15	17	21		
14%	9	9	10	11	11	13	14	17	21	
15%	8	8	9	9	10	11	12	14	16	20

of years your assets will last if they are growing at a slower rate than they are being withdrawn. For example, a widow aged 65 with a life expectancy of slightly more than 17 years, should plan on making her capital last for about 26 years. That means that on assets that are earning and appreciating at a combined 9 percent annual rate, she could safely withdraw 10 percent of her principal each year.

In Conclusion

We've covered a lot of alternatives in this chapter, and you would be forgiven if you were somewhat confused by the array of options open to you. Don't panic. But it's because of the number of decisions you'll have to make that we suggested at the outset of the chapter that you start considering them at least a year in front of your retirement date.

We can't tell you exactly how to make these decisions, of course. What we've tried to do here is lay out the options, note their pros and cons, and give you an idea of what they'll do—and won't do—for you.

You have to put together a package you're comfortable with, one that doesn't keep you awake at night worrying about the risks, or one that isn't so complicated that you have to stay up nights managing it. Some people can live with more risk than others, so they won't lose sleep over a plan that would turn the next guy into an insomniac. Others really enjoy a plan that gives them something to do, like managing an investment portfolio or a piece of rental property.

We suggest that you retain as much flexibility as you can in your plan, so you'll be able to roll with any punches that come your way, and so you can change the program to meet any changing needs that come with advancing age.

Chapter 45 Estate Planning

EVEN IF you have done a good deal of estate planning—and most of us have done at least some—there's a chance you haven't gone over your program lately. If that's the case, it could well be out of date. An estate plan isn't something you can do and, having done it, say, "That's that." It needs adjustment from time to time to take into account changed conditions in your family and business situations. Furthermore, estate planning must be an ongoing concern regardless of the size of your estate or the seeming simplicity of your individual situation. Finally, your estate is something that quite likely needs the help of a variety of qualified advisers—your attorney, banker, accountant, insurance agent, and investment adviser.

This chapter will give you a starting point for a full-scale review of your own program. It will help you spot areas that need special attention. After this preliminary work, you'll be in a better position to call upon your various advisers for specific application.

The best place to start the review is to find out how much you're worth. Besides determining how much you're currently worth, as we discuss in Chapter 38, you ought to find out how much your estate would be worth. The difference can be substantial, of course, because of proceeds from insurance policies and other death benefits, plus lump sum distributions from pension and profit-sharing programs where you work.

Net estate worth is the starting point from which estate taxes will be calculated. How much of a bite these taxes—federal and state—take will largely rest on how well you have designed your program. The difference between taxes on an estate subjected to little or no planning and one that is carefully thought out can be staggering.

Keeping Your Will Current

After you find out how much your estate would be worth, you have to think about what you want done with this wealth. The front line of protection in this regard is a will. You do have one, don't you? Is it current?

Dying intestate—that is, without leaving a will—could be one of the most thoughtless, tragic, and expensive errors in your estate planning. It means that the courts, using an impersonal and rigid formula set out by state law, will decide who gets what, regardless of how you or your heirs might have wanted things.

Almost as bad is leaving behind a will that is so far out of date or so carelessly planned as to be inadequate, invalid, or inappropriate to your own current wishes and family's best interests. No matter how simple or clear-cut you think your situation is, you ought to spell out with a will your desires regarding the disposition of your wealth as specifically as possible. Another thought: While you can draw up your own will, there's a better than even chance that such a homemade document would not stand up in court. It's always safest to have the work done by an attorney.

Choosing an Executor

Choosing the right executor is nearly as vital as the drafting of a proper will. Yet the choice of an executor too often is left more to chance and sentiment than to common sense. A hasty and ill-considered decision ultimately can undo much of your otherwise careful planning and estate building efforts.

Many persons almost automatically name their spouse, other close family member, or friend as executor, with little contemplation of the risks that will fall to this individual or the qualifications with which he would confront them.

On the other hand, an attorney specializing in estate management or a bank or trust company might not be as close to the family situation as a relative or friend, and might make decisions quite alien to your own desires or, possibly, to the real needs of the family.

But there is a way to have your cake and eat it too. That is to name your spouse or other relative as co-executor with a bank or trust company. In such an arrangement, you could give your kin the final say in any decision, thus providing continuity in your family's lifestyle, while the professional executor would provide the good management, attend to the details, and be available to offer expert counsel.

As with other things, there is a difference in the quality of service between one institution and another. The better you know the bankers in your community, the better you'll be able to decide which one to choose. Your family lawyer can help you, too. Another way many persons get a feel for how a trust department would handle their estate is to establish a living, revocable trust with the bank as co-trustee. The way the bank handles that trust is a good indication of how it would handle the estate.

An executor's task is not one to be taken lightly. In a small estate, with no major complications, where the will's intentions are clearly spelled out and there is not much property to dispose of or heirs to offer dispute, the job can be relatively easy. But in an estate of any substance, where there are children or elderly dependents and their continuing financial security to consider, or where family quarrels erupt, the job can be far from routine.

In such cases, the availability of an executor could be required over the span of several years. Can you be sure the person of your choice would meet this test? He could die or move away or be otherwise unable to carry on. In this event, a new executor would have to be appointed, at considerable expense to the estate. One way around this eventuality would be to name a successor executor at the time you draw up your will. Unless you had designated an alternate choice, a court-appointed replacement might handle the estate at a variance with your wishes.

Furthermore, an executor should have experience in this type of work. He should have the ability to conserve the estate's assets and administer them prudently. He should be financially responsible. To be sure, an executor can be held legally responsible for the estate's assets if he carelessly handles them or illegally diverts them. He can be held liable for actions he fails to take as well as for oversights that result in losses. However, if he is financially unable to make restitution, the heirs would be the ultimate losers.

You are in the best position to know who will serve your family's interests well in your stead, if that ever becomes necessary. But you should make the choice only after considerable thought, and possibly with some advice from professionals. Your decision can be as important as the care you take in preparing your will.

Can You Use a Trust?

We mentioned trusts above. Do they have a place in your estate plan? They are not only for the super-rich. More and more persons of modest means are using trusts to accomplish a variety of estate planning aims, from lowering taxes to helping charity.

The first step in deciding whether trusts are for you is to determine just what you want them to accomplish. The second is to understand some of the basic differences between various types of trusts.

Here are some of the things trusts can do for you. Provide financial support for a relative. Split family income and thus the total family tax bill. Divide an estate among heirs. Retain family privacy. Help minimize estate taxes. Provide professional management of assets. Protect a family business. Make gifts. Assure bequests of specific property. Help charity.

There are basically two kinds of trusts, those that are in effect while you are alive, or "inter vivos trusts," and those that become operative upon your death, called "testamentary trusts." Living trusts can be revocable (those in which you retain control of the assets) or irrevocable (those in which you permanently give up control). The distinction is an important one, particularly in estate planning.

Trusts can be used to assure a lifelong stipend for a spouse or other relative from the income generated by the trust assets, with the assets themselves going, say, to a child or grandchild on the income beneficiary's death. This serves two valuable functions. First, it assures an income for someone who might not otherwise possess enough financial acumen to use the capital wisely. Second, it can save a good deal in estate taxes because, in effect, the assets are taxed only once, while serving twice.

In the chapter on financing a college education, we discussed short-term trusts in this regard. Short-term trusts can also be used to provide income for an aged parent or other older dependent. These revocable trusts are of no use in reducing the size of your estate, since if you die while one is in force, the assets are counted among your own. This is the case with any revocable trust—any trust in which you retain the power to change any of the provisions or to dissolve it and reacquire the assets.

However, if the trust is irrevocable, its assets will not be counted in your estate because you have given them away totally and permanently. You might find that you incur a gift tax liability when establishing and contributing to such trusts.

Where can you get specific advice about trusts? A good place to begin is with the trust department of your local bank. They can tell you whether your idea has merit, perhaps offer alternatives if it's questionable. They can also give you a picture of total cost. You should also talk with your lawyer early on; you'll need one for just about any kind of trust you set up. You might want to bring your tax counsel into the talks, too. He could have some insights into your financial picture that the lawyer might not have.

Pros and Cons of Joint Ownership

There are many valid reasons for married couples to hold property jointly. If their total estate is so small that taxes would be minimal or avoided entirely, many of the negative effects of joint ownership probably would be nonexistent—and possibly even be more than offset by certain benefits.

Here are some advantages of joint ownership: It can give a sense of family security. It can provide a safe and easy way to maintain and liquidate bank accounts. It can reduce estate administration costs and speed up the settlement of the estate, since property passes at once to the survivor. It can reduce or eliminate the need for probate.

One important thing you should realize about joint ownership is that it does not take the place of a will. Whether you choose joint or separate ownership, each spouse should have a will; that's the only sure way of seeing that your wishes are carried out after death.

There are many types of joint ownership, and a quick review here might prove useful. *Joint tenancy* permits co-ownership of real estate and other types of property, with right of survivorship. In other words, the survivor receives total title of ownership at the death of the other co-owner. *Tenancy by the entirety* is limited to joint ownership by husband and wife, and in many states to real estate only, with the right of survivorship. *Tenancy in common* permits two or more persons to own undivided shares in real or personal property; co-owners' shares pass to heirs or beneficiaries, not to surviving co-owners. *Community property* is the assumption in eight states that each partner in marriage has an automatic right to half the couple's assets, regardless of who provided how much. (The eight community property states are Arizona, California, Idaho, Louisiana, Nevada, New Mexico, Texas, and Washington.) Business arrangements such as partnerships, syndicates, and joint ventures are yet other forms of joint ownership.

For most married couples, joint ownership means joint tenancy and/or tenancy by the entirety, where right of survivorship is a principal element. Many couples believe this arrangement is all they need in the way of estate planning. Here are some reasons why that can be a dangerously shortsighted assumption.

One. It restricts your estate planning options. Because assets pass automatically from one spouse to the other on death of one, you cannot spell out in a will conditions under which your "share" of the property can be distributed.

Two. It can be inconvenient. Both owners must give their OK to any changes in the property—changing the ownership status, disposing of it, and the like. This means signatures of both, say, when selling jointly held stocks and bonds.

Three. It could increase estate taxes. Although the gift and estate tax laws have been liberalized with regard to the marital deduction and joint ownership, there are circumstances where maximum use of the tax provisions cannot be made because property is held jointly.

Four. It can have gift tax implications. If one spouse contributed all or most of the assets, he or she is, in effect, making "gifts" to the other. Many couples, ignorant of this obligation, can find themselves facing unexpected taxes or penalties for failing to declare the gifts.

What, if anything, can be done to unspring these potential traps? First, it isn't such a bad idea, under most circumstances, to keep the house in joint names. That way, the survivor acquires it at once on the spouse's death. Likewise for a savings account with enough money in it to carry the survivor over the first rough months until the estate is settled, or at least sufficiently organized to permit the disbursement of some funds. Second, you could decide to divide all other property equally, including securities and other real estate, by changing from joint tenancy to tenancy in common, dropping the right of survivorship. This way, each can dispose of his or her share by will. Any gift tax liability of one spouse should be far less than the estate taxes that would result from not dividing the property. As with other such maneuvers, the guidance of professional counsel is advised.

The Marital Deduction

For most couples, the marital deduction represents a major estate tax tool. You should be careful not to blunt its effectiveness on a technicality. First, some basics. To qualify for the marital deduction, a couple must be married at the time of death of one spouse. Thus, divorced persons may not claim a marital deduction. Furthermore, the property must pass into the full control of the surviving spouse. It is on this point that many estate planning efforts founder.

To help avoid problems as you explore the possible benefits of the marital deduction in your own situation, consider these potential traps:

Trap one: too many strings. For instance, a man can't leave property to his wife for her lifetime and specify what must be done with it at her death. She must be given the right to specify for herself.

Trap two: secondary disqualification. Watch for strings not included in the will or trusts. For instance, stocks in a closely held corporation which were left to the surviving spouse under a separate agreement not to sell or transfer except back to the company would likely be barred from the marital deduction.

Trap three: life insurance survivorship clauses. Since a large part of many estates consists of life insurance proceeds, particular attention should be paid to them. To qualify for the marital deduction, the proceeds must be payable to the surviving spouse either in a lump sum or in installments at least annually starting no later than 13 months after the insured's death. The surviving spouse alone must have power to dispose of proceeds. If any of your policies provide for secondary beneficiaries, check to make sure that if there is an overriding provision it gives the surviving spouse the specific exercise of power of appointment over any proceeds you wish to qualify for the marital deduction.

Trap four: a will that is too specific. If you make bequests of specific property or in specific dollar amounts, you run the risk of not fully utilizing the marital deduction or of forcing your executors to include property other than that which might bring greater benefit. A better approach might be to merely instruct the executor to make the marital deduction as large as possible, then make bequests and other distributions from the remainder. You also should allow your spouse to choose specifically from the estate's assets those which he or she wants, either within or outside the marital deduction limits. (You may be challenged by the tax people on this latter point, though it has been supported by at least one court case.)

Trap five: unduly burdening the spouse's estate. Sometimes use of the marital deduction can be counterproductive in the long run, saving taxes the first time around only to have substantially larger taxes imposed later. This is particularly true where each spouse has considerable independent wealth.

Trap six: creating a liquidity problem in the spouse's estate. Leaving assets under the marital deduction that would force the spouse to sell at a substantial loss to raise needed capital might more than offset any tax benefits.

Trap seven: using the marital deduction for tax savings when it should be avoided for other reasons. An example would be the splitting of a controlling block of stock or other division of a family-owned business to place a portion under the marital deduction.

Trap eight: presuming the order of demise. When considering the marital deduction, of course, you must presume that the spouse with the most property will die first, allowing fullest use of the benefit. However, it is prudent to have some standby plans at the ready in the event the other spouse should predecease.

Trap nine: failure to make provision for simultaneous death. It is possible by will to designate one spouse as having predeceased the other for probate purposes in the event of simultaneous death. The wills thus should be constructed so this presumption yields the maximum marital deduction benefit.

Trap ten: failure to make periodic review. Unless you examine your estate planning program from time to time, you run the risk that changed circumstances will arise to minimize or eliminate any benefits in your most thoughtful earlier plans.

How Gifts and Estates Are Taxed

Since much of your estate planning strategy involves cutting the federal tax bite, some idea of how the tax works should be of help. Of course, Congress has a way of playing havoc with the rules, so it's impossible to get too specific here.

The first thing you ought to remember about the federal gift and estate tax structure is that it is progressive. This means the rate gets higher as the taxable estate gets larger. It's an important point, because it increases the potential for tax savings through reductions in the size of the estate.

Because of this incentive to reduce the size of the taxable estate, the Internal Revenue Service has evolved a body of rules covering the way in which these reductions may be made. Basically, IRS is telling you that you can't have your cake and eat it, too. You either must dispose of your property—outright and with no strings—or your estate will be taxed on it.

That means that any property you transfer to someone else on which you reserve the income or the right to "use and enjoy" is not acceptable by the tax people as a transfer. Further, any property you transfer to someone else less than three years before death generally is counted in your estate as well, minus any gift tax paid or credit applied. Also counted in your estate are proceeds from any life insurance policies you own. Likewise, any property transferred to someone else after death via a will is counted in the estate. However, any amount bequeathed to a qualified charitable organization is deductible from the gross estate.

Property included in the gross estate must be appraised at fair market value. The executor generally may value the property either at the date of death or an alternate valuation date. If he uses the alternate date, he must apply it to all assets, not just to some. Present law places the alternate valuation date as six months from the date of death. Unless he is granted extensions, an executor must file an estate tax return no later than nine months after death.

In 1976, Congress extensively rewrote the gift and estate tax laws. In 1978, it "refined" some of these changes. Without getting too deeply into specifics, here is what the new legislation did:

It scrapped the old separate gift and estate tax tables and separate lifetime exemptions. It replaced them with a unified tax rate on both gifts and estates. In place of the separate exclusions, it instituted a unified tax credit. The value of gifts now is tallied cumulatively and deducted from the unified credit when the estate's final accounting is made. However, please note that the annual $3,000 gift tax exclusion was not touched by the 1976 law and remains available to you.

The new unified gift and estate tax credit, in effect, shears the top off the old tax tables. Where the minimum rate used to be 3 percent, it is now 18 percent. The top rate remains 70 percent. But the new unified tax credit is much larger than the old gift and estate tax exemptions, with the result that many more estates escape any taxation at all. The new law phases in the new credit, so that by 1982, taxable estates of $175,000 or less will be exempt from tax.

The new law also ruled out so-called generation-skipping transfers as a means of holding down estate taxes on property passed by a decedent to more than one generation successively. Such property now is taxed at all levels of transfer. However, the law allows a certain amount of property to be passed along to grandchildren without incurring this extra tax. It did a lot of other things, too, that threw a good many estate plans out of kilter.

The new law also provided for taxation of capital gains that previously had escaped taxation upon the death of the property owner. Under a so-called "fresh-start" rule, the decedent's tax basis would become that of the beneficiary. But such a hue and cry arose that the plan was first delayed by the Revenue Act of 1978, then dropped altogether as a provision of the Windfall Profit Tax of 1980.

Changes in the law, many times much less dramatic, as well as issuance of new regulations and judicial decisions continually add new shadings to that vast and complicated body of law concerned with estate planning. Those, as well as the evolution of your own family situation, are the main reasons your plan needs periodic review.

Chapter 46 Financial Planning for Singles

FOR THE man or woman who decides to forgo connubial bliss, a special set of financial planning considerations presents itself. He or she is confronted with a much stiffer federal income tax bill than married friends who file jointly. This means that singles reach the higher brackets rather quickly—a fact that could affect their approach to investing and the deployment of their resources.

Although it would appear logical that single persons—with fewer mouths to feed, fewer backs to clothe, and fewer educations to buy—would have much healthier savings accounts than their colleagues who are raising families, this is not always true. For often the difference is eaten up with more frequent nights out, more new wardrobes, more travel, and more expensive hobbies. And it's not all that much less expensive to provide a roof overhead for one than it is for four, five, or six.

Yet, savings for the single person might be more important than for a family person, because often there is no one readily at hand to help if the going gets rough. If you're single, you have every bit as much reason as anyone else to look forward to a long and happy retirement. Thus, you have as much reason to provide for the probable gap between pension and Social Security income and your actual financial needs in retirement.

There are some things you can do to establish a savings and investment program if you haven't already done so, and some ways to make your existing program more productive. Here are a few:

Boost your retirement fund. If you still have some years before retirement, start building onto your pension fund now. Some alternatives: An individual retirement account to shelter income from current taxation (up to 15 percent of earned income to an annual $1,500 limit) if you are employed but not participating in a qualified plan where you work. A Keogh plan if you're self-employed (that

458

can shelter up to 15 percent to a $7,500 limit annually). A "mini" Keogh if you do consulting or other work on your own (up to $750 a year may qualify regardless of percentage limitations).

Start an investment portfolio. Inflation plays no favorites—it will hit you as hard as anyone else. Chances are, you're the cautious type when it comes to savings. If so, you probably have lots of your assets in bank accounts, savings bonds, and other "safe" investments. Or, because of your freer lifestyle, you might be a "swinger" when it comes to investments. You like a high flyer, you play the long shots. Either way, you could profit over the long term by diverting a portion of your earnings into a portfolio of high-quality growth stocks. That way, you'd be protecting yourself now against inflation tomorrow. Furthermore, the growth is not taxable until you sell the stocks.

Buy a home. This is another good way to achieve tax savings and protect against inflation. You get the deductions on interest payments and property taxes—and other things if you use part of the property to provide rental income. You also have an asset that probably is appreciating faster than average and that shows promise of continuing to do so. If you don't like the idea of putting up with the headaches of maintaining a house, consider a condominium. You get the same tax breaks and—if it's carefully chosen—the same chances for capital appreciation.

Cut your taxes. As a single, you're the hardest hit when it comes to federal income taxes and often state taxes as well. There are some things you can do to ease the bite. Pumping as much income as possible into your tax-sheltered retirement program and buying a home as noted above are two ways. You may be able to save money by stacking two years' worth of deductibles like charitable gifts into every other tax year and itemizing, then taking the standard deduction in alternate "stripped" years. If you contribute at least half the cost of maintaining a home for a parent or provide at least half the cost of supporting an unmarried relative in your own home, you may qualify as "head of household" and thus a lower tax rate. If you contribute at least 10 percent of the cost of supporting a relative, and you and other contributing family members together provide more than half of that relative's support, you can collectively agree to let one claim the dependent as an exemption.

Planning for Retirement

What happens when you as a single man or woman reach retirement age? Like anyone else, you must be prepared to provide a steady inflow of funds to cover living expenses. As with any other retiree, you'll most likely draw the major portion of retirement income from Social Security benefits and a check from your company's pension plan. As with a good many other retirees, you'll most likely find these to be inadequate.

What other sources are at hand? The biggest probably is the nest egg you've been building up over the years. Now, in retirement, how best can you utilize it?

The answer depends somewhat on how you've built it, how large it is, and what kind. If you've been putting your savings into a deferred annuity, where income earned during the accumulation period has not been taxed, you'd probably be best off to convert it to an income annuity. To take a lump sum distribution of the assets would impose a hefty tax payment that would eat mightily into the size of the nest egg.

If you haven't been salting away funds in an annuity, but think perhaps you should buy one now, you should examine the decision carefully. For one thing, if you're fairly young, say 60 to 68, you'll quite likely find that you can obtain as good a return on your money by investing in a portfolio of good-quality stocks and bonds as you can with an annuity. And you'll have your principal to draw upon in an emergency, where with an annuity you irrevocably trade those assets for an assured life income. If you're a woman, your annuity dollars will buy about the same income as for a man five years your junior, because of women's greater longevity.

As you grow older, an annuity begins to make more sense. For one thing, the return on investment becomes much more attractive. For another, it provides you with an assured income and frees you from management headaches at a time when you may be becoming less able to handle them.

Back to that investment portfolio. If you've never dabbled in the stock market, you shouldn't let the prospect of investing frighten you. With some careful homework and a hefty dose of common sense, you should be able to do respectably well. You can put together a package that will yield you an adequate annual income and still provide protection against inflation. There is some risk to such an alternative, of course. But it can be minimal when investments are made in the best and most solid corporations.

After Retirement

Aside from your savings and perhaps gifts and inheritances, about the only alternative open to you for filling an income gap after retirement is to work. It could be the most exciting thing that ever happened to you. In "retirement," with a good part of your income assured via Social Security and pension, you have a golden opportunity to pursue enterprises foreclosed to you during your "working" years. Furthermore, you have more room to gamble on them—not so much to lose if they don't pan out or if you wish later to try something else.

If you can line something up before you begin drawing Social Security benefits, you can put off taking those benefits; and then when you do start receiving them, they'll be higher. Meanwhile, you won't have forfeited any benefits by exceeding the earnings limitations.

Finally, in retirement, don't neglect your protection. With the stringencies of a retirement budget, it would be tempting to drop your insurance coverage, or to buy "bargain" coverage. You shouldn't overspend, of course, but neither should you skimp on the important things. Foremost is the adequate medical coverage, particularly that which closes the biggest Medicare gaps. Then, be sure you're adequately covered against loss of your possessions and for personal liability. A fire or burglary could leave you stripped of worldly belongings and a legal settlement against you could severely deplete your savings.

Estate Planning

Now let's turn to another consideration that many single persons might tend to overlook—estate planning. If you're someone who never married and had a family, and your own parents or other aging relatives are no longer here and dependent upon you, it would be easy for you to conclude that there really isn't much need for you to give much thought to estate planning.

That would be a shortsighted—and potentially tragic—conclusion. For, in its broadest sense, estate planning embraces much more than determining how your wealth and possessions should be divided after your death. It includes the drafting and maintaining of a plan to utilize these assets most effectively during your own lifetime. Furthermore, it involves preparing for some potentially traumatic contingencies while you are still able to do it rationally.

For the single retired person without heirs or dependents, those considerations should be of utmost importance. Regard these possibilities: A prolonged illness and/or recuperation could well impose extraordinary financial burdens; the absence of close family members heightens the chance you'll need to pay for nursing care. Incapacitation could, without prior planning, place you in the hands of virtual strangers via a court-appointed guardian or conservator, or in the hands of family members not totally committed to your welfare or in sympathy with your desires and comfort. The same situation could place you in a home for the aged that might not be the one you would have chosen.

In addition to these lifetime concerns, there is the usual one regarding final distribution of your estate after death. In the absence of a valid will, this distribution could be made in a way that is not in accord with your desires or philosophy. In fact, this is more likely to be the case than for someone with heirs and close family.

So, what steps should you take to prepare and maintain an estate plan? First, make a will. In it, you can be sure that close friends and your favorite charitable organizations are remembered. You can also use it to leave specific instructions regarding funeral and burial, and the like, that might not otherwise be known or considered in the absence of close family.

Choose an executor. A relative in whom you have confidence, or a close friend. Perhaps your attorney, if you'd feel more secure. If there is considerable property involved and its disposition is likely to take several years, consider a bank as executor or co-executor with the relative or friend. Inform your executor-designate of your wish that he serve, and keep him informed as to the location of your will and any other documents he might need. A letter of instruction, providing more detailed information than included in the will, should be prepared and kept with the will.

Consider trusts. One way to prepare against the possibility of your becoming unable to handle your own affairs because of mental incompetence or physical incapacity is to create a living trust, where you and someone in whom you have utmost confidence are the co-trustees. As long as you are able to function, you retain full control over your affairs, but if and when you are not, someone of your own choice stands ready to take over immediately in your behalf. Trusts can also be used to distribute your property after death.

Make contingency plans. Even though you don't believe it will ever happen, give thought to what you would do if you should need to move to a nursing home or a place where care is provided for the elderly. You don't need to do a thorough investigation; that's impractical. But at least have an idea of what's available in your area, what kind of service is provided and what kind of costs are involved.

Review your estate plan periodically. Making such a plan is never something you can do and then put aside forever. Your life is in a constant state of flux. Conditions change. Your ideas change. You must make certain that your plan keeps abreast of these changes.

Chapter 47 "Women's Lib" and Financial Planning

THE CHANGING role of women in our society is challenging some traditional precepts of family financial planning. The growing numbers of women pursuing careers, either instead of or in conjunction with having families, means more women have more need to involve themselves with money management. The addition of a wife's income to the family budget adds yet other implications to financial planning. The rising divorce rate likewise has forced many women to join the labor force. The continuing trend of wives outliving husbands makes it prudent for women to prepare for the financial aspects of widowhood.

Many modern couples have cast aside the so-called traditional family roles where the husband and father is the sole breadwinner and the wife and mother stays home to keep house and raise the children. In most cases this means that the wife has taken a paying job and added to the family income. This also means that with more financial resources, and therefore frequently more to allocate to savings, the family's money management must become more sophisticated. As a contributor to the income side of the financial statement, the wife likewise should become an active participant in the decisions regarding the outgo side, if she isn't already.

A wife should also establish a credit rating of her own. In the past, most married women have simply assumed the rating of their husbands—until they lost their husbands, either through death or divorce. Then they found themselves cast adrift in the financial seas, frequently with substantial wealth and resources, but without access to credit when its use would be helpful. New federal law allows wives to establish their own credit rating whenever they and their husbands use joint charge accounts and the like. All wives, whether newlyweds, in the middle years of their marriage, or later on, should take steps to establish their own credit records. Their husbands, if they are sincere in their wish to leave their wives financially self-sufficient, should wholeheartedly push for its implementation.

Emphasizing "Togetherness"

Many modern couples are also assuming new attitudes toward life insurance. Instead of loading the husband up with coverage beyond a certain basic amount, they use the money that would have gone into extra premiums to provide protection against other future uncertainties.

One of these is more insurance coverage for the wife, especially in families with young children. In some ways, her death would create more financial hardship for the family than her husband's. A widow with children would probably qualify for mother's benefits under Social Security; a widower of a woman who was not qualified under Social Security would not. In addition, someone would probably have to be hired to do many of the tasks the wife performed.

Where the wife does not work outside the home, the couple might invest in education to arm her with some "marketable" skill—teaching, nursing, accounting, law. That way, she could go to work if need be to support herself and the children. Or she could pursue a career that would add to the family's income and help build a savings and investment program.

At any rate, the emphasis should be on "togetherness" when it comes to managing the family's finances. Whether the wife produces income or not, the devastating effects of inflation on family budgets dictate that more attention be paid to strict and thoughtful budgeting. This task frequently falls to the wife. But the feminist movement has broadened women's horizons beyond that; more wives want a larger part in planning the big picture, and this is as it should be. The more both partners know about the family's total financial situation, the better.

Are You Ready for Widowhood?

In many "old-fashioned" families, it's the husband who makes all the major money decisions, doling out a certain amount of cash to the wife for current expenses. It isn't always a matter of male chauvinism; sometimes the wife just isn't interested in finances. The husband opens the bank accounts, buys the stocks and bonds, picks out the insurance policies, and even possibly stashes the whole bundle away someplace without bothering to say where. Bowing to statistical imperatives, he dies before his wife, leaving to her the task of finding his hidden assets and untangling them as best she can. Then, unversed in wise deployment of the inheritance, she has to learn fast or depend upon someone else or, quite possibly, squander the assets her late husband worked a lifetime to accumulate.

No thoughtful husband would want such a scenario to be played out in his absence. The best way to prevent it is to make sure the wife is closely involved in the family's financial affairs all along. Not only is she then more adequately prepared for the emotion-shattering prospect of widowhood, but she is also able to contribute another point of view to the thinking that goes into the family's financial program. Frequently, her better understanding of monetary affairs can make for a more harmonious marriage as well.

Aside from the wife's involvement in finances, what other guidance can be offered to help ease the burden of transition to widowhood? The first suggestion is this: Don't ignore the possibility that it will happen to you. Unsettling though it is to contemplate, if you're a woman, your chances are five times those of your husband that you will become widowed.

Obviously, it is impossible to anticipate every need, every circumstance, every emotion that would occur in widowhood. But in the cool analytical climate that is more likely to prevail before such an occurrence, it is possible to prepare a course of action. By doing this, you will eliminate the necessity of making major decisions when you are extremely susceptible to errors in judgment. It will buy you some time to get your bearings, to see how things are going, to decide what you want to do.

The first rule should be adhered to with determination. Do nothing in haste. Make no major decisions (aside from those immediately relating to the funeral) during the initial phases of bereavement. Hold firmly to this rule, despite the advice, either well-meaning or self-serving, of family and friends. If you and your husband have planned properly together, there should be no need for hasty action. You should give yourself ample time to gather your thoughts.

The second rule is to stay put. Many people will advise you to "get away" for a while to gather yourself up. It may not necessarily be the wisest course, for it may only delay the making of adjustments that inevitably must be made at home—socially, emotionally, and financially. Moving away immediately is generally a mistake, for moving is another of life's more stressful experiences, and undertaking it at a time like this would only serve to pile one traumatic experience on another.

Don't be afraid to vent your emotions. You'll have them aplenty; and don't be surprised if some are not what you would regard as the most "honorable." Guilt that you may have contributed to your husband's death. Anger that he "left" you alone. Shame that you have such feelings. They're natural; nearly every woman who has gone through the experience can tell you she has felt the same things. Those who hold them all in—the "perfect" widows—are only putting up a brave front.

Once you regain your bearings, you will have to start getting your new life in order. Among the priority items will be to get a firm grip on your day-to-day finances. We've all heard sad tales of widows flush with new inheritances going on spending sprees, only to discover themselves a short time later destitute and alone. Or of others, afraid to spend lest they not have money enough, who are found cold and starving—with a fortune in the mattress.

These are extremes, fortunately, but the situations do represent what actually happens to a good many widows, though to a much lesser degree. Assets ineptly deployed are too quickly—or too slowly —consumed, robbing their intended beneficiaries of a much more comfortable life.

At the risk of being repetitious, we again emphasize the importance of prior planning as a means of easing the shock of traumatic changes in your life. While it is impossible to anticipate precisely what shape these changes will take, it is possible to get a workably accurate picture. The more thoroughly this is done beforehand, the easier the transition will be.

But whether or not you have done this, your first task in sorting out your financial affairs in widowhood is to find out where you stand. You'll have to determine which sources of income will shrink or disappear. You'll have to discover what additional assets will become available.

Here are some of the ways your income is likely to shrink: Your Social Security benefit almost certainly will drop. Even if you have worked long enough to draw a benefit of your own, it won't be as big as that drawn by your husband and you together. A widow's benefit is the amount of the husband's primary benefit—but there won't be that additional 50 percent wife's benefit paid while he was alive.

The pension benefit from your husband's former employer might drop—or discontinue altogether. Deferred compensation or other business "income" might halt. Income earned by your husband through part-time employment will no longer come in. Certain annuity payment options may provide for a drop when one partner dies.

But there might be factors that offset any such reductions. Proceeds from life insurance policies. Lump sum distributions of pension benefits or deferred compensation. Proceeds from buy-out agreements among business partners. Sale of personal or business property from the husband's estate.

Where Do You Get Help?

Where can you get the advice you need to put these assets to their most productive use? That's a tough question to answer. As many other women in your situation can tell you, you will be overwhelmed by offers to "help," once word of your widowhood gets around. Many will be sincere, others will have obvious motivation, still others will represent designs upon your wealth not immediately apparent. So where do you turn?

Your best bet, if you're up to it—and anyone with average intelligence and determination should be—is to make your own decisions, based on as wide a range of "intelligence" as possible. Tap many sources for advice. Your family lawyer. The executor of your husband's estate. Your banker, accountant, life insurance agent, stockbroker. From all these sources you can distill information and ideas to help you decide what your needs are, and to draft a program tailored to fill them.

If you simply don't feel up to the task, then perhaps you should consider getting a professional manager. But take great pains to select someone whose philosophy is compatible with your own, someone with whom you feel comfortable and in whom you have supreme confidence.

One approach would be to have a trust set up to manage the assets and provide you with regular income checks. By making it a revocable trust, you can retain ultimate control of the assets; you merely shift the burden of management onto someone else. Remember, though, it will cost something to set up and keep operating. Weigh these costs in your decision. Your lawyer and/or banker can help you with specifics.

Another approach would be to have your stockbroker help you set up a portfolio of income-oriented securities. If you choose this option, you must be aware of the possible risks as well as the potential advantages. And you must choose a broker who will serve your interests best, not his.

Or you could use the assets to purchase an annuity that would provide regular income for as long as you live. If you do this, you must be aware of the negatives about annuities, as well as the positives. (See Chapter 43.) Finally, some combination of these approaches might be the best all-around solution.

Weigh Your Financial Alternatives

Here are some things you should *not* do: Don't succumb to temptations to invest in "sure things" that promise instant wealth. As a new widow, you'll be a prime target of con artists offering such "investments." Don't make investments without first reaching some clear objectives. By all means, don't simply do nothing at all. By doing nothing with these idle assets, you will be needlessly robbing yourself of the income they could be earning, or the security they could be providing.

But before committing any of your assets, sit down and draft a plan for them. Decide what you need these assets to do. Provide immediate income? Serve as a safety cushion against future expenses? Protect you against inflation? Some combination of these things? Here are some of your alternatives.

Annuities. These can provide you with an assured income for life.

But once you commit your assets to an annuity, you cannot retrieve them should you need them for something else. So, you limit your financial flexibility.

Savings accounts. While these provide the ultimate in safety, they do little to extend your wealth. They may not even keep up with inflation. And, if you commit savings to those longer-term accounts to obtain higher interest, you'll have to pay a penalty to get at them if you need them before they mature.

U.S. Savings Bonds. Again, ultra-safe. Again, limited return. Series E Bonds allow you to accumulate interest without paying income taxes on it until you cash them in; Series H Bonds make periodic interest payments to you.

Other U.S. government and agency bonds. These are as safe as Savings Bonds, but they pay a bit more interest. They come in varying maturities, but generally cannot be purchased for less than $1,000; some come in $5,000, $10,000, and even $25,000 and $100,000 minimum denominations.

Corporate bonds. These provide varying amounts of safety, depending upon the company issuing them. Highly rated ones can be extremely "safe," and they tend to yield greater returns than government issues.

Common stocks. Depending on which ones are chosen, they can provide dividend income, capital growth, or some combination of the two. But their prices and dividends can also go down, so they do not possess the safety of bonds or savings accounts. However, carefully chosen common stocks can be a valuable part of your financial security program, for they offer an excellent way to help beat inflation.

Mutual funds. They offer the same things as common stocks, but allow you to diversify your holdings with less investment, and they offer continuing management of your assets. Mutual funds consisting solely of bonds are available, too.

How do you choose from among this dazzling array of possibilities? Again, back to your basic plan. If you want an assured life income and if you aren't concerned about committing assets to provide it, you'll probably choose an annuity. If you're already well provided with income from a pension program, you might prefer instead to use your assets to hedge against inflation, so you'll probably put together a portfolio of common stocks. If you want a bit more income to supplement what you already have, but also want to protect against the future rise in prices, you'll perhaps put together a program that includes a combination of annuities and bonds for assured income, and common stocks for capital growth.

Where do you get advice about investing that nest egg? Don't be afraid to keep your own counsel. With some homework and a good helping of common sense, you should be able to handle it. Get as much input from others as you can, but reserve final judgments for yourself. If you're a novice, this book will serve as a good primer. Read the investment columns in the newspapers to get a "feel" for the market. If you want to get more deeply involved, consider subscribing to an investment advisory service. Avoid those that tout a single investment approach or that recommend offbeat stocks.

Deciding how to invest your assets isn't all you'll have to do. Choosing the proper mix for a nest egg can be as important as picking the right investments. A number of factors will bear on the decisions you must make as to how you distribute the proceeds from your husband's estate. Your income requirements. Your age. Your need to provide inflation protection. Your ability to undertake financial risk. And, of course, the size of the nest egg itself.

You Might Have to Work

In the final analysis, you might have to work to make ends meet. But a job can reap rewards beyond the financial. Many younger couples these days have predicated their long-range plans on the fact that the wife would work in case of the husband's premature death, and they already have charted their contingencies. But many older couples have not operated on that premise, and indeed are of an era when the wife's place was strictly in the house. So she may feel ill prepared to seek and hold a job.

But the realities of inflation have severely strained that attitude in a great many instances. Funds are harder to set aside for a widow's financial security, and those that are saved simply won't do the job. And they grow ever less adequate as time goes on.

The result is that many widows who might not have contemplated the need to provide their own income will be confronted with that necessity. You should not ignore the possibility that you might be one of them.

If so, don't panic. Many widows who have had to go to work have found the experience an opening to an exciting new facet of their lives. Indeed, a job can be an excellent way to help you adapt to your drastically changed life. Even if you don't absolutely need to go to work, you should give it serious thought. Becoming a contributing member of the business world can have many rewards of its own.

Where to begin? Start by assuming a positive attitude. Look on a job as an opportunity, not as a cross to bear. Then assess your strengths and weaknesses. Consider brushing up on former skills, even if they're two or three decades old. Or, if experience and interests acquired since then indicate a new direction, begin collecting credentials.

If you're not yet widowed, discuss the idea with your husband. Togetherness, again, is a keynote to planning. If it's not absolutely necessary for you to go to work right now, but if the prospect shimmers in the future, consider wetting your toes with something on a part-time basis. Substitute teaching. Seasonal sales. Temporary secretary. Free-lance writing or designing, if they're your field. Volunteer work in social agencies, hospitals, schools—and even in politics —can often lead to a paying job.

Where do you find a job? Once you've decided what your experience and aptitude suit you for, get word around among your friends. Contact your family lawyer and banker. Don't overlook your husband's business connections, either. They might yield a sympathetic ear, helpful counsel, and even a job. Then, of course, there are the usual sources—the want ads and employment agencies. Many state employment offices also maintain job listings.

If you work through an agency, and there are some that specialize in finding positions for women, be absolutely sure that you fully understand the conditions beforehand. They charge a fee; that's how they make their living. But in most cases these days, the employer picks up the tab. Try to find such a situation if you can. However, if you must pay the fee, be sure it's reasonable; 5 to 7 percent of annual salary is a good rule of thumb. Be sure, too, that any contract you sign with an agency contains some provision for refund or adjustment in case the job doesn't work out during the first three months.

How do you land a job? Write a resume. Include your educational background, academic honors, earlier career accomplishments, if any, and personal information; but omit your age and graduation year, to prevent a prejudiced employer from rejecting you sight unseen. However, don't hedge about your age in an interview. Don't forget to mention volunteer work that might have helped equip you for a paying career. Make the resume brief and to the point. A single typewritten page is best, if possible, but in no case should it be longer than two pages. Present it in outline form, but you might include a short paragraph about why you feel qualified for the position.

When you're interviewed, exude confidence, even if your knees are like jelly. Mention your maturity and the fact that you'd be more likely than a younger person to remain on the job. And, since you are mature, you'll show up for the interview appropriately—but not overly—dressed. Answer questions firmly and forthrightly. Emphasize your skills, but don't overplay them.

There are some realities that you should understand. Because of the break in your employment record, you are likely to be taking a job at the entry level at first. Don't expect the same pay as a career woman of your age. Gain experience and confidence first, then look for advancement in both pay and position. Don't be too pushy about getting raises, but don't be too bashful, either.

Above all, remember this: Many employers will be glad to see you coming. They already know the merits of employing older women, and with them you won't have to "sell" yourself so hard to beat out the younger crowd.

Part VII SPEAKING THE LANGUAGE
OF THE BULLS AND BEARS

An extensive and exhaustive glossary of investment, economic, business, legal, and financial terms of importance to investors.

Glossary

Account executive. Another name for a broker or dealer.

Acid test (also known as quick assets ratio or liquidity ratio). The ratio of current assets less inventories to current liabilities. The acid test provides a better test of a firm's current operations than the current ratio, since inventories often do not prove liquid enough to service current debt. *See* Current ratio.

Advance-Decline Index. The net result of all advances and declines which have occurred on the NYSE or other exchange since a particular starting point. The ratio derived from relating advances to declines provides an overbought/oversold index.

Advisory service. An organization offering information, generally buy and sell advice, to investors for a fee.

American Depositary Receipts (ADR's). Negotiable receipts issued by an American depositary bank stating that a certain number of foreign shares have been deposited with the overseas branch of the depositary or with a custodian. Since foreign stock is often in bearer form, the ADR facilitates such matters as the receipt of dividends by the shareholder.

American Stock Exchange. The second largest securities exchange; located in New York City. The AMEX's volume is approximately as heavy as that of all the regional exchanges combined.

Amortization. The gradual liquidation annually of the cost of an intangible asset such as a patent or of a debt. Amortization is a bookkeeping entry and does not require an outlay of cash.

Annual report. The formal financial statement issued yearly by a corporation to its shareholders.

Annuity. Payment made to an annuitant at some regular interval for either a specified or indefinite length of time. Annuity contracts are sold by life insurance companies. "Annuity" also refers to the contract under which the payments are made.

Arbitrage. The act of purchasing a particular security or commodity in one market and simultaneously selling it in another market at a higher price. The arbitrageur profits when the price differential between the two markets exceeds the cost of the operation. Also, the purchase and sale of related securities—common and convertible—for profit on price differentials.

Assets. Physical properties or intangibles of value owned by an individual or a business.

Authorized stock. The maximum amount of stock which can be issued by a corporation according to its certificate of incorporation, which may at any time be amended by stockholders' vote.

Balanced fund. A mutual fund which diversifies its portfolio holdings over common stocks, bonds, preferreds, and possibly other forms of investment. Holdings of defensive securities are proportionately increased when the market outlook appears unfavorable, and aggressive positions are stressed when the market seems to be headed upward.

Balance sheet. An accounting statement showing the amount of a company's assets, liabilities, and owners' equity as of a given date.

Bar chart. A form of chart used extensively by technicians. The horizontal axis represents time and the vertical axis represents price. Vertical lines are drawn at each time period, with the top and bottom of each bar plotted at the high and low prices for the period. A small horizontal line is drawn across the bar at the closing price. Many charts also include a vertical scale at the bottom depicting trading volume.

Basis point. A unit used to measure changes in interest rates and bond yields. One basis point equals .01, or $\frac{1}{100}$ of 1 percent.

Bear. One who believes that the market is headed downward. One theory of the term's origin holds that the old proverb "to sell a bear's skin before one has caught the bear" describes what the short seller (bear) is doing, because the short seller does not own the stock he is selling. The terms "bull" and "bear" were both used on the London Stock Exchange in the early eighteenth century. *See* Bull.

Bearer bond. A bond which does not have the name of the owner registered in the books of the issuer, but on which interest and principal are paid to the bearer. *See* Coupon bond, Registered bond.

Beta. A measure of the sensitivity of a stock's price to fluctuations in a particular average. A volatile stock has a high beta, and a low-risk stock generally has a low beta. If a stock tends to move the same as the average, it has a beta of one.

Bid price. The highest amount a prospective buyer is willing to bid or pay for a security at a given time.

Big Board. Another name for the New York Stock Exchange.

Blue chip stocks. High-quality stocks of major companies which have long, unbroken records of earnings and dividends, good growth prospects, well-regarded management, and a conservative financial structure.

Blue List. A daily trade publication for dealers in municipal bonds listing the names and amounts of municipal bonds that dealers all over the country are offering for sale.

Blue sky laws. Laws various states have enacted to protect the public against securities frauds.

Bond. Evidence of a debt on which the issuing company usually promises to pay the bondholders a specified amount of interest for a given length of time, and to repay the loan at the expiration date.

Book value. A company's total assets less its liabilities and the liquidating value of its preferred stock. The result is divided by the number of common shares outstanding, to put the measure on a per-share basis.

Broad tape. A machine operated by Dow Jones & Co. which prints important financial news on an enlarged form of the ticker tape. *See* Ticker.

Broker. An agent who handles buy and sell orders for securities or commodities for a commission charge.

Bull. One who believes that the market is headed upward. One theory of origin holds that the way a bull tosses things up with its horns describes the action of a bull on the exchange. *See* Bear.

Business cycle. Regularly recurring periods of economic activity encompassing prosperity, recession, depression, and recovery.

Businessman's risk. The risk involved in securities transactions which a businessman appears able to undertake. The term generally denotes securities entailing greater than average risk, but not so much as speculative issues.

Callable. A bond or preferred issue, all or part of which may be redeemed by the issuing corporation under definite conditions prior to maturity. Many high-coupon bonds are vulnerable to call in periods of declining interest rates.

Call option. A contract which allows its owner to buy a certain number of shares of stock at a specific price, within a given period of time. The term also refers to commodity contracts.

Capital gain or capital loss. Profit or loss from the sale of a capital asset. Tax considerations are different from those on ordinary income.

Capital goods. Material goods used in the production of other goods.

Capitalization. The total amount of securities (bonds, preferred stock, and common stock) issued by a corporation, plus its retained earnings.

Cash flow. The reported net income of a corporation plus the amount charged off for depreciation, depletion, amortization, and other charges which are bookkeeping deductions and which do not entail actual payout of dollars and cents.

Certificate. The actual piece of paper which is evidence of ownership of stock in a corporation.

Certificate of deposit. A certificate for money deposited in a commercial bank for a specified period of time and earning a specific rate of return.

Certified Financial Planner (CFP). A designation conferred upon those individuals who have demonstrated competence in analyzing and developing personal and business financial plans. Candidates complete a broad study program and demonstrate their proficiency by completing five comprehensive examinations.

Channels. A technical analysis term. Channels are drawn on a chart by connecting a series of highs and a series of lows to make parallel lines. Characteristically, a stock will trade within ascending and descending channels.

Chartered Financial Analyst (CFA). A professional designation awarded to those financial analysts who have passed a series of three examinations requiring knowledge of accounting, financial statement analysis, economics, and finance, as well as competence in investment management and securities analysis.

Chicago Board Options Exchange. A market established in 1973 for the formalized trading of put and call options.

Chicago Board of Trade (CBT). One of the oldest and largest organized commodity exchanges in the U.S. Officially chartered by the Illinois state legislature in 1859, the CBT provides facilities for trading in selected cash and futures markets.

Churning. Excessive trading in a customer's account without adequate or proper justification. Churning is usually done to generate additional commissions.

Clearing house. A corporation which takes the opposite side of all trades. The clearing house becomes the buyer to all sellers and the seller to all buyers.

Clifford trust. A short-term trust. Assets placed in the trust return to the donor after a specified period, as long as that period extends at least ten years and one day, or upon the death of the beneficiary. Meanwhile, income earned by the assets is taxable to the beneficiary.

Coinciding indicators. Economic indicators which tend to move directly with the business cycle. *See* Lagging indicators, Leading indicators.

Commercial paper. Unsecured short-term negotiable promissory notes of well-known business concerns and finance companies.

Commission. The amount paid to a broker or other agent to buy or sell securities or commodities.

Commission broker. A broker who owns a seat on the exchange and executes transactions on the floor for customers of his member firms.

Commodity contract. A firm legal agreement between the buyer or seller and the commodity exchange's clearing house.

Commodity futures market. A market in which contracts for the future delivery of commodities or foreign exchange are bought and sold. The most important function of the futures market is that it provides a means of insurance against the risk of adverse price fluctuations between the time of the production of the commodity and its utilization.

Commodity Futures Trading Commission. The agency created in 1974 by the federal government to regulate the commodity business, as the SEC oversees the securities industry.

Common stock. Securities which represent ownership interest in a corporation. Preferred stock normally has prior claim in regard to dividends and, in the event of liquidation, assets. Common stockholders assume greater risk for potentially greater reward.

Common stock equivalent. All stock options and warrants, plus all convertible securities which at time of issue have a cash yield of less than two thirds of the then current prime rate.

Confirmation. A formal memo delivered to a client of a brokerage house which bears all data relevant to a securities transaction executed for the client.

Conglomerate. A diversified corporation with operations in a number of varied industries.

Contractual plan. A plan under which a mutual fund investor signs a contract agreeing to invest a specific sum of money in a particular fund at regular intervals for a definite period of time. Since, according to law, 20 percent of the first year's investment may be deducted as a sales charge, there is a monetary loss in dropping out of the plan prior to completion.

Conversion parity. The point at which the price of a convertible security is equal to the value of the common shares into which it can be converted.

Conversion value. The worth of a convertible bond, preferred stock, or warrant if it were converted into common stock under the terms of the conversion privilege and if the common stock obtained by conversion were sold at its current market price.

Convertible security. A bond, debenture, or preferred stock which may be exchanged by the owner for common stock or another security, usually of the same company.

Coupon bond. A bond with interest coupons attached. The coupons are clipped as they come due and are presented by the holder to a bank for payment. *See* Bearer bond, Registered bond.

Covered option. An option written against securities already owned. *See* Naked option.

Cumulative preferred. Preferred stock on which unpaid dividends accrue. Dividends in arrears on a cumulative preferred stock must be paid before any common dividend.

Current ratio. The ratio of current assets to current liabilities. This measure is used to evaluate a firm's liquidity. *See* Acid test.

Cushion bond. A premium bond, selling above its call price. Because of the possibility of call, it does not tend to rise as much in price as other bonds of a similar maturity when interest rates decline. It therefore does not decline as much when rates rise. Thus price action is cushioned by the call feature.

Custodian account. An account—brokerage, bank, Keogh, mutual fund, etc.—held in the name of the custodian for the benefit of another.

Cyclical stocks. Stocks of companies whose earnings fluctuate with the business cycle. Cyclical industries include steel, cement, paper, machinery, and autos.

Day order. An order to buy or sell which is good for one day only.

Dealer. An individual who acts as principal, in contrast to a broker who acts as an agent. A dealer buys securities for his own account and then sells them to a customer from his own holdings. Profit or loss is the difference between the price he paid for the security and the price at which he sells it.

Debenture. A promissory note backed by the general credit of a company and usually not secured by a mortage or lien on any specific property.

Debt to equity ratio. The relationship of long-term debt and other long-term liabilities to common shareholders' equity. This measure is commonly used to indicate leverage.

Defensive stocks. Stocks of companies in steady businesses which are relatively unaffected by the ups and downs of the business cycle. Examples of defensive industries are electric and telephone utilities and food suppliers.

Deferred annuity. An annuity purchased as a single-premium or annual-premium annuity on which income distributions begin at some future date.

Depletion. Charges against earnings to reflect the gradual exhaustion of natural resources, such as ore, oil, and timber. It is a bookkeeping entry and does not require a cash outlay.

Depreciation. Charges against earnings to write off the cost, less salvage value, of an asset over its estimated useful life. Like depletion, it is a bookkeeping entry.

Discount. Amount by which a security may be purchased that is below its redemption value, as in Savings Bonds, Treasury bills, and some corporate bonds.

Discount broker. A broker who charges a smaller commission than that of a full-service broker. Generally no investment advice is given by a discount broker.

Discount rate. The interest rate the Federal Reserve Board charges member banks for loans.

Discretionary account. An account in which the broker determines the timing for buying and selling as well as the selections and number of shares to be bought and sold.

Disintermediation. The outflow of money from savings banks and savings and loan associations to higher-yielding vehicles.

Diversification. Spreading investments among different companies in a variety of industries, and/or among different types of securities or investments in order to spread risk.

Dividend. A payment designated by the board of directors of a corporation to be distributed to shareholders on a pro rata basis.

Dividend payout ratio. The percentage of earnings which are paid out in cash dividends.

Dollar cost averaging. An investment plan under which an investor purchases an equal dollar amount of a given stock or stocks at regular time intervals.

Double tops and bottoms. A technical analysis term which refers to chart formations in which the stock fluctuates, hitting the same top or bottom on two and sometimes three or four successive occasions. The breakout from such a pattern is the clue to the action to be taken.

Dow Jones Industrial Average. An average of 30 blue chip stocks. The average was originally published in 1897, based on twelve stocks. Adjustments in the divisor are currently used to reflect stock splits or stock dividends.

Dow Jones Transportation Average. An average of 20 transportation stocks.

Dow Jones Utility Average. An average of 15 utility stocks.

Dow Theory. A theory of market analysis based on performance of the Dow Jones Industrial and the Dow Jones Transportation averages. According to the theory, the market is in a basic uptrend if one of these averages advances above a previous important high, accompanied or followed by a similar advance in the other. When the averages drop below previous important lows, a confirmation of a basic downtrend occurs.

Downtick. A term which designates a transaction made at a price lower than the preceding transaction in a particular stock.

Dual funds. Publicly traded investment companies with two classes of stock—capital shares and income shares. Capital shareholders are entitled to all of the capital appreciation but no income. Income shareholders receive all of the income from the portfolio of holdings.

Dual listing. The listing of a stock on both the NYSE and the American Exchange.

Efficient market. The theory which holds that stock prices always reflect all available relevant information.

Employee Retirement Income Security Act of 1974 (ERISA). The law which created a uniform federal standard for fiduciary conduct relating to the establishment and maintenance of corporate employee benefit plans.

Exchange privilege. The right to exchange shares of one mutual fund for shares of another fund under the same sponsorship at net asset value or at a reduced sales charge.

Ex-dividend date. The date when the stock sells "ex" or without the dividend. On or after this date, the buyer of a stock does not receive a previously declared dividend.

Federal funds rate. The interest rate charged on loans from one member bank of the Federal Reserve System to another.

Federal Reserve Board. The seven-member board of governors of the Federal Reserve System, the central bank of the United States.

FIFO (first in, first out). The method of inventory valuation in which those goods purchased first are assumed to be sold first. *See* LIFO.

Fiscal policy. The use of a government's spending and revenue-producing activities to achieve certain objectives.

Fiscal year. A corporation's accounting year. Because of the nature of their particular business, some companies do not use the calendar year for their bookkeeping. Retailing concerns, for instance, generally end their year on January 31, because of the Christmas rush.

Flat. A bond which trades flat, trades without interest accruals. Bonds which are in default of interest or principal are traded flat. Income bonds trade flat, since interest is not paid on a regular basis but only when earned. Most bonds trade "plus interest," with the buyer paying the seller the interest that has accrued since the previous payment date.

Floating supply. The proportion of the listed capital stock of a corporation available for trading purposes; usually excludes shares closely held by management.

Flower bonds. Certain U.S. Treasury bonds which can be purchased at a discount and turned in at par for payment of federal estate taxes if the bonds are actually owned by the decedent at the time of death.

Form 10-K. A report which a corporation must file with the SEC within 90 days after the end of each fiscal year. The 10-K contains certified financial statements and is more detailed than the annual report.

Fully diluted earnings. The earnings figure that gives effect to all securities which could be converted into common stock and which would reduce earnings per share. *See* Primary earnings.

Fundamental analysis. The study and evaluation of such basic elements as earnings and dividend growth potential, and the varied impact of economics and politics on the market as a whole or a particular industry or company.

General obligation bond. A major type of municipal bond backed by the full faith and credit of the issuer.

Good-until-canceled (GTC) order. An order to buy or sell which remains in effect until it is either executed or canceled.

Government Retirement Bonds. A special series of U.S. individual retirement bonds issued by the federal government under the provisions of the Second Liberty Bond Act. These bonds come in $50, $100, and $500 denominations and pay interest at the rate of 6 percent compounded semiannually.

Gross national product (GNP). A measure of the nation's total output of goods and services.

Growth stock. Stock of a company whose sales and earnings are expanding faster than the general economy. Retained earnings are largely plowed back into the business to facilitate expansion.

Head and shoulders. A technical formation whose name is derived from the appearance given by the pattern of a head and right and left shoulders. If one has not previously sold on the higher head level, he should take advantage of the rally which forms the right shoulder, because price deterioration on reduced volume can set in quickly.

Hedge. To try to minimize risk by taking certain steps to offset the risk. In commodities, hedging is taking a position in the futures market that is equal to but opposite from an existing or soon to exist position in the cash market.

Hedge funds. Mutual funds which always keep a portion of their portfolios in a "short" position.

Holding company. A corporation that owns the majority of stock or securities of one or more other corporations for purposes of control rather than investment.

Hypothecation. The pledging of customers' securities as collateral for loans to brokers and dealers.

Income bond. A bond which promises to repay principal but pays interest only when earned.

Income stock. Common stock which pays out a relatively large portion of earnings in dividends, and thus provides a high yield to investors.

Indenture. A written agreement under which debt securities are issued. It sets forth the maturity date, interest rate, call provisions, security, and any other factors affecting those bonds.

Index funds. Mutual funds whose portfolios either duplicate the structure of the S&P 500 or other selected average or consist of 100 or more S&P issues to track the average. The indexing concept concedes that since it is difficult to beat the average consistently, analysis and investment fees should be reduced and the performance of the average matched.

Indicator Digest Average. Equal dollar investment–type average of all stocks traded on the Big Board.

Individual retirement account (IRA). Accounts which may be set up by individuals who are not participants in any qualified retirement plan. Up to 15 percent of earned income may be contributed, up to a $1,500 annual limit. Contributions may be deducted from gross income before federal income taxes are figured.

Insiders. Directors, officers, and principal securities holders of a corporation. Principal holders are those who own 10 percent or more of a publicly traded company's stock. The SEC requires insiders to report their initial position and details of any significant change in their holdings.

Institutional investor. An institution, such as a bank, life insurance company, or pension fund, whose investments constitute an important part of overall operations.

Intestate. Without a will.

Investment banker. The intermediary in the money markets who assists corporations in raising capital from investors. A profit is made on the difference between the price paid to the corporation and that at which the securities are sold to the public.

Investment company. A corporation which sells its own securities to the public and invests the proceeds in other securities in keeping with an indicated objective. *See* Mutual fund.

Investment Company Act of 1940. The basic federal law governing the registration and regulation of investment companies.

Investment tax credit. A tax break which enables a business to credit a percentage of the cost of new equipment against its income tax. Legislated by Congress to encourage spending to spur the economy.

Joint and survivor annuity. An annuity which pays income over the lifetime of two individuals.

Junk bonds. Lower quality bonds, generally below investment grade, which provide exceptionally high yields with commensurately high risks.

Keogh plan. A retirement plan set up under the Self-Employed Individuals Tax Retirement Act of 1962 (HR-10). Currently, a self-employed individual may place 15 percent of earned income, up to $7,500 per year, in such an account. Contributions are sheltered from current income taxes.

Lagging indicators. Indicators of economic activity which change direction subsequent to moves in overall economic activity.

Leading indicators. A group of indicators of economic activity which tend to turn in advance of general economic activity.

Leverage. The effect obtained when borrowed funds are added to invested equity in a financial venture.

Liabilities. Claims against the assets of a corporation or individual.

LIFO (last in, first out). The method of inventory valuation in which those goods last acquired are assumed to be sold first. LIFO reduces earnings in periods of rising prices. *See* FIFO.

Limited partnership. A form of investment often employed because of favorable tax consequences. The limited partnership limits both the risks and the rewards of the investor but puts the planning and decision-making in the hands of a professional management team.

Limit order. An order in which the buyer or seller indicates to his broker the price at which it is to be executed. A limit order to buy specifies a price below the market; a limit order to sell indicates a price above the market. *See* Stop order.

Liquidation. The process of converting securities or other property into cash.

Liquidity. The cash or near-cash position of a corporation. Also, the term refers to the ability of the market in a particular security to absorb a reasonable amount of buying or selling at reasonable price changes.

Listed stock. Stock of a corporation which is traded on a securities exchange.

Living trust. A trust which is in effect during the life of the testator, also called an inter vivos trust. A living trust may be revocable (control is retained over assets) or irrevocable (control is permanently forfeited).

Load. The sales charge a buyer of mutual funds may have to pay in addition to the actual net asset value of the shares.

Management fee. The fee deducted from the gross income of an investment company prior to any distributions to shareholders. Generally it amounts to ½ of 1 percent of the fund's net asset value. Also, the fee charged by an investment counselor for his service.

Margin. The value of securities and cash in a brokerage account against which an investor may purchase more stock. Margin requirements in the past twenty years have ranged from 40 percent of the purchase price to 100 percent. In commodity jargon, margin refers to funds put up as security or guarantee of contract fulfillment.

Margin call. A call from a broker asking for additional cash in order to bring the equity in a customer's margin account at least up to the margin maintenance requirements stipulated by the exchange. The margin call is made when the value of securities in an account declines.

Market order. An order to buy or sell a stated amount of a security at the most advantageous price obtainable after the order is presented on the trading floor.

Monetary policy. The management by a central bank of a nation's money supply to insure the availability of credit in line with national objectives.

Money market. The arena in which short-term funds (less than one year) are channeled. Money market instruments include promissory notes and bills of exchange, commercial paper, bankers' acceptances, Treasury bills, short-term tax-exempts, dealer paper, and negotiable certificates of deposit.

Money market funds. Mutual funds which invest in money market instruments.

Money supply. The sum total of money stock. Common measures are M_1, which is currency in circulation plus demand deposits (checking accounts), and M_2, which is M_1 plus time deposits at commercial banks other than large certificates of deposit.

Mortgage bonds. Bonds which are secured by a conditional lien on part or all of a corporation's property.

Moving average. One of the popular methods for determining market and individual stock strength or weakness. A moving average is obtained by adding up the prices for a certain number of days and dividing the total by the number of days involved. For the next figure, the price for the earliest day or week is dropped and the current one added.

Municipal bond. A bond issued by a state or political subdivision, or by a state agency or authority. Interest from municipal issues is exempt from federal income tax.

Mutual fund. An investment company which enables its shareholders to pool their capital into a single large professionally managed account. *See* Investment company.

Naked option. An option written against stock which is not currently owned. *See* Covered option.

NASD (National Association of Securities Dealers). A national organization which provides for the self-regulation of the over-the-counter market.

NASDAQ (National Association of Securities Dealers Automated Quotation system). A computerized communications system that collects, stores, and displays up-to-the-second quotations from a nationwide network of over-the-counter dealers making markets in stocks included in the NASDAQ system. Certain requirements must be met in order for a stock to be included.

Net asset value. The total market value of a mutual fund portfolio less liabilities divided by the number of shares of the fund outstanding.

New York Stock Exchange. The largest national securities exchange.

New York Stock Exchange Index. The unweighted average of all stocks listed on the New York Stock Exchange.

Odd lot. A trade of fewer than 100 shares. *See* Round lot.

Open-end investment company. An investment company in which the price is determined by the per-share net asset value of the portfolio. There is no fixed number of shares. These funds make a continuous offer of shares for sale to the public, and at any time will buy back outstanding shares at net asset value.

Open market operations. The purchase or sale of government bonds in the open market (mostly in New York) by the Federal Reserve Board. Open market operations are the chief stabilizing tool of the Fed.

Option. The right to buy or sell specified securities at a set price within a stated time period.

Option Clearing Corporation. The organization which acts as buyer to all sellers and vice versa for all traded options.

Over-the-counter market. A negotiation market which has a dollar volume greater than the total of all stock exchanges.

Par value. The amount stated on the face of a bond, preferred stock, or common stock. Interest or dividends are often stated as a percentage of par in the case of bonds and preferreds, and bonds are generally redeemed at par on their maturity date. In the case of common stock, however, par value bears no real relationship to the market price or underlying value of the shares.

Pink Sheet. A daily publication of the National Quotation Bureau. Prices on over-the-counter securities are listed along with the names and telephone numbers of those firms which make a market in them. Prices quoted by these firms are not definite bids and offers.

Pits. Platforms on the trading floor of a commodity exchange in which traders and brokers stand as they trade in particular commodities.

Point and figure chart. A technical chart which shows a compressed picture of significant price changes. These charts are designed to show strength of price movement and to emphasize changes in direction.

Portfolio. The total securities held by an institution or private individual.

Preferred stock. A class of stock which has preference over the common stock of a corporation in respect to the payment of dividends. In the event of liquidation, preferred shareholders usually have priority over common shareholders in the distribution of assets.

Premium. The amount by which a security, bond, convertible, etc., sells above its redemption or conversion value.

Price-earnings multiple. The current market price of a share of stock divided by earnings per share for a twelve-month period. (Also called Price-earnings ratio.)

Primary earnings per share. Net income after preferred dividends, divided by common shares outstanding plus the shares that would be outstanding if common stock equivalents were actually converted.

Primary issue. The original sale of stock, where proceeds revert to the issuing company.

Prime rate. The rate of interest charged by commercial banks for short-term loans extended to their best customers.

Private placement. The selling of securities directly to one or more large investors, without the services of an underwriter or an SEC registration.

Profit margin (pre-tax). Pre-tax income divided by net sales. This figure is a measure of the efficiency of a company, although profit margins vary from industry to industry and company to company.

Prospectus. A communication which offers a security for sale. The prospectus contains salient parts of the registration statement, which gives all information relevant to the issue.

Proxy statement. Information required by the SEC to be given stockholders as a prerequisite to solicitation of proxies for a security subject to requirements of the Securities Exchange Act of 1934.

Prudent man rule. The rule which enables a trustee to use his own judgment in making investments as long as he acts in a prudent manner. The rule comes from an 1830 court decision.

Put option. A contract which gives its owner the right to sell a certain number of shares of stock at a specific price, within a defined time period.

Random walk. A theory which states that the size and direction of a stock market or individual stock price action cannot be predicted from the size and direction of previous moves.

Ratio writing. Writing calls on more shares than are actually owned.

Real Estate Investment Trust (REIT). A professionally managed portfolio of real estate properties and/or mortgages.

Record date. The date on which a shareholder must be registered on the books of a corporation to receive a declared dividend or vote on company affairs.

Red herring. A preliminary prospectus which does not include the price at which the securities are to be offered to the public. It is issued to obtain an indication of interest in an offer. It gets its name from the statement, printed in red ink on its front cover, that it is a preliminary prospectus.

Refunding. Replacing an outstanding debt obligation with a new obligation.

Registered bond. A bond which is recorded on the books of the issuer in the name of the owner. It can be transferred only when endorsed by the registered owner. *See* Bearer bond, Coupon bond.

Registered representative. Another name for a broker or dealer in securities.

Registrar. A trust company or bank charged with the responsibility of preventing the issuance of more stock than is authorized by a company.

Regular way transaction. A transaction in which delivery of a stock certificate is made at the office of the purchaser on the fifth full business day following the transaction date.

Regulation Q. The banking regulation that sets interest rate ceilings that banks in the U.S. can pay on deposits.

Relative strength. The relationship of the price of a stock to the Dow Jones Industrial Average or some other market average. The resulting percentage, multiplied by a factor to bring the plotting closer to the price bars on the chart, shows by the direction of the curve whether the stock is performing better than, worse than, or the same as the market average used.

Replacement cost accounting. An accounting concept which espouses valuing assets at their replacement—or current value—cost.

Resistance level. A price area which attracts selling sufficient to keep the price of a stock from rising above it on repeated occasions. Once it has been broken through on the upside, the old resistance area becomes a new support level. *See* Support level.

Retained earnings. Profits remaining in the company after payment of preferred and common stock dividends that have been accumulated over the years. Retained earnings provide an important internal source of capital for business expansion.

Return on equity. Net income available for the common stock divided by the previous year's shareholders' equity.

Return on total capital. Earnings before interest and taxes divided by total capitalization.

Revenue bond. A municipal bond on which interest and principal are payable from receipts obtained from the operation of the project they finance rather than from general tax receipts.

Revocable trust. A trust in which control of assets is retained.

Rights (pre-emptive). Short-term options granted to existing shareholders of a company to purchase new stock issues, generally at reduced price levels.

Ring. *See* Pit.

Round lot. Normally 100 shares of stock; for bonds, $100,000 face value.

Rule 390. The New York Stock Exchange rule which states that NYSE-listed shares may not be traded by member firms on other exchanges.

Savings Bonds. Nonmarketable bonds issued by the U.S. Treasury. Series E Bonds are issued at a discount and mature in five years. Series H Bonds pay interest semiannually and mature in ten years.

Securities Act of 1933. The law which states what information is required in a registration statement and prospectus.

Securities Exchange Act of 1934. The law which created the Securities and Exchange Commission. It requires registration with the SEC of many organizations dealing in securities and sets down rules for hypothecation of customers' securities.

Securities Investor Protection Corporation (SIPC). An insurance corporation organized under the Securities Investor Protection Act of 1970 to protect the assets of brokerage accounts in the event of a brokerage company bankruptcy. Operating funds are provided by assessments on brokerage firms' earnings.

Selling against the box. Short selling against stock which is owned by an investor. The short sale may be covered by purchasing additional shares or by delivering the shares already owned.

Semilogarithmic chart. A chart drawn on semilogarithmic graph paper. On this paper, the horizontal scale is drawn arithmetically, but the vertical scale is constructed so that equal distances represent equal percentage changes.

Serial bonds. A bond issue which is sold with serial maturity dates and commensurate interest rates.

Short interest ratio. The figure obtained by relating the monthly short interest (total number of shares sold short) to the average daily trading volume in the period concerned.

Short selling. Selling stock which one does not already own, in the belief that the price will decline. The broker borrows the stock so that he can deliver the shares to the buyer. Later, the short seller must cover his position by buying the same amount of stock borrowed for return to the buyer.

Single premium annuity. An annuity contract purchased with only one payment or premium.

Sinking fund. Money set aside by a company to redeem its bonds, debentures, or preferred shares periodically as specified in the indenture or charter.

Specialist. A member of an exchange whose first function is to maintain an orderly market in the stocks in which he is registered as a specialist. To do so, the specialist is expected to buy or sell for his own account when there is a temporary disparity between supply and demand.

Special situation. A term which encompasses several types of unusual investment opportunities, including merger or takeover candidates, new-product development, spin-offs, or liquidations.

Speculation. The assumption of above-average risk in anticipation of commensurately higher return.

Speculative Index. The relationship of American Stock Exchange volume to New York Stock Exchange volume expressed as a percentage. Presumably, the lower the figure, the closer the market is to a bottom; and the higher the figure, the closer it is to a peak.

Standard & Poor's 500 Composite Stock Price Index. Weighted average of 500 stocks, consisting of 400 industrial, 40 financial, 40 utility, and 20 transportation stocks.

Standing margin (commodities). The amount of money a clearing house member keeps on deposit with the clearing house for each net open position at the end of the trading day.

Stock dividend. A dividend paid in securities rather than cash. It may be additional shares of the issuing company or shares of another company (usually a subsidiary) held by the company.

Stockholders' equity. *See* Book value.

Stock split. The allotment of additional shares to stockholders to represent their ownership interest in a corporation. Often stock splits are designed to broaden interest in a high-priced stock. A shareholders' proportionate interest in a company is not altered by a stock split.

Stop order. An order which specifies a particular price at which a stock should be bought or sold. A stop order to buy specifies a price above the market; a stop order to sell indicates a price below the market. A stop order automatically becomes a market order once the security reaches the specified price.

Straddle. The purchase of a put and a call on the same underlying stock having identical striking prices and expiration dates.

Straight life annuity. An annuity which provides a predetermined amount of income periodically for the life of the annuitant. *See* Joint and survivor annuity.

Street name. Securities held in the name of a broker instead of the owner's name. Sometimes this arrangement is done for convenience; stocks bought on margin must always be left in a street name.

Striking price. The price at which a call or put option is written. In the case of a call option, it is the price at which the stock named in the contract may be bought; in the case of a put, it is the price at which the stock may be sold.

Subordinate debenture. A debt issue whose claim on corporate assets comes after that of debentures in a liquidation.

Support level. A technical analysis term which denotes a price area in which there is demand for a stock sufficient to keep the price from dropping below it on repeated occasions. Once there is a break below the area, a new support level is created. *See* Resistance level.

Syndicate. A group of investment bankers formed to underwrite and distribute a securities issue. Also, a group of individuals and/or concerns who combine to undertake a particular investment. *See* Investment banker.

Tax-free rollover. Using an individual retirement account to channel retirement funds from one qualified pension program to another, with no immediate tax consequences.

Tax loopholes. Gaps in the tax structure through which clever taxpayers and special interest groups can maneuver. Use of tax loopholes is not illegal.

Tax shelter. Any means whereby income receives preferential tax treatment.

Technical analysis. The study of phenomena internal to the market, such as patterns of price movement, in an attempt to forecast the future movement of the market as a whole or of individual stocks.

Tenancy in common. The title jointly held by two people, usually unmarried, to a given piece of property. Each person retains control over his individual share of the property.

Tenancy by the entirety. The form of property ownership which exists when the names of both husband and wife appear on the deed to property, with rights of survivorship.

Tender offer. An offer by a corporation to buy back its own shares, or an offer by an outsider interested in acquiring control to buy up shares in a company.

Ticker. The electronic system which prints prices and volume of security transactions in cities and towns throughout the U.S. and Canada within minutes after each transaction.

Transfer agent. A bank or trust company that keeps a record of the name of each registered shareowner, his address, and the number of shares owned, and who sees that certificates presented to his office for transfer are properly canceled and new certificates issued in the name of the transferee.

Treasury bills. U.S. government securities maturing in one year or less, usually in three months or six months. They are sold at weekly auctions at a discount from par, and redeemed at par.

Treasury bonds. U.S. government securities with a maturity of greater than five years.

Treasury notes. U.S. government securities with a maturity of one to seven years.

Treasury stock. Stock issued by a company but later reacquired by the same company and held in its treasury.

Trend line. Line drawn on a chart which indicates the direction in which a particular stock or the general market is trending.

Trust. An agreement whereby the person who establishes the trust gives property to a trustee to invest and manage for the advantage of the beneficiary.

Trustee. An individual or institution designated to oversee the handling and distribution of a trust fund.

Unit trust. An investment entity that issues only redeemable certificates that represent individual interests in a fixed portfolio with a specified life span and no continuing management.

Unweighted average. Stock market average in which higher-priced issues do not have more influence on the average than lower-priced issues. *See* Weighted average.

Upside-downside volume. Tabulation of the shares traded on the New York Stock Exchange at prices higher or lower than the previous day's close.

Uptick. A term which designates a transaction made at a price higher than the preceding transaction in a particular stock.

Value Line Index. The unweighted average based on equal dollar investments in a list of 1,665 stocks.

Variable annuity. An annuity in which a specified portion of the principal is invested in common stocks.

Volume. The number of transactions occurring during a given period of time.

Warrant. A certificate giving the holder the right to purchase securities at a stipulated price within a specified time limit or perpetually.

Wash sale. A wash sale is said to occur if securities or options to buy them are obtained within thirty days before or after a sale of substantially the same securities. No tax loss may be taken in such cases.

Weighted average. An average which gives greater weight to stocks with a higher market value—S&P, NYSE averages.

"When issued." A new issue of securities that has been authorized but not actually issued to purchasers in a split. Shares are bought and sold in the market, with all transactions settled only when, as, and if the securities are finally issued.

Withdrawal plan. An arrangement under which investors in mutual funds can regularly receive monthly or quarterly payments of a specified amount.

Working capital. Current assets minus current liabilities. Working-capital needs vary among industries and among firms in the same industry.

Yield. The dividends or interest paid on a particular security expressed as a percentage of the current price or as a percentage of cost price, or as related to the maturity of a bond.

Yield to maturity. The return earned on a bond if it is held to maturity.

Index